T0191686

BEHAVIORAL SPECIFICATIONS OF BUSINESSES AND SYSTEMS

THE KLUWER INTERNATIONAL SERIES
IN ENGINEERING AND COMPUTER SCIENCE

BEHAVIORAL SPECIFICATIONS OF BUSINESSES AND SYSTEMS

edited by

Haim Kilov
Genesis Development Corporation
U.S.A.

Bernhard Rumpe
Technische Universität München
Germany

Ian Simmonds
IBM T J Watson Research Center
U.S.A.

SPRINGER SCIENCE+BUSINESS MEDIA, LLC

Electronic Services <http://www.wkap.nl>

Haim Kilov - *hkilov@gendev.com*
Bernhard Rumpe- *rumpe@informatik.tu-muenchen.de*
Ian Simmonds - *simmonds@us.ibm.com*

Library of Congress Cataloging-in-Publication Data

Behavioral specifications of businesses and systems / edited by Haim
    Kilov, Bernhard Rumpe, Ian Simmonds.
       p.   c.m -- (Kluwer international series in engineering and
computer science ; SECS 523)
      "The second volume of papers based on a series of workshops held
alongside ACM's [Association for Computing Machinery] annual
conference on Object Oriented Programming Systems Languages and
Applications (OOPSLA) and European Conference on Object-Oriented
Programming (ECOOP)"--Pref.
    Includes bibliographical references and index.
    ISBN 978-1-4613-7383-4   ISBN 978-1-4615-5229-1 (eBook)
    DOI 10.1007/978-1-4615-5229-1

    1. Object-oriented programming (Computer science) 2. System
design. I. Kilov, Haim. II. Rumpe, Bernhard. III. Simmonds, Ian,
1966-   . IV. Series.
QA76.64.B42 1999   99-40807
005.1'17--dc21   CIP

CONTENTS

PREFACE

'Thinking again?' the Duchess asked, with another dig of her sharp little chin.

'I've a right to think,' said Alice sharply, for she was beginning to feel a little worried.

'Just about as much right,' said the Duchess, 'as pigs have to fly; and the m—'

But here, to Alice's great surprise, the Duchess's voice died away, even in the middle of her favourite word 'moral,' and the arm that was linked into hers began to tremble. Alice looked up, and there stood the Queen in front of them, with her arms folded, frowning like a thunderstorm.

'A fine day, your Majesty!' the Duchess began in a low, weak voice.

'Now, I give you fair warning,' shouted the Queen, stamping on the ground as she spoke; 'either you or your head must be off, and that in about half no time! Take your choice!'

The Duchess took her choice, and was gone in a moment.

'Let's go on with the game,' the Queen said to Alice.

Lewis Carroll

WHY IS THIS BOOK OF INTEREST TO YOU?

This book is about thinking in specification reading, writing and understanding.

The teaching of specifications (in the same way as the teaching of programming) is the teaching of thinking. The teaching of programming has little to do with the teaching of a particular programming language; and in the same way, the teaching of specifications has nothing to do with the teaching of a particular methodology, notation, or tool. When features of a notation are emphasized, "[t]he student is made to believe that the more [language] ideosyncrasies he understands, the better a programmer he will be." [D76] However, these "powerful features belong more to the problem set than to the solution set", and as a result the student becomes "an expert coder of trivial [usually given] algorithms" [D76]. Thus, "the really tough problems are way beyond his mental horizon". Such tough problems, both in programming and in specifications, are about understanding and proper structuring of (often large amounts of) information. Clear thinking is needed to formulate and solve these problems.

WHAT TO SPECIFY, AND WHY

There is no need for contrived or toy examples to demonstrate that apparently complex business situations can be specified in an abstract, precise, clear and explicit manner. Consider Adam Smith's 1776 description [S1776], provided in *italics*, of the centuries old workings of a market economy:

> *The produce of industry is what it adds to the subject or materials upon which it is employed. In proportion as the value of this produce is great or small, so will likewise be the profits of the employer.*

A business or system specification describes the things and relationships of the domain. The structure of the domain — i.e., the shape of its relationships — is more fundamental than the particular things that participate in these relationships. The semantics of relationships ought to be clear from their specification; and it is much deeper than the cardinalities that we are so used to.

> *But it is only for the sake of profit that any man employs a capital in the support of industry; and he will always, therefore, endeavour to employ it in the support of that industry of which the produce is likely to be of the greatest value, or to exchange for the greatest quantity either of money or of other goods.*

Since information systems involve people, we must understand something of their motives both as individuals and as part of larger social systems. In more modern terms, the Enterprise Viewpoint of the RM-ODP systems specification standard "focuses on the purpose, scope and policies" of the system which may or may not be wholly an IT system [ISO95a].

> *But the annual revenue of every society is always precisely equal to the exchangeable value of the whole annual produce of its industry, or rather is precisely the same thing with that exchangeable value.*

When large things are composed of smaller things, some properties of the larger things are determined by those of the smaller. Such composition relationships are common. Properties of a composite may be determined by those of its components and the way that those components are combined [ISO95a]. Here the property determination is simple — it can be expressed as a simple formula.

> *As every individual, therefore, endeavours as much as he can both to employ his capital in the support of domestic industry, and so to direct that industry that its produce may be of the greatest value; every individual necessarily labours to render the annual revenue of the society as great as he can.*

The purpose and behavior of a component must also be understood and specified and within the context of the compositions of which it is a part. In this particular case, had Smith not included the word 'necessarily' he could have been accused of writing romantic nonsense. However, he chose his words very carefully. The word 'necessarily' is elaborated as 'the invisible hand' of his following sentences:

He generally, indeed, neither intends to promote the public interest, nor knows how much he is promoting it. By preferring the support of domestic to that of foreign industry, he intends only his own security; and by directing that industry in such a manner as its produce may be of the greatest value, he intends only his own gain, and he is in this, as in many other cases, led by an invisible hand to promote an end which was no part of his intention.

The 'invisible hand' is — in the more modern terminology of RM-ODP — the way that the components are combined within the composition. The 'invisible hand' is not algorithmic, is not supposed to be, but nevertheless is the way that determines some properties of the composite. The "glue" between components is in part defined very carefully by contract law and, more generally, by business law, the main concepts and constructs of which have remained unchanged for centuries and perhaps millennia.

Nor is it always the worse for the society that it was no part of it. By pursuing his own interest he frequently promotes that of the society more effectually than when he really intends to promote it.

Adam Smith was able to give a precise, elegant, concise and abstract specification of a market economy in 1776. Such specifications are even more important for computer-based information systems. This book contributes to that goal.

ONLY OO?

The papers presented here are not about traditional OO "Analysis and Design". You will often encounter useful and sometimes elegant concepts, good practices (in programming and in specifications), and solid underlying theory that is of interest and importance to all of us. At times, these ideas and concepts will be represented in (and flavored by) contexts that are there for various technical, political and other reasons; but we hope that you will be able to distinguish semantics issues from various representations.

PRACTICE

This book is not unique: developments of the kind presented here are encountered in practice, described in international standards (such as RM-ODP [ISO95a] and GRM [ISO95b]) and in some cases have even become new buzzwords. Whilst several years ago the concepts of pre- and postconditions and invariants were considered inappropriate for business specifications (we often heard that "nobody could ever understand them"), now they are often used in various specifications, standards, and even "CASE tools". Users, including business SMEs (subject matter experts), do understand and successfully apply such concepts. Perhaps now is the turn of applied concepts of category theory; some papers in this book describe how category theory can be used.

Having said that, we want to emphasize that many concepts shown in this book have been used, and successfully, in real industrial projects. In the same manner as mathematics and physics is the basis of traditional engineering knowledge and activities, (possibly different areas of) mathematics are the basis of software engineering — and this includes specification! — knowledge and activities.

WHERE DO THE PAPERS COME FROM?

This is the second volume of papers based on a series of workshops held alongside ACM's annual conference on Object Oriented Programming Systems Languages and Applications (OOPSLA) and European Conference on Object-Oriented Programming (ECOOP). The first volume — *Object-Oriented Behavioral Specifications*[1], edited by Haim Kilov and William Harvey [KH96] — was also published by Kluwer, in 1996. It was based on the first four workshops, held from 1992-1995. While several of this volume's authors contributed to the first volume, there are also many new names.

We have tried to ensure that the workshops on behavioral semantics represent and bring together a wide variety of voices. They range from the practitioner and business thinker through to the academic and (almost pure) mathematician. Some papers also use (and may even quote) foundational material like Wittgenstein's ideas (e.g., [W33]). We encouraged this kind of diversity, and therefore not all authors (including the editors) agree with everything included in this book.

FROM THE HIGHLY THEORETICAL TO THE EXTREMELY PRAGMATIC

Don't be scared by the mathematics that appears in some papers. In all cases the authors were asked to demonstrate the relevance of their work in the simplest possible terms. As E.W. Dijkstra suggested, mathematics is "the art and science of effective reasoning". So is the art of programming — "the art of organising complexity, of mastering multitude and avoiding its bastard chaos as effectively as possible" [D72], and the art of business specifications.

We all deal with the increased complexity of businesses and systems. This complexity should never be(come) artificial: the basics of many businesses were perfectly specified centuries ago, and these specifications can be succesfully (re)used now. At the same time, it only recently became possible to articulate the common mathematical ideas underlying different branches of mathematics and probably engineering: to quote a recently published introduction to category theory used (among others) by high school classes, "the ideas we'll study have been employed for thousands of years, but they first appeared only as dimly perceived analogies between subjects" [LS97]. These fundamental insights, both in category theory and in run-of-the-mill specification and programming areas, lead to better understanding and thus to delivering products that are what all concerned want them to be (rather than what was rapidly hacked together and often hated by the customer).

By bringing these papers together in one volume we hope to show you that these seemingly different papers address different aspects of a single problem. In our workshops we had a similar mixture, which turned out to be very fruitful for inspring discussions during and after the workshops. The papers are all about better understanding of business enterprises and of the software systems that they rely upon.

While it is always tempting to determine a classification scheme for a collection of papers, once again we admit defeat. We used a lexical rather than semantic classification: the papers are in alphabetical order of their first author's last name.

INVITATION

On behalf of our fellow authors, we invite and encourage you to tell us what you think of this book and its contents.

Firstly, each paper includes the e-mail addresses of all authors. Please send any comments or questions to the relevant authors.

Secondly, we invite you to submit papers to future workshops in the OOPSLA and ECOOP series. As we mentioned above, we encourage a wide variety of contributions, from academics and practitioners. Perhaps you will contribute a paper to the next book in *this* series? You can find details of OOPSLA and its workshops at: http://www.acm.org/sigplan/oopsla or by contacting one of the editors of this book.

ACKNOWLEDGEMENTS

As editors and organizers of the above mentioned workshops, we would like to thank the organizers of the conferences ECOOP'97, OOPSLA'97, ECOOP'98 and OOPSLA'98 for their wonderful assistance in running the workshops, as well as Samer AlHunaty and the authors of the book's articles for their help in putting the work together (despite layout-problems).

We would like to thank our loved ones for their help, support, encouragement and tolerance of hours and days of virtual (e-mail) and physical (workshop) absence, and partly also for their active assitance in putting the workshops and the book together.

We also want to express our sincerest thanks to the Technische Universität München for allowing and encouraging the reuse of parts of the articles and of full articles of the following four workshop proceedings in enhanced form:

- TUM-I9725, ECOOP'97 Workshop on Precise Semantics for Object-Oriented Modeling Techniques,
- TUM-I9737, OOPSLA'97 Workshop on Object-Oriented Behavioral Semantics,
- TUM-I9813, Second ECOOP Workshop on Precise Behavioral Semantics, and

- TUM-I9820, Seventh OOPSLA Workshop on Behavioral Semantics of OO Business and System Specifications.

The work was partially supported by the Bayerische Forschungsstiftung under the FORSOFT research consortium and by the DFG under the Leibnizpreis program.

June, 1999

Haim, Bernhard, Ian

Haim Kilov, Genesis Development Corporation
Bernhard Rumpe, Technische Universität München
Ian Simmonds, IBM T J Watson Research Center

References

[D72] E.W.Dijkstra. Notes on structured programming. In: O.-J.Dahl, E.W.Dijkstra, C.A.R.Hoare. *Structured programming*. Academic Press, 1972, pp. 1-82.

[D76] E.W.Dijkstra. The teaching of programming, i.e. the teaching of thinking. In: *Language hierarchies and interfaces* (ed. by F.L.Bauer and K.Samelson), Lecture Notes in Computer Science, Vol. 46 (1976), pp. 1-10, Springer Verlag.

[ISO95a] ISO/IEC JTC1/SC21, Open Distributed Processing - Reference Model: Part 2: Foundations (IS 10746-2 / ITU-T Recommendation X.902, 1995).

[ISO95b] ISO/IEC JTC1/SC21, Information Technology. Open Systems Interconnection - Management Information Services - Structure of Management Information - Part 7: General Relationship Model, 1995. ISO/IEC 10165-7.2.

[KH96] H.Kilov and W.Harvey (Eds.). *Object-oriented behavioral specifications*. Kluwer Academic Publishers, 1996.

[LS97] F.William Lawvere, Stephen H. Schanuel. *Conceptual mathematics: A first introduction to categories*. Cambridge University Press, 1997.

[S1776] Adam Smith. *An Inquiry into the Nature and Causes of the Wealth of Nations*. 1776.

[W33] Ludwig Wittgenstein. *Tractatus Logico-Philosophicus*. 2nd corrected reprint. New York: Harcourt, Brace and Company; London: Kegan Paul, Trench, Trubner & Co. Ltd., 1933.

Endnotes

1. Behavior is defined in RM-ODP [ISO95a] as "[a] collection of actions with a set of constraints on when they may occur." Many papers deal with these constraints expressed (in a precise and abstract manner) in different ways.

Chapter 1

OBJECT-ORIENTED TRANSFORMATION

Kenneth Baclawski

Northeastern University
Boston, Massachusetts 02115
kenb@ccs.neu.edu

Scott A. DeLoach

Air Force Institute of Technology
Wright-Patterson AFB, Ohio 43433
Scott.DeLoach@afit.af.mil

Mieczyslaw M. Kokar

Northeastern University
Boston, Massachusetts 02115
kokar@coe.neu.edu

Jeffrey Smith

Sanders, a Lockheed Martin Company
Nashua, New Hampshire
jeffrey.e.smith@lmco.com

Abstract   Modern CASE tools and formal methods systems are more than just repositories of specification and design information. They can also be used for refinement and code generation. Refinement is the process of transforming one specification into a more detailed specification. Specifications and their refinements typically do not use the same specification language. Code generation is also a transformation, where the target language is a programming language. Although object-oriented (OO) programming languages and tools have been available for a long time, refinement and transformation are still based on grammars and parse trees. The purpose of this paper is to compare grammar-based transformation with object-oriented transformation and to introduce a toolkit that automates the generation of parsers and transformers. A more specific objective is to apply these techniques to the problem of translating a CASE repository into logical theories of a formal methods system.

Keywords: CASE tool, formal methods, specification, modeling language, transformational reuse, code generation, context-free grammar

1. INTRODUCTION

In this chapter, we discuss the problem of transformation of object-oriented representations into formal representations. We encountered such a problem while attempting to translate UML diagrams [BRJ97a, BRJ97b] into formal specifications expressed in the formal specification language Slang [W+98]; this step was part of the process of formalization of the UML. In order to simplify this rather complex task, we wanted to take advantage of existing translation tools, like Refine[1] [Ref90]. Our goal, in addition to the translation, was also to establish a formal semantics for the UML and to prove the correctness of the translation.

It is well known that UML diagrams, by themselves, are insufficient for representing the semantics of a software system. Additional conditions (such as pre- and post-conditions) are required. Establishing a formal semantics for the UML would clarify the meaning and limitations of the diagrams as well as eliminate ambiguities and conflicts between different diagrams.

One possible way of performing such a translation would be to translate data models of UML directly into expressions in the Slang grammar – a one-big-leap-transformation approach. Such a direct translation would be quite complex. The complexity of this step can be reduced by decomposing it into a number of smaller simpler steps. Another reason for such a multi-step approach is that there is no single tool that could be used in this process. On the other hand, a number of excellent tools exist that could be used for smaller steps.

There are then two ways to achieve our goal: either represent UML as a context-free grammar and then perform the translation(s) in the category of context-free grammars, or perform translation(s) of UML using only object-oriented representations, representing the result using a context-free grammar as the last step if necessary.

In this paper, we argue for the latter solution. In Section 2, we show an example of an object-oriented diagram and discuss the difficulties with representing this kind of diagram using context-free grammars. Then in Section 3 we describe a system, called nu&, developed at Northeastern University by K. Baclawski. The nu& toolkit is the basis for our object-oriented approach to parsing and transformation. This process is decomposed into a number of smaller stages, each of which involves translation, parsing and symbol table manipulation. The two processing paths mentioned above – translation of data models and translation of context-free grammars – are discussed in detail. In Section 4, a specific example is used to illustrate the steps in the transformation pipeline of Section 3. The intent here is to show that the process of transformation of object diagrams is much simpler if it is carried out directly on the object level than by continually constructing linear textual representations which must be parsed before the next stage of the transformation may be performed.

Simplifying the transformation pipeline is one of the main themes of this paper. Certainly simplification has many obvious benefits. Simplification makes it easier to construct the transformation and to prove that it is correct. Simplification also makes it easier to comprehend the transformation and to compare alternatives. This is especially important for a formalization of the UML because the UML is only a semi-formal modeling language. For example, the concept of inheritance varies from one programming language to another, and there can be several alternatives within a single language such as virtual and nonvirtual derivation in C++.

2.   COMPARISON OF GRAMMARS WITH OBJECT-ORIENTED DATA MODELING LANGUAGES

Translation from one language to another begins with parsing, when the source language is defined by a context-free grammar (also known as abstract syntax trees or ASTs). The grammar is said to define the *syntax* of the language, while the subsequent phases of compilation are said to represent the *semantics* of the language. Excellent tools are available that automate the task of generating a parser from a grammar. Such tools are often called "compiler-compilers" even though they only automate the generation of the parser. To specify the semantics of the language with a compiler-compiler, one must specify the action associated with each grammar rule.

The result of parsing is often referred to as the *parse tree*. A parse tree is a hierarchical representation of information that conforms to a data model defined by the grammar. The fact that a grammar defines a data model was first observed by Gonnet and Tompa [GT87], whose p-string data model has powerful query operations for grammatical data models. Since then, there has been much work on elaborate grammatical data modeling languages, such as SGML and HTML/XML. For a detailed discussion of the limitations of grammars as data models see [Bac91]. The reverse of parsing represents a parse tree as linear text. This process is *linearization* or "pretty printing."

The rest of this section presents an example to compare the modeling power of grammars with object-oriented modeling languages.

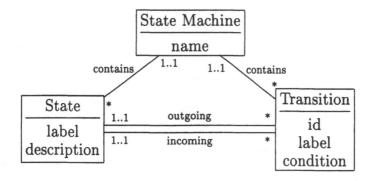

Figure 1   State Machine Data Model

Consider the example of a database of state machines as specified in Figure 1. This figure uses a simplified form of the UML notation to define a data model. The data model in the figure is similar to the UML state machine concept, but it is not the same, for the sake of simplicity. Each state and each transition is contained in a state machine, and each transition links exactly two states. State machines, states and transitions have various attributes. The name of a state machine is unique. The identifier of a transition is unique within the state machine that contains it. A transition is allowed to join states in different state machines. This raises the issue of which state machine such a transition should be contained in. In an actual UML state machine diagram one of the state machines would be nested within another state machine, and the transition would belong to the parent state machine.

One can represent an instance of the state machine data model as a parse tree in a variety of ways. One could represent it as a list of state machines, each of which contains a list of states and transitions. In addition, each transition is related to exactly one incoming state and exactly one outgoing state. This suggests that the following grammar represents the state machine data model:

$$
\begin{aligned}
\text{Root} &\leftarrow \text{State\_Machine}^* \\
\text{State\_Machine} &\leftarrow \text{string State}^* \text{ Transition}^* \\
\text{State} &\leftarrow \text{string string} \\
\text{Transition} &\leftarrow \text{string string string State State}
\end{aligned}
$$

A subtle problem with the above grammar is that the state objects contained in a transition object are different objects from the ones contained in the state machine objects and those contained in the other transition objects. The nonterminals of a grammar represent nodes in a tree, and the nodes that occur below a Transition nonterminal cannot occur below a State_Machine nonterminal or below another Transition node. Such an arrangement would violate the requirement that the parse tree be a tree. One could, in theory, add the constraint that each state linked by a transition must have the same information as one of the states contained in a state machine. Aside from the huge amount of redundancy that is caused by this design, it is also ambiguous because there could be states that have exactly the same attributes, since there is no uniqueness condition imposed on the states.

Alternatively, one might try to represent the relationships between states and transitions by including lists of incoming and outgoing transitions in each state, but now it is the transition objects that are being redundantly represented. Yet another possibility is to represent the two relationships as two independent entities. This design is even worse than the others, for now one is representing both the state objects and the transition objects redundantly.

In order to represent the incoming and outgoing relationships of the state machine data model, it is necessary to introduce some kind of reference mechanism. For example, instead of having two state objects within each transition object, one might specify that each transition object contain two state identifiers. This would work if states had unique identifiers, but there is no uniqueness condition on the state attributes. In the grammar above, transition objects are uniquely identified within each state machine, so a compound identifier consisting of a state machine name and a transition id will uniquely identify each transition, because state machine names are unique. Assuming that most transitions will be contained in the same state machine as the states being linked, one should also allow transition references to consist of just a transition id which can be disambiguated by the context. The following is the grammar in this case:

$$
\begin{aligned}
\text{Root} &\leftarrow \text{State\_Machine}^* \\
\text{State\_Machine} &\leftarrow \text{string State}^* \text{ Transition}^* \\
\text{State} &\leftarrow \text{string string transition\_ref}^* \text{ transition\_ref}^* \\
\text{Transition} &\leftarrow \text{string string string} \\
\text{transition\_ref} &\leftarrow \text{string} \mid \text{string string}
\end{aligned}
$$

It appears that one has, at last, fully represented the original data model of Figure 1 as a grammar. However, a number of important considerations are not included in the grammar specification. The strings occurring in each transition reference must occur as state machine names or as transition ids with the following additional constraints:

1. If just one string occurs, then it represents the transition id of a transition in the same state machine as the state.

2. If two strings occur, then the first must be a state machine name and the second is the transition id of a transition in that state machine.

These constraints must be enforced by actions triggered by the grammar rules.

If this example seems a little contrived, exactly the same issues arise in programming languages for which identifiers are used for variables and methods within classes and the same identifier may be used in different classes. In programming languages the disambiguation of identifiers is a very complex problem.

This example also shows that expressing an object-oriented data model in terms of a grammar typically results in a grammar that is much more complex and awkward than the data model. However, tree representations of data do have some advantages. There are easily available tools for automatically generating parsers from a grammar, and there are several tools for transforming trees in one grammar to trees in another grammar.

3.   A NEW APPROACH TO TRANSFORMATIONS

The purpose of the nu& Project [Bac90a, Bac90b, BMNR89] is to provide automated support for transformations from one language to another with emphasis on object-oriented modeling languages. This project combined the advantages of automated parser generation with the modeling power of object-oriented data models. Like grammar-based compiler-compilers, the nu& tools automatically generate parsers. However, the nu& toolkit uses the more powerful object-oriented data models rather than grammars, and the nu& toolkit transforms linear text directly into an object-oriented data structure. The toolkit can also be used to linearize an object-oriented database. Parsing and linearization of object-oriented data structures are similar to the marshaling and unmarshaling of data structures in remote procedure call mechanisms. The main distinction between RPC and the nu& toolkit is that nu& allows one to specify details about the grammar that is produced so that the resulting linear representation is readable. RPC linear representations, by contrast, are neither flexible nor intended to be read by people.

While the automated generation of parsers and linearizers is a useful feature, the main function of the nu& toolkit is to support transformations from one modeling language to another. In this respect, the nu& toolkit is similar to transformational reuse systems, such as Refine [Ref90], except that nu& supports a large variety of data modeling languages, including object-oriented data models while existing transformational reuse systems are grammar-based.

One of the problems with traditional approaches to transformations is the insistence on communicating using linear text. This is fine for simple transformations and has proved to be very effective in environments, such as the Unix shell, where "pipelines" join together relatively simple transformations to form more complex transformations. For example, `sort file | uniq -c | sort -nr | head -20` will compute the 20 most commonly occurring lines in a file. However, this technique becomes increasingly unwieldy as the complexity of the textual representation increases. For more complex languages, one requires a parser to produce a parse tree from the text, after which the identifiers in the parse tree must be disambiguated using a *symbol table*, and finally an internal (sometimes called an *intermediate* representation) is constructed. The intermediate representation is then processed to produce linear text to be used in the next stage of the pipeline.

Consider the problem of transforming a CASE tool diagram to a formal methods language. The traditional approach requires a series of transformational stages, each consisting of a series of steps. Each step involves processing output of the previous step. The whole process forms a pipeline of steps. To simplify the transformation, the diagram is first transformed to an object-oriented formal methods language, which is then transformed to a more traditional formal methods language. The formal specification can then be used to generate code in a programming language.

To illustrate the traditional transformational pipeline, we will use the example of the Slang formal methods language[W+98], and the O-SLANG object-oriented formal methods language [DeL96]. The O-SLANG language was developed in [DeL96] as a target structure that could be later transformed into Slang.

The full pipeline looks like that depicted in Figure 2. The middle column in this figure consists of the various linear representations that act as the communication language between the processing modules in the pipeline. The original diagram is dumped to a standard format of some kind. This standard format is parsed, and the identifiers placed in a symbol table, so that when one is encoun-

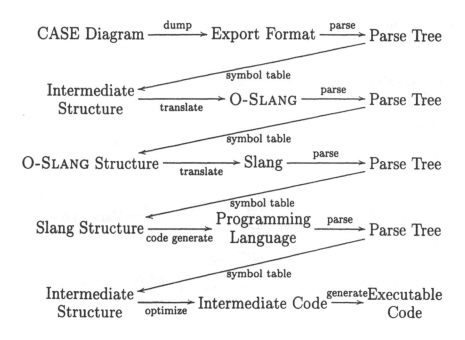

Figure 2 Transformation Pipeline

tered, it can be replaced with a reference to the object being referenced. The result is an intermediate structure which is essentially equivalent to the original diagram. This structure is then translated to the O-SLANG object-oriented formal methods language and given to the O-SLANG compiler. The same kind of parsing and symbol table manipulation is then performed so that O-SLANG can be translated to the Slang formal methods language, which is then used to generate code in a programming language. Finally, the programming language is compiled. A specific example of the transformation pipeline in Figure 2 is given in Section 4 below.

While many of the steps in the pipeline of Figure 2 are important, many of them represent duplication of effort. None of the steps in the traditional transformational pipeline are easy for nontrivial languages, and any one of the steps is a source of error. Proving the correctness of the entire pipeline is a difficult task. Reducing the number of steps is certainly desirable in itself, and this is one of the primary motivations for the nu& approach.

Using the nu& toolkit, one can make significant simplifications to the transformational pipeline of Figure 2. In Figure 3, the CASE diagram is isomorphic to a CASE tool's intermediate object structure. This structure is typically translatable to any kind of new structure by a vendor-provided scripting language. Rather than translate the CASE diagram to text in any form (as suggested by Figure 2), the nu& approach is to translate directly to the O-SLANG structure using object-oriented techniques and to continue to translate entirely

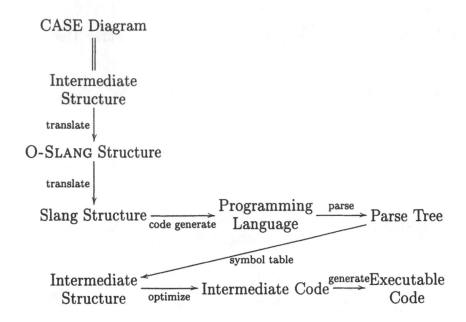

Figure 3 Simplified Transformation Pipeline

at the level of data structures (i.e., the left column of Figure 3). Unfortunately, it is difficult to streamline the entire transformation pipeline because one rarely has access to all of the internal data structures. For example, it is not currently possible to circumvent the parser of a compiler and present it with its intermediate representation directly.

Another possibility for simplifying Figure 2 would be to transform at the level of the parse tree (i.e., the right column in Figure 2). This is the approach taken by traditional transformational code generation systems such as Refine [Ref90] and GenVoca [BO92, BG97]. While this approach is certainly simpler than the original pipeline, it has the disadvantage that the translation code must deal with the table of identifiers, so that identifier lookup and resolution must be handled at the same time as the transformation. Another disadvantage is that the parse tree structures (right column in Figure 2) are generally more complex and unwieldy than the internal data structures (left column in Figure 2).

4.   STATE MACHINE EXAMPLE

In this section, we will give an example of the traditional transformational pipeline outlined in the previous section. We then compare it to the nu& approach.

Traditional Pipeline Approach

This example is derived from [DeL96]. In UML, a state diagram is one technique for describing the behavior of a class. The objective in this example is to convert a state machine diagram to its corresponding O-SLANG specification. In this example, we will use the class *pump* whose state diagram is given in Figure 4.

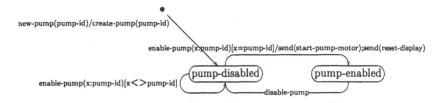

Figure 4 Pump State Diagram

The CASE tool used by DeLoach was a commercially available object-oriented drawing package, ObjectMaker[2]. The textual output from Object-Maker is parsed into a Refine parse tree using a Refine-based parser. Once in Refine, a rule-based conversion program translates the ObjectMaker parse tree into a Generic parse tree which is isomorphic to the original CASE diagram.

Once in the Generic parse tree, a rule-based transformation program implementing the transformation rules translates the Generic parse tree into an O-SLANG parse tree within the Refine environment. Once in a valid O-SLANG parse tree, the Dialect pretty printer is used to produce a textual representation of the O-SLANG parse tree. The actual transformation is performed by creating the root node of the O-SLANG parse tree and then automatically translating each class and association, one at a time, from the Generic parse tree to the O-SLANG parse tree.

The actual Refine transformation code is more complex than even Figure 2 suggests. The Export Format of ObjectMaker has a structure that is complex enough to require an additional transformation stage. The actual transformation from CASE Diagram to O-SLANG consists of the pipeline shown in Figure 5. The Refine tool allows some of the steps in the pipeline to be combined, but it is still necessary to write (and debug) five separate Refine specifications to achieve the entire transformation from CASE Diagram to O-SLANG. Several hundred lines of code are needed for specifying the rules for transforming a state machine diagram. We now show some excerpts from this code.

The grammar for the dynamic model portion of a Generic class is the following:

```
Generic-Class = <name, {Superclass}, [Connection], {Attribute},
        {State}, {Transition}, {Axiom}, {Operation}, {Function}>
State = <name, {State}, {Axiom}>
Transition = <name, [Parameter], Axiom, {Action},
```

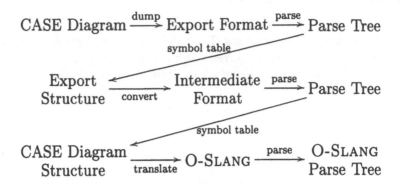

Figure 5 Actual Transformation Pipeline from CASE Diagram to O-SLANG

```
                FromState, ToState>
FromState = name
ToState = name
Action = <name, [Parameter], {Action}>
Parameter = <name, datatype>
```

A simplified version of the O-SLANG grammar is shown below. Notice that both StateAttr and State are defined as functions. StateAttr is a function that takes an object as its domain and returns a state value as its range. States are defined as nullary functions that return specific values of the state attribute.

```
Class = <name, ClassSort, {Operation}, {Import}, {Sort},
  {Attribute}, {Method}, {StateAttr}, {Event}, {State}, {Axiom}>
StateAttr = Operationdecl
State = Operationdecl
Operationdecl = <name, [Domain-Ident], [Range-Ident]>
Axiom = complex definition of 1st order predicate logic
```

There are three distinct steps to transforming the dynamic model from the Generic parse tree to the O-SLANG parse tree: (1) creation of state attributes, (2) creation of state values, and (3) creation of axioms that implement the transitions. For simplicity, we will just consider the axioms for transitions. Translation of the Generic Transitions into O-SLANG axioms is performed by breaking down each Generic Transition object and processing it in five parts: the current state, transition guard, new state, method invocation, and the sending of any new events.

```
function create-oslang-transition-axiom (x: Transition) :
  Axiom-Def = let (s:object=undefined)
    s <- Make-OslangAxiom(
          concat(create-oslang-current-state-string(x),
          create-oslang-guard-string(x),
```

```
          create-oslang-new-state-string(x),
          create-oslang-method-invocation-string(x),
          create-oslang-send-event-string(x),
          ")"))
```

The five parts are concatenated into a string which is parsed into an O-SLANG axiom parse tree by the Make-OslangAxiom function of the form

old-state ∧ *guard-condition* ⇒ *new-state* ∧ *method-invocations* ∧ *event-sends*

The final result of the pipeline is an O-SLANG parse tree which can be linearized into the following textual form:

```
class Pump is
  class-sort Pump
  import Pump-Id, Reset-Display, Start-Pump-Motor, Pump-Aggregate
  sort Pump-State
  attributes
    pump-id : Pump -> integer
    pump-state : Pump -> Pump-State
  operations
    attr-equal : Pump, Pump -> Boolean
  states
    pump-disabled : -> Pump-State
    pump-enabled : -> Pump-State
  events
    ...
  methods
    ...
  axioms
    pump-disabled <> pump-enabled;
    attr-equal(P1, P2) <=> (pump-id(P1) = pump-id(P2));
    (pump-state(P) = pump-enabled) =>
      (pump-state(disable-pump(P)) = pump-disabled);
    (pump-state(new-pump(P, A)) = pump-disabled
      & attr-equal(new-pump(P, A), create-pump(A)));
    ...
end-class
```

Object-Oriented Transformation

By contrast the transformation code using the nu& toolkit simply constructs each of the components occurring in the O-SLANG data structure as objects. One can use either rules or a series of nested loops to express the transformation. The following are some fragments of the code that illustrate the nu& nested loop approach:

```
for every c in allClasses {
  OSlangClass oclass = new OSlangClass (c.name);
  ...
  for every state in oclass.states {
    oclass.states.add (new State (state.name));
    ...
    for every transition in state.outTransitions {
      oclass.events.add (new Event (transition.name));
      oclass.axioms.add
        (new Axiom (transition.currentState && transition.guard,
            transition.newState && transition.methodInvocation
            && transition.sendEvent));
      ...
    }
  }
}
```

In addition to requiring fewer steps, the nu& approach involves much simpler code that focuses on the fundamental issues rather than myriad syntactic and symbol table issues.

5.   RELATED WORK

Several authors have proposed techniques for transforming informal system requirements and specifications into formal specifications. Babin, Lustman, and Shoval proposed a method based on an extension of Structured System Analysis. The method uses a ruled-based transformation system to help transform the semi-formal specification into a formal specification [B+91]. Fraser, Kumar, and Vaishnavi proposed an interactive, rule-based transformation system to translate Structured Analysis specifications into VDM specifications [F+94]. In both cases, the output of the process is a text-based formal specification that would require parsing for further automated refinement.

Specware [Spe94] is a transformational program derivation system based on Slang [W+98] which is the end target for this work. Specware provides the automated tool support for developing and transforming specifications using the Slang formal specification language. Once defined in Slang, all transformations – including algorithm design and optimization, data type refinement, integration of reactive system components, and code generation – are performed on an internal AST-based representation of Slang. However, Specware does not provide the front end as described in our research: an object-oriented, graphically-based semi-formal, community accepted representation.

Although not specifically concerned with formalization, there have been many research efforts and commercial products that support transformations from one language to another. Such tools are called transformational code generators or generative reuse tools. Krueger [Kru92] has a survey of such tools. Some of the most prominent among these tools are Batory's Gen-Voca [BO92, BG97], Neighbors' Draco [Nei84], and Reasoning Systems' Refine [Ref90]. While the output of these transformational systems can be object-oriented (e.g., by using components from and generating code in an object-oriented programming language), all of these systems use a specification language that is grammar-based. The nu& toolkit, by contrast, not only can generate object-oriented data structures, but also supports object-oriented specifications. As noted in Section 3, transforming object-oriented data structures is simpler, more powerful and less error-prone than transforming parse trees.

6. CONCLUSIONS

While object-oriented languages have become very popular in both programming and software specification, the formalism for representing their structure is still that of a context-free grammar, even though this formalism was developed mainly for a different kind of language. In this paper, we argued that for object-oriented representations data models are better suited than such context-free grammars. We showed with an example the difficulties involved in representing an object-oriented diagram using a context-free grammatical representation. We analyzed two possibilities for transforming object-oriented representations (UML diagrams) into formal non-object-oriented representations (Slang specifications):

1. Transform the data model of UML into a context-free grammar and then perform consecutive transformations in the realm of context-free grammars using CASE tools available for such translations, and

2. Translate the UML data model into an intermediate object-oriented representation and perform consecutive translations in the object-oriented domain, while translating into the context-free target language as the last step.

We argued for the latter approach. We showed that this approach is simpler in the sense that it consists of fewer transformational steps, and thus is less error-prone.

Notes

1. Refine is a trademark of Reasoning Systems Inc. Palo Alto California
2. ObjectMaker is a registered trademark of Mark V Systems Limited Encino California

References

[B+91]   G. Babin et al. Specification and design of transactions in information systems: A formal approach. *IEEE Transactions on Software Engineering*, 17:814–829, August 1991.

[Bac90a]   K. Baclawski. The nu& object-oriented semantic data modeling tool: intermediate report. Technical Report NU-CCS-90-18, Northeastern University, College of Computer Science, 1990.

[Bac90b]   K. Baclawski. Transactions in the nu& system. In *OOPLSA/ECOOP'90 Workshop on Transactions and Objects*, pages 65–72, October 1990.

[Bac91]   K. Baclawski. Panoramas and grammars: a new view of data models. Technical Report NU-CCS-91-2, Northeastern University College of Computer Science, 1991.

[BG97]   D. Batory and B. Geraci. Composition validation and subjectivity in Gen-
            Voca generators. *IEEE Transactions on Software Engineering*, 23:67–82, 1997.
            DARPA and WL supported project under contract F33615-91C-1788.

[BMNR89]   K. Baclawski, T. Mark, R. Newby, and R. Ramachandran. The nu& object-
            oriented semantic data modeling tool: preliminary report. Technical Report
            NU-CCS-90-17, Northeastern University, College of Computer Science, 1989.

[BO92]   D. Batory and S. O'Malley. The design and implementation of hierarchical
            software systems with reusable components. *ACM TOSEM*, October 1992.

[BRJ97a]   G. Booch, J. Rumbaugh, and I. Jacobsen. *UML Notation Guide, Version 1.1*,
            September 1997.

[BRJ97b]   G. Booch, J. Rumbaugh, and I. Jacobsen. *UML Semantics*, September 1997.

[DeL96]   S. DeLoach. *Formal Transformations from Graphically-Based Object-Oriented
            Representations to Theory-Based Specifications*. PhD thesis, Air Force Institute
            of Technology, WL AFB, OH, June 1996. Ph.D. Dissertation.

[F$^+$94]   M. Fraser et al. Strategies for incorporating formal specifications. *Communica-
            tions of the ACM*, 37:74–86, 1994.

[GT87]   G. Gonnet and F. Tompa. Mind your grammar: a new approach to modelling
            text. In *Proc. 13th VLDB Conf.*, pages 339–346, Brighton, UK, 1987.

[Kru92]   C. Krueger. Software reuse. *ACM Computing Surveys*, 24:131–183, June 1992.

[Nei84]   J. Neighbors. The Draco approach to constructing software from reusable com-
            ponents. *IEEE Trans. Software Engineering*, pages 564–574, Sept. 1984.

[Ref90]   *Refine 3.0 User's Guide*, May 25, 1990.

[Spe94]   *Specware^{TM} User Manual: Specware^{TM} Version Core4*, October 1994.

[W$^+$98]   R. Waldinger et al. *Specware^{TM} Language Manual: Specware^{TM} 2.0.2*, 1998.

About the Authors

Kenneth Baclawski is an Associate Professor of Computer Science at Northeastern University. His research interests include Formal Methods in Software Engineering, High Performance Knowledge Management, and Database Management. He has participated in and
directed many large research projects funded by government agencies including the NSF,
DARPA and NIH. He is a co-founder and Vice President for Research and Development
of Jarg Corporation which builds Internet-based, high performance knowledge management
engines.

   Scott A. DeLoach is currently an Assistant Professor of Computer Science and Engineering and Director of the Agent Lab at the Air Force Institute of Technology (AFIT).
His research interests include design and synthesis of multiagent systems, knowledge-based
software engineering, and formal specification acquisition. Prior to coming to AFIT, Dr. De-
Loach was the Technical Director of Information Fusion Technology at the Air Force Research
Laboratory. Dr. DeLoach received his BS in Computer Engineering from Iowa State Univer-
sity in 1982 and his MS and PhD in Computer Engineering from the Air Force Institute of
Technology in 1987 and 1996.

   Mieczyslaw M. Kokar is an Associate Professor of Electrical and Computer Engineering at Northeastern University. His technical research interests include formal methods in
software engineering, intelligent control, and information fusion. Dr. Kokar teaches graduate
courses in software engineering, formal methods, artificial intelligence, and software engineering project. Dr. Kokar's research has been supported by DARPA, NSF, AFOSR and
other agencies. He has an M.S. and a Ph.D. in computer systems engineering from Technical
University of Wroclaw, Poland. He is a member of the IEEE and of the ACM.

   Jeffrey Smith is a Senior Principle Engineer at Sanders and PhD candidate in Computer Systems Engineering at Northeastern University. His research interests include Formal Methods in Software Engineering, Operating Systems and High Performance Computing
Frameworks. He has applied his research in defense based applications, as both a practitioner
and manager for more than twenty years.

Chapter 2

BEING SERVED: THE PURPOSES, STRENGTHS AND LIMITATIONS OF FORMAL SERVICE MODELLING

Bernard Cohen

School of Informatics, City University
Northampton Sq. London EC1V 0HB
b.cohen@city.ac.uk

Abstract   Although the Object-Oriented community is now largely committed to formal service description, its ramifications have yet to be widely appreciated. A formal service description is a model (constructed by an observer: the analyst) of a service desired by an agent (in the context of the agent's world model). The assessment of its validity involves subjecting it to such operations as 'horizontal' composition (with models of other services with which it should interoperate), 'vertical' composition (with models of platforms on which servers propose to implement it), closure (to determine its possible behaviours), and restriction (to more limited ontologies, e.g. with respect to 'legacy' systems). These acts of analysis can reveal flaws both in the observer's understanding and in the agent's world model. In the latter case, the effects are clinical (as in psychoanalysis), altering the agent's world model, and the services desired, along a 'trajectory' in the space of all models. Although most of the mathematical frameworks familiar to Computer Science (e.g. set theory, abstract algebra, modal logic) are suitable vehicles for formal service modeling, none can represent such 'higher order' trajectories. Formal service modeling therefore presents a serious challenge both to our theory and to our praxis.

1. INTRODUCTION

A service is a system that one agent (a 'server') offers to another (a 'client'). The description of a service constitutes a contract between them, the server promising to supply , and the client agreeing to accept, some implementation that satisfies the description. A service description should be 'underdeterined', or 'weak', in that it specifies only those properties that are essential to it. in isolation.

But the client's demand for services is usually expressed in the context of the client's situation in which several services are to interoperate. Any description of a service in isolation may therefore have to be modulated by the various contexts in which it might be exploited. Similarly, a server's design for a service may be influenced by particular properties of the 'platform' on which it is to be implemented, which may also modulate the description of the isolated service.

These, and other related, considerations give rise to a class of phenomena which are manifest in many business domains but are particularly well manifested in telelcommunications systems, where they are known as 'feature interactions'. Although these phenomena are often experienced as 'mere' technological difficulties (e.g. software problems), they provide evidence of much deeper issues, involving philosophy, psychology and mathematics, that are not well understood by either the 'clients' or the 'servers' in the domains in which they arise.

In the following section, we provide some anecdotes of actual occurences of feature interactions, in telecoms and elsewhere, which we will use to motivate a case for formality in service description. Then we will address the problems of formalisation itself, in particular those associated with the composition of formal descriptions, and investigate how these problems affect the relationship between the modeler (i.e. an analyst) and the subject of the model (i.e. an enterprise, be it client, or server, or both). Finally, by considering the enterprise as its own analyst, we will take the discussion into the realms of strategy, where it becomes necessary to model not only the interoperation of services within and among enterprises, but the evolution of those enterprise, of their services, and of the agents who offer and invoke them.

2. FEATURE INTERACTION

Telecommunications systems offer services to their clients in behavioural packages called 'features'. These services are said to interact with each other when their behaviour in concert differs from their behaviour in isolation. When this behavioural modification is deemed to be beneficial, the features are said to 'interoperate', or to exhibit 'emergent' properties. However, when a behavioural property promised by one feature, and exhibited by it in isolation, is absent from the composite behaviour, we call the interaction 'destructive'.

Since Bellcore first publicized this problem [BDCGHL89], over one hundred destructive interactions among familiar telephony features have been discovered, all empirically. Here are a few examples, presented as anecdotes:

2.1 Call Waiting and Calling Number Identification

Mary received an obscene phone call. Deciding to take matters into her own hands, she used her 'Calling Number Identification' service to trace the call. When she called the number reported by the system, Ann answered. Mary, assuming that this was the partner of the obscene caller, demanded that she tell her husband to cease his disgusting practice. Ann, shocked at this accusation, called her best friend, who was none other than Mary! What had happened?

While the obscene caller has been on the line, Ann had called Mary and, of course, found her busy. Now Mary also subscribed to the 'Call Waiting' service, which recorded Ann as the 'last caller', so that when Mary invoked 'Calling Number

Identification', she received Ann's number.

It is tempting to think of this as a mere technical difficulty that could be resolved by, for example, having Calling Number Identification retain a list of calling parties instead of just the last one. However, this will not do. How would the subscriber know which number referred to which call?

The problem is one of semantics, not technology. The behaviours of these services satisfy their users' expectations of them in isolation, but violate those expectations when composed.

Some suppliers have tried to deal with this problem by analysing the interactions among all pairs of features: a large task, but a finite one.

However, this will not do either, because some destructive interactions occur among groups of more than two features.

2.2 Unlisted Number, Automatic Recall and Itemized Billing

Fred called John while John was busy talking to Al. Fred invoked John's 'Automatic Recall' feature, so when John's line became free, the system made a connection from John to Fred. Now Fred had the 'Unlisted Number' feature and John had 'Itemized Billing'.

Question: Should Fred's phone number appear on John's phone bill?

Answer: Yes and no! Either will violate one of the features. The composition of their specifications is logically inconsistent.

2.3 Emergency Services and Mobiles

A repairman had just arrived at a house call when he noticed a neighbour having a heart attack. Being a good citizen, he called the emergency services using his brand new mobile phone. The emergency operator responded immediately and sent the ambulance to the ground station of the mobile network!

Why? Because emergency operators had always been advised by the system of the caller's 'location', which was assumed to be that of the (fixed) instrument. Mobile telephony violates this ontological assumption.

Ontological problems arise frequently in the database world, as the following non-telephonic example demonstrates.

2.4 Patient Records

An epidemiologist working with a large repository of patient records held by an insurance company was startled to discover that, of those patients with post partum complications (conditions arising shortly after childbirth), some 40% were male!

The explanation is trivial: the genders recorded were those of the patients' husbands — the policy holders who, from the insurance company's perspective, are more significant than the patients.

Nor are 'feature interactions' restricted to information systems. A tragic instance occurred in automotive design.

2.5 Safety and Security

An armoured automobile, carrying a senior politician, was ambushed. The occupants wisely stayed behind the locked doors. The assailants, having failed to break a window, took a lever to the front bumper and located the microswitch that inflated the airbags. A safety feature ensured that it also threw open all four doors!

Here, safety and security features were mutually inconsistent: satisfying one violated the other.

3. FORMAL SERVICE MODELLING

An analysis of these and many other 'feature interactions' [CC96] suggested a classification according to their origins in the development process.

This process is conceived (see figure 1) as starting with a 'requirements analysis' in which the analyst constructs an isolated formal model of the required service that seeks to respect the client's ontology and semantics, but that omits all other services whether in the context in which it would be deployed or in any platform on which it might be implemented.

Of course, the formal model of any isolated service may itself be constructed as a composition of models. This gives rise to the hierarchy of description known as 'abstraction', which may also be inverted, with higher level service models being 'decomposed' into lower level ones, in the process of 'design'.

These *service descriptions* must be subjectable to the following formal operations:
- **horizontal composition** with models of other services in the client's context, to reveal inconsistencies that would, were they to occur in use, violate users' expectations;
- **restriction** to the earlier ontologies of systems already deployed, to reveal those problems usually encountered when integrating 'legacy' systems;
- **vertical composition** with models of the platforms on which the service is to be implemented, to reveal the effects of implementation constraints on the behaviour of the service as required; and
- **closure** and **projection** to reveal behaviours that, although derivable from the model, would be unacceptable to the client.

Since set theory offers all these operations, it has often been used (thinly disguised as Z, VDM, relational algebra, etc.) as the formal framework for the construction of such models. Both the object-oriented and distributed-systems communities have acknowledged the need for set-theoretic models of services, witness the recent introduction of semantic extensions to UML ('OCL', version 1 of which was issued in September 1998) and CORBA ('CDL' as proposed by the Business Object Domain Task Force), although their analytical implications are not yet widely appreciated.

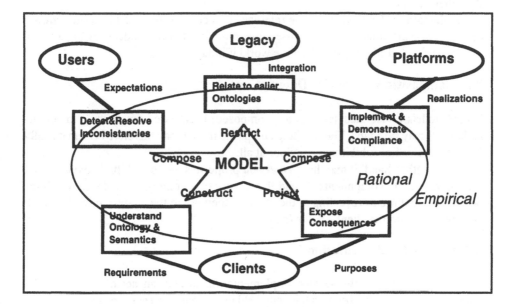

Figure 1: Rôles of Formal Models

3.1 State-based Models

Such set-theoretic, or 'state-based', models are schemata with state components and events, corresponding roughly to the attributes and methods, respectively, of the classes of object-oriented models. The state components are restricted by invariants and the events by pre- and post-conditions. Each schema must be demonstrably consistent in that no sequences of events may lead from a state that satisfies the invariant to one that violates it. A schema thereby defines a *topology* on its state space.

There is no 'message-passing' in set theory. Instead, multiple inheritance establishes a product state-space in which erstwhile isolated models interoperate. Inter-method (i.e. inter-event) communication occurs only through the sharing of parameters, so that event composition may be interpreted as concurrency..

A state-based model describes a service by virtue of its *ontology* — the (names of) things-in-the-world that are attributed to its state components and events. These correspond to 'reference' and 'sense', respectively, in Frege's theory of meaning.

Such models admit additional interpretations, as follows:

• **behavioural,** where each schema specifies a service whose behaviour comprises the set of all traces of the schema's events, as in process algebra;

• **deontic,** where each schema's invariants, preconditions and postconditions identify

obligations and responsibilities for those **agents** who would offer services satisfying the schema; and
•   **anticipatory** [R87] where, if the reference of a composite model is an **enterprise**, then its sense articulates the enterprise's theory of itself, whose adequacy determines the enterprise's ability to survive in the world it inhabits.

3.2 Composition of Service Descriptions

When models of isolated services are composed, new state components, invariants and events may be added. The resulting composite model may therefore be semantically inconsistent — i.e. exhibit no behaviour at all.

On the other hand, it may have *emergent* properties — i.e. exhibit behaviours not seen in any of its components — and the *closure* of a composite model may exhibit behaviours that are as revealing to the client as they are to the analyst, providing both with insights into the client's *value ladder* (see below).

3.3 Service Implementation

From this point of view, service implementation is also an act of formal model composition (not, as has been traditionally held in computer science, one of *refinement*). To implement a formal service model (composite or not), one must:
•   select *platforms* that already supply (implement, embody) certain services;
•   *compose* the required service model with models of the platforms' services, introducing appropriate relations and invariants among those components;
•   *verify* that the resulting composite model is consistent and that its closure is acceptable; and finally
•   *construct* the composite model on the platforms.

Unless the implemented service has emergent properties not exhibited by any of the platforms it exploits, it is merely an *aggregate*, not a *system*. Clearly, then, the value added by implementation resides in its composition of the models of the platforms' services with that of the required service.

4. SERVICES, AGENTS AND ENTERPRISES

The resolution of problems arising from model composition may entail changes in either:
•   the client's theory of the world (*Weltanschauung*), which is a clinical operation performed on the client; or
•   the analyst's model of the client, which is a formal operation (the application of *theory morphism*) on the model.

This suggests that the task of the analyst is to construct a theory of the knowledge of an agent qua client-for-services (see figure 2) and that agents themselves are,

simultaneously:
- *clients* who, as users of services, see only the service models and are responsible for assessing the fitness of those models for their own purposes;
- *servers* who, as providers of services, see both the model and the implementation of services and are responsible for guaranteeing conformance between them; and
- *members* of enterprises, in which they collaborate with other agents, respecting the mutual obligations and responsibilities articulated in the enterprise's composite model, so as to accomplish the enterprise's mission.

Since the enterprise's mission always includes the provision of services to its clients, every enterprise is itself an agent.

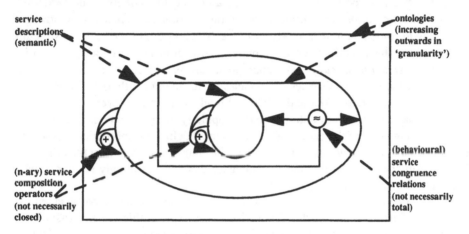

Figure 2: Theory of Agent qua Client

4.1 Value Ladders and Process Chains

Value ladders are directed graphs of service models expressed in terms of composition operators and congruence relations over an observer's model of an agent's knowledge.

Value ladders descend, from the unknowable roots of the agent's desires to the agent's expressed requirements for services to be supplied by others, by successive decomposition.

A model at any level in a value ladder may be:
- *overdetermined*, in that exactly one satisfactory decomposition can be conceived; or
- *underdetermined*, in that it admits more than one satisfactory decomposition; or
- *impossible*, in that no refinement, or implementation, could satisfy it.
  Impossibilities, or 'lacks in demand' [BC98], may arise because:
- due to flaws in the agent's knowledge, a service model, or the composition of a set of service models, is demonstrably inconsistent; or
- having reached an ontological boundary, the agent cannot further decompose the

model of some service; or
• the agent identifies some service as being desirable but cannot articulate a 'higher level' service of which it is a component.

Process chains similarly ascend from the *capabilities* of agents by the successive composition of the implemented (or embodied) platforms that these capabilities provide. They may be under- or overdetermined at any level and may suffer from impossibilities ('lacks in supply') for similar reasons of ignorance or error.

4.2 Enterprise Modelling

An enterprise may be modelled [BC98] as a composition of its value ladders (a *referential articulation*) and process chains (an *existential articulation*), arranged according to some common *business structure*. The purpose of the business structure is to distribute the authority to choose among underdetermined behaviours by imposing constraints (a *deontic articulation*) at appropriate 'layers' of that structure. The deontics also include the enterprise's rules and policies for resolving conflicts within itself.

In general, the referential and existential models at a given layer of the business structure may differ both in ontology and in topology. In order to compose them, the corresponding layer of the deontic articulation must define the appropriate constraints as invariants over a new ontology together with maps from from it to the other two. This construction, which is typical of category theory, is strikingly similar to what Fiadeiro calls 'superposition' [FA96].

The *closure* of such an enterprise model denotes all the knowledge that an enterprise can have of itself in its world. Enterprises may explore this closure (usually in extension, and therefore incompletely) in order to evaluate the anticipated effects of their possible courses of action. Such enterprises are *anticipatory* systems.

The enterprise is also a *reflective* system in that it can change its model of itself. To model such a system, we must construe it as being its own observer. This requires the modeller to take a position, with respect to the endo/exo cut [AWA95], that is radically different from that of classical systems theory.

A business sector consists of a collection of such enterprises that compete and collaborate in the provision of services to each other. In this context, an enterprise needs to respond to evolutionary pressures — from competition, technological change and customer preference — by changing its models of itself and, mutatis mutandis, the deontic context of its own agents. Such an enterprise is an *adaptive* system whose closure is the set of its possible trajectories through the space of its own potential models of itself (see figure 3).

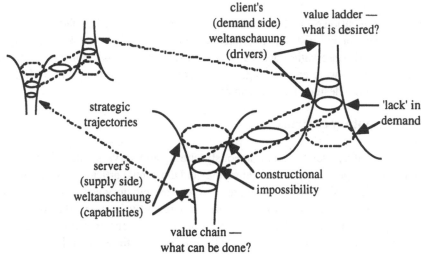

Figure 3: Trajectories through Model Space

5. A RESEARCH AGENDA

Agents and enterprises, as defined above, are members of the class of composite, anticipatory, reflective, adaptive systems — a class that lies beyond the expressive and analytical limits of classical systems theory. Nevertheless, engineers and strategic consultants are currently being charged with the analysis and design of such systems. It is not surprising that they encounter serious conceptual, analytical and synthetical problems, of which 'feature interaction' is just a symptom.

Although research programmes currently under way address some aspects of the agent/enterprise modelling problem, they are relatively fragmented. A full research agenda for this increasingly important class of problems should investigate all the following issues:

5.1 Theory morphism

As a reflective system, the agent/enterprise can change its own model of itself. These changes are theory morphisms which an appropriate modelling framework would have to be able to express *inside* the formal system. This is beyond the scope of first order models. Category theory seems to be indicated [F96] but it is not yet clear what categorical structures could express triply articulated enterprise/agent models, their closures, their reflections and their trajectories.

5.2 Refinement

The free composition of implementations that separately satisfy isolated service models. does not necessarily satisfy the restricted composition of those models [MC95]. This relatively trivial observation deals a serious blow to the well-established principle of refinement in software engineering. What methodological principles should replace refinement in the design of agents and enterprises?

5.3 Anticipatory Systems

Agents and enterprises are simultaneously clients and servers, characterised by the composition, respectively, of their referential and existential articulations as constrained by their deontic articulations. They are therefore anticipatory systems, members of a class that has attracted considerable attention recently in many disciplines, from cosmology to biology. Can enterprise modelling benefit from mathematical frameworks, such as *hyperincursion* [D98], developed in these other disciplines?

5.4 Higher Order Cybernetics

In information systems analysis, the complaint is often heard that 'the requirement specification changed all the time' because 'the client kept changing his mind'. However annoying it might be to the analyst, this behaviour is not only natural but essential to the enterprise, which must make choices among trajectories through a space of models of anticipatory systems. Strategic development is the rule, not the exception. The classical approaches to systems analysis derive from the precepts of cybernetics as they were formulated in the '50s. But this 'first-order' cybernetics is not applicable to our model of enterprise. What will be the precepts of a second or third order cybernetics, and how will they govern systems analysis?

5.5 Modelling as a Clinical Activity

The nature of the discourse between systems analyst and client, when the client is taken to be an enterprise, has much in common with *psychoanalysis*. This praxis is concerned with eliciting 'lacks' in the client's desires, with their relationships to the client's sense of identity, and with the clinical treatment of developmental problems that the client suffers therefrom. It is subject to certain pitfalls, such as rejection and transference, that the psychoanalyst is trained to recognise and avoid. This training has not traditionally been provided to the systems analyst who, as a result, may expose the client to potential clinical damage. Should the training of systems analysts be changed accordingly, and should a register be maintained of those who are qualified to practise?

References

[BDCGHL89] Bowen TF, Dworak FS, Chow CH, Griffeth ND, Herman GE, Lin Y-J. *The Feature Interaction Problem in Telecommunication Systems.* Proc. 7th IEE Int. Conf. on Software Engineering for Telecommunications Systems, 1989.

[BC96]   Cohen B, Cameron J. *Formal Approaches to Feature Interactions.* Tutorial Notes, Proc. FORTE/PSTV '96, Kaiserslautern, 1996.

[R87]   Rosen, R. Anticipatory Systems. Pergamon, 1987.

[BC98]   Boxer P, Cohen B. *Analysing the* lack *of Demand Organisation..* Proc. Computing Anticipatory Systems, Daniel M. Dubois, ed. Conference Proceedings 437, pp157-181, American Inst. Phys., Woodbury, NY, 1998.

[AWA95]   Atmanspacher H, Wiedenmann G, Amann A. *Descartes Revisited — The Endo/exo- Distinction and its Relevance for the Study of Complex Systems.* Complexity 1(3), pp. 15-21, 1995.

[MC95]   Menezes PB, Costa JF. *Compositional Reification of Concurrent Systems.* Journal of the Brazilian Computer Society, No. 1, Vol. 2, pp. 50-67, July 1995.

[F96]   Fiadeiro JL. *On the Emergence of Properties in Component-Based Systems.* Proc. AMAST 96, LNCS 1101, pp. 421-443, Springer 1996.

[D98]   Dubois D. *Computing Anticipatory Systems with Incursion and Hyperincursion..* Proc. Computing Anticipatory Systems, Daniel M. Dubois, ed. Conference Proceedings 437, pp.3-30, American Inst. Phys., Woodbury, NY, 1998.

About the Author

Bernard Cohen is Professor of Computing at City University in London. He graduated from Glasgow University in 1965. For the next 18 years, he designed telephone switching systems software for ITT in the UK, Belgium, France and the USA, latterly founding the Software Research Group in STL, ITT's UK laboratory. He held the Racal Chair in Information Technology at the University of Surrey from 1984 to 1990, and was Business Development Manager for Rex, Thomson and Partners, UK, from 1990 until he took his present post in 1991. His research interests are in the formal modelling of enterprises and in the relationships between systems analysis and psychoanalysis, in which he collaborates with Boxer Research Ltd. Some of the work reported here was supported by a grant from the RENOIR programme.

Chapter 3

WHAT VS. HOW OF VISUAL MODELING: THE ARROW LOGIC OF GRAPHIC NOTATIONS

Zinovy Diskin
F.I.S. Group, Latvia
zdiskin@acm.org
diskin@fis.lv

Boris Kadish
ZAKAZ.COM, Inc.
bkadish@zakaz.com
cadish@fis.lv

Frank Piessens
Dept. of Computer Science
K.U.Leuven, Belgium
frank@cs.kuleuven.ac.be

Abstract   The goal of the paper is to explicate some universal logic underlying various notational systems used in visual modeling. The idea is to treat the notational diversity as the diversity of visualizations of the same basic specificational format. It is argued that the task can be well approached in the arrow-diagram logic framework where specifications are directed graphs carrying a structure of diagram predicates and operations.

1.   INTRODUCTION

People like drawing pictures in order to explain something to others or to themselves. Concise graphical images – *visual models* – presenting various aspects of the universe of discourse are a very natural (for humans) means of communication and comprehension, and proved their practical helpfulness in a wide range of design activities: from thinking out how to knock a shack (where a drawing is useful yet optional) to design of high-rise buildings of business/software systems (impossible without visual models). The history of graphic notations invented in various scientific and engineering disciplines is rich and instructive but it is software/business engineering where for the last years one can observe a Babylon diversity of visual modeling languages and methods: ER-diagrams and a lot of their dialects, OOA&D-schemas in a million of versions and, at last, the recent UML which itself comprises a host of various notations. There is a plenty of literature on the subject and a huge amount of papers were written to advance a few basic ideas in one or another direction or polish them up to one or another level of details.

In this respect, what we would like to say clearly from the very beginning is that we see the present paper as *not* yet another one towards greater generality or a bit more well-defined semantics. Our goal is much more ambitious: to clarify the basic semantic foundations of visual modeling (VM) on a whole, and present an integrated framework where many problems of VM can be approached consistently, or, as our experience shows, even be eliminated at all by a proper formulation. Our concern is about *what* we actually do by visual models rather than inventing any particular, even "the best one", VM-notation. However, a clearly defined *what* induces certain guidelines for *how* and we will point to some basic principles of building VM-notations, which our analysis of semantic foundations suggests.[1] We call the corresponding graphic format *sketch* following mathematical category theory (CT) where (somewhat different) sketches were invented for specifying mathematical structures.[2]

Let S be a specification in some language $\mathcal{L}$ whose details are not essential, particularly, $\mathcal{L}$ can be some VM-notation and S is a graphic schema (we prefer to call graphic specifications schemas rather than diagrams because the term *diagram* has special technical meaning in the sketch language). If one is well satisfied with informal intuitive meaning of S, we have almost nothing to say about benefits of sketches. However, as soon as one is interested in some abstract, intuition-free, description of the meaning of S, the sketch format immediately appears. Indeed, a lesson one can learn from modern mathematics is that formal semantics of any notation should be searched in the world of abstract homogeneous sets and functions, and sketches are nothing but a graphical language for specifying this world and its constructs. Moreover, a surprising result proved in CT states that *any* formal construction can be expressed by a sketch and, thus, as soon as S has a meaning described formally, it can be expressed by some sketch S_0 as well. As for S, its syntax can be arbitrary (and even not graphical at all) but, in principle, we can consider it as a syntactic visualization sugar over the basic sketch structure S_0 behind S. Generally speaking, this visualization superstructure is independent of S_0 but the meaning of S would be much more transparent if some parallelism between formal logical specification S_0 and its visual appearance S holds. This at once leads to a useful principle of graphic notation design: in a reasonable language $\mathcal{L}$, any schema S appears as $V(S_0)$ with S_0 a logical sketch specification behind S and V a mapping of specificational constructs into their visualizations.

Despite the absolute expressiveness of the sketch language, its vocabulary of basic terms is extremely brief. Roughly, a *sketch* is a directed graph in which some diagrams (graph's fragments closed in a certain technical sense) are marked with labels taken from a predefined *signature*; these labels (markers) are predicate symbols and marked diagrams are nothing but predicate declarations. So, a sketch specification consists of only three kinds of items: (i) nodes, (ii) arrows, (iii) marked diagrams. Formally, it can be presented by a tuple $[G, P_1(D_1), \ldots, P_n(D_n)]$ with G a graph, P_i diagram predicate symbols and $P_i(D_i)$ predicate declarations for diagrams D_i in G (to be read as "diagram D_i of sets and functions possesses the property P_i"). In addition, some of predicate symbols may denote diagram operations (similar to presenting, say, addition of integers by a ternary predicate); thus, (iv) an attribute of being *basic* or *derived* should be defined for all items of a sketch. The four constructs we mentioned exhaust the basic sketch vocabulary.

In the sketch framework the task of designing a VM-notation in some applied field (semantic data modeling, behavioral modeling, business modeling, X-modeling with X an arbitrary domain of discrete nature) is reduced to the following two subtasks:

(i) design of sufficiently expressive and convenient signature of diagram predicates to build *logical* sketches S_0,

(ii) design of appropriate way of external presentation of sketch specifications, that is, design of sketch *visualization mechanism V* to build graphic specifications, *visual* sketches, $S = V(S_0)$.

This clear formulation is in sharp contrast with the current practice of VM-notation design often based on shaky and *ad hoc* logical foundations (if any).

The task (i) needs formal explication of domain specific constructs in the sketch language: it is a typical applied mathematics setting similar to, for example, application of calculus in mechanical or electric engineering. The absolute expressive power of sketches does guarantee feasability of this task (at least, in principle, but of course within the very limits of intuitive domain formalizability). However, for real practical applications of some notation $\mathcal{L}$, more important than the expressive power of $\mathcal{L}$ are naturality of $\mathcal{L}$-specifications for the domain, their practical effectiveness and convenience, and such an immaterial (yet integral and we believe very important for vitality of complex intellectual systems including notations) property as elegance. In this respect, the visualization part of notation design is of extreme importance but it is far beyond formal logic and the sketch format as such, actually, it is a non-trivial problem of general cognitive nature. Nevertheless, the rigor and clear specification pattern provided by sketches allows to approach this problem by mathematical methods, in particular, to consider visualization V as a morphism from some structure of specificational primitives into a similar structure of visual primitives.[3]

Well, the sketch language is expressive but we emphasize that, as any other logical machinery, it does not solve the two major problems (i),(ii) above and, given some particular discipline of VM, the virtual possibility of expressing its modeling constructs in the sketch language has nothing to do with effective usage of sketches in the field. However, the clear formulation of graphic notation problems in the sketch framework, its brevity and the semantic guidelines it suggests are themselves helpful and organize the design activity on reasonable (and mathematically justified) foundations. At any rate, they allow to focus on resolving actual problems having real semantic meaning rather than fighting with pseudo-problems generated exclusively by using an unsuitable *ad hoc* language and existing only within that language. A typical example is the infamous problem of integrating ER and OO that has been widely discussed in the literature on conceptual data modeling but at once disappears as soon as one approaches it in a proper semantic framework [DK].

As always with applications of abstract mathematics to engineering problems, applying sketches to system/business modeling is an art rather than science and much depends on heuristic issues that cannot be formally deduced or predicted. So, discussing practical benefits of adopting sketches for visual modeling in a particular field $\mathcal{F}$ we can speak only about expectations rather than assert firmly, and only real "case studies" of notations invented in $\mathcal{F}$ and problems they should help to manage can confirm or refute our "sketch thesis". In this respect our current experience is promising: in domains where we applied sketches they appeared as a precise, and practically useful, logical refinement and generalization of the existing notation rather than an external imposition upon it. In particular, in semantic data modeling sketches can be seen as a far reaching yet natural generalization of functional data schemas, ER-diagrams and OOA&D-schemas ([DK]), in meta-specification modeling they appear as essential generalization of schema grids developed by the Italian school [BBS93] (see [Dis98a] for the sketch treatment of meta-modeling) and we expect that in process modeling sketches will be a natural development of interaction diagrams [Abr94].

The rest of the paper consists of bits of additional explanations, few examples and few comments to points mentioned above, all are necessarily very brief because of space limitations. In section 2.1 we explain the distinction between logical specification as such and its visual presentation. We believe that this issue is of principle importance for VM but often is not properly understood. Then we briefly discuss current approaches to building semantic foundations of VM and their principle shortcomings, and explain basics of the sketch solution we suggest, particularly, its benefits for unification goals (section 3.). Section 4. is a very brief outline of the semantic data specifications in the sketch framework. It is only one example of refining a VM-practice with sketches but hopefully it gives a general notion how the machinery works. In particular, in 4.3 we will compare notational mechnisms of our sketches and two particular kinds of UML-diagrams.

2.   FORMAL SEMANTICS FOR GRAPHIC NOTATIONS

To be really useful as business and software specifications, and as a means of communication between many people of diverse backgrounds involved in design of complex systems, VM-diagrams (VMDs) should have clear and unambiguous semantic meaning. However, semantic meanings of VMDs' items live in the world of abstract concepts, they cannot be "pointed out by finger" and must be described in some special language, necessarily symbolic to be able to refer to abstract concepts. Certainly, since the description should be unambiguous the language for specifying semantics must be extremely precise, in ideal, formal or ready to be formalized.

So, the academic problem of formal semantics for a given VM-notation attains a real practical value, and many attempts were made to build precise semantic foundations under ER-modeling, OO-modeling and, in particular, now we can observe an explosion of semantic research for the UML-modeling. All these attempts can be roughly divided into the two large groups briefly discussed below in sections 2.2 and 2.3 but to make the discussion substantial we first need some methodological preparation in section 2.1.

2.1   GRAPH-BASED VS. STRING-BASED LOGICS

It is crucial for understanding the purposes of the present paper to recognize the distinction between string-based and graph-based logics. The point is that any specification – as it is presented to its reader – is actually a *visual presentation* of a certain underlying *logical specification* as such. In general, there are possible graphical visualizations of string-based logical specifications and, conversely, linear string visualizations of graph-based specifications.

Let us consider, for example, an expression "$(a+b) \times c$" where a, b, c denote elements of some predefined domain and symbols $+, \times$ denote binary operations, say, *plus* and *prod*, over the domain. The expression denotes the result of applying *prod*-operation to the pair (r, c) where r denotes the result of applying *plus*-operation to the pair (a, b). So, the logical specification hidden in the visual expression $(a + b) \times c$ is a parsing tree which can be presented in the bracket notation by the formula $prod(plus(a, b), c)$.

This specification can be extracted from the visualization above if the parser knows that operations *plus* and *prod* have (arity) shapes as shown in the Version1-column of the table below (bullets • denote place-holders for which elements of the domain are to be substituted). If one takes other visualizations of the shapes, one will get other visualizations of the same logical specification (see the table for examples).

	Version1	Version2	Version3
Visual shapes of operations	• + •, • × •	• + •, $\prod(•, •)$	$\overset{+}{\underset{• \quad •}{\wedge}}, \overset{\times}{\underset{• \quad •}{\wedge}}$
Visual presentation of specification $prod(plus(a, b), c)$	$(a + b) \times c$	$\prod(a + b, c)$	$\overset{\times}{\underset{\underset{a \quad b}{\wedge} \quad c}{+}}$

In shapes of operations above one can distinguish the logical part – a set of place-holders called the *arity* of operation, and the visualization part – the mutual arrangement of place-holders and the symbol (marker) of the operation. To distinguish different place-holders in an arity shape it is reasonable to label them by natural numbers and then an arity appears as a string of place-holders. Hence, the logic we consider is string-based. As for the visualization mechanism, it can be linear (*eg*, columns 1,2 of the table) or two-dimensional (column 3). Correspondingly, the specification above will be visualized by a linear string or a two-dimensional image as is shown in the bottom row of the table. In the Version3-case the image is a graph but it does not mean that the logic itself is graph-based. More complex yet real examples of the same notational phenomenon are the so called conceptual graphs [MMS93] and graphical interfaces to relational database schemas employed in many design tools. Conversely, graph-based logic specifications can be presented in a linear plain form: after all, a graph is an ordinary two-sorted mathematical structure well specified by formulas.

So, in considering graphic notational systems one should carefully distinguish between specification and visualization, and graph-based logics should be carefully distinguished from graphical interfaces to string-based logics. Any logic with string-like arities is a string-based logic, no matter how graphical its visualization looks.

2.2   FOREIGN FORMAL SEMANTICS: VISUAL MODELS AS STRING-BASED ELEMENT-ORIENTED THEORIES

With the approach in the title, visual models are considered as theories in some string-based logical formalism built along the lines the ordinary many-sorted predicate calculus ($\mathcal{PC}$) is built. Examples (just to mention few) are $\mathcal{PC}$-like formalization of OO built in [KLW95], of ER in [GH91] and of UML fragments in [LB98, WJS94]. However, $\mathcal{PC}$-like formalizations of graphic notations used in conceptual modeling fail to capture the two key ideas behind VM:

(i) in syntax, stating *graph-based logic* as the main apparatus,

(ii) in semantics, viewing the world as a system of objects and object classes inter-related by associations/references between them.

Indeed, syntax of $\mathcal{PC}$ is based on sets (strings) rather than graphs though, as it was shown above, these string specifications can be graphically visualized. As for semantics, $\mathcal{PC}$ enforces one to view the world in terms of elements and operations/relations over these elements, that is, constitutes an *elementwise* approach (where, for example, tuples are primary while relations are derivative – they are sets of tuples). In contrast, the OO-modeling necessarily leads to viewing the world as a collection of homogeneous variable sets (classes) and functions (references) between them while internal structure of elements (objects) is derivative: for example, first a set R is somehow declared to be a relation over domains $D_1, \ldots D_n$ and only then elements of R can be considered as $D_1 \times \ldots \times D_n$-tuples. This OO-view is somewhat opposed to the elementwise one and, thus, the $\mathcal{PC}$-approach does give precise semantics but for something different than modern VM-notations.

2.3   NATIVE NAIVE SEMANTICS: VISUAL MODELS AS GRAPH-BASED OO-DESCRIPTIONS

In this approach, semantic meaning of VM-diagrams has been explicated in some direct way by considering VMDs immediately as graphic specifications with their intended OO-interpretations. These attempts are very different technically but share the naive approach to the problem when formal semantics for a graphic notation has been built in an *ad hoc* way based on common sense and intuition. We call these approaches naive since actually the issue is highly non-trivial and hardly can be properly developed from scratch. Indeed, it was in a focus of CT research in 1960s-70s and stating a proper basic framework required serious efforts of the mathematical community. The corresponding foundations are now well known in CT under the name of *topos theory* and, in fact, the most advanced studies in searching VMD-semantics resulted in rediscovery of particular topos-theoretic concepts in a naive way. However, as a rule, approaches of this second kind provide "semantics" that is just a different yet again highly informal re-description of intuitive meaning (the UML Semantics [RJB99] is an example).

2.4   NATIVE FORMAL SEMANTICS: VISUAL MODELS AS SKETCHES

The only way to describe something abstract in an unambiguous way is to describe this thing in some also abstract yet commonly understandable basic terms. For a long time this problem was in a focus of mathematical studies and to the present day two frameworks are established. One is the classical set-theoretical framework based on the key notions of *set* and its *elements* related with the fundamental *membership* predicate. This is the ground of $\mathcal{PC}$-semantics and elementwise thinking referred above. The second framework is more recent, it was developed in CT and is based on two other key concepts: of *object* (*eg*, set) and of *morphism* (*eg*, mapping). Syntactically, specifications in this second framework take the form of directed graphs consisting of nodes (objects) and arrows (morphisms), and the entire approach is often called *arrow logic* and even *arrow thinking* since its applications assume a special ability of specifying any universe of discourse by arrows.

It should be stressed that the difference between the two approaches is not only in that specifications in the former are strings while in the latter they are graphs. Much more important is the substantial difference in the intended semantic interpretations. Normally, items of string specifications are interpreted by elements of some predefined domain (or several domains), and by constructs built from elements. In contrast, items of the arrow specifications are normally interpreted by set-like (for nodes) and mapping-like (for arrows) objects of some predefined universe of domains and mappings between them. As for some internal "elementwise" structure of these objects, it is characterized externally via adjoint arrow diagrams: all that one wants to say about an object one has to say via arrows related to this object (in section 4. we will show a few simple examples how it can be done).[4] As it was formulated by one of the founders of the arrow thinking Bill Lawvere, "to objectify means to mappify". In contrast, in the first framework, to "objectify" something means to point out elements of this thing.[5]

A fundamental result proved in CT is that expressive powers of the two languages are equal: any set-element specification can be converted into an object-arrow one expressing the same semantics and vice versa. In addition, this common expressive power is *absolute*: by a basic dogma of modern mathematics, the very notion of formalizability means the possibility to be described via sets and elements, hence, via objects and arrows as well. So, for *any* universe of discourse, as soon as one needs to build its formal model, one can well consider the universe as a system of nodes and arrows, which, in addition, carries a certain structure of arrow diagram predicates; that is, as a category theorist would say, to consider the universe as a *topos*. Then visual models of the universe are nothing but finite specifications of the topos (in general, infinite) and, as such, can be *naturally* considered as sketches we described in introduction: indeed, sketches are nothing but finite presentations of toposes.

3. TOPOSES AND SKETCHES: SEMANTIC DIVERSITY IN THE SAME SPECIFICATIONAL FORMAT

3.1 SKETCHES AND THEIR INTERPRETATIONS

A topos is an abstract mathematical structure whose items (nodes, arrows, markers) can be manipulated in an abstract algebraic way. In concrete applications, one deals with concrete toposes consisting of, for example,

(*i*) sets (data types) and functions (procedures), in *functional programming*;

(*ii*) variable sets (object classes) and variable functions (references), in *semantic data modeling / OO analysis and design*;

(*iii*) propositions and proofs, in *logic/logic programming*;

(*iv*) interfaces and processes, in *process modeling*.

In other words, when one specifies a universe in a discipline above by a sketch, nodes and arrows of the sketch can be interpreted, in function of context, as pointed. One can also say that sketch nodes and arrows are formal parameters while their interpretations above are actual parameters.

A special and important interpretation is when nodes and arrows are considered as

(*v*) specifications and mappings between them (*meta-modeling*).

It was shown in [Dis98a] that in this way the basic notions of view and refinement of specification can be modeled and, thus, the arrow language turns out to be very natural for meta-modeling.

So, in different applications we have different toposes yet they are instances of the same abstract construct. Then, all the semantic diversity above can be managed within the same mathematical and notational framework. For example, a relation between

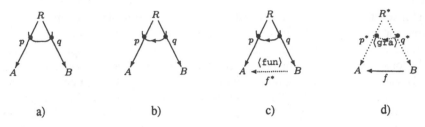

Figure 3.1 Relations via arrows

two objects A and B of whatever sort they are (for example, A, B can be data types, or object classes, or process interfaces, or data schemas) is specified in the same way by an arrow span shown on schema (a) Fig. 3.1. In this figure, R is an object similar to A, B, which is to be thought of as consisting of pairs (links, relationships) of items of A, B, and p, q are projection morphisms (references, processes, schema mappings) to be thought of as extracting the first and the second components of the pairs. In addition, a special predicate *Rel* should be declared for the triple (R, p, q) to ensure that R-items can be indeed thought of as pairs of A-items and B-items. A natural way to express such a declaration $Rel(R, p, q)$ syntactically is to mark the arrow diagram (p, q) by some label, say, an arc, as shown on schema, in fact, a sketch, (a). The description is generalized for n-ary relations in a straightforward way: consider arrow n-spans $(R, p_1, ..., p_n)$ over domains $A_1, ..., A_n$.

Specifically, the property of being a functional relation, say, from B to A, can be expressed by another predicate declared for the same diagram; syntactically, it can be presented as, *eg*, shown on sketch (b), Fig. 3.1. In this case there is a mapping $f: B \to A$ derived from the relation. In fact, one has a *diagram operation* producing an arrow from a span marked with the functional relation label, see schema (c), where the marker $\langle \text{fun} \rangle$ denotes the operation in question and the dotted body of the f^*-arrow denotes that it is derived (by the operation). Conversely, from a given arrow (reference, process, schema mapping) $f: B \to A$, one can derive its graphic (R^*, p^*, q^*). Formally this can be expressed as application of the operation $\langle \text{gra} \rangle$ to the arrow f as shown on (d) where all derived items are marked with the *-superscript. So, in the arrow framework relations can be specified, and manipulated, in an abstract way without considering their elements but via their arrow interfaces, (p, q) in the example.

3.2   SKETCHES VS. HETEROGENEITY OF VISUAL MODELS

In the previous section we discussed possibilities of the unifying sketch format across different fields where VM is applied. However, even within the same field usually there are many different VM-methodologies resulting in different notational systems. For example, in conceptual data modeling there are sets of ER-based and of OO-based notations, and many "this-vendor-tool-based" ones. With the current trend to cooperative/federal information systems, one necessarily encounters severe problems of integrating specifications describing (overlapping fragments of) the same universe but in different notational systems.   In fact, the famous UML recently adopted as a standard in OO analysis and design, is nothing but an attempt to solve this sort of problems "once and for ever". No doubts that the UML is a significant achievement towards unification but, from the logical view point, it is just another (very bulky) notational system rather than a framework to manage the heterogeneity problem.

In the sketch framework the heterogeneity problem can be approached as follows. First of all we note that actually any sketch is a Π-sketch, where Π denotes some predefined signature of diagram predicates and operations (markers) that can be declared in the sketch. Very different signatures are possible, and each of them determines its own notational subsystem within the same sketch language.

Now, given some field $\mathcal{F}$ of applying VM, let $\mathcal{M}$ be a particular VM-methodology used in the field. One can arrange $\mathcal{M}$-vocabulary of specificational constructs into a signature, $\Pi_{\mathcal{M}}$, so that $\mathcal{M}$-specifications become convertible into $\Pi_{\mathcal{M}}$-sketches. Thinking semantically, this is always possible since a given $\mathcal{M}$-specification and its $\Pi_{\mathcal{M}}$-sketch counterpart are nothing but different presentation of the same semantic universe, that is, of the same topos (of $\mathcal{F}$-sort). Moreover, by adjusting visualizations of $\Pi_{\mathcal{M}}$-predicates one can make visual presentations of $\Pi_{\mathcal{M}}$-sketches close to $\mathcal{M}$-schemas as they are seen externally. In this way the *diversity* of VM-models (used in $\mathcal{F}$) can be transformed into the *variety* of sketches in different signatures. Indeed, sketches in different signatures are nevertheless sketches, and they can be uniformly compared and integrated via relating/integrating their signatures. Though the latter task is far from being trivial, it is precisely formulated and can be approached by methods developed in CT.[6] Anyway, in many interesting particular cases the signature integration is easy.

The methodology of the sketch approach can be illustrated by the following analogy. Let us consider applications of sketches to semantic data modeling. The place of sketches in the heterogeneous space of semantic meta-models is comparable with that of the modern positional notations for numbers in the general space of such notations (we will call them numeral systems) including also zeroless positional systems (*eg*, Babylonian, Mayan) and a huge diversity of non-positional *ad hoc* systems (Egyptian, Ionian, Roman *etc*). The analogy we mean is presented in the table below.

Specification paradigm	Data to be specified	Language		Minimal language
		Predefined base	Specification	
Positional numeral systems	Finite cardinalities	Base of numeral system, k	Positional k-number	Binary numbers
Sketches	Collections of sets and functions	Signature, Π	Π-sketch	Original categorical sketches

In the context of this analogy, many conventional notations used for semantic data modeling are similar to *ad hoc* non-positional numeral systems like, *eg*, Roman. The question about expressive power of sketches is analogous to the question of whether a positional system can emulate an arbitrary numeral system. The positive answer is evident to everybody but it would not be so if one considers the question within the pure syntactical frame: thinking syntactically, it is not so obvious how to translate Roman numbers into decimal. The question above is easy because of our inherited habit to think about numbers semantically: any Roman number is a presentation of some finite cardinality, and a decimal number can express the latter as well.

The situation with sketches is similar: thinking semantically, any data schema is a specification of a system of sets and functions, and the latter can be expressed by a sketch as well. Of course, a specialist in semantic modeling who has the habit to think of conceptual schemas in pure relational terms will have doubts whether an arbitrary complex logical formula can be expressed by a diagram predicate. The translation is indeed far from being evident but nowadays can be found in any textbook on categorical logic (*eg*, [BW90]).

Well, sketches do provide a principle possibility to manage heterogeneity of visual models in a consistent way by translating any model into a sketch. However, for practical applications the crucial question is how easy and natural such a translation could be, and whether the visual appearance of the model and its sketch counterpart could be a good match. The latter is important since a given visual notation often accumulates some useful experience and VM-techniques developed in the field; at any rate, it is habitual for the community and useful notational habits surely should be kept. As for semantic data modeling, it was shown in [Dis98b] how one can put conventional notational constructs into the sketch pattern by considering them as either special visualizations of diagram markers or as special abbreviations. In sections 4.3, 4.4 below we will present an example of such a case study by sketching two familiar UML-constructs.

4.   EXAMPLE OF SKETCHING A VM-DISCIPLINE: SEMANTIC DATA MODELING VIA SKETCHES

The main idea underlying the sketch approach to data modeling is to consider object classes as plain sets consisting of internally unstructured (homogeneous) elements whereas all the information about their type is moved into certain arrow (reference) structures adjoint to classes.

4.1   COMPLEX TYPES VIA ARROW DIAGRAMS

The arrow way of specifying basic complex types (tuple type, set type, variant type) was presented in [Dis98b]. Here we will reproduce the tuple type description to make the paper selfcontained on the first reading level.

Instead of saying that a set X consists of n-tuples over a list of domains $D_1, \ldots, D_n$, one can equivalently say that there is a *separating* family of functions, $f_i \colon X \longrightarrow D_i (i = 1, \ldots, n)$, that is, a family satisfying the following condition:

(Sep)   for any $x, x' \in X$, $x \neq x'$ implies $f_i(x) \neq f_i(x')$ for some i

Indeed, in such a case the tuple-function $f = \langle f_1 \ldots f_n \rangle$ into the Cartesian product of domains,

$$f = \langle f_1 \ldots f_n \rangle \colon X \longrightarrow D_1 \times \cdots \times D_n, \quad fx \stackrel{\text{def}}{=} \langle f_1 x, \ldots, f_n x \rangle$$

is injective so that elements of X can be considered as unique names for tuples from a certain subset of $D_1 \times \ldots \times D_n$, namely, the image of f. In fact, elements of X can be identified with these tuples so that X is a relation up to isomorphism. In the classical ER-terminology, if the domains D_i's are entity sets then f_i's are *roles* and any $x \in X$

is a relationship between entities $f_1(x), \ldots, f_n(x)$. Since, conversely, for any relation the family of its projection functions is separating, the very notions of a tuple set and separating source (of functions) are equivalent.

Correspondingly, on the syntax level, to specify a node as a relation one may leave the node without any marking but label instead the corresponding source of outgoing arrows by some marker (say, an arc) denoting the (Sep)-constraint.

4.2   INTERPRETATION OF ARROWS

The key point in semantics of sketches is how to interpret arrows. In the former considerations we interpreted arrows by ordinary functions, *ie*, totally defined single-valued functions. This is the standard category theory setting. In contrast, in semantic modeling it is convenient (and common) to use optional and multivalued attributes/references, and so other interpretations of arrows arise: by partially defined functions (*p-functions*) and by multivalued functions (*m-functions*); of course, interpretations by partially defined and multivalued, *pm-functions*, are also possible.

Note, m-functions and p-functions are not ordinary functions subjected to some special constraints. Just the opposite, a single-valued function is a special m-function $f : A \longrightarrow B$ when for any $a \in A$ the set $f(a) \subset B$ consists of a single element. Similarly, a totally defined function is a special p-function $f : A \circ\!\longrightarrow B$ whose domain $D_f \subset A$ coincides with the entire source set A. So, to manage optional multi-valued attributes and references in the sketch framework we assume that

(i) all arrows are by default interpreted by pm-functions,

(ii) there is an arrow predicate (marker) of being a single-valued function,

(iii) there is an arrow predicate (marker) of being a totally defined function.

It is convenient to visualize constraintless arrows (without markers) by $\circ\!\longrightarrow\!\!\!\!\rightarrow$ whereas $\longrightarrow\!\!\!\!\rightarrow$ and $\circ\!\longrightarrow$ are denotations of arrows on which markers are hung: the ordinary tail is the marker of being totally defined and the ordinary head is the marker of being single-valued. Of course, superposition of these markers is also legitimate and it is natural to visualize it by the arrow $\longrightarrow$. Thus, visualization of predicate superposition equals superposition of visualizations: here we have a simple instance of applying a useful general principle that reasonable graphic notation should follow. (Actually, it gives rise to a consistent mathematical framework for building graphic notation we mentioned in introduction).

4.3   SIMPLE EXAMPLES: SKETCHES VS. UML-DIAGRAMS

We will consider two very simple examples to give some, actually very rough, notion of conceptual modeling with sketches.

The UML-diagram D_1 on Fig. 3.2(i) describes a very simple universe: each *Villa*-object has one or more owners from the class *Person* and a *Person*-object may own none or only one *Villa*; *Ownership* is a corresponding association class as they are understood in the UML [BJR99].

The corresponding sketch specification is presented on the right. Two arrows out of the *Ownership*-node with the arc-marker hung on them (section 4.1) show that *Ownership*-objects can be considered as pairs (v, p) with $v \in [\![Villa]\!]$ and $p \in [\![Person]\!]$, here $[\![\ ]\!]$ denotes semantic mapping assigning sets to nodes and functions

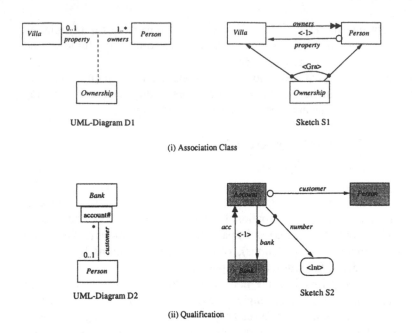

Figure 3.2   Sketches vs. UML: two examples

to arrows. Tails and heads of the horizontal arrows (section 4.2) declare the same constraints as the left and right superscripts over the association edge on the UML-diagram. Marker $\langle-1\rangle$ hung on the pair of horizontal arrows denotes the predicate of being mutually inverse functions. Marker $\langle\text{Gra}\rangle$ means that $[\![\ Ownership\ ]\!]$ is the graph of (each of) these functions, that is, if $(v,p) \in [\![\ Ownership\ ]\!]$ then $v = [\![\ property\ ]\!]\ (p)$ and $p \in [\![\ owners\ ]\!]\ (v)$.

Another example is presented on Fig. 3.2(ii). The UML-diagram D_2 models the so called *qualification* construct when two coupled nodes are attached to the same end of an association edge: this means that in order to select an object on the other end of the association one should point out a value of the qualifier. In the example, *account#* (smaller rectangle) is a qualifier and thus, for a given *Bank*-object b, while $b.customer$ is the set of b-customers, $b[55555].customer$ is the single *Person*-object having account #55555 at the bank b.

Sketch specification of the same data semantics is presented on the right. A peculiarity of sketch S_2 is that it has two kinds of nodes. Rectangles denote object classes (in the database context, extension of these nodes should be stored and it is suggestive to fill-in them with dots) while stadions denote value domains (computable rather than storable).

Semantics of this latter kind of nodes is *a priori* known to the DBMS and, thus, for the sketch approach, $\langle\text{Int}\rangle$ is a *marker* hung on the corresponding node and denoting the corresponding constraint (predicate). Indeed, if a node is marked by $\langle\text{Int}\rangle$ its intended semantics is constrained to be the predefined set of integers. At the same time, *Person* and *Bank* are *names* labeling nodes without imposing any constraints.

Actually, specifications we have just considered capture only a very poor projection of real semantic phenomena of association and qualification. The point is that semantic meaning of major conceptual modeling constructs (object identity, IsA- and IsPartOf-relationships, various association and qualification relationships) can be precisely explicated only in the framework of *variable* sets semantics for sketches ([DK], see also [Dis98b] for a shorter presentation). In this framework, sketch nodes and arrows are interpreted by sets and functions changing in time while markers denote invariant (constant in time) properties of variable set-and-function diagrams. This interpretation enriches conceptual modeling with a new – dynamic, or evolutionary, – dimension and in the much more rich dynamic world (well known in CT under the name of *topos of variable sets*) there are several kinds of dynamic separation predicates and several kinds of dynamic "simply functions", correspondingly, there are several kinds of dynamically different associations and qualifications. For example, a few different *Ownership*-associations are possible, but when one interprets sketch items by static sets and functions, all this variety is degenerated into a purely structural, and much more poor, picture which we have specified by sketch S_1. In Appendix the basic idea is very briefly motivated and outlined.

4.4   VISUALIZATION ASPECTS

Having two given notational samples for comparison, the question which one is "more right" is incorrect: any notation with unambiguously specified semantics can be used. However, the question of which notation is more clear and transparent w.r.t. its intended semantic meaning is quite reasonable.

Compare, for example, UML-diagram D_1 and sketch S_1 on Fig. 3.2(i), which express the same semantics. On a whole, the sketch presents a more detailed specification – all functions involved are shown explicitly – while the UML-diagram can be considered as a special abbreviation. In fact, in D_1 we have two different abbreviations. One is the presentation of two mutually inverse functions by one undirected edge each of whose ends carries the corresponding name and multiplicity constraint. It is a reasonable abbreviation, it makes the graphical image more compact and multiplicity expressions are as good as special arrow heads and tails, or even better w.r.t. mnemonic efforts. Note, however, that when one considers compositions of many references, undirected visualization can lead to mistakes. As for abbreviating the arrow span out of node *Ownership* in the sketch S_1 by an edge going into another edge in D_1, it is a purely syntactical trick hardly clarifying semantic meaning of the association class *Ownership*. In addition, such a way of presenting binary associations does not work for multiple (greater than 2) arity associations. In contrast, in the sketch language arbitrary n-ary association are presented by n-arrow spans in a uniform way.

Diagram D_2 on Fig. 3.2(ii) is even a more powerful abbreviation: four nodes and four arrows of the actual semantic picture (specified by sketch S_2 in detail) are compressed in a graphical image with only three nodes and one edge. However, the distance between visual schema D_2 and its semantic meaning ("congruently" specified by sketch S_2) is so large and meandering that diagram D_2 hardly can be considered as presenting a good visualization mechanism.

Of course, the issue we are discussing is of complex cognitive nature and such culture-dependent points as notational habits, preferences, notions of elegance can play significant role; analysis of such things goes far beyond the sketch formalism as such. Nevertheless, we believe that clear logical structure of sketch specifications and the presence of well-defined semantics for them make the sketch format a proper foundation for building a really good graphic notational system upon it.

Finally, concerning visualization of sketches, it must be emphasized that visualization on a computer display is much clearer than visualization on paper. Colours can be used to distinguish between basic and derived items in the sketch. Dynamic highlighting of marked diagrams is very useful if one has to deal with complex sketches with many markers. In that case, it can be difficult to visualize on exactly which diagram each marker is hung. On a computer display, a satisfactory solution is to highlight a marked diagram in response to a click on the marker.

5.   CONCLUSION: IS IT OF REAL PRACTICAL INTEREST?

The platform we have outlined provides VM with consistent and mathematically justified semantic foundations. However, as it was quite justly noted in [KR98], the user of visual models does not need to use (or even see) the underlying framework. In this respect we would like to stress specially that the sketch-topos view has also quite immediate practical consequences for VM even in its current, mainly *ad hoc*, state. The major of them is that VM-diagrams should be directed graphs while in the majority of VM-notations undirected edges are employed. Another one is that many markers used in graphical schemas could, and should, be considered as denoting diagram predicates and operations in, generally, a variable sets-and-functions world. At least, clear separation of predicate/operation markers from those performing another, for example, meta-specificational or purely syntactic-sugar function is quite necessary. Also, explicit notational distinction of the fundamental difference between basic and derivable items is very important for VM.

On a whole, the topos-sketch view we suggest gives rise to a whole program of refining the VM-vocabulary, making it precise and consistent, and unified. In the topos framework for semantics, *any particular VM-notation appears as a particular visualization of the same common specificational format* – the format of sketches. Besides this unifying function, an essential advantage of the sketch format is the extreme brevity of its conceptual vocabulary. Nevertheless, as it was discussed in the paper, the sketch language is absolutely expressive and possesses a great flexibility. So, sketches enjoy a nice (in fact, unique) amalgamation of graphical evidence, rigor and expressiveness.

Acknowledgments

We are indebted to Ilya Beylin (Chalmers University) for many disputes on the sketch notation, which always were stimulating and substantial. We are also grateful to our colleagues at F.I.S, George Sheinkman and Vitaly Dzhitenov, for encouragement-from-practitioners helpful in both technical and moral aspects. Special thanks go to Joseph Goguen for a few brief yet substantial discussions by correspondence, which clarified some important aspects of the problem we approach. Finally, most of all we are indebted to Haim Kilov with whom the ideas presented in the paper were repeatedly discussed, considered and re-considered from very different viewpoints; in particular, these discussions made the structure and presentation of our material in the paper much clearer.

Appendix: Formalizing mysterious object identity

Real world sets are changeable and consist of changeable objects. For example, the set of persons of some community at a time moment t, $[\![\,Person\,]\!]^t$, and conceptually the same set at another moment u, $[\![\,Person\,]\!]^u$, are physically different. Speaking accurately, elements of the sets $[\![\,Person\,]\!]^t$, $[\![\,Person\,]\!]^u$ are *states* of persons at the moments t, u rather than persons themselves and hence, in general, the sets $[\![\,Person\,]\!]^t$ and $[\![\,Person\,]\!]^u$ are even disjoint. However, these sets are not mutually independent: they are inter-related by identifying different elements, say, $p' \in [\![\,Person\,]\!]^t$ and $p'' \in [\![\,Person\,]\!]^u$, as different states of the same person, say, p. In this case we write $p' = p(t)$ and $p'' = p(u)$.

What is p? In the ER data model a suitable concept is that of entity, in the OO-paradigm p would be called an object identity (o-id). However, in these and other data models the notion is not formally explicated and remains intuitive. In contrast, we take the constructive ontology view point that "to be" means to be observed, and so the identity is the *observable* identity. That is, if there are some verified reasons (a constructive proof as a mathematician would say) to consider p' and p'' to be (the two different states of) the same entity, this should be declared in an explicit form. Such declarations, irrespectively to ways how the information could be obtained, can be expressed by a family of binary inter-state relations

$$ {}^t[\![\,Person\,]\!]^u \subset [\![\,Person\,]\!]^t \times [\![\,Person\,]\!]^u, \ t < u \text{ are time moments,}$$

so that $p' \in [\![\,Person\,]\!]^t$ and $p'' \in [\![\,Person\,]\!]^u$ have to be considered as different states of the same entity if and only if $(p', p'') \in {}^t[\![\,Person\,]\!]^u$.

Of course, object identity is a construct for building a logical model of a universe rather than writing its chronicle: time moments s, t, u should be treated generally as indexes of real world states, and their precedence is logical rather than physical. Correspondingly, the logical time is branching: it is ordered partially rather than linearly.

Definition. Let $\mathcal{T} = (T, \leq)$ be a logical time and $\mathcal{O}$ be a class of *observable states* of objects. A $(\mathcal{O}, \mathcal{T})$-*variable set* C is a family of sets $[\![\,C\,]\!]^t \subset \mathcal{O}$, $t \in T$, taken together with a family of binary *interstate relations* ${}^t[\![\,C\,]\!]^u \subset [\![\,C\,]\!]^t \times [\![\,C\,]\!]^u$, $t \leq u$, such that the following *transitivity* condition holds for any $s \leq t \leq u \in T$:

$$(\text{Trans})_{s \leq t \leq u} \qquad\qquad {}^s[\![\,C\,]\!]^t \bowtie {}^t[\![\,C\,]\!]^u = {}^s[\![\,C\,]\!]^u,$$

here $\bowtie$ denotes the operation of relational composition.

When the context $(\mathcal{O}, \mathcal{T})$ is fixed, we call $(\mathcal{O}, \mathcal{T})$-variable sets simply variable sets, or *varsets*. C is the name of the varset in question, $[\![\,C\,]\!]^t, t \in \mathcal{T}$ are *states of* C and elements of $[\![\,C\,]\!]^t$ are *states of C-objects*.

The objects themselves are nothing else than sets of their states indexed by time moments. In particular, if objects do not merge nor split and so all the interstate relations are of one-to-one type, an object c is represented by a trajectory in the space of observable states:

$$c = [c(t_1), c(t_2), c(t_3) \ldots],$$

where $[c(t_i), c(t_{i+1})] \in {}^{t_i}[\![\,C\,]\!]^{t_{i+1}}$ and $t = t_1$ is the first moment when some element from $[\![\,C\,]\!]^t$ was identified as (state of) c.

Thus, in the variable sets framework an object *is* a trajectory as above and the meta-physical absolute o-id is replaced by a constructive notion of observable trajectory in the space of observable states.

Definition. Let C be an object class, that is, a varset. C-objects are called:

- *Static*, when for any $t \leq u$, $[\![\,C\,]\!]^t \cap [\![\,C\,]\!]^u$ is not empty and ${}^t[\![\,C\,]\!]^u$ is its diagonal, then object trajectories are glued into points; examples are values like integers or strings.

- *Proper*, when all ${}^t[\![\,C\,]\!]^u$ are of one-one type; examples are entities in the conventional sense like *persons* or *villas*.

- *Legacyless* or *snapshots*, when ${}^{t}[\,C\,]^{u} = \varnothing$ for all $t < u$ and so each object trajectory is defined only for a single time moment – such objects have neither a history nor future; examples are relationships in the sense of the ER-model like *ownerships* between *persons* and *villas*.

Examplifying legacyless objects by conventional relationships needs explanation. What we have said is that there is a certain view on *ownerships*, say, *R-view*, in which pairs $(p', v') \in$ $[\,Person\,]^{t} \times [\,Villa\,]^{t}$, $t \in T$ are temporally discrete. This means that the question of whether the same pair (p', v') in two different (but related) states, $t < u \in T$,

$$(p', v') \in [\,Person\,]^{t} \times [\,Villa\,]^{t} \text{ and } (p', v') \in [\,Person\,]^{u} \times [\,Villa\,]^{u},$$

represents the same *ownership* or another *ownership* of the same objects is not stated, or considered incorrect (an example of different *ownerships* between the same p and v is when p sold his villa v but then purchased it again in another terms).

Of course, there is another view on the ownership, *E-view*, when identity of *ownerships* is traced through time. Then the question of identifying two pairs of the same objects is legitimate, moreover, mandatory, and we consider the ownership as an entity association rather than a legacyless relationship.

Remark. In both cases, when a varset C is legacyless and when it is a value domain, o-id trajectories of C-objects are points, but note an essential difference. In the first case trajectories are defined only for a single moment, in fact, the very notion of trajectory is degenerated. In the second case we have trajectories but they are of special kind: they are reduced to points.

Finally, it should be stressed that predicates of being a snapshot, or a value, or a proper object, are determined by observer's (user's) needs or possibilities rather than intrinsic properties of objects. More details of the varset taxonomy can be found in [DK, section 4].

The formal framework provided by ideas described above is still not sufficient for proper semantic data specifications. Indeed, the real world is full of ontological inter-dependencies between objects: objects may form associations, may be parts of other objects, may be views to other objects and so on. Variable set semantics explicates the notion of object identity but what is to do with dependencies between objects like those listed above?

Fortunately, the answer is an almost immediate consequence of the varset idea. Indeed, because of identity of C-objects is explicated by interstate relations ${}^{t}[\,C\,]^{u}$, $t \leq u$, one can say that ontology of C-objects is given by C-interstate relations. Then, a natural way to explicate that C-objects somehow ontologically depend on objects of other classes $D_1, D_2, \ldots, D_n$ is to state that interstate relations for C depend on those for D_i, that is, ${}^{t}[\,C\,]^{u}$ can be somehow derived from ${}^{t}[\,D_i\,]^{u}$, $i = 1, \ldots, n$, for each pair of moments $t \leq u$. For example, given object classes *Employee* and *Person*, the meaning of declaration "any *employee* is a *person*" (usually it is expressed by declaring *Employee* to be an IsA-subclass of *Person*) is that object identity of *employee* coincides with that of *persons*. Formally this can be expressed as follows: (i) there is an arrow (reference) $f: Employee \rightarrow Person$, which is semantically interpreted by a variable one-one function

$$[\,f\,]^{t}\colon\ [\,Employee\,]^{t} \rightarrow [\,Person\,]^{t},$$

and (ii) interstate relations for *Employee* are directly determined by those for *Person*:

$$(e', e'') \in {}^{t}[\,Employee\,]^{u} \text{ iff, \textbf{by definition}, } (e'.[\,f\,]^{t}, e''.[\,f\,]^{u}) \in {}^{t}[\,Person\,]^{u}$$

for any $t \leq u \in T$, $e' \in [\,Employee\,]^{t}$, $e'' \in [\,Employee\,]^{u}$. In other words, object identity of the class *Employee* is derived from that of *Person* via the function f.

What was just described for the IsA-relation between objects is a general idea. It is shown in [DK] (see [Dis98b] for a shorter presentation) that in a similar way semantic constructs of association, aggregation, qualification, IsPartOf relationships can be explained and formalized. So, what is intuitively perceived as ontological difference can be formally explicated dynamically in the varset framework.

Notes

1. Of course, VM is a complex human activity and should be considered in the corresponding contexts, including, in particular, highly non-trivial issues of cognitive and social nature far beyond formal logic and technical semantics for VM-diagrams (cf. [Gog96]). The latter are not only specifications but also political documents (especially, if we consider high-level visual models) and thus some fuzziness and vagueness are unavoidable, and even useful [Gog98]. Nevertheless, we believe that clear technical semantics picture is helpful anyway, in particular, it prevents some technical problems with serious social consequences. On the other hand, as was noted by one of the editors of this book, some room for manoeuvres so important for political documents can be also achieved by using quite precise yet incomplete specifications admitting a few possible realizations. At any rate, in the present paper we focus on the specificational half of visual models leaving social aspects aside.

2. References to CT-literature should be an important component of the present paper. However, we are not aware of CT-books suitable for software engineers or business modeling people. And indeed, a good book of such kind could only be the result of certain experience of applying CT to practical problems and teaching CT to the corresponding audience. Unfortunately, the former is still very rare, and the latter does not exist at all, at least, in a systematic form. Moreover, as soon as one starts to apply CT to real problems in business/software engineering, (s)he at once realizes that the arrow machinery – as it was developed in mathematical CT – itself needs serious adaptation and development towards generalizations helpful in practice, some consideration on this issue can be found on first pages of [Dis97]. So, we restrict ourselves by a single reference [BW90]: it is a good source of required CT-results, and is very well written from the view point of theoretical computer science though not very suitable for a non-initiated reader.

3. Close ideas were developed by Goguen and his group in their studies of building reasonable graphical interfaces [Gog97].

4. Interpretations of arrow specifications when nodes are interpreted by elements (object instances rather than classes) are also possible, then arrows are binary relationships of partial order or instances of logical consequence. In this framework, propositional logic can be sketched.

5. Arrow diagrams adjoint to a node C can be considered as interfaces to the class C and so the idea of the approach can be phrased as that objects show themselves only through arrow diagram interfaces. Such a setting appears to be a precise realization of the basic OO principle of encapsulation, the more so that arrows can be treated as formal counterparts of references, attributes and methods. Thus, conceptually, objects in the OO sense and objects in CT have much in common.

6. Quite briefly, there is some set of basic diagram operations such that semantic meaning of any diagram predicate can be defined in terms of these operations and equations; as a result, any signature of diagram predicates can be considered as an essentially algebraic theory over some common set of basic operations. This makes it possible (at least, in principle) to relate and compare sketches in different signatures in some unified way.

References

[Abr94] S. Abramsky. Interaction categories and communicating sequential processes. In A.W. Roscoe, editor, *A Classical Mind: Essays in honour of C.A.R.Hoare*, pages 1–15. Prentice Hall Int., 1994.

[BBS93] C. Batini, G. Battista, and G. Santucci. Structuring primitives for a dictionary of entity relationship data schemas. *IEEE Trans.Soft.Engineering*, 19(4):344–365, 1993.

[BJR99] G. Booch, I. Jacobson, and J. Rumbaugh. *The Unified Modeling Language user guide*. Addison-Wesley, 1999.

[BW90] M. Barr and C. Wells. *Category Theory for Computing Science*. Prentice Hall International Series in Computer Science, 1990.

[Dis97] Z. Diskin. Generalized sketches as an algebraic graph-based framework for semantic modeling and database design. Technical Report M9701, University of Latvia, 1997.

[Dis98a] Z. Diskin. The arrow logic of meta-specifications: a formalized graph-based framework for structuring schema repositories. In B. Rumpe H. Kilov and I. Simmonds, editors, *Seventh OOPSLA Workshop on Behavioral Semantics of OO Business and System Specifications)*, TUM-I9820, Technische Universitaet Muenchen, 1998.

[Dis98b] Z. Diskin. The arrow logic of visual modeling and taming heterogeneiuty of semantic models. In H. Kilov and B. Rumpe, editors, *Second ECOOP Workshop on Precise Behavioral Semantics (with an Emphasis on OO Business Specifications)*, TUM-I9813, Technische Universitaet Muenchen, 1998.

[DK]   Z. Diskin and B. Kadish. Variable set semantics for generalized sketches: Why ER is more object-oriented than OO. To appear in *Data and Knowledge Engineering*

[GH91]   M. Gogolla and U. Hohenstein. Towards a semantic view of an extended entity-relationship model. *ACM Trans.Database Systems*, 16(3):369–416, 1991.

[Gog96] J. Goguen. Formality and informality in requirement engineering. In *Requirement engineering, 4th Int. Conference*, pages 102–108. IEEE Computer Society, 1996. (keynote address).

[Gog97] J. Goguen. Semiotic morphisms. Technical report, University of California at San Diego, 1997. TR-CS97-553.

[Gog98] J. Goguen. Personal letter, 1998.

[KLW95] M. Kifer, G. Lausen, and J. Wu. Logical foundations of object-oriented and frame-based languages. *Journal ACM*, 42(4):741–843, 1995.

[KR98]   H. Kilov and B. Rumpe. Overview of the Second ECOOP Workshop on Precise behavioral semantics (with an Emphasis on OO business specifications). In *The Europian Conference on Object-Oriented Programming, ECOOP'98*, LNCS 1543. Springer, 1998.

[LB98]   K. Lano and J. Bicarregui. Formalising the UML in structured temporal theories. In H. Kilov and B. Rumpe, editors, *Second ECOOP Workshop on Precise Behavioral Semantics (with an Emphasis on OO Business Specifications)*, TUM-I9813, Technische Universitaet Muenchen, 1998.

[MMS93] G.W. Mineau, B. Moulin, and J.F. Sowa, editors. *Conceptual graphs for knowledge representation*. Number 699 in LNAI. Springer, 1993.

[RJB99] J. Rumbaugh, I. Jacobson, and G. Booch. *The Unified Modeling Language Reference Manual*. Addison-Wesley, 1999.

[WJS94] R. Wieringa, W. de Jonge, and P. Spruit. Roles and dynamic subclasses: a modal logic approach. In *European Conference on Object-Oriented Programming, ECOOP'94*, Springer LNCS, 1994.

About the Authors

Zinovy Diskin got MSc in mechanical engineering from Bryansk Inst. of Transport Engineering (Russia) in 1981 and worked in the wagon-building industry for 8 years. In 1992 he got PhD in mathematics from the Omsk State University (Russia) and in 1994 Dr. Math. from the University of Latvia. Current research interests are in graphical specification languages and notations, semantic data modeling and database semantics, abstract algebraic logic and categorical logic. In 1992-1997 he headed Lab. for database design at F.I.S. Currently, he works as a consultant in conceptual and business modeling.

Boris Kadish graduated from the Riga Polytechnic Institute in 1980. In 1986 he defended his Dissertation on database design at the State SRI for Problems of Computer Technique and Informatics in Moscow (Russia). In 1992 the University of Latvia conferred the Dr. of Computer Science degree on him. Since 1991 he has been a scientific advisor of the group supported by Grant No.45 from the Science Council of Latvia "Methods and Integration Tools for Heterogeneous Database Design". In 1992 he was the initiator and the program chair of the international conference "Methods of Database Design". He has a numerous year experience in creating large database systems in Latvia and in former USSR countries. Since July 1998 he is living in California. Since September 1998 he is a co-owner and the president of Californian company ZAKAZ.COM, Inc.

Frank Piessens obtained a Master of Engineering in Computer Science degree from the Katholieke Universiteit Leuven in 1991. He obtained a PhD in Computer Science from the same university in 1996. He is currently a Postdoctoral Fellow of the Belgian National Fund for Scientific Research. His research has focused on applications of category theory to computer science.

Chapter 4

META-MODELLING
SEMANTICS OF UML

Andy Evans
University of York, UK
andye@cs.york.ac.uk

Kevin Lano
Imperial College, UK
kcl@doc.ic.ac.uk

Robert France
Colorado State University, US
france@cs.colostate.edu

Bernhard Rumpe
Munich University of Technology
Germany
rumpe@in.tum.de

Abstract   The Unified Modelling Language is emerging as a de-facto standard for modelling object-oriented systems. However, the semantics document that a part of the standard definition primarily provides a description of the language's syntax and well-formedness rules. The meaning of the language, which is mainly described in English, is too informal and unstructured to provide a foundation for developing formal analysis and development techniques. This paper outlines a formalisation strategy for making precise the core semantics of UML. This is achieved by strengthening the denotational semantics of the existing UML metamodel. To illustrate the approach, the semantics of generalization/specialization are made precise.

1.   INTRODUCTION

The Unified Modeling Language (UML) [BRJ98, RJB99] is rapidly becoming a de-facto language for modelling object-oriented systems. An important aspect of the language is the recognition by its authors of the need to provide a precise description of its semantics. Their intention is that this should act as an unambiguous description of the language, whilst also permitting extensibility so that it may adapt to future changes in object-oriented analysis and design. This has resulted in a Semantics Document [OMG99], which is presently being managed by the Object Management Group, and forms an important part of the language's standard definition.

The UML semantics is described using a meta-model that is presented in terms of three views: the abstract syntax, well-formedness rules, and modelling element semantics. The abstract syntax is expressed using a subset of UML static modelling notations. The abstract syntax model is supported by natural language descriptions of the syntactic structure of UML constructs. The well-formedness rules are expressed in the *Object Constraint Language* (OCL) and the semantics of modelling elements are described in natural language. The advantage of using the meta-modelling approach is that it is accessible to anybody who understands UML. Furthermore, the use of object-oriented modelling techniques helps make the model more intuitively understandable.

A potential advantage of providing a precise semantics for UML is that many of the benefits of using a formal language such as Z [S92] or Spectrum [BFG$^+$93] might be transferable to UML. Some of the major benefits of having a precise semantics for UML are given below:

Clarity: The formally stated semantics can act as a point of reference to resolve disagreements over intended interpretation and to clear up confusion over the precise meaning of a construct.

Equivalence and Consistency: A precise semantics provides an unambiguous basis from which to compare and contrast the UML with other techniques and notations, and for ensuring consistency between its different components.

Extendibility: The soundness of extensions to the UML can be verified (as encouraged by the UML authors).

Refinement: The correctness of design steps in the UML can be verified and precisely documented. In particular, a properly developed semantics supports the development of design transformations, in which a more abstract model is diagrammatically transformed into an implementation model.

Proof: Justified proofs and rigorous analysis of important properties of a system described in UML require a precise semantics in order to determine their correctness.

Unfortunately, the current UML semantics are not sufficiently formal to realise these benefits. Although much of the syntax of the language has been defined, and some static semantics given, its semantics are mostly described using lengthy paragraphs of often ambiguous informal English, or are missing entirely. Furthermore, limited consideration has been paid to important issues such as proof, compositionality and rigorous development. A further problem is the extensive scope of the language, all of which must be dealt with before the language is completely defined.

This chapter describes work being carried out by the precise UML (pUML) group and documented in [PUML99, FELR98, EFLR98]. PUML is an international group of researchers and practitioners who share the goal of developing UML as a precise (formal) modelling language, thereby enabling it to be used in a formal manner. This chapter reports on work being carried out by the group to strengthen the existing semantics of UML. In Section 2., a formalisation strategy is described (developed through the experiences of the group) that aims to make precise the existing UML semantics. A core UML semantics model is identified in Section 3. as a first step towards achieving this goal. Section 4. then describes how the formalisation strategy has been applied to the development of a precise understanding of a small yet interesting part of the UML semantics - generalization/specialization hierarchies. Finally, the paper concludes with a brief overview of some future directions of the group's work.

2.   FORMALISATION STRATEGY

In order to implement the pUML approach it is necessary to develop a strategy for formalising the UML. This is intended to act as a step by step guide to the formalisation process, thus permitting a more rigorous and traceable work program.

In developing a formalisation strategy for UML it has been necessary to consider the following questions:

1. Is the meta-modelling approach used in the current UML semantics suitable for assigning a precise semantics to UML?

2. Should the existing UML semantics be used as a foundation for developing a precise semantics for UML?

3. Given the large scope of UML, which parts should be formalised first?

Suitability of meta-modelling

There are many approaches used to assign semantics to languages. One of the best known (and most popular) is the denotational approach (for an in-depth discussion see [S86]). The denotational approach assigns semantics to a language by giving a mapping from its syntactical representation to a meaning, called a denotation. A denotation is usually a well-defined mathematical value, such as a number or a set. Typically, functions are used to define mappings between syntax and denotations. For example, the meaning of a simple language for adding and subtracting natural numbers might be described in terms of two functions, add and subtract, and the result of each would be a single integer value.

The use of a language to give a 'meta-circular' description of its own denotational semantics is well known in Computer Science. For example, the specification language Z has been given a meta-circular semantics using a simple subset of Z [S92]. Unfortunately, the meta-modelling approach opens itself to the criticism that it doesn't really define anything. Informally, if a reader does not understand UML, then it is unlikely that they will understand the meaning of UML when written in UML.

The justification given for using meta-modelling in these contexts is that, in principle at least, it should be possible to give a formal interpretation to a meta-description in terms of a more basic language such as predicate logic. This argument can also be applied to UML, as it seems likely that it can be given a more fundamental interpretation in terms of sets and predicate logic. Indeed, a significant amount of work has already been done to describe the semantics of UML class diagrams and OCL like expressions [BR98] in Z. There is also an important pragmatic reason for choosing UML to describe the denotational semantics of UML: Because UML is designed to provide an intuitive means for constructing models, using UML to help better understand UML is likely to be a useful way of testing the expressiveness and power of UML as a modelling language.

Given that UML can be used to describe its own semantics, how should these semantics be presented in order to emphasise the denotational approach? As described in the introduction, the current UML semantics already makes a distinction between syntax and semantics (as in the denotational approach). However, it mainly uses English prose to describe the semantic part. The pUML approach advances this work by using associations (and constraints on associations) to map syntactical elements to their denotations. This approach has also been used in the UML semantics to a limited extent. For example, associations are described by the set of possible object links they are associated with. The distinguishing feature of the pUML approach is its emphasis on obtaining *precise* denotational descriptions of a much wider selection of UML modelling elements.

Working with the standard

Assuming that a meta-modelling approach is adopted to describe the UML semantics, two approaches to developing a precise semantics can be adopted. The first approach is to ignore the existing semantics documentation and develop a new model. This has the advantage that the modeller is completely free to develop a semantics that is appropriate to their needs. For example, greater emphasis might be placed on obtaining a simple semantic model, or one that will readily support a particular proof technique.

The second approach is to adopt the existing semantics as a foundation from which a precise semantics can be obtained. Some good reasons for adopting this approach are as follows:

1. It recognises that considerable time and effort has been invested in the development of the existing UML semantics. It cannot be expected that a radically different semantic proposal will be incorporated in new versions.

2. Without working within the constraints of the existing semantics it is easy to develop models that are incompatible with the standard or omit important aspects of it.

An important aspect of the pUML approach is its aim of eventually contributing to the emerging standard. Therefore, it is the second approach that has been adopted. This is why the remainder of the paper will focus on developing an approach to incrementally clarifying the *existing* semantics of UML.

Clarifying a core semantics

To cope with the large scope of the UML it is natural to concentrate on essential concepts of the language to build a clear and precise foundation as a basis for formalisation. Therefore, the approach taken in the group's work is to concentrate on identifying and formalising a core semantic model for UML before tackling other features of the language. This has a number of advantages: firstly, it makes the formalisation task more manageable; secondly, a more precise core will act as a foundation for understanding the semantics of the remainder of the language. This is useful in the case of the many diagrammatical notations supported by UML, as each diagram's semantics can be defined as a particular 'view' of the core model semantics. For example, the meaning of an interaction diagram should be understandable in terms of a subset of the behavioural semantics of the core.

Formalisation strategy

The formalisation strategy consists of the following steps:

1. Identify the core elements of the existing UML semantics.

2. Iteratively examine the core elements, seeking to verify their completeness. Here, completeness is achieved when: (1) the modelling element has a precise syntax, (2) is well-formed, and (3) has a precise denotation in terms of some fundamental aspect of the core semantic model.

3. Use formal techniques to gain better insight into the existing definitions as shown in [FELR98, EFLR98].

4. Where in-completeness is identified, we attempt to address it in a number of ways, depending on the type of omission found.

> Model strengthening - this is necessary where the meaning of a model element is not fully described in the meta-model. The omission is fixed by strengthening the relationship between the model element and its denotation.

> Model extension - in certain cases it is necessary to extend the meta-model to incorporate new denotational relationships. This occurs when no meaning has been assigned to a particular model element, and it cannot be derived by constraints on existing associations. For example, this is necessary in the case of *Operation* and *Method*, where the meaning of a method is defined in terms of a *procedureExpression* and Operation is given no abstract meaning at all.

> Model simplification - in some cases, aspects of the model are surplus to needs, in which case we aim to show how they can be omitted or simplified without compromising the existing semantics.

5. Feed the results back into the UML meta-model, with the aim of clarifying the semantics of a core part of the UML.

6. Disseminate to interested parties for feedback.

Finally, it is important to consider how the notion of *proof* can be represented in the semantic model. This is essential if techniques are to be developed for analysing properties of UML models. Such analysis is required to establish the presence of desired properties in models [E98]. The need to establish properties can arise out of the need to establish that models adhere to requirements or out of challenges posed by reviewers of the models. Proof is also important in understanding properties of model transformations in which a system is progressively refined to an implementation [BHH+97].

3.   THE CORE SEMANTICS MODEL

The question of what should form a core precise semantics for UML is already partially answered in the UML semantics document. It identifies a 'Core Package - Relationships' package and a number of 'Common Behaviour' packages. The Core Relationship package defines a set of modelling elements that are common to all UML diagrams, such as ModelElement, Relationship, Classifier, Association and Generalization. However, it only describes their syntax. The Common Behavior (Instances and Links) package gives a partial denotational meaning to the model elements in the core package. For instance, it describes an association between Classifier and Instance. This establishes the connection between the representation of a Classifier and its meaning, which is a collection of instances. The meaning of Association (a collection of Object Links) is also given, along with a connection between Association roles and Attribute values.

To illustrate the scope, and to show the potential for realising a compact core semantics, the relevant class diagrams of the two models are shown in the Figures 4.1 and 4.2. Well-formedness rules are omitted for brevity.

An appropriate starting point for a formalisation is to consider these two models in isolation, with the aim of improving the rigor with which the syntax of UML model elements are associated with (or mapped to) their denotations.

4.   FILLING THE SEMANTIC GAP

In this section, we illustrate how the pUML formalisation approach has been applied to a small part of the core model. The modelling concept that will be investigated is generalization/specialization.

4.1   DESCRIPTION

In UML, a generalization is defined as "a taxonomic relationship between a more general element and a more specific element", where "the more specific element is fully consistent with the more general element" [OMG99], page 2-34 (it has all of its properties, members, and relationships) and may contain additional information.

Closely related to the UML meaning of generalization is the notion of direct and indirect instances: This is alluded to in the meta-model as the requirement that "an instance is an indirect instance of ... any of its ancestors" [OMG99], page 2-56.

UML also places standard constraints on subclasses. The default constraint is that a set of generalizations are disjoint, i.e. " (an) instance may have no more than one of the given children as a type of the instance" [OMG99], page 2-35. Abstract classes

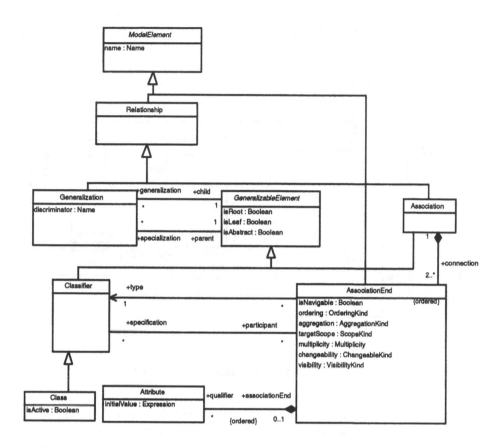

Figure 4.1   Fragment of the core relationships package

enforce a further constraint, which implies that no instance can be a direct instance of an abstract class.

We now examine whether these properties are adequately specified in the UML semantics document. In this paper, we will only consider properties that relate to Classifiers: the UML term for any model element that describes behavioural and structural features. Classes are a typical specialisation of Classifiers.

4.2   EXISTING FORMAL DEFINITIONS

France et al. [BR98] have defined a formal model of generalization that fits very well with that adopted in UML. Classes are denoted by a set of object references, where each reference maps to a set of attribute values and operations. generalization implies inheritance of attributes and operations from parent classes (as expected). In addition, class denotations are used to formalise the meaning of direct and indirect instances, disjoint and abstract classes. This is achieved by constraining the sets of

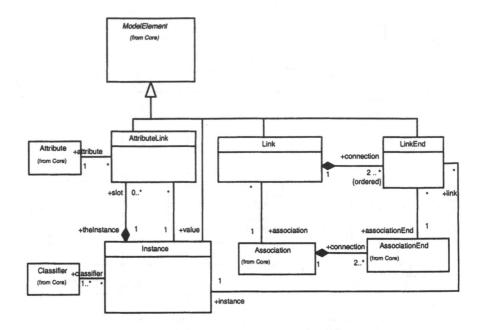

Figure 4.2   Fragment of the common behaviour package

objects assigned to classes in different ways depending on the roles the classes play in a particular generalization hierarchy. For example, assume that a_i is the set of object references belonging to the class a, and b and c are subclasses of a. Because instances of b and c are also indirect instances of a, it is required that $b_i \subseteq a_i$ and $c_i \subseteq a_i$, where b_i and c_i are the set of object references of b and c. Thus, a direct instance of b or c must also be an *indirect* instance of a. A direct instance is also distinguishable from an indirect instance if there does not exist a specialised class of which it is also an instance.

This model also enables constraints on generalizations to be elegantly formalised in terms of simple constraints on sets of object references. In the case of the standard 'disjoint' constraint on subclasses, the following must hold: $b_i \cap c_i = \emptyset$, i.e. there can be no instances belonging to both subclasses. For an abstract class, this constraint is further strengthened by requiring that b_i and c_i partition a_i. In other words, there can be no instances of a, which are not instances of b or c. Formally, this is expressed by the constraint: $b_i \cup c_i = a_i$.

We will adopt this model in order to assign a precise denotational meaning to generalization/specialization.

4.3   SYNTAX AND WELL-FORMEDNESS

The abstract syntax of generalization/specialization is described by the meta-model fragment in Figure 4.3 of the core relationships package:

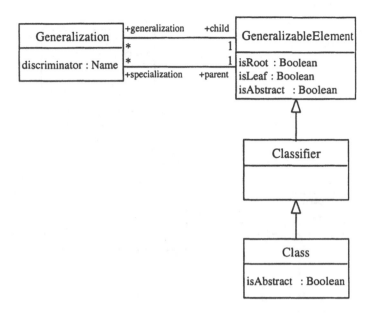

Figure 4.3   Meta-model fragment of Generalization/Specialization

The most important well-formedness rule which applies to this model element, and is not already ensured by the class diagram, is that circular inheritance is not allowed. Assuming allParents defines the transitive closure of the relationship induced by self.generalization.parent, which happens to be the set of all ancestors, then it must hold that:

```
context GeneralizableElement
not self.allParents -> includes(self)
```

4.4   SEMANTICS

The completeness of the semantic formalisation vs. the desired properties of generalization is now examined. We concentrate on determining whether the following properties of generalization are captured in the meta-model:

- instance identity and conformance.

- direct and indirect instantiation of classifiers.

- disjoint and overlapping constraints on sub-classifiers.

- abstract classes.

As noted in Section 3., the UML meta-model already describes a denotational relationship between Classifier and Instance. The meta-model fragment in Figure 4.4 describes this relationship.

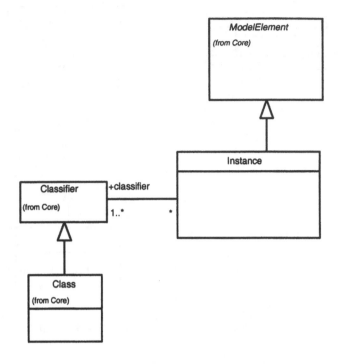

Figure 4.4   Meta-model fragment for Class and Instance relationship

However, unlike the formal model described above, the UML meta-model does not describe the constraints that generalization implies on this relationship. For example, an *Instance* can be an instance of many classifiers, yet there are no constraints that the classifiers are related. Thus, the meta-model must be strengthened with additional constraints on the relationship between model elements and their denotations.

4.5   MODEL STRENGTHENING

The first aspect of the model to be strengthened relates to the meaning of indirect instances. As stated in Section 4.1, an instance of a classifier is also an *indirect* instance of its parent classifiers. This property, which we term as 'instance conformance' can be precisely stated by placing an additional constraint on the relationship between the instances of a classifier and the instances belong to the classifier's parents. It is specified as follows:

```
context c :  Classifier
invariant
    c.generalization.parent -> forall(s :  Classifier |
        s.instance -> includesAll(c.instance))
```

This states that the instances of any Classifier, c, are a subset of those belonging to the instances of its parents.

4.5.1   Direct instances.   Given the above property, it is now possible to precisely describe the meaning of a direct instance:

```
context i :  Instance
isDirectInstanceOf(c :   Classifier)  :  Boolean
isDirectInstanceOf(c) =
                c.allParents -> union(Set(c)) = i.classifier
```

A direct instance directly instantiates a single class and indirectly instantiates all its parents. This definition is in fact a more precise description of the OCL operation oclIsTypeOf, i.e.

```
context i :  Instance
oclIsTypeOf(c :  Classifier)  :  Boolean
oclIsTypeOf(c) = i.isDirectInstanceOf(c)
```

A similar operation can be used to assign a precise meaning to the OCL operation oclIsKindOf:

```
context i :  Instance
oclIsKindOf(c :  Classifier)  :  Boolean
oclIsKindOf(c) - i.oclIsTypeOf(c) or
                c.allSupertypes ->
                     exists(s :  Classifier | i.oclIsTypeOf(s))
```

Finally, an OCL operation which returns the Classifier from which an instance is directly instantiated from can be defined:

```
context i :  Instance
direct :  Classifier
direct = i.classifier -> select(c | i.isDirectInstanceOf(c))
```

4.5.2   Indirect instances.   Once the meaning of a direct instance is defined, it is straightforward to obtain an OCL operation that returns all the Classifiers that an instance indirectly instantiates.

```
context i :  Instance
indirect :  Set(Classifier) :
indirect = i.classifier - Set(i.direct)
```

The set of indirect classes is the difference of the set of all classifiers instantiated by the instance and the direct classifier.

4.5.3   Instance identity.   Unfortunately, the above constraints do not guarantee that every instance is a direct or indirect instance of a related classifier. For example, consider two classifiers that are not related by generalization/specialization. The current UML semantics do not rule-out the possibility of an instance being instantiated by both classifiers.

Thus, an additional constraint must be added in order to rule out the possibility of an instance being instantiated from two or more un-related classes. This is the unique identity constraint:

```
context i :  Instance
invariant
    i.classifier = i.direct -> union(i.indirect)
```

This states that the *only* classifiers that an object can be instantiated from are either the classifier that it is directly instantiated from or those that it is indirectly instantiated from.

4.5.4   Disjoint subclasses.   Once direct and indirect instances are formalised, it is possible to give a precise description to the meaning of constraints on generalizations (for example the disjoint constraint).

The disjoint constraint can be formalised as follows:

```
context c :  Classifier
invariant
    c.specialization.child -> forall(i,j :  Classifier |
        i <> j implies i.instance ->
            intersection(j.instance) -> isEmpty)
```

This states that for any pair of direct subclasses of a class, i and j, the set of instances of i will be disjoint from the set of instances of j.

4.5.5   Abstract classes.   Finally, the following OCL constraint formalises the required property of an abstract class that it can not be directly instantiated:

```
context c :  Classifier
invariant
    c.isAbstract implies
        c.specialization.child.instance -> asSet = c.instance
```

Note, the result of the `specialization.child` path is a bag of instances belonging to each subclass of c. Applying the asSet operation results in a set of instances. Equating this to to the instances of c implies that all the instances of c are covered by the instances of its subclasses. This, in conjunction with the disjoint property above, implies the required partition of instances.

4.6   MODEL EXTENSION

The above definition of the 'disjoint' constraint is adequate provided that it applies across all generalizations, and indeed this is the default assumption in UML. However, UML also permits overlapping constraints to be applied across subclasses as shown in Figure 4.5.

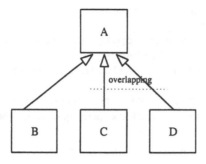

Figure 4.5 Partly overlapping subclasses

Here, instances of C and D may overlap, but they must be disjoint from instances of B (the default disjoint constraint still exists between B and C and B and D). Thus, the overlapping constraint is viewed as overriding the existing default constraint.

Unfortunately, overlapping constraints are not explicitly encoded in the existing semantics. Therefore, it is necessary to extend the meta-model with an explicit overlapping constraint in order to be able to formalise its meaning. This is shown in Figure 4.6.

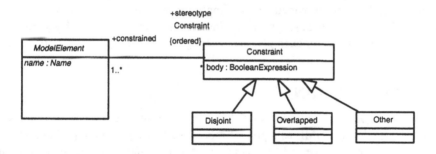

Figure 4.6 Fragment of the meta-model with extended Constraint

Here, overlapping constraints are modelled as a subclass of *Constraint*. Because overlapping constraints must be applied across more than one subclass, the following additional well-formedness rule must be added:

```
context o :  Overlapping
invariant
    o.constrained -> size > 1
```

An improved version of the disjoint constraint can now be given:

```
context c :  Classifier
invariant
```

```
c.specialization -> forall(i,j :  Generalization |
   (i <> j and
   not (i.hasSameOverlappingConstraint(j)))
   implies i.child.instance ->
        intersection(j.child.instance) -> isEmpty)
```

This states that the instances of two or more generalizations are disjoint unless they overlap. Note that the same overlapping constraint must be applied to the generalizations.

The operation hasSameOverlappingConstraint is defined as follows:

```
context i :  Generalization
hasSameOverlappingConstraint(j :  Generalization) :  Boolean

hasSameOverlappingConstraint(j) =
   ((i.stereotypeConstraint -> asSet) ->
       intersection(j.stereotypeConstraint -> asSet) ->
           exists(c :  Constraint | c.oclType = Overlapping))
```

This operation is true if a pair of generalizations share the same overlapping constraint.

This completes the formalisation examples. Although not complete, they indicate the benefits of adopting a denotational emphasis in modelling the UML semantics. In particular, they have provided a much improved understanding of some important aspects of UML. They have also provided a foundation from which to clarify many other aspects of the language, for example, the meaning of the OCL operations oclIsKindOf and oclIsTypeOf.

5.   CONCLUSION

This paper has described ongoing work by members of the precise UML group, who are seeking to develop UML as a precise modelling language. By applying previous knowledge and experience in formalising OO concepts and semantic models, it has been shown how important aspects of the current UML semantics can be clarified and made more precise. A formalisation strategy was also described, with the aim that it will act as a template for exploring further features of UML and for developing new proof systems for the standard language.

In the longer term, our intention is to give a semantics to the complete notation set, by mapping into the core, extending the core only when there is not already a concept which suffices. Of course one role of semantics is to clarify and remove ambiguities from the notation. Therefore we will not be surprised if we find that the notation needs to be adjusted or the informal semantics rewritten. However, we will be able to provide a tightly argued, semantically-based recommendation for any change deemed necessary.

Some consideration also needs to be given to quality insurance. There are at least three approaches we have identified:

1. peer review and inspection

2. acceptance tests

3. tool-based testing environment

So far the only feedback has come from 1. Since a meta-model is itself a model, acceptance tests could be devised as they would be for any model. Perhaps "testing" a model is a novel concept: it at least comprises devising object diagrams, snapshots, that the model must/must-not accept. Better than a list of acceptance tests on paper would be a tool embodying the meta-model, that allowed arbitrary snapshots to be checked against it.

Finally, we re-iterate the factors driving the work outlined in this paper. Given the UML's intended role as a modelling notation standard, it is imperative that it has a well-founded semantics. Only once such a semantics is provided can the UML be used as a rigorous modelling technique. Moreover, the formalisation of UML constructs is an important step towards gaining a deeper understanding of OO concepts in general, which in turn can lead to the more mature use of OO technologies. These insights will be gained by exploring consequences of particular interpretations, and by observing the effects of relaxing and/or tightening constraints on the UML semantic model.

Acknowledgments

This material is partially based upon work supported by: the National Science Foundation under Grant No. CCR-9803491; the Bayerische Forschungsstiftung under the FORSOFT research consortium and the DFG under the Leibnizpreis program, and the Laboraturio de Methodos Formais of the Departamento de Informatica of Pontificia Universidade Catolica do Rio de Janeiro.

References

[BFG+93] M. Broy, C. Facchi, R. Grosu, R. Hettler, H. Hußmann, D. Nazareth, F. Regensburger, O. Slotosch, and K. Stølen. The Requirement and Design Specification Language SPECTRUM, An Informal Introduction, Version 1.0, Part 1. Technical Report TUM-I9312, Technische Universität München, 1993.

[BHH+97] Ruth Breu, Ursula Hinkel, Christoph Hofmann, Cornel Klein, Barbara Paech, Bernhard Rumpe, and Veronika Thurner. Towards a formalization of the unified modeling language. In Satoshi Matsuoka Mehmet Aksit, editor, *ECOOP'97 Proceedings*. Springer Verlag, LNCS 1241, 1997.

[BR98] J-M. Bruel and R.B.France. Transforming UML models to formal specifications. In *UML'98 - Beyond the notation*, LNCS 1618. Springer-Verlag, 1998.

[BRJ98] G. Booch, J. Rumbaugh, and I. Jacobson. *The Unified Modeling Language User Guide*. Addison-Wesley, 1998.

[EFLR98] Andy Evans, Robert France, Kevin Lano, and Bernhard Rumpe. Developing the UML as a formal modelling notation. In Jean Bezivin and Pierre-Allain Muller, editors, *UML'98 Proceedings*. Springer-Verlag, LNCS 1618, 1998.

[E98]   A. S. Evans. Reasoning with UML class diagrams. In *WIFT'98*. IEEE
           Press, 1998.

[FELR98] R. France, A. Evans, K. Lano, and B. Rumpe. The UML as a formal
           modeling notation. *Computer Standards & Interfaces*, 19, 1998.

[OMG99] Object Management Group. OMG Unified Modeling Language Specifica-
           tion, version 1.3r2. found at: http://www.rational.org/uml. 1999.

[PUML99] The   pUML   Group.   The   precise   UML   web   site:
           http://www.cs.york.ac.uk/puml. 1999.

[RJB99]   J. Rumbaugh, I. Jacobson, and G. Booch. *The Unified Modeling Language
           Reference Manual*. Addison-Wesley, 1999.

[S86]   D. A. Schmidt. *Denotational Semantics: A Methodology for Language
           Development*. Allyn and Bacon, 1986.

[S92]   J.M. Spivey. *The Z Reference Manual, 2nd Edition*. Prentice Hall, 1992.

About the Authors

Andy Evans has taught and researched in the area of formal methods and their application
to object-oriented and real-time systems. He is co-founder of the precise UML group and
forthcoming co-chair of UML'2000. He has authored and co-authored papers on formalising
UML and object-oriented standards.

Robert France is currently an Associate Professor in the Computer Science Department at
Colorado State University. Currently, his primary research activities revolve around the formalization of object-oriented modeling concepts and the development of rigorous software
development techniques.

Kevin Lano has carried out research and development using formal methods both in industry
and academia. He is the author of "Formal Object-oriented Development" (Springer, 1995) and
"The B Language and Method" (Springer, 1996). His current research is on the integration of
formal methods and safety analysis techniques, and on the formalisation of UML.

Bernhard Rumpe has taught and supervised research in the area of object-oriented modelling
and programming, formal methods and embedded systems. His work includes refinement and
composition techniques for structural as well as behavioral notations, methodical guidelines,
and the development of formalisation approaches for UML. He co-authored and co-edited three
books. He is program chair of UML'99.

Chapter 5

COMBINING JSD AND CLEANROOM FOR OBJECT-ORIENTED SCENARIO SPECIFICATION

Marc Frappier
Richard St-Denis
Département de mathématiques et d'informatique
Université de Sherbrooke
2500, boul. Université
Sherbrooke (Québec) Canada J1K 2R1
Marc.Frappier@dmi.usherb.ca
Richard.St-Denis@dmi.usherb.ca

Abstract   A black box specification process useful for the requirements analysis phase of object-oriented methods is presented. It provides a notation for structuring the description of a system's external behavior as input-output traces using process algebra and entities from the Jackson System Development method. Such a notation allows black box specifications to be an acceptable substitute or supplement for use cases, scenarios, and interaction diagrams. The specification process is divided into four phases – declaration of input and output spaces, specification of entities composing the system, definition of constraints on well-formed input sequences, and specification of input-output behavior.

1.   INTRODUCTION

Several object-oriented methods propose *use cases* as a notation for analyzing and documenting user requirements. According to the UML definition [R97]:

> The use case construct is used to define the behavior of a system without revealing the entity's internal structure. Each use case specifies a sequence of actions, including variants, that the entity can perform, interacting with actors of the entity.

Most OO practitioners suggest using plain English to describe use cases. An interaction diagram (sequence diagram or collaboration diagram) is used to graphically illustrate message exchanges between objects [BRJ99]. The former gives a representation of use cases that does not allow significant leverage in reasoning about properties

of a system or in building case tools for scenario generation and scenario validation [O98]. The latter can contain informal indications, local variables, and pseudo
code that can be misinterpreted or intentionally considered as internal structures of the
software system.

In Cleanroom [MLH86], black box specifications play exactly the same role as
use cases. They describe, in an abstract manner, the external, user-visible system
behavior solely in terms of stimulus histories (input traces or input sequences) and
corresponding responses (outputs), without defining design internals such as system
states, classes, or software structures [L94].

The black box specification process described in detail in this paper differs from
the counterpart of Cleanroom in many aspects. Process algebra [BB87, H85, M89]
is used, in a style inspired by the Jackson System Development (JSD) method [J83],
to describe input sequences that the system may accept in a structured way. First
of all, a process algebra expression defines input sequences or traces of an entity,
which is a concept drawn from the JSD method. Then, parallel compositions of
traces, with synchronization on common inputs, give well-formed input sequences.
Finally, valid input sequences are obtained by adding constraints on well-formed input
sequences. The whole process yields a specification of the system's input-output
behavior expressed in terms of axioms on valid input sequences rather than functions
between input sequences and outputs as in Cleanroom.

Structured black box specifications are close, in spirit, to documents produced
during the requirements analysis phase of object-oriented methods. Because they are
more expressive, they can be used in conjunction with, or as a substitute for, object-
oriented notations, like use cases and interaction diagrams. Complex input sequences
can be described in a concise manner. When an entity reveals behavior that includes
selections, interleaving, and iterations, it is almost impossible to adequately define
equivalent interaction diagrams. In practice, it seems that OO practitioners describe
the most typical but not all scenarios, because this would require too many diagrams.
Finally, the new specification process allows a smooth transition to object-oriented
modeling, because classes naturally emerge from black box specifications. Entity
types are candidates for classes. Typically, an entity type corresponds to a class, but
in some cases, several entity types may be merged to form a single class. Objects of a
class correspond to entities of an entity type. Some associations between classes may
be derived from the relationships between entities. Finally, entity traces correspond to
object values. Identification of specialization relationships between classes are not as
obvious to derive from entity types.

2.   TRACE-BASED SPECIFICATIONS

A system is specified as a black box, considering only its inputs and its outputs, and
abstracting from internal state transitions. In information systems, inputs are typically
called *atomic operations* or *functions*. In this context, a trace-based specification
defines how each sequence of inputs is related to an output.

2.1   INPUT AND OUTPUT SETS

Inputs are described by using set theory and Cartesian products. Let us consider a banking system (B) as a running example. After an initial analysis of this system, the following input sets emerge.

$$X_1 \triangleq \{\text{Register}\} \times \text{Client\_Name} \times \text{Client\_Id}$$
$$X_2 \triangleq \{\text{Open\_Account}\} \times \text{Client\_Id} \times \text{Account\_Id}$$
$$X_3 \triangleq \{\text{Get\_Balance}\} \times \text{Account\_Id}$$
$$X_4 \triangleq \{\text{Deposit}\} \times \text{Account\_Id} \times \text{Amount}$$
$$X_5 \triangleq \{\text{Withdraw}\} \times \text{Account\_Id} \times \text{Amount}$$
$$X_6 \triangleq \{\text{Transfer}\} \times \text{Account\_Id} \times \text{Account\_Id} \times \text{Amount}$$
$$X_7 \triangleq \{\text{Close\_Account}\} \times \text{Account\_Id}$$
$$X_8 \triangleq \{\text{Unregister}\} \times \text{Client\_Id}$$
$$X_9 \triangleq \{\text{List\_Accounts}\}$$

For instance, the tuple $\langle\text{Transfer}, aId_1, aId_2, amount\rangle$ denotes an input that belongs to X_6. This input corresponds to a transfer of money ($amount$) by a client from one account (aId_1) to another (aId_2). The first component Transfer is the input *label*.

The input set for this system is the union of these sets: $X \triangleq \bigcup_{i=1}^{9} X_i$. Sets like **Account_Id** are assumed to be defined. For the purpose of specifying the input-output behavior, the actual definition of these sets is not relevant.

The output sets are defined in a similar manner.

$$Y_1 \triangleq Y_2 \triangleq Y_4 \triangleq Y_5 \triangleq Y_6 \triangleq Y_7 \triangleq Y_8 \triangleq \{\tau\}$$
$$Y_3 \triangleq \textbf{Amount}$$
$$Y_9 \triangleq (\textbf{Account\_Id} \times \textbf{Client\_Id} \times \textbf{Amount})^*$$

Given an input from input set X_i, the system should produce an output from output set Y_i. Symbol τ denotes an output that is not visible to the user. Typically, update functions deliver an invisible output or a confirmation message, since their only effect is to modify the internal system state which is not visible to the user. For simplicity, it is assumed that τ is always produced when update functions are invoked. To display information about the system state, the user typically invokes inquiry functions, which normally provide a visible output. For instance, given an input from X_9, the system should produce an output from Y_9, that is, a list (a sequence represented by the operation *) of accounts with their owner and balance. The output set is given by $Y \triangleq \bigcup_{i=1}^{9} Y_i$.

In an object-oriented model, messages submitted from the environment to a system object correspond to inputs of X; messages sent from a system object to the environment correspond to outputs of Y; internal messages exchanged between system objects are not part of the input space nor the output space. The signature of a method corresponds to a definition like $X_i \times Y_i$. It should be noted that our approach does not encourage specification in terms of signatures only. The semantics of atomic operations is given by a relation between the set of finite sequences over X and output set Y.

Table 1   An input-output history for the banking system

i	Input x_i	Output y_i
1	$\langle$Register, $Mary, c_1\rangle$	τ
2	$\langle$Open_Account, $c_1, a_1\rangle$	τ
3	$\langle$Deposit, $a_1, 50\rangle$	τ
4	$\langle$Open_Account, $c_1, a_2\rangle$	τ
5	$\langle$Get_Balance, $a_1\rangle$	$\langle 50\rangle$
6	$\langle$Register, $Paul, c_2\rangle$	τ
7	$\langle$Open_Account, $c_2, a_3\rangle$	τ
8	$\langle$Transfer, $a_1, a_2, 30\rangle$	τ
9	$\langle$Deposit, $a_3, 100\rangle$	τ
10	$\langle$List_Accounts$\rangle$	$\langle a_1, c_1, 20\rangle \cdot \langle a_2, c_1, 30\rangle \cdot \langle a_3, c_2, 100\rangle$

2.2   INPUT-OUTPUT TRACES

Let X^+ be the set of nonempty, finite sequences built using elements of X. Given input set X and output set Y of a system, the set of input-output traces is given by $X^+ \times Y$. As an example, let us consider Table 1. Assume that the system has just started, thus it is in its initial state, and input x_1 is submitted. The system processes this input and delivers output $y_1 = \tau$. The input-output trace corresponding to this behavior is $\langle\langle$Register, $Mary, c_1\rangle, \tau\rangle$. Another example of input-output trace is

$$\langle\langle\text{Register}, Mary, c_1\rangle \cdot \langle\text{Open\_Account}, c_1, a_1\rangle \cdot \langle\text{Deposit}, a_1, 50\rangle \cdot$$
$$\langle\text{Open\_Account}, c_1, a_2\rangle \cdot \langle\text{Get\_Balance}, a_1\rangle, \langle 50\rangle\rangle.$$

A trace-based specification is a relation R between X^+ and Y and $s \triangleleft R \triangleright y$ denotes that the pair $\langle s, y\rangle$ is an element of relation R. The two examples given above are input-output traces that belong to the specification of the banking system. Let $s[i]$ denote the ith element of sequence s. A trace-based specification is interpreted as follows. A program is said to be a correct implementation of a specification R if, for any input sequence $s = s[1] \cdot \ldots \cdot s[n] \in dom(R)$, the program satisfies the following two properties: i) input sequence s is accepted by the program and ii) after processing the last input $s[n] \in X_i$, the program delivers an output $y \in Y_i$ such that $s \triangleleft R \triangleright y$.

Using relations instead of functions is a slight generalization of the initial Cleanroom model of black box specifications. It allows a simple form of nondeterminacy in specifications. A more powerful form of nondeterminacy is possible if relations are defined between input histories and output histories (i.e., relations between X^+ and Y^+). For a large class of information systems, relations between X^+ and Y are, however, sufficient and easier to manage, as it is not necessary to deal with output histories. The reader is referred to [BDD92] and [WP94] for additional details on these alternative models.

3. MATHEMATICAL NOTATIONS

In order to have a self-contained text, let us introduce the strict mathematical notations for specifying traces. In JSD, Jackson uses regular expressions, but process algebras are slightly more expressive for this task. For the purpose of making the specification process easier, we have selected a suitable subset of CSP [H85] and LOTOS [BB87], which corresponds, roughly speaking, to regular expressions plus parallel composition with synchronization. Semantics of the chosen operations has been simplified and concepts such as nondeterminacy, arbitrary recursion, and the silent action (denoted by τ in CCS) have been deliberately omitted. An operational semantics of these operations in the CCS style [M89] can be found in [FS99].

Predicates are written using the language of first-order logic with the usual connectives in the following binding order from highest to lowest: $\neg, \wedge, \vee, \{\Leftarrow, \Rightarrow\}, \Leftrightarrow, \{\forall, \exists\}$. Binding order is modified by means of parentheses. As usual, free variables in axioms are implicitly universally quantified. Let $e(x)$ be a term where variable x may occur. A commutative, associative binary operation Φ is extended by quantifying over a set of values satisfying a predicate p. This is denoted "$\Phi x : p(x) : e(x)$" and variable x is bound by operation Φ. This notation is equivalent to $\Phi_{\{x|p(x)\}}e(x)$, but is more readable when the quantification predicate contains long names.

Given an alphabet Σ, elements of $\Sigma \cup \{\epsilon\}$ represent *elementary* process expressions (PE's). Variables and the special symbol "_" may be used in the specification of an elementary PE. Variables are useful for defining PE's over an infinite alphabet. The special symbol "_" is useful for creating expressions with "don't care" values; this reduces the number of variables required to write an expression. Process expressions are typically defined over an alphabet structured as the Cartesian product of sets. Thus, a tuple-like notation is used to define elementary PE's. For example, tuple $\langle a, \_ \rangle$ is equivalent to $| b : \langle a, b \rangle \in \Sigma : \langle a, b \rangle$, where "$|$" is the choice operation. Symbol π_i refers to the projection function on the ith coordinate of a tuple.

A process expression may be constructed using elementary PE's and the following operations: $\cdot, +, *, |, |[\,]|, ||, |||$. Operations $\cdot, +, *$ denote the usual concatenation, positive closure, and Kleene closure of regular expressions. Operation $E_1 | E_2$ is a choice between E_1 and E_2; it is drawn from regular expressions and CSP [H85]. Operation $E_1 |[A]| E_2$ is the parameterized parallel composition of E_1 and E_2 with synchronization on elements of set A; it is drawn from LOTOS [BB87]. Operations $||$ and $|||$ are, respectively, the parallel composition and the interleave of CSP [H85]; they are special variants of $|[\,]|$. The set of all traces defined by a PE E is noted $\mathcal{T}(E)$. As an example of a PE over alphabet $\Sigma = \{a, b, c\}$, let us consider $E \triangleq a \cdot b |[\{b\}]| b \cdot (a | c)$. Then, $\mathcal{T}(E) = \{a, ab, aba, abc\}$.

Finally, useful operations on sequences are introduced. A finite sequence over X is written as $s = s[1]s[2]\ldots s[n]$, where $s[i]$ is its ith element and n its *length* (denoted $\#s$). The *empty sequence* is noted ε. The functions $first(s)$, $last(s)$, $front(s)$, and $tail(s)$ respectively denote the first element, the last element, all but the last element, and all but the first element of sequence s, provided s is not empty. The expressions $x \dashv s$, $s \vdash x$, and $s_1 \cdot s_2$ denote the *left append* of element x to sequence s, *right append* of element x to sequence s, and concatenation of sequences s_1 and s_2, respectively. The function $prefix(s)$ denotes the set of prefixes of sequence s, that is,

$prefix(s) \triangleq \{s_1 \mid \exists s_2 : s = s_1 \cdot s_2\}$. For simplicity, a one-element sequence and its corresponding element are interchangeable.

4.   SPECIFICATION PROCESS

Specifying the external behavior of an information system with the help of an input-output relation requires a process structured into four steps:

1. definition of input and output spaces X and Y;

2. definition of *entities* from which well-formed input sequences are automatically produced using process expressions;

3. definition of *constraints* on well-formed input sequences;

4. definition of relation R using axioms on input-output pairs.

The purpose of steps 2 and 3 is to define *valid* input sequences. Step 4 defines an input-output relation between valid input sequences and outputs.

An invalid input sequence contains an input that causes an error when it is processed. For instance, let us consider input element $\langle \text{Deposit}, a_5, 25 \rangle$. If this input is submitted after any input in Table 1, the system should display an appropriate message as an output, because account a_5 has not been opened before this operation. It should process subsequent inputs as if this erroneous input never happened. Taking into account invalid input sequences significantly increases specification size and reduces readability, while providing little added value for understanding the system behavior. It is more cost-efficient to first define the behavior for valid input sequences, and then refine the specification to provide meaningful error messages for invalid input sequences in a later stage.

4.1   DEFINITION OF ENTITIES

The second step of the specification process is largely inspired from the *entity structure step* of the JSD method [J83]. First, the entities composing the system are identified. Then, the behavior of each entity is described using a process expression. Finally, the semantics of entities is given in terms of a set of well-formed input sequences.

4.1.1   Process Expressions. Let $E \triangleq \{e_1, \ldots, e_n\}$ be the set of entity types of the system, and X and Y its input and output sets. Let $\mathcal{PE}$ be the set of process expressions over $X \cup \{\epsilon\}$. A set of keys K_e is associated to each entity type $e \in E$. A key makes it possible to uniquely identify each entity of type e. Furthermore, for each $e \in E$, a total function $f_e \in K_e \rightarrow \mathcal{PE}$ gives some ordering constraints on inputs. A trace of $\mathcal{T}(f_e(k))$, called an *entity trace*, is specific to the entity of type e with key k.

There are four entity types in the banking system: account, client, transfer, and query. The entity types account and client appear naturally and

$$K_{\text{account}} \triangleq \text{Account\_Id} \qquad K_{\text{client}} \triangleq \text{Client\_Id}.$$

The behavior of an entity of type account is given by the following simple process expression:

$$f_{\text{account}}(aId) \triangleq account(\_, aId)$$

where $account(\_, aId)$ is an auxiliary process expression with two arguments that belong to K_{client} and K_{account}, respectively. The underscore ("$\_$"), as first argument, denotes that any value for "client identifier" is acceptable. This expression describes all the possible input sequences that the account with key aId could execute during its life. It is defined as:

$$account(cId, aId) \triangleq \langle \text{Open\_Account}, cId, aId \rangle \cdot$$
$$($$
$$\langle \text{Get\_Balance}, aId \rangle \mid \langle \text{Deposit}, aId, \_ \rangle \mid$$
$$\langle \text{Withdraw}, aId, \_ \rangle \quad \mid \langle \text{Transfer}, aId, \_, \_ \rangle$$
$$)^* \cdot$$
$$\langle \text{Close\_Account}, aId \rangle$$

It is structured as a concatenation (sequence) of three process expressions. The first one corresponds to the opening of an account by a client. The second one is an iteration over a choice between common operations on the same account. Finally, the third one allows the account to be closed.

It should be noted that an entity of type account deals only with transfers from an account. Transfers to an account are handled by entities of type transfer, in order to properly state that the source and destination accounts must exist before executing a transfer. It is not an appropriate solution to add PE $\langle \text{Transfer}, \_, aId, \_ \rangle$ in the choice expression of $account(cId, aId)$, because of our semantics of entities (see Section 4.1.3). This solution would only state that the source account *or* the destination account must exist, but not necessarily both.

Process expression $account(cId, aId)$ is reused in the following definition associated to the entity type client:

$$f_{\text{client}}(cId) \triangleq \langle \text{Register}, \_, cId \rangle \cdot$$
$$(\|\|\| aId : \text{Account\_Id} : account(cId, aId)) \cdot$$
$$\langle \text{Unregister}, cid \rangle$$

The second term of the concatenation describes how a client performs operations on its accounts. It uses a new operation, the bounded interleave ($\|\|\|$), whose formal definition is omitted. In short, this term is an abbreviation of the following process expression:

$$account(cId, aId_1) \|\| \cdots \|\| account(cId, aId_n),$$

with $aId_i \in \text{Account\_Id}$ and $n \geq 0$. The use of expression $account(cId, aId)$ is an example of process abstraction, which allows an incremental construction of entities.

The entity type transfer makes it possible to ensure that the destination account of a transfer operation has been previously opened and differs from the source account. An entity of this type has a destination account identifier as key and its behavior is given by a process expression that will allow synchronization of the source account with the destination account on a transfer operation:

$$K_{\text{transfer}} \triangleq \text{Account\_Id}$$

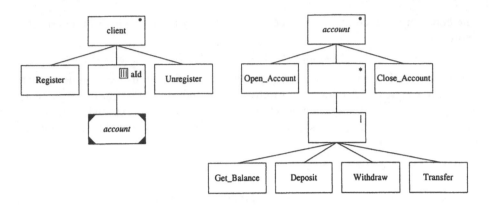

Figure 1   Structure diagrams for a client

$$f_{\mathsf{transfer}}(daId) \triangleq \langle \mathsf{Open\_Account}, \_, daId \rangle \cdot$$
$$($$
$$| \; saId : saId \in \mathbf{Account\_Id} - \{daId\} :$$
$$\langle \mathsf{Transfer}, saId, daId, \_\rangle$$
$$)^* \cdot$$
$$\langle \mathsf{Close\_Account}, daId \rangle$$

Finally, the entity type query takes into account inquiries from the system administrator. Query inputs typically do not have strong ordering constraints. They may be submitted at any time by the user and they do not influence the state of the system. For the sake of simplicity, queries are typically grouped into a single entity. This entity has no "natural" key, but to keep the mathematical framework uniform and simple, a key is required. Hence,

$$K_{\mathsf{query}} \triangleq \{1\} \text{ and } f_{\mathsf{query}}(1) \triangleq \langle \mathsf{List\_Accounts}\rangle^*.$$

A process expression of an entity describes a subset of operations that may be submitted to the system in a specific order. It may be graphically represented by a syntax tree, called a *structure diagram*, to enhance specification readability. Figure 1 provides the structure diagrams for the entity type client and its auxiliary process expression. To make the diagram clearer and simpler, input parameters are omitted, leaving only input labels and operators. The top right corner of a rectangle contains an operator. A leaf corresponds to either an input or an auxiliary process expression; the latter is identified by triangled corners. The purpose of a diagram is to give a quick overview; to get further details, the reader may consult the formal textual definition of the corresponding process expression.

This way of defining entities provides a good idea of possible *scenarios* of a system. For instance, they describe how clients and accounts are managed. Furthermore, it is quite intuitive from diagrams in Figure 1 that the entity type client should become a class in an object-oriented model. Moreover, the fact that an entity of type account is implicitly referenced in an entity of type client indicates that they are associated. One may even infer that a client is related to several accounts (i.e., a one-to-many relationship), because of the bounded interleave on accounts. In complex modeling situations, two entity types could be refined by two classes or merged into a single class; this is a design issue.

4.1.2 Examples of Entity Traces. An entity trace specific to the entity of type e with key k is a trace that belongs to $\mathcal{T}(f_e(k))$. Let us deduce the entity traces of the input sequence in Table 1. There are two client traces denoted t_1 and t_2, respectively.

$t_1 = \langle$Register, $Mary, c_1\rangle \cdot \langle$Open_Account, $c_1, a_1\rangle \cdot \langle$Deposit, $a_1, 50\rangle \cdot$
$\qquad \langle$Open_Account, $c_1, a_2\rangle \cdot \langle$Get_Balance, $a_1\rangle \cdot \langle$Transfer, $a_1, a_2, 30\rangle$

$t_2 = \langle$Register, $Paul, c_2\rangle \cdot \langle$Open_Account, $c_2, a_3\rangle \cdot \langle$Deposit, $a_3, 100\rangle$

The remaining entity traces of the input sequence in Table 1 are given below.

account traces: $t_3 = \langle$Open_Account, $c_1, a_1\rangle \cdot \langle$Deposit, $a_1, 50\rangle \cdot$
$\qquad\qquad\qquad \langle$Get_Balance, $a_1\rangle \cdot \langle$Transfer, $a_1, a_2, 30\rangle$

$\qquad\qquad t_4 = \langle$Open_Account, $c_1, a_2\rangle$

$\qquad\qquad t_5 = \langle$Open_Account, $c_2, a_3\rangle \cdot \langle$Deposit, $a_3, 100\rangle$

transfer trace: $t_6 = \langle$Open_Account, $c_1, a_2\rangle \cdot \langle$Transfer, $a_1, a_2, 30\rangle$

query trace: $t_7 = \langle$List_Accounts$\rangle$

4.1.3 Semantics of Entities. Entity traces must be combined to form system input sequences (e.g., input sequence in Table 1). To achieve that, all traces of entities of the same type are interleaved. For example, if there are two clients, it does not matter in which order they evolve because the two clients are self-sufficient. The resulting traces for each entity type are then composed in parallel, but they must be synchronized on common inputs. For example, the input sequences that can be generated from entity traces $t_1, \ldots, t_7$ are defined by the process expression $(t_1 \;|||\; t_2) \;||\; (t_3 \;|||\; t_4 \;|||\; t_5) \;||\; t_6 \;||\; t_7$. This process expression has several possible system traces. The input sequence in Table 1 is one of them.

The parallel composition operator $||$ between entity types acts like a conjunction: an input sequence must satisfy all the ordering constraints specified for each entity. For example, let us consider entity trace t_1' which is a permutation of t_1:

$t_1' = \langle$Register, $Mary, c_1\rangle \cdot \langle$Open_Account, $c_1, a_1\rangle \cdot \langle$Deposit, $a_1, 50\rangle \cdot$
$\qquad \langle$Get_Balance, $a_1\rangle \cdot \langle$Transfer, $a_1, a_2, 30\rangle \cdot \langle$Open_Account, $c_1, a_2\rangle$

Note that t_1' is a correct trace of $\mathcal{T}(f_{\text{client}}(c_1))$. However, it transfers an amount of money from account a_1 to account a_2 that does not exist yet. This results in a deadlock in system behavior because t_1' and t_6 cannot synchronize. This example illustrates that it is not possible to generate an input sequence that does not satisfy all the ordering constraints specified by the entities.

The set of all *well-formed input sequences* resulting from the association of entities is constructed by combining all possible sets of traces for each entity and is formally defined as follows:

$$S_E \triangleq \mathcal{T}(\;||\; e : e \in E : \textstyle\prod k : K_e : f_e(k)).$$

4.2   SPECIFICATION OF CONSTRAINTS

Process expressions may not be sufficient to represent all the necessary constraints on input sequences. Additional constraints on well-formed input sequences must sometimes be added. This task constitutes the third step of the specification process. For this purpose, the set $\mathbf{Valid}_E$ of valid input sequences is defined as follows:

$$\mathbf{Valid}_E \triangleq \{s \mid s \in S_E \wedge p_1(s) \wedge \ldots \wedge p_n(s)\}$$

where $p_1, \ldots, p_n$ are predicates in first-order logic that represent constraints on well-formed input sequences. An input sequence is *valid* if it is well-formed and each p_i holds. It should be noted that constraints are similar to *safety* properties, as they require a property to hold for any *prefix* of a well-formed input sequence.

4.2.1   Extracting Entity Traces.   Basic predicates are introduced to extract entity traces from a well-formed input sequence. Let $s \in S_E$ and T be a set of 3–tuples of the form $\langle e, t, k \rangle$, where t is an entity trace specific to the entity of type e with key k. Predicate $entity\_traces(s, T)$ holds if input sequence s is constructed from all the elements of T. For each entity type e, predicate $e(t, k, T)$ holds iff t is an entity trace specific to the entity of type e with key k according to a set T, that is, $e(t, k, T) \Leftrightarrow \langle e, t, k \rangle \in T$. Formal definitions of these predicates can be found in [FS99].

As an example, let s be the well-formed input sequence in Table 1. Predicates $entity\_traces(s, T)$ and $\mathsf{client}(t_1, c_1, T)$ hold with

$$T = \{\langle \mathsf{client}, t_1, c_1 \rangle, \langle \mathsf{client}, t_2, c_2 \rangle, \langle \mathsf{account}, t_3, a_1 \rangle,$$
$$\langle \mathsf{account}, t_4, a_2 \rangle, \langle \mathsf{account}, t_5, a_3 \rangle, \langle \mathsf{transfert}, t_6, a_2 \rangle, \langle \mathsf{query}, t_7, 1 \rangle\}.$$

4.2.2   Example of a Constraint.   The following predicate ensures that an account never has a negative balance.

$$Positive\_Balance(s) \Leftrightarrow \forall s', aId, T : s' \in prefix(s) \wedge entity\_traces(s', T) \wedge$$
$$\mathsf{account}(\_, aId, T) \Rightarrow balance(aId, s') \geq 0$$

where the function *balance* is recursively defined as:

$$balance(aId, s) \triangleq \mathbf{case}\ last(s)\ \mathbf{of}$$

$\langle \mathsf{Deposit}, aId, m \rangle$	:	$m + balance(aId, front(s))$;
$\langle \mathsf{Withdraw}, aId, m \rangle$	:	$balance(aId, front(s)) - m$;
$\langle \mathsf{Transfer}, \_, aId, m \rangle$	:	$m + balance(aId, front(s))$;
$\langle \mathsf{Transfer}, aId, \_, m \rangle$	:	$balance(aId, front(s)) - m$;
$\langle \mathsf{Open\_Account}, \_, aId \rangle$	:	0;

$\qquad\qquad\mathbf{otherwise}$
$\qquad\qquad balance(aId, front(s))$.

Basic predicates and the function *balance* make it possible to formulate axioms that are useful in the specification of the input-output behavior. Given $s \in S_{\mathsf{B}}$ and T such that $entity\_traces(s, T)$, the following predicate holds if the account with key aId has not been closed.

$$active\_account(aId, t, T) \Leftrightarrow \textsf{account}(t, aId, T) \wedge$$
$$Label(last(t)) \neq \textsf{Close\_Account}$$

4.3   SPECIFICATION OF INPUT-OUTPUT BEHAVIOR

In the last step of the specification process, the input-output behavior is defined with a set of axioms on valid input sequences. A typical input-output axiom has the following form:

$$s\vdash x \in \textbf{Valid}_E \wedge \text{conjunction} \Rightarrow s\vdash x \triangleleft R_E \triangleright y.$$

Variable x denotes the last element of an input sequence. A *complete* specification should have a set of axioms that defines an output for each input sequence of $\textbf{Valid}_E$, that is, $\textbf{Valid}_E \subseteq dom(R_E)$ should hold. Moreover, an output should belong to the output set associated to the input set of the last input, that is, $s\vdash x \triangleleft R_E \triangleright y \wedge x \in X_i \Rightarrow y \in Y_i$.

When an input sequence ends with an element of X_i whose corresponding output set Y_i is a singleton, the output is specified in a generic manner with the following axiom:

$$s\vdash x \in \textbf{Valid}_E \wedge x \in X_i \wedge Y_i = \{y\} \Rightarrow s\vdash x \triangleleft R_E \triangleright y.$$

For example, in the banking system, this axiom suffices to specify the output for any input sequence ending with an input from sets X_1, X_2, or X_4 to X_8. It remains to specify the output for an input sequence ending with $\langle \textsf{Get\_Balance}, aId \rangle$ or $\langle \textsf{List\_Accounts} \rangle$.

4.3.1   Balance of an Account.   The following simple axiom gives the output for an input sequence ending with $\langle \textsf{Get\_Balance}, aId \rangle$. It uses the auxiliary predicate $active\_account(aId, t, T)$ previously defined.

$$s\vdash \langle \textsf{Get\_Balance}, aId \rangle \in \textbf{Valid}_B \wedge entity\_traces(s, T) \wedge$$
$$active\_account(aId, \_, T) \Rightarrow s\vdash \langle \textsf{Get\_Balance}, aId \rangle \triangleleft R_B \triangleright balance(aId, s)$$

This axiom checks if a trace of the active account with key aId appears in sequence s. If this is the case, then the output is the current balance of this account.

4.3.2   List Accounts.   The next axiom defines the output for an input sequence ending with input $\langle \textsf{List\_Accounts} \rangle$. The output is a list of active accounts with their owner and current balance, sorted by account identifier.

$$s\vdash \langle \textsf{List\_Accounts} \rangle \in \textbf{Valid}_B \wedge entity\_traces(s, T) \wedge$$
$$O = \{o \mid \exists aId, t : active\_account(aId, t, T) \wedge$$
$$o = \langle aId, Client\_Id(first(t)), balance(aId, s) \rangle \} \wedge$$
$$sorted(out, \pi_1, O)$$
$$\Rightarrow$$
$$s\vdash \langle \textsf{List\_Accounts} \rangle \triangleleft R_B \triangleright out$$

This axiom defines set O of 3–tuples $\langle aId, cId, amount \rangle$. A 3–tuple is generated by selecting a trace t of an active account. Its owner is extracted by using a projection function on the first input $\langle$Open_Account, $cId, aId\rangle$ of entity trace t. Note that, as a convention, the name of the set defining the domain of an attribute (e.g., **Client_Id**) is used as a projection function (e.g., $Client\_Id$) that returns the value of the attribute for a given input. The sort criteria and the transformation of the set into a sequence according to the sort criteria are expressed using predicate $sorted(out, \pi_i, O)$. Informally, this predicate states that out is a list of all elements of O sorted on the ith attribute given by projection function π_i.

4.4   SPECIFYING ERRORS

A typical information system produces an error message when an invalid input is received, and processes the subsequent inputs as if they were not preceded by invalid inputs. This behavior can be specified in a generic manner by defining a robust specification. Function $robust$ takes a relation R, between X^+ and Y, which deals only with valid input sequences, and extends it to a total relation between X^+ and $(Y \cup \textbf{ErrorMsg})$.

$$robust(R) \triangleq \{(s,y) \mid (red(front(s), R) \cdot last(s), y) \in R \ \vee$$
$$red(front(s), R) \cdot last(s) \notin dom(R) \ \wedge$$
$$y \in \textbf{ErrorMsg}\}$$

where $red(s, R)$ is defined as follows:

> **if** $s = \varepsilon$ **then**
> $red(s, R) = \varepsilon$
> **else if** $s \in dom(R)$ **then**
> $red(s, R) = s$
> **else if** $red(front(s), R) \cdot last(s) \in dom(R)$ **then**
> $red(s, R) = red(front(s), R) \cdot last(s)$
> **else** $red(s, R) = red(front(s), R)$

5.   CONCLUSION

The primary advantage of this new specification process is that it combines several specification paradigms in a fruitful manner. A specification is incrementally constructed into several layers, each layer providing a different view-point. First, the specification of inputs is decoupled from the specification of outputs, deviating from a purely process algebraic approach in which inputs and outputs are catered for at the same time. This makes the specification easier to understand, because there are fewer details to handle at once. Second, input sequences are structured into entity traces. This structure can be used to describe system outputs in a style very similar to state-based specifications like B [A96] or Z [S88], but without the burden of defining state variables and updating them in each operation. In fact, entities and constraints are sufficient to specify the behavior of update operations that do not produce visible outputs. One only has to specify the output of inquiry operations using input-output axioms. Consequently, specifications can be shorter (up to 40 %) than equivalent model-based specifications written in B.

Trace-based specifications also provide a good alternative for the precise description of use cases. They satisfy the abstraction goal that use case proponents pursue, without requiring the definition of objects and classes like interaction diagrams do. Furthermore, this abstraction level does not hinder the definition of an object-oriented model, because entity types are naturally refined to become classes. Entities are also more expressive than interaction diagrams, because they allow a complete description of system scenarios.

We are currently working on a prototype for executing specifications in order to facilitate their validation. We have implemented an interpreter in Prolog for a library specification written using our notation. This interpreter can determine if an input sequence is valid, that is, if it satisfies the ordering constraints and global constraints. When the input sequence is valid, the interpreter can compute the corresponding output. An input sequence may be decomposed into entity traces, which facilitates the validation process. We are currently working on a generalization of this interpreter, in order to interpret a larger class of specifications.

Acknowledgment

The research described in this paper was supported in part by the Natural Sciences and Engineering Research Council of Canada (NSERC) and the Fonds pour la formation de chercheurs et l'aide à la recherche of Québec (FCAR).

References

[A96]   Abrial, J.-R. (1996) *The B-Book*, Cambridge University Press.

[BB87]   Bolognesi, T., E. Brinksma (1987) Introduction to the ISO Specification Language LOTOS, *Computer Networks and ISDN Systems* 14(1) 25–59.

[BRJ99]   Booch, G., J. Rumbaugh, I. Jacobson (1999) *The Unified Modeling Language User Guide*, Addison-Wesley.

[BDD92]   Broy, M., F. Dederichs, C. Dendorfer, M. Fuchs, T.F. Gritzner, R. Weber (1992) The Design of Distributed Systems - an Introduction to FOCUS, Technische Universität München, Institut für Informatik, TUM-I9203.

[FS99]   Frappier, M., R. St-Denis (1999) Specifying Information Systems through Structured Input-Output Traces, Université de Sherbrooke, Département de mathématiques et d'informatique, Technical Report 233.

[H85]   Hoare, C.A.R. (1985) *Communicating Sequential Processes*, Prentice Hall.

[J83]   Jackson, M. (1983) *System Development*, Prentice Hall.

[L94]   Linger, R.C. (1994) Cleanroom Process Model, *IEEE Software* 11(2) 50–58.

[MLH86]   Mills, H.D., R.C. Linger, A.R. Hevner (1986) *Principles of Information Systems Analysis and Design*, Academic Press.

[M89]   Milner, R. (1989) *Communication and Concurrency*, Prentice Hall.

[O98]   Odell, J.J. (1998) *Advanced Object-Oriented Analysis & Design Using UML*, Cambridge University Press.

[R97]   Rational Software (1997) Unified Modeling Language Summary, version 1.1, September 1, http://www.rational.com/uml/.

[S88]   Spivey, J.M. (1988) *Understanding Z: A Specification Language and its Formal Semantics*, vol. 3 of Cambridge Tracts in Theoretical Computer Science, Cambridge University Press.

[WP94]   Wang, Y., D.L. Parnas (1994) Simulating the Behavior of Software Modules by Trace Rewriting, *IEEE Transactions on Software Engineering* **20**(10) 750–759.

About the Authors

Marc Frappier is a professor of computer science at the Université de Sherbrooke. He earned a Ph.D. in computer science from the University of Ottawa in 1995. His research interests include the mathematics of software development and the use of measures for software cost estimation and quality management. He held several positions in industry prior to his academic career, both at technical and management levels. He is also an independent industrial consultant.

Richard St-Denis received the B.Sc. and M.Sc. degrees in computer science from the Université de Montréal in 1975 and 1977, respectively, and the Ph.D. degree in applied sciences from École Polytechnique de Montréal in 1992. He is currently a professor of computer science at the Université de Sherbrooke, where his research interests include discrete-event systems, software engineering, and artificial intelligence. He has published a book in French on programming with the *Sparc* assembly language.

Chapter 6

WHAT IS BEHIND UML-RT?

Radu Grosu

Institut für Informatik, TU München, D-80290 München

grosu@in.tum.de

Manfred Broy

Institut für Informatik, TU München, D-80290 München

broy@in.tum.de

Bran Selic

ObjecTime Limited, K2K 2E4 Kanata, Ontario

bran@ObjecTime.com

Gheorghe Stefănescu

Faculty of Mathematics, University of Bucharest, RO-70109 Bucharest

ghstef@stoilow.imar.ro

Abstract   The unified modeling language (UML) developed under the coordination of the Object Management Group (OMG) is one of the most important standards for the specification and design of object oriented systems. This standard is currently tuned for real time applications in the form of a new proposal, UML for Real-Time (UML-RT), by Rational Software Corporation and ObjecTime Limited. Because of the importance of UML-RT we are investigating its formal foundation in a joint project between ObjecTime Limited, Technische Universität München and the University of Bucharest. Our results clearly show that the visual notation of UML-RT is not only very intuitive but it also has a very deep mathematical foundation. In a previous paper (see [GBSS98]) we presented part of this foundation, namely the theory of flow graphs. In this paper we use flow graphs to define the more powerful theory of interaction graphs.

1.   INTRODUCTION

The specification and design of an interactive system is a complex task that has to work out data, behavior, intercommunication, architecture and distribution aspects of the modeled system. Moreover the specification has to assure the successful communication between the customer and the software expert. In order to fulfill these requirements, an UML-RT specification for an interactive system (see [SR98]) is a combined visual/textual specification, called a *capsule class,* which is built hierarchically as shown in Figure 6.1, left.

A capsule class has associated two visual specifications: a *structure* specification and a *behavior* specification. The structure specification gives the architecture of the capsule in terms of other capsules and *connectors* (or duplex channels) between capsules. The connectors are typed, i.e., they have associated *protocol classes* defining the messages allowed to flow along the connectors. The types of the messages and the protocols themselves, are defined in terms of *data classes* or directly in C++. The

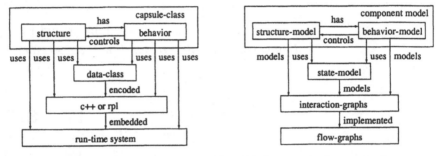

Figure 6.1   The layers of UML-RT and their semantic characterization

behavior of a capsule is controlled by a state transition diagram. The *state variables* and the *functions* occurring in this diagram are also defined in terms of data classes or in C++. Moreover, the detailed description of the *actions* associated to a transition are given in C++. Hence, the UML-RT visual specifications build on top of a *sequential object oriented language.* Special actions like sending a message or setting a timer are performed by calling the run time system. Hence, UML-RT also builds upon a communication and synchronization model. Since a sender may always send a message this is an *asynchronous* communication model.

The semantics we currently define for UML-RT in a joint project between ObjecTime Limited, Technische Universität München and the University of Bucharest, follows a similar hierarchy, as shown in Figure 6.1, right. It consists of a *structure model,* a *behavior model* and a *state model.* Each model interprets an associated *interaction graph.* These graphs closely resemble the UML-RT visual specifications. However, they are completely formalized and this makes them an ideal candidate for the semantics of UML-RT.

The structure model defines the structure of a capsule class in terms of other capsules and connectors between these capsules. It also defines the synchronization between capsules. The behavior model defines the behavior of a capsule in terms of hierarchical states and transitions between these states. The state model is the equivalent of the data classes and the object oriented languages. It allows us to define arbitrary data

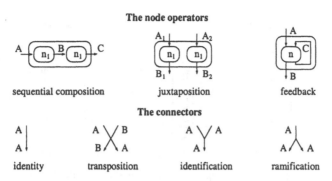

The node operators

sequential composition   juxtaposition   feedback

The connectors

identity   transposition   identification   ramification

Figure 6.2 Flow graphs

types and functions processing these types. Hence, it is used both by the structure and the behavior models. In contrast to UML-RT, this is also a model for interaction graphs. Hence, using our semantics, one can make UML-RT completely visual and independent from any particular programming language.

Finally, interaction graphs are implemented by *flow graphs*. In contrast to interaction graphs which are appropriate for high level design, the later ones are low level graphs which make causality explicit.

In our earlier paper (see [GBSS98]) we presented the theory of flow graphs. In this paper we use flow graphs to define the theory of interaction graphs. This theory is characterized by three elements: a *visual notation,* a *textual notation* and a *calculus.* The visual notation consists of a set of graph construction primitives presented in a visual form. They define the *user interface* to an abstract editor for diagrams. The textual notation consists of the same set of graph construction primitives, presented in a textual form. They define an abstract *internal representation* of the above primitives. The textual form is *automatically generated* from the visual form, and it is usually hidden from the user. It can be roughly understood as the program that actually runs on the computer. Finally, the calculus is the engine that allows us to *transform* a diagram into another diagram that has the *same meaning* but optimizes time and/or space. Moreover it *determines* whether two diagrams are equivalent. The calculus consists of a set of equations which identify semantically equal graphs. This immediately allows us to compare diagrams. Orienting the equations (e.g. from left to right) one obtains a *rewriting calculus,* i.e., an interpreter.

The rest of the paper is organized as follows. In Section 2 we revise the basic elements of the theory of flow graphs. In Section 3 we first motivate the need for interaction graphs. Then we use the theory of flow graphs to define interaction graphs and their associated properties. Finally in Section 4 we draw some conclusions.

2.   FLOW GRAPHS

Flow graphs (see [GBSS98]) are constructed by using, as shown in Figure 6.2, three operators on nodes – *sequential composition, juxtaposition* and *feedback* and four connectors – *identity, transposition, identification* and *ramification.*

The node operators and the connectors have a rich set of algebraic properties that basically reflect our visual intuition about flow graphs. In the following we review these properties and point out how they fit in the general setting of category theory. However,

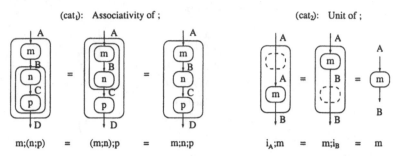

(cat₁): Associativity of ;   (cat₂): Unit of ;

$$m;(n;p) \quad = \quad (m;n);p \quad = \quad m;n;p \qquad\qquad i_A;m \quad = \quad m;i_B \quad = \quad m$$

Figure 6.3   Properties of sequential composition

as Figures 6.3, 6.4 and 6.5 clearly show, no background in category theory is really necessary to understand them and the interested reader may consult [GBSS98] for a complete treatment. Moreover, these properties are not a prerequisite to understand the rest of the paper. We give them here basically for reference purpose and to establish the connection with other work in the semantics of concurrent processes. They are also needed in the proofs of similar properties for interaction graphs.

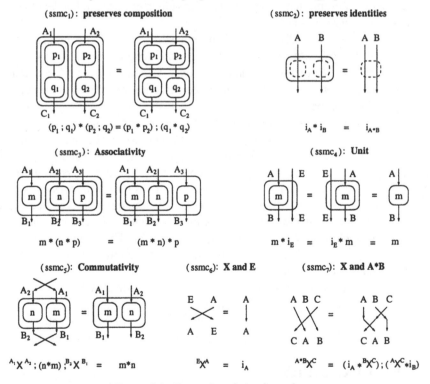

(ssmc₁): **preserves composition**

$$(p_1 ; q_1) * (p_2 ; q_2) = (p_1 * p_2) ; (q_1 * q_2)$$

(ssmc₂): **preserves identities**

$$i_A * i_B \quad = \quad i_{A*B}$$

(ssmc₃): **Associativity**

$$m * (n * p) \quad = \quad (m * n) * p$$

(ssmc₄): **Unit**

$$m * i_E \quad = \quad i_E * m \quad = \quad m$$

(ssmc₅): **Commutativity**

$$^{A_1}X^{A_2} ; (n*m) \overset{B_2}{;} X^{B_1} \quad = \quad m*n$$

(ssmc₆): **X and E**

$$^E X^A \quad = \quad i_A$$

(ssmc₇): **X and A*B**

$$^{A*B}X^C \quad = \quad (i_A * {}^B X^C) ; ({}^A X^C * i_B)$$

Figure 6.4   Properties of visual attachment

As shown in Figure 6.3, sequential composition is associative and has identities as neutral elements. Hence, in mathematical terminology, nodes equipped with sequential composition define a *category*. As shown in Figure 6.4, juxtaposition is defined both on arrows and on nodes in such a way that it preserves identities and composition. In mathematical terminology, it is a *functor*. Moreover, it is associative, has a neutral element and commutes with transposition. It therefore defines a strict *symmetric monoidal category*. As shown in Figure 6.5, feedback also allows to construct loops and its properties extend the strict symmetric monoidal category to a *trace monoidal category*.

The *tightening* equation allows to tighten the scope of the feedback. In mathematical terminology one says that the feedback $\uparrow^C_{A,B}$ is *natural* in the arrows A and B, i.e., in the arrows that are not fed back. The *sliding* equation allows to slide n along the feedback loop. In mathematical terminology the feedback operator $\uparrow^C_{A,B}$ is *natural* also in the feedback arrow C. The *superposing* equation says that feedback superposes over visual attachment and the *yanking* equation shows how feedback relates to transposition. Finally, the *vanishing* equations show how to decompose the feedback loop.

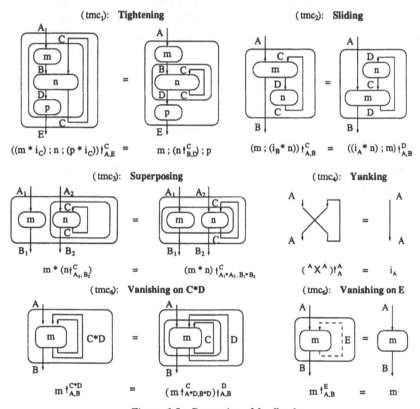

Figure 6.5 Properties of feedback

Identification is associative, has neutral elements and commutes with transposition. Hence, it mathematical terms, it defines a *monoid structure* on each arrow. Ramification is coassociative has neutrals element and commutes with transposition. Mathematically speaking, it defines a *comonoid structure* on each arrow. Moreover, identification preserves ramification and the other way around, i.e., identification is a comonoid morphism and ramification is a monoid morphism. Hence they define a *bimonoid structure* on each arrow.

3.   INTERACTION GRAPHS

Flow graphs are a very basic formalism that allows us to describe the structure of any interactive system. However, they are too low level to directly cope with the constructs occuring in UML-RT. In particular they cannot directly express UML-RT *protocol types*, *duplex ports* and *duplex channels*.

For example, consider the following UML-RT protocol type Tel between a telephone and its associated telephone driver, *defined from the point of view of the driver*:

> **protocol** Tel = { **input**   = {offH, onH, tlk, (dig, N)}
>   **output** = {dtB, dtE, rtB, rtE, tlk}}

where offH, onH, tlk, dig, dtB, dtE, rtB and rtE stand for off hook, on hook, talk, digit, dial tone begin/end and ring tone begin/end respectively. The digit message contains additional data $x \in N$ where $N = \{0, \ldots, 9\}$. Then the interconnection between the telephone and the driver is given in a UML-RT capsule diagram as shown in Figure 6.6. The driver contains a duplex port d of type Tel and

Figure 6.6   A simple telephone architecture in UML-RT

the telephone contains a duplex port t having the *dual type* Tel*. By duality it is meant that input and output are interchanged. These ports are connected by a duplex bend channel whose ends have dual type. By convention, duplex (or bidirectional) channels are drawn without any arrow head.

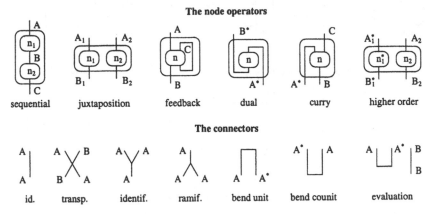

Figure 6.7   The node operators and the connectors

To model this structure directly, we need a graph formalism that includes both duality and bend connectors with dual ends. We call such a graph formalism *interaction graphs*. The reason for this name is that each arrow in these graphs defines a *two way* communication. In other words, it defines an *interaction*. As shown in Figure 6.7, the mere introduction of duality and of bend connectors with dual ends immediately allows to define six operators on nodes – *sequential composition, juxtaposition, feedback,*

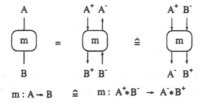

$$m : A \rightarrow B \quad \hat{=} \quad m : A^{+} * B^{-} \rightarrow A^{-} * B^{+}$$

Figure 6.8 Translation of interaction graphs nodes to flow graph nodes

dual, curry and the *higher order nodes* constructor and seven connectors – *identity, transposition, identification, ramification, bend unit, bend counit* and *evaluation*.

As we show in the next sections, interaction graphs are implemented by flow graphs in the same way higher order programming languages are implemented by assembler languages. Hence, each interaction graph could be analyzed by translating it to a flow graph. However, this analysis could be very cumbersome. It is therefore much better to prove once and for all a set of core properties for interaction graphs which allows to manipulate them directly in a similar way to flow graphs. In fact, *all properties* of flow graphs naturally extend to interaction graphs. Moreover, the introduction of bend connectors and dual types is the source of new graph operators and connectors and of a rich set of new properties. They allow us to adjust the component interaction interfaces and to dynamically manipulate both procedures and capsules.

In the following sections we show the implementation of interaction graphs in terms of flow graphs and the new properties of interaction graphs. Both the proofs and the properties similar to flow graphs are not given because of obvious space limitations.

3.1 ARROWS

Let X and Y be flow graph arrows. An *interaction graphs arrow* is defined as a *pair* (X, Y) of flow graph arrows where X has a top down orientation and Y has a bottom up orientation. By using such pairs, interaction graphs can deal simultaneously with three kinds of arrows: *unidirectional top down* arrows, *unidirectional bottom up* arrows and *bidirectional arrows*. Unidirectional top down arrows are pairs (X, E) where E is the flow graphs empty arrow. Unidirectional bottom up arrows are pairs (E, X) and bidirectional arrows are pairs (X, Y). To simplify notation and to make the connection between the components of the pair more explicit we denote interaction graphs arrows by A, B etc., and annotate their top down and bottom up components with a *plus* and respectively a *minus* sign. Hence we write A for (A^{+}, A^{-}). Visually, we distinguish bidirectional arrows from unidirectional arrows, by drawing them without any head. Moreover, since everything proved for bidirectional arrows also holds for unidirectional arrows we shall work in the following sections only with bidirectional arrows.

3.2 NODES

A node $n : A \rightarrow B$ in an interaction graph maps the interaction arrow $A = (A^{+}, A^{-})$ to the interaction arrow $B = (B^{+}, B^{-})$, as shown in Figure 6.8, middle. The interaction arrow A is the *client interface*. The interaction arrow B is the *server interface*. Going from flow graphs to interaction graphs is actually a switch of programming paradigm. We abandon the *input/output* paradigm in favor of the *client/server* paradigm.

However, since as in programming, each interaction graphs arrow is defined by a pair of flow graphs arrows, for each interaction graphs node there is a corresponding flow graphs node as shown in Figure 6.8, right. We take these flow graphs nodes as the *implementation* (or representation) of the interaction graphs nodes. When looking at the implementation of an interaction graphs connector in the next sections, keep in mind this translation because it determines a unique interface of the corresponding flow graphs connector.

Using this implementation, each interaction graph may be implemented by a flow graph. Moreover, as we see later, each interaction graphs operator may be implemented by a composition of flow graphs operators. Formally, implementing an interaction graph node $m : (A^+, A^-) \rightarrow (B^+, B^-)$ by a flow graphs node $m : A^+ * B^- \rightarrow A^- * B^+$ can be described by a representation function (or relation) *rep* such that:

$$rep(m : (A^+, A^-) \rightarrow (B^+, B^-)) = m : A^+ * B^- \rightarrow A^- * B^+$$

Abstracting (or embedding) a flow graphs node $m : A^+ * B^- \rightarrow A^- * B^+$ to an interaction graphs node $m : (A^+, A^-) \rightarrow (B^+, B^-)$ can be formally described by an *abstraction* function (or relation) *abs* such that:

$$abs(m : A^+ * B^- \rightarrow A^- * B^+) = m : (A^+, A^-) \rightarrow (B^+, B^-)$$

Taking $abs(A) = (A, E)$ each flow graph may be embedded into an interaction graph with arrows pointing only top down (with the exception of the feedback arrow). As a consequence, each flow graph node operator and each flow graph connector has a corresponding interaction graph node operator and connector, respectively. Instead of inventing for each a new notation, we use the same symbols in the interaction graphs, too. In other words, we *overload* the node operators and connectors. Moreover, instead of dealing explicitly with the representation function, i.e., instead of writing $rep(m : (A^+, A^-) \rightarrow (B^+, B^-)) = m : A^+ * B^- \rightarrow A^- * B^+$ we shall simply write $m : (A^+, A^-) \rightarrow (B^+, B^-)) \,\hat{=}\, m : A^+ * B^- \rightarrow A^- * B^+$, which can be read as a *definition*. Since in most cases we will not make the types explicit one should keep in mind that the symbol on the left of the definition is an interaction graphs symbol, whereas the same symbol on the right of the definition is a flow graphs symbol.

3.3   OPERATORS ON NODES

Sequential Composition.   As shown in Figure 6.9, left, the most basic way to *connect* two interaction graphs nodes is *sequential composition*. By this we connect the server interface of one node to the client interface of the other node, if they have the same type. Textually we denote this operator also by ; (hence ; is an overloaded operator). As shown in Figure 6.9, right, given $m{:}A{\rightarrow}B$ and $n{:}B{\rightarrow}C$ we define (implement) the interaction graphs composition $m;n : A{\rightarrow}C$ in terms of the flow graphs sequential composition, transposition and feedback. As in flow graphs, the composition in interaction graphs defines both a *connection* and a *containment* relation.

Using the properties of flow graphs one can easily show that sequential composition is associative and has the identities as neutral elements. Hence interaction graphs nodes equipped with sequential composition define a *category*.

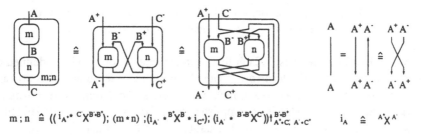

$$m;n \triangleq ((^{i_{A^{.+}}{}^{C}X^{B^{.}B^{.}}); (m*n) ;(i_{A^{.}} \bullet{}^{B^{.}}X^{B^{.}} \bullet i_{C^{.}}); (i_{A^{.}} \bullet{}^{B^{.}B^{.}}X^{C^{.}}))^{B^{.}B^{.}}_{A^{.}.C^{.} A^{.}.C^{.}} \qquad i_{A} \triangleq{}^{A^{.}}X^{A^{.}}$$

Figure 6.9 Sequential composition and identity

Juxtaposition. By *juxtaposition* we mean that nodes and corresponding arrows are put one next to another, as shown in Figure 6.10, left. To obtain a textual representation

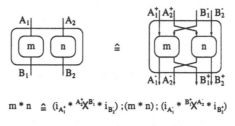

$$m*n \triangleq (i_{A_1^+} *{}^{A_2^+}X^{B_1^-} * i_{B_2^-}) ;(m*n); (i_{A_1^-} *{}^{B_1^+}X^{A_2^+} * i_{B_2^+})$$

Figure 6.10 Juxtaposition

for juxtaposition, we need therefore a juxtaposition operator defined both an arrows and on nodes. We denote this operator also by $*$ (hence $*$ is an overloaded operator). Given two arrows A_1 and A_2 their juxtaposition is expressed by $A_1 * A_2$ and defined in terms of flow graphs juxtaposition by $(A_1^+ * A_2^+, A_1^- * A_2^-)$. Given two nodes $m:A_1 \to B_1$ and $n:A_2 \to B_2$ their juxtaposition is expressed as $m*n:A_1*A_2 \to B_1*B_2$ and defined, as shown in Figure 6.10, in terms of flow graphs juxtaposition. Similarly to sequential composition, juxtaposition also defines a containment relation.

As with flow graphs, two nodes m and n may be visually attached in two different ways: $m*n$, i.e., with m on the left or $n*m$, i.e., with n on the left. Since we are mainly interested in the "one near the other" relation, these two attachments should be equivalent modulo a *transposition* isomorphism $^{A}X^{B} : A*B \to B*A$. We define the interaction graphs transposition $^{A}X^{B}$ in terms of flow graphs transposition as shown in Figure 6.11, right.

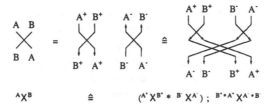

$$^{A}X^{B} \triangleq (^{A^{.}}X^{B^{.}} * {}^{B^{.}}X^{A^{.}}) ; {}^{B^{.}\bullet A^{.}}X^{A^{.}\bullet B^{.}}$$

Figure 6.11 Interaction graphs transposition

Using the properties of flow graphs it is easy to show that juxtaposition is defined both on arrows and on nodes such that it preserves identities and composition. Hence it is a *functor*. Moreover, it is associative, has a neutral element and commutes with transposition. It therefore defines a *strict symmetric monoidal category*.

Duality and bend connectors. Each line A in the interaction graphs is defined by a pair (A^+, A^-) of flow graphs arrows, with A^+ pointing in top down direction and A^- pointing in bottom up direction. It makes therefore sense to think of reversing the direction of these arrows. This is accomplished by a *duality operator* $(.)^*$ defined as follows: $A^* = (A^+, A^-)^* = (A^-, A^+)$. Duality is involutive since $A^{**} = A$.

In order to extend duality to nodes we need two bend connectors: the *bend unit* $\sqcap_A : \mathbb{E} \rightarrow A*A^*$ and the *bend counit* $\sqcup_A : A^**A \rightarrow \mathbb{E}$. The bend unit and counit are

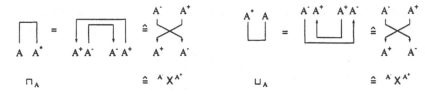

Figure 6.12   Unit and counit bends

defined, as shown in Figure 6.12, by using the flow graphs transposition connector. It is interesting to note that $\sqcap_A$ and $\sqcup_A$ have the same definition (or implementation) in the flow graphs category. However, their type in the interaction graphs category is different which means that they are used in different contexts.

Nodes duality. Using the bend connectors one can extend the duality operation to nodes. Given $m : A \rightarrow B$ we define $m^* : B^* \rightarrow A^*$, as shown in Figure 6.13, left. The

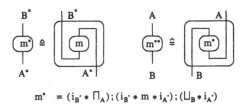

$$m^* = (i_{B^*} * \sqcap_A) ; (i_{B^*} * m * i_{A^*}) ; (\sqcup_B * i_{A^*})$$

Figure 6.13   Duality extended to nodes

duality on nodes is also involutive if $m^{**} = m$. As shown in Figure 6.13, this is indeed the case if the unit $(igCcc_1)$ and counit $(igCcc_2)$ axioms in Figure 6.14 hold. This can be easily checked by using their definition. Moreover $(igCcc_1)$ and $(igCcc_2)$ also say that $(i_{A^*})^* = i_A$ and $(i_A)^* = i_{A^*}$, i.e., that duality preserves identities. It is also easy to check that the involutive duality operators preserves sequential composition. Hence, in mathematical terminology, duality is an *involutive functor*. Since this functor reverses the direction of arrows and consequently the direction of composition, it is called a *contravariant* functor. The contravariant duality functor enriches the interaction graphs with the structure of a *compact closed category* (abbreviated as igCcc). This structure is very rich and allows us to define feedback, curry and the data nodes constructor as derived operators.

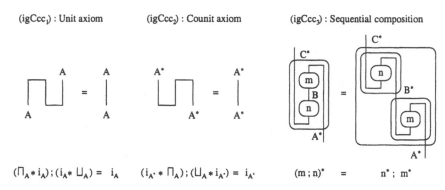

$$(\Pi_A * i_A) ; (i_A * \sqcup_A) = i_A \qquad (i_{A^*} * \Pi_A) ; (\sqcup_A * i_{A^*}) = i_{A^*} \qquad (m ; n)^* = n^* ; m^*$$

Figure 6.14 Functor properties of duality

Nodes as Data. Using the bend connectors one can move any client arrow of an interaction graphs node to its server side and any server arrow to its client side. In particular, one can move all arrows either on the client side or on the server side. Moving all arrows on the client side one obtains nodes very similar to the architecture nodes in UML-RT. In this case, it is possible to connect two nodes only by using the bend unit and the transposition connectors. As a consequence, the connected arrows are requested to be *dual*. This is exactly what the graphical editor for UML-RT architecture diagrams checks.

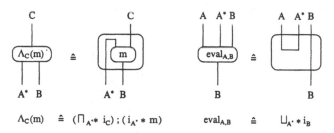

$$\Lambda_C(m) \triangleq (\Pi_{A^*} * i_C) ; (i_{A^*} * m) \qquad eval_{A,B} \triangleq \sqcup_{A^*} * i_B$$

Figure 6.15 Curry isomorphism and eval connector

Moving all the arrows of an interaction graphs node to its server side transforms this node into a *data node*. Why is it a data node? Because its client interface becomes empty and therefore no other client node may be sequentially connected to it anymore. To use this node one needs therefore an evaluation operator, which applies the data node to its input (or routes the data to the input). However, since changing the interface of a node is merely a matter of convenience, the visual intuition tells us that between real nodes and data nodes there should be a *one-to-one* correspondence.

The correspondence is given by an isomorphism $\Lambda_C : (A*C \rightarrow B) \rightarrow (C \rightarrow (A^* * B))$, known as *curry* and a distinguished connector $eval_{A,B} : A*(A^* * B) \rightarrow B$, as shown in Figure 6.15. Their definition is as expected a straight forward use of the bend connectors. Using the properties of these connectors, one can easily check that the relation between *curry* and *eval* is the one shown in Figure 6.16. The β-axiom says that *bending* an input arrow of a node twice does not change the meaning of the node. The η-axiom says that *bending* an output arrow of a node twice does not change the meaning of a node. The λ-calculus equivalent for the β-axiom is

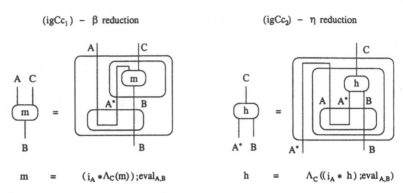

$(igCc_1) - \beta$ reduction

$(igCc_2) - \eta$ reduction

$$m = (i_A * \Lambda_C(m)) ; eval_{A,B}$$

$$h = \Lambda_C((i_A * h) ; eval_{A,B})$$

Figure 6.16   The curry-eval axioms

$m(a, c) = eval(a, \lambda x.m(x, c))$. Since $eval(a, f)$ is often written as $f(a)$ the above equation is also written as $m(a, c) = (\lambda x.m(x, c))(a)$. The λ-calculus equivalent of the η-axiom is $h = \lambda x.eval(x, h)$ or with the above convention $h = \lambda x.h(x)$. The identifier x is supposed to not occur free in h.

Higher order nodes.   An element of $A^* * B$ is a data node $f : \mathbb{E} \to A^* * B$. In order to emphasize that $A^* * B$ contains data nodes we also use for it the arrow like notation $A{-\circ}B$. Hence $-\circ$ maps a pair of interaction arrows A and B to an interaction arrow $A{-\circ}B$. But what about nodes?

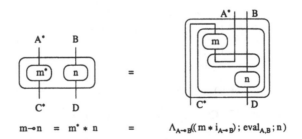

$$m{-\circ}n = m^* * n = \Lambda_{A{-\circ}B}((m * i_{A{-\circ}B}) ; eval_{A,B} ; n)$$

Figure 6.17   The definition of $-\circ$

Consider a pair of nodes with arrows in opposite (dual) directions, as shown in Figure 6.17, left. Textually, we denote this construction by $m{-\circ}n : (A{-\circ}B) \to (C{-\circ}D)$. It takes *data nodes* in $A{-\circ}B$ as input and delivers data nodes in $C{-\circ}D$ as output. Using *curry* and *eval* the meaning of $m{-\circ}n$ is defined as shown in Figure 6.17, right. Since $A{-\circ}B$ is defined in terms of juxtaposition and duality, it inherits the properties of both these operators, as shown in Figure 6.18. In mathematical terminology, $-\circ$ is a *functor* changing the direction of arrows in the first argument (the argument where duality is applied). This functor is a consequence of the compact closure of interaction graphs and the structure it determines together with *eval* and *curry* on these graphs is that of a *closed category* (igCc stands for interaction graphs closed category). Closed categories are models for the λ-*calculus,* the calculus underlying all higher order functional programming languages.

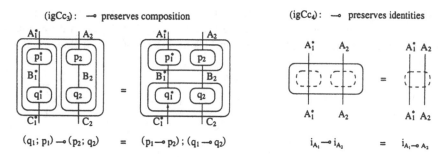

$(igCc_3):$ — preserves composition $(igCc_4):$ — preserves identities

$(q_1; p_1) \multimap (p_2; q_2) = (p_1 \multimap p_2); (q_1 \multimap q_2)$ $i_{A_1} \multimap i_{A_2} = i_{A_1 \multimap A_2}$

Figure 6.18 The functor axioms for —o

Feedback. The bend connectors allow us to define the *feedback operator* for interaction graphs in a very simple way as shown in Figure 6.19. Using the properties of

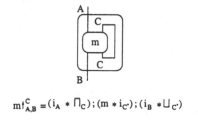

$$mf_{A,B}^C = (i_A * \sqcap_C); (m * i_{C'}); (i_B * \sqcup_{C'})$$

Figure 6.19 Feedback in a compact closed category

the bend connectors it is easy to show that the interaction graphs feedback also defines a *trace monoidal category* structure on the underlying category (see [GBSS98]).

3.4 CONNECTORS

In the previous sections we already introduced four connectors: *identity* i_A, *transposition* $^A\mathsf{X}^B$, *bend unit* $\sqcap_A$ and *bend counit* $\sqcup_A$. While the bend connectors are new, the identity and transposition connectors are extensions of the analogous flow graphs connectors to interaction graphs. A similar extension is possible for the *identification* connector $\vee_A$ and the *ramification* connector $\wedge^A$.

Identification. The definition of the interaction graphs *identification* connectors $\top_A :$ $E \to A$ and $\vee_A : A * A \to A$ is shown in Figure 6.20. It is based on flow graphs identification, ramification and transposition. Using the properties of flow graphs it is

$V_A \triangleq (V_{A^+} * \wedge^{A^-}); ^{A^+}\mathsf{X}^{A^-} \bullet_{A^-}$ $T_A \triangleq (T_{A^+} * i_{A^-}); ^{A^+}\mathsf{X}^{A^-}; (\bot^{A^-} * i_{A^+})$

Figure 6.20 Interaction graphs identification

easy to show that identification is associative, has neutral element and commutes with transposition. Hence, it defines a *monoid structure* on each arrow.

Ramification. The definition of the interaction graphs *ramification* connectors $\perp^A$: $A \to E$ and $\wedge^A : A \to A * A$ is shown in Figure 6.21. It is based on flow graphs identification, ramification and transposition. Using the properties of flow graphs it

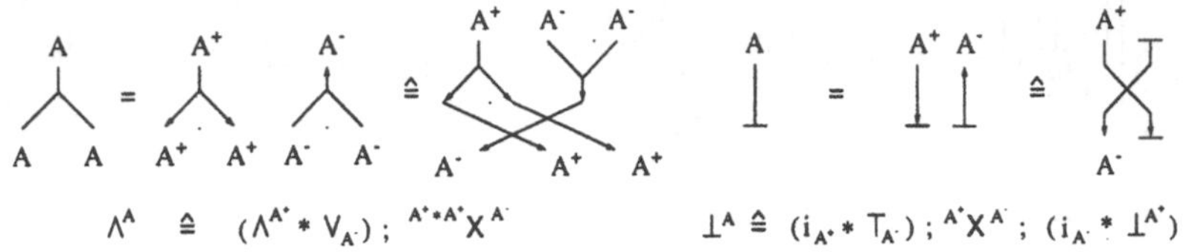

$$\wedge^A \; \triangleq \; (\wedge^{A^+} * \vee_{A^-}) \; ; \; {}^{A^+ * A^-}X^{A^-} \qquad\qquad \perp^A \triangleq (i_{A^+} * T_{A^-}) \; ; \; {}^{A^+}X^{A^-} \; ; \; (i_{A^-} * \perp^{A^+})$$

Figure 6.21   Interaction graphs ramification

is easy to show that ramification is coassociative has neutral element and commutes with transposition. Hence, it defines a *comonoid structure* on each arrow. Moreover, identification preserves ramification and the other way around, i.e., identification is a comonoid morphism and ramification is a monoid morphism. Hence they define a *bimonoid structure* on each arrow.

4.   CONCLUSIONS

The main benefits of the graph theory defined in this paper can be summarized as follows. First, it introduces a set of graph construction primitives in a *consistent way*. This diminishes the arbitrariness in the choice of these primitives. Second, it provides a mathematically *precise semantics* for these primitives. This is very useful as a *reference* both for tool designers and for system development engineers because it *eliminates misinterpretation*. Third, it provides a calculus which allows us to *compare* and to *optimize designs* and even to do *rapid prototyping*. While the visual notation is the interface to system engineers, the textual notation is the interface to tool developers.

The calculus of flow graphs (see [GBSS98]) is a simpler, more general and more intuitive presentation of the one given in the context of flow charts in [CS90]. Models of flow graphs were studied independently in the context of flow charts in [CS90] and in the context of data flow networks in [B87, GS96]. In [GSB98a] we show how to combine these models to obtain a semantics for ROOM. This semantics is extended for the hierarchical specification of hybrid systems in [GSB98b].

The calculus of interaction graphs is a simpler, more intuitive and more general formulation of interaction categories (see [AGN94]) that uses ideas from [JSV96]. It is not only closer to UML-RT but, in our opinion, a better foundation for the theory of typed concurrent systems. This was only possible by having in mind the concrete implementation of UML-RT. A semantic model for this calculus is given in [GBSR99]. It is also inspired by the UML-RT implementation. Since it defines a game semantics for interaction graphs, it is very general too and it may be used to understand concurrency.

The use of the interaction graphs theory in the context of visual formalisms, in particular for UML-RT is new. It clearly shows that visual formalisms are not only intuitive but also can have a deep underlying formal theory. In fact, we are using this theory to compare, optimize and execute designs. Moreover, it is the best starting point for verification techniques. In fact, we use this theory in the project Mocha (see [AHM+98]) for modular model checking. More generally, because of the deep connection between interaction graphs and linear logic (see [A96]) other analysis and verification techniques may be used as well.

References

[A96]   S. Abramsky. Retracing some paths in process algebra. In *Seventh International Conference on Concurrency Theory (Concur'96), Lecture Notes Computer Science 1055*, pages 21–33, 1996.

[AGN94]   S. Abramsky, S. Gay, and R. Nagarajan. Interaction categories and the foundations of typed concurrent programming. To appear in Proc. Marktoberdorf Summer School, 1994.

[AHM+98] R. Alur, T. A. Henzinger, F.Y.C. Mang, S. Qadeer, S. K. Rajamani, and S. Tasiran. Mocha: Modularity in model checking. To appear in the Proceedings of the Tenth International Conference on Computer-aided Verification (CAV 1998), Lecture Notes in Computer Science, Springer-Verlag, 1998.

[B87]   M. Broy. Semantics of finite and infinite networks of concurrent communicating agents. *Distributed Computing*, 2:13–31, 1987.

[CS90]   V.E. Căzănescu and Gh. Stefănescu. Towards a new algebraic foundation of flowchart scheme theory. *Fundamenta Informaticae*, 13:171–210, 1990.

[GBSR99] R. Grosu, M. Broy, B. Selic, and B. Rumpe. A formal foundation for UML-RT. To Appear, July 1999.

[GBSS98] R. Grosu, M. Broy, B. Selic, and Gh. Stefanescu. Towards a calculus for UML-RT specifications. In H. Kilov, B. Rumpe, and I. Simmonds, editors, *Seventh OOPSLA Workshop on Behavioral Semantics of OO Business and System Specifications, Vancouver, Canada, Monday, October, 19th*. TUM-I9820, 1998.

[GS96]   R. Grosu and K. Stølen. A Model for Mobile Point-to-Point Data-flow Networks without Channel Sharing. In *Proc. of the 5th Int. Conf. on Algebraic Methodology and Software Technology, AMAST'96, Munich*, pages 505–519. LNCS 1101, 1996.

[GSB98a] R. Grosu, Gh. Stefanescu, and M. Broy. Visual formalisms revisited. In *CSD '98, International Conference on Application of Concurrency to System Design, Aizu-Wakamatsu City, Fukushima*. IEEE, March 1998.

[GSB98b] Radu Grosu, Thomas Stauner, and Manfred Broy. A modular visual model for hybrid systems. In *Formal Techniques in Real Time and Fault Tolerant Systems (FTRTFT'98)*. Springer-Verlag, 1998.

[JSV96]   A. Joyal, R. Street, and D. Verity. Traced monoidal categories. *Math. Proc. Camb. Phil. Soc.*, 119:447–468, 1996.

[SR98]   B. Selic and J. Rumbaugh. Using UML for modeling complex real-time systems. Available under http://www.objectime.com/uml, April 1998.

About the Authors

Radu Grosu studied computer science at the Technical University of Cluj. In 1994 he received his PhD at the Technical University of Munich where he became a scientific assistant. Since 1998 he is also a visiting researcher at the University of Pennsylvania. His research interests include theoretical and practical aspects in the design and analysis of reactive, real-time and hybrid systems. In particular he is interested in the formal foundation of the software engineering's visual formalisms and worked in several projects on this issue. Currently at the University of Pennsylvania he is investigating the analysis potential of visual formalisms both for reactive and for hybrid systems.

Manfred Broy is full professor of computing science at the Technical University of Munich. His research interests are theory and practice of software and systems engineering aspects includind system models, specification and refinement of system components, specification techniques, development methods and verification. He leads a research group working in a number of industrial projects that try to apply mathematically based techniques and to combine practical approaches to software engineering with mathematical rigor. Professor Broy is a member of the European Academy of Sciences. In 1994 he received the Leibniz Award by the Deutsche Forschungsgemeinschaft.

Bran Selic is Vice President of Advanced Technology, at ObjecTime Limited. He has over 25 years of experience in real-time software, focussing on distributed systems and object-oriented development. He is the principal author of the textbook, "Real-Time Object-Oriented Modeling" and is a core member of the team that defined the Unified Modeling Language (UML), a standard for object-oriented analysis and design that was issued by the Object Management Group (OMG). Bran is currently working on applying UML to real-time development. He is also co-chair of the Real-Time Analysis and Design Working Group within the OMG.

Gheorghe Stefănescu completed his university studies at the University of Bucharest, receiving a PhD degree in 1991. He spent 15 years as a researcher at the Institute of Mathematics at the Romanian Academy. Currently he is Professor of Computer Science at the University of Bucharest. He was visiting professor/researcher at various universities, including Technical University Munich, Kyushu University, University of Amsterdam, and Utrecht University. His main research interests are in formal methods applied to distributed computing and object-oriented systems, especially using algebraic methods.

Chapter 7

Applying ISO RM-ODP in the Specification of CORBA® Interfaces and Semantics to General Ledger Systems

Jack Hassall, John Eaton

Stanford Software International, The Hollygate, Chestergate,
Stockport, Cheshire, SK3 0BD, UK
jack_hassall@omg.org
john_eaton@omg.org

Abstract   This chapter describes how the ISO Reference Model of Open Distributed Processing (ISO RM-ODP) was successfully used in the specification of an internationally agreed standard for software interfaces to the General Ledger component of Financial Accounting business systems. This standard, called the General Ledger Facility, is currently in the latter stages of formal adoption by the Object Management Group (OMG) and will become part of its global CORBA standard. Technology submissions to OMG typically represent only a fragment (with minimal emphasis on semantics) of the ISO RM-ODP Computational Viewpoint. In some cases, these can be incomplete and difficult to understand, particularly if the reader is not familiar with the default assumptions surrounding the subject matter. The approach described was used to enhance understandability and precision in support of the goals of creating long-lived and widely applicable domain specifications. The OMG General Ledger Facility specification incorporates all five RM-ODP viewpoints: Enterprise, Information, Computational, Engineering and Technology.

1. BACKGROUND

The Object Management Group (OMG) is the world's largest software development consortium. It was conceived in 1989 in response to the shared view of ten or so people that software development in its 1989 incarnation was a mess and did not work. OMG has since grown from 10 or so supporters to over 800 members. It has created a global standard for software interfaces across multiple hardware and software platforms. This standard (CORBA) has been publicly adopted by over 600 companies, the International Standards Organisation (ISO), the US Department of Defence and some of the largest software development organisations in the world. OMG's prime mission is the establishment of global technology standards to facilitate distributed application interoperability. The OMG General Ledger Facility defines the interfaces, and their semantics, that are required to enable interoperability between General Ledger systems and accounting applications.

The business accounting function (of which, General Ledger is the common core) is a statutory requirement for all commercial organisations and individual proprietorships. The vast majority of General Ledger systems are proprietary, non-standard and non-interoperable, even though the underlying accounting concepts have been stable for over 500 years. Applications such as Payroll systems and Report Writers frequently need to interoperate with General Ledger systems. However, this is often a tedious, difficult and error prone task, due to the general lack of technology standardisation.

1.1 ISO RM-ODP Viewpoint Approach

The ISO RM-ODP Standard [ISO96a-d] provides a short, clear and explicit specification of concepts and constructs that define semantics, independently of representation, methodologies, tools and processes. The RM-ODP standard specifies a conceptual framework that may be used to manage complexity through a "separation of concerns", by addressing a particular problem from different points of view. Specifically; from the ODP Enterprise, Information, Computational, Engineering and Technology "viewpoints". All viewpoints are considered of equal significance and it is only when all viewpoints are considered together, that one has a "complete" ODP description of the system.

Furthermore, while ODP is frequently applied to automated information systems, this need not always be the case. The ODP conceptual framework is non-prescriptive and makes no requirements as to "how" things are actually imple-mented. This is an entirely context dependent issue that may assume many forms, depending on how the ODP standard itself is applied, as well as what it is applied to. However, for the purposes of actually applying the ODP standard to an OMG Technology submission, the ODP approach is instantiated specifically into the OMG/CORBA context and environment.

As all OMG Specifications are based on the use of CORBA technologies, the corresponding ODP Computational, Engineering and Technology "Viewpoint Specifications" are based on the use of CORBA ORBs and IDL, Common Object Services and Common Facilities, and are not elaborated further. However, the semantics of the various ODP viewpoints need to be specified precisely and as completely as possible. Please note that the examples given are partial. The reader wishing to more fully explore this approach should consult the reference section given at the end of this chapter. The formal OMG General Ledger Facility specification itself [OMGGL98] is publicly available on the OMG's web server: www.omg.org in the documents: finance/98-12-03 and finance/99-02-01. However, please also note that at this time (May '99), significant clarifications and enhanced revisions of the specification are planned.

2. ISO RM-ODP ENTERPRISE VIEWPOINT

The ODP Enterprise Viewpoint is concerned with the contextual purpose, scope and policies of a system or service and how that system or service relates to the overall environment. It covers the role of the system or service in the business and the human user roles and policies related to the service. As stated previously, in an ODP context, it is possible to create an Enterprise Viewpoint specification for non-computer based systems (such as a business, for example) and it is also equally possible (and applicable) to create an Enterprise Viewpoint specification for a purely computer based information system (such as a relational database). Part of the overall contextual purpose for the General Ledger Facility (i.e. financial accounting for businesses) was described in the GL Facility's Enterprise Viewpoint specification with a quote from the famous German economist, Ludwig Von Mises [LVM63].

> "Monetary calculation is the guiding star of action under the social system of division of labour. It is the compass of the man embarking upon production ... [It] is the main vehicle of planning and acting in the social setting of a society of free enterprise directed and controlled by the market and its prices ... Our civilisation is inseparably linked with our methods of economic calculation. It would perish if we were to abandon this most precious intellectual tool of acting. Goethe was right in calling book-keeping by double entry 'one of the finest inventions of the human mind'."

2.1 GL Facility - Purpose

The purpose of the OMG GL Facility is to provide both a reference architecture and specification for implementations of automated information systems, each of which acts as a "repository of commercial information about an enterprise" - i.e. information about an enterprise or other organisational entity's financial inputs and outputs, also called its General Ledger Transactions. This information (i.e. managed by the GL Facility) may also later be retrieved and processed in many different ways in order to create "general purpose financial statements". An enterprise or other organisational entity engaging in such activities is called the "reporting enterprise" in this specification. A "reporting enterprise" is also defined as an enterprise (or other organisational entity) for which there are users who rely on general purpose financial statements as their major source of information about the enterprise. The primary purpose of the GL Facility is to store information related to GL Transactions so that this information may subsequently be retrieved by a reporting enterprise for inclusion in general purpose financial statements.

Financial statements are a structured financial representation of the financial position of an enterprise and the financial transactions undertaken by that enterprise. The objective of general purpose financial statements is to provide information about the financial position, performance and cash flows of an enterprise that is useful to a wide range of users in making economic decisions. Financial statements also show the result of management's stewardship of the resources entrusted to it. To meet this objective, financial statements provide information about an enterprise's: assets and liabilities; equity; income and expenses (including gains and losses) and cash flows. The Board of Directors and/or other governing body of an enterprise is responsible for the preparation and presentation of its financial statements. The users of general purpose financial statements include present and potential investors, employees, lenders, suppliers and other trade creditors, customers, governments and their agencies and the public. They use general purpose financial statements for their own, specific purposes. These include:

Investors - the providers of risk capital and their advisers are concerned with the risk inherent in, and return provided by, their investments. They need information to help them determine whether they should buy, hold or sell. Shareholders are also interested in information which enables them to assess the ability of the enterprise to pay dividends.

Employees - employees and their representative groups are interested in information about the stability and profitability of their employers. They are also interested in information which enables them to assess the ability of the enterprise to pay dividends.

Lenders - lenders are interested in information that enables them to determine whether the loans, and the interest attaching to them, will be paid when due.

Suppliers and other trade creditors - suppliers and other creditors are interested in information that enables them to determine whether amounts owing to them will be paid when due. Trade creditors are likely to be interested in an enterprise over a shorter period than lenders unless they are dependent upon the continuation of the enterprise as a major customer.

Customers - customers have an interest in information about the continuance of an enterprise, especially when they have a long term involvement with, or are dependent on, the enterprise.

Governments and their agencies - governments and their agencies are interested in the allocation of resources and, therefore, the activities of enterprises. They also require information in order to regulate the activities of enterprises, determine taxation policies and as the basis for national income and similar statistics.

Public - enterprises affect members of the public in a variety of ways. For example, enterprises may make a substantial contribution to the local economy in many ways including the number of people they employ and their patronage of local suppliers. General purpose financial statements may assist the public by providing information about the trends and recent developments in the prosperity of the enterprise and the range of its activities.

2.2 GL Facility - Scope

The scope of the GL Facility is limited to the external interfaces, relationships and semantics that are required for accounting application interoperability with General Ledger systems. It does not specify the internal interfaces of General Ledger systems or other functions that are not required for general interoperability with other applications. The scope of the GL Facility is limited exclusively to the General Ledger component of the OMG Accounting Facility. A single instance of the GL Facility is responsible for the containment and management of a collection of entities called General Ledgers. There are one to many General Ledgers constrained and managed by a single instance of a GL Facility. Each General Ledger has an associated "Chart of Accounts", which is the collection of (zero to many) GL Accounts associated with a single General Ledger name. Each GL Account is subsequently associated with zero (or more) GL Transactions. Each GL Transaction references two (or more) GL Entries each of which references one (or more) source and destination GL Accounts within a single, specific General Ledger.

2.3 GL Facility - Policies

An ODP policy statement provides behavioural specifications. The policy statement may relate to various constraints or degrees of empowerment. An ODP policy statement includes statements of permissions, prohibitions and obligations for the various roles or other enterprise objects. These statements relate to: the environmental contracts governing the system; the creation, use and deletion of resources by enterprise objects; the configuration and allocation of enterprise objects and interactions between enterprise objects fulfilling roles. The following examples make specific reference to (part of) the GL Facility's assumed environment. Additional supporting clarifications for each statement given here were also included in the specification. These have been omitted with the specific intention of giving the reader a variety of concrete examples within the available space.

- The GL Facility assumes that GL client authentication for the security policy domain has occurred prior to access to GL Facility interfaces.

- The GL Facility assumes that access controls will be applied according to system domain policies prior to and during GL client sessions. For example, the passing of clear-text parameters in operation invocations will be protected from unauthorised access or disclosure.

- The only interface provided to GL clients prior to GL session establishment is the GL Arbitrator interface. The environment shall not disclose other GL interfaces to GL clients. That is the responsibility of the GL Arbitrator interface. For example, only the GL Arbitrator interface shall be advertised in the Trader Service and Name Service. Other GL interfaces are provided by the GL Profile interface, subsequent to GL client session establishment. (Note: the OMG Trader and Naming Services are not part of the GL Facility itself).

- There is a one-to-one mapping between each General Ledger and each Chart of Accounts in each GL Facility instance. This "single set of books" constraint is conformant with International Accounting Standards [IASC98]. However, a GL Facility is not responsible for enforcing this constraint in federation with other GL Facility installations.

- Operations performed during each GL client session are constrained by session-specific GL policies.

2.4 GL Facility – Obligations, Permissions and Prohibitions

The ODP Enterprise viewpoint states that obligations, permissions and prohibitions need to be identified. In the specific case of GL systems, these objects include

General Ledgers, GL Accounts, GL Transactions and GL Entries. The following examples specify these types of constraint for each of these objects. As with the previous examples, the additional semantics provided in the formal GL Facility specification have been omitted.

- The specified names of General Ledgers to be constrained and managed by the GL Facility must be unique. The duplication of General Ledger names is prohibited. The naming of specific General Ledgers is usually carried out by privileged GL Facility administrators.

- The decision to remove a specific General Ledger, GL Account, GL Transaction or GL Entry from the GL Facility is set by organisational and environment specific policies.

- The currently selected General Ledger's reporting currency is determined by organisational policy. A reporting currency is the nominated currency used by a reporting enterprise and is used in the presentation of general purpose financial statements. The reporting enterprise is an enterprise or other organisational entity, for which there are users who rely on general purpose financial statements as their major source of information about the enterprise. A single General Ledger constrained by a GL Facility implementation may support only a single reporting currency.

2.5 GL Facility - Transactions

The sum of all GL Entry debits and credits constrained by any GL Transaction must be equal (i.e. "balanced"). GL Transactions which are unbalanced are prohibited. If the debit and credit accounts of the GL Entries constrained by a single GL Transaction are the same, implementations will ensure that the debit takes place before the credit in the audit trail.

2.6 GL Facility - Entry Invariants

A single GL Entry constrained by a single GL Transaction and posted to a specific General Ledger constrained by the GL Facility has an identifier which must be unique. This identifier represents the "audit trail" number of each GL entry. A single GL Entry constrained by a single GL Transaction and posted to a specific General Ledger constrained and managed by an instance of the GL Facility has an identifier which specifies the precise nature of that GL Entry. Implementations claiming conformance with this specification shall provide each GL Entry a type with a unique GL Entry type code which semantically differentiates between the various types of GL related financial accounting transactions for example; "Journal Debit" or "Journal Credit".

2.7 GL Facility - Qualitative Characteristics

The users (i.e. communities) of general purpose financial statements may include present and potential investors, employees, lenders, suppliers and other trade creditors, customers, governments and their agencies and the public. However, all these communities use general purpose financial statements (which may be derived from information contained by the GL Facility) in order to satisfy some of the different needs for information. This section covers the qualitative characteristics of the information recorded by a General Ledger constrained and managed by an instance of the GL Facility for all communities (federated or otherwise) and independently of the role of the specific community. Qualitative characteristics are the attributes that make the information provided in [general purpose] financial statements useful to users. The four principal qualitative characteristics are understandability, relevance, reliability and comparability.

Understandability - An essential quality of the information provided in [general purpose] financial statements is that it is readily understandable to users. For this purpose, users are assumed to have a reasonable knowledge of business and economic activities and accounting and a willingness to study the information with reasonable diligence. However, information about complex matters that should be included in the [general purpose] financial statements because of its relevance to the economic decision making needs of users should not be excluded merely on grounds that it may be too difficult for certain users to understand.

Relevance - To be useful, information must be relevant to the decision making needs of users. Information has the quality of relevance when it influences the economic decisions of users by helping them evaluate past, present or future events or confirming, or correcting, their past evaluations.

Materiality - The relevance of information is affected by its nature and materiality. In some cases, the nature of the information alone is sufficient to determine its relevance. Information is material if its omission or misstatement could influence the economic decisions of users taken on the basis of the general purpose financial statement(s).

Reliability - To be useful, information must also be reliable. Information has the quality of reliability when it is free from material error and bias and can be depended upon by users to represent faithfully that which it either purports to represent or could reasonably be expected to represent. Information may be relevant but so unreliable in nature or representation that its recognition may be misleading. To be reliable, information must represent the transactions and other events it either purports to represent or could reasonably be expected to represent.

Comparability - Users must be able to compare the financial statements of an enterprise through time in order to identify trends in its financial position and performance. Users must also be able to compare the financial statements of different enterprises in order to evaluate their relative position, performance and changes in financial position. An important implication of the qualitative characteristic of comparability is that users be informed of the accounting policies employed in the preparation of the financial statements, any changes in these policies and the effects of such changes. Compliance with International Accounting

Standards, including the disclosure of the accounting policies used by the enterprise, helps to achieve comparability.

Constraints On Relevant And Reliable Information - If there is undue delay in the reporting of information it may loose its relevance. Management may need to balance the relative merits of timely reporting and the provision of reliable information. To provide information on a timely basis it may often be necessary to report before all aspects of a transaction or other events are known, thus impacting reliability. Conversely, if reporting is delayed until all aspects are known, the information may be highly reliable but of little use to users who have has to make decisions in the interim.

3. ISO RM-ODP INFORMATION VIEWPOINT

The ODP Information Viewpoint is concerned with the semantics of information and information processing. An Information viewpoint specification is modelled in terms of three different but related schemas: invariant, static and dynamic schemas. It is important to note that the static and dynamic schemas are subject to the assertions and constraints of the invariant schema, which (in practice) is typically much larger than the others.

- The invariant schema describes assertions, information and constraints that must always be true. ODP [Part 3] states that an Invariant Schema is: "A set of predicates on one or more information objects which must always be true. The predicates constrain the possible states and state changes of the objects to which they apply." Thus, an invariant schema is the specification of the type of one or more information objects that will always be satisfied by whatever behaviour the objects might exhibit.
- The static schema describes assertions, information and constraints that must be true at a single point in time. ODP [Part 3] states that a Static Schema is: "A specification of the state of one or more information objects at some particular point in time, subject to the constraints of any invariant schemata." These types are subtypes of the types specified in the invariant schema.
- The dynamic schema describes how information can evolve as the system operates. ODP [Part 3] states that a Dynamic Schema is: "A specification of the allowable state changes of one or more information objects at some particular point in time, subject to the constraints of any invariant schemata." A General Ledger contains a set (chart) of General Ledger Accounts, each of which have associated with them zero or more General Ledger transactions which are a composition of (for example) Journal Credits and Debits and other GL Entry types such as a Bank Payment, for example.

3.1 Invariant Schema

- A Chart of Accounts is a predefined set of General Ledger (GL) Accounts, which are created and maintained by the role of financial manager which is identified in the management community of the accounting domain.

- Each GL Account must have a unique identifier that is never duplicated. GL Accounts or GL transactions may not be deleted at any time.

3.2 Static Schema

- When a GL Accounting Period is closed, changes are made to the GL Accounts in such a manner that certain attributes are set to zero. Note: just the fact (predicate) "accounting period closed", implies the fact (predicate) that "certain attributes (denoting XXX...) are zero".
- When a fiscal year is closed, changes are made to various GL Accounts in such a manner that certain attributes (depending on national practice) are set to zero.

3.3 Dynamic Schema

- When a GL transaction is posted to a specified GL Account, the ac-count_balance attribute of that GL Account must be updated accordingly.
- When a GL transaction is posted to a specified GL Account, the set of associated GL transactions is increased by one.

4. ISO RM-ODP COMPUTATIONAL VIEWPOINT

The Computational Viewpoint is concerned with the interaction patterns between the components (i.e. services) of the system which are described through their interface definitions. The Computational Viewpoint specification of a service is a model of the service interface seen from a client perspective, and the potential set of other services that this service requires. The computational object model defines types of interfaces (e.g. operation, stream, signal); bindings of interfaces and legal actions for objects. In the context of a Technology Proposal to the OMG, the ODP Computational Viewpoint relates to a set of OMG IDL interface definitions (and their constraints) which focuses on interoperability and flexibility. The computational viewpoint should contain a description of the "top level" architecture reference model of the facility itself, as well as the interfaces in the specification. Furthermore, the reference model should always be accompanied by understandable prose. An example of this taken directly from the GL Facility specification is shown here.

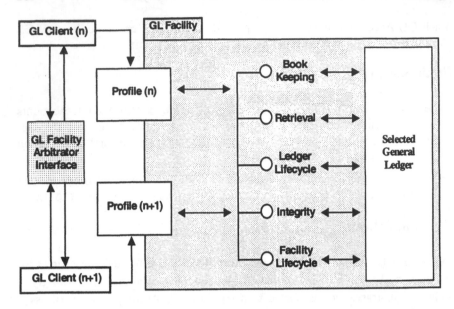

Figure 1: illustrates the different interfaces that comprise the GL Facility. The intention of the diagram is to show that one or more GL clients make a request for a new GL client session from the GL Facility's Arbitrator interface. If the invocation was successful, the GL Arbitrator::open_session() operation returns a GL Profile interface which provides information about the current session, as well as making provision for controlled access to the various interfaces and operations supported by the GL Facility

The intention behind the previous model was to present a high level reference model of the proposed computational architecture. The following text was also included in the computational viewpoint specification and was intended to represent a brief description of the facility, but purely from the computational viewpoint.

> The General Ledger (GL) Facility specifies interfaces that encapsulate distributed object frameworks implementing accounting General Ledgers, these GLs are conformant with International Accounting Standards for double entry book-keeping. The GL interfaces comprise a framework (in the object-oriented sense), that supports the implementation of accounting client applications. Example include: Accounts Payable, Accounts Receivable, Payroll, and so forth. The architectural intention is to facilitate the convenient implementation of interoperable accounting applications, referred to as "clients" in this specification. The overall intention is to provide as complete a set of GL services as possible in order to support the implementation of accounting clients that need to interoperate with one or more GL Facility implementations..

4.1 Operation And Interface Descriptions

Every operation in every interface of the GL Facility is specified by using the pattern presented in the following example. This shows the Computational viewpoint specification of the method `get_all_account_info()` which belongs to the GL Facility's `Retrieval` interface.

In this simple example, the reader may be puzzled as to why (for example) the Pre and Post conditions are "None", even though the signature states that an exception may be raised. It is true that should the specified exception occur (`PermissionDenied`), then there has to be some sort of Postcondition. However, if the specified environmental contract has been met in full, then this exception should never be raised. This (interestingly) ignores the fact that other exceptions from the system may also be raised, such as a "memory exhausted" system exception from the ORB (for example) - which would also cause a Postcondition(s) to exist in the same way that the `PermissionDenied` exception would. Part of the GL Facility's Computational Viewpoint specification contains a section detailing each exception and the policies relating to them.

> The following section gives detailed information about the various operation exception conditions that may be raised by the various GL Facility interface operations. The exception declaration comes first, immediately followed by information specific to the exception. Many of these exceptions are used both individually and in combination in this specification. These exceptions may only be raised by the various GL Facility operations described in this specification and are distinct from CORBA "system exceptions".

However, there are certain interface operations in the specification where Pre and Post conditions did apply. "Input Parameters" represent parameters that in OMG IDL signatures are qualified by "in". The same applies for "Output Parameters". In this example there are none. We see from the example that an `AccountInfoList` is returned by the operation, therefore this is documented in the pattern.

4.2 GL Retrieval Interface Operation ::get_all_account_info()

```
AccountInfoList
get_all_account_info()raises(PermissionDenied);
```

Description
This operation invocation retrieves a sequence of all GL Account references and descriptive names that exist in the currently selected General Ledger. If the operation was successful, the GL client has access to a list of all GL Accounts in the currently selected General Ledger. The data type `AccountInfoList` contains information which describes the name and purpose of all GL Accounts in the currently selected General Ledger.

Preconditions

None.

Input Parameters
None.

Output Parameters
None.

Return Value
This operation invocation returns an `AccountInfoList`, each member of which contains a GL Account reference and descriptive name (i.e. purpose) of an individual GL Account, for all GL Accounts in the currently selected General Ledger.

Exceptions
The exception `PermissionDenied` is raised if (and only if) the GL client has not successfully established a valid GL client session with `Arbitrator::open_session()` prior to the call or does not have permission to use this interface.

Postconditions
None.

5. ISO RM-ODP ENGINEERING AND TECHNOLOGY VIEWPOINTS

The ODP Engineering Viewpoint is concerned with the design of distribution-oriented aspects, i.e. the infrastructure required to support distribution. The ODP Technology Viewpoint is concerned with the provision of an underlying technology infrastructure. The ODP Technology viewpoint defines how a system is structured in terms of hardware and software components and the underlying and supporting infrastructures. ODP defines a framework for defining infrastructures supporting distribution transparencies that mask the complexities of distribution from the client. As mentioned previously, ODP itself makes no specific recommendations with regard to "how" specific systems should be implemented. However, in the context of an OMG Domain Technology Proposal, the Computational, Engineering and Technology viewpoints are assumed to be handled by CORBA itself which supports many of the distribution transparencies specified by ODP. ODP defines access, failure, location, migration, relocation, replication, persistence and transaction transparencies and many of these transparencies are already addressed by the CORBA platform infrastructure.

6. SUMMARY

This chapter has described an approach for creating specifications based on RM-ODP concepts. The work presented here will be further refined and developed in several projects with the goal of achieving a better understanding of the various aspects of system development, with a focus on distributed information systems and components.

Acknowledgements

The authors wish to sincerely acknowledge and thank Haim Kilov for his kind assistance and support over the years and we'd also like to thank Arne-Jorgen Berre and Tor Neple of SINTEF as well as the co-submitters of the OMG General Ledger Facility, Real Objects, The Software Box and Economica. Special thanks must also go to Thomas J. Mowbray and Mr. Eric Leach as well as all the OMG members and staff from all over the world.

References

[ISO96a] ISO/IEC, "ISO/IEC 10746-1 Information Technology – Basic reference model of Open Distributed Processing – Part 1: Overview" ISO ITU-T X.901 – ISO/IEC DIS 10746-1, 1996

[ISO96b] ISO/IEC, "ISO/IEC 10746-2 Information Technology – Open Distributed Processing – Reference Model: Foundations", 1996

[ISO96c] ISO/IEC, "ISO/IEC 10746-3 Information Technology – Open Distributed Processing – Reference Model: Architecture", 1996

[ISO96d] ISO/IEC, "ISO/IEC 10746-4 Information Technology – Open Distributed Processing – Reference Part 3: Architectural semantics", 1996

[IASC98] International Accounting Standards, 1998 – ISBN 0 905625 56 0

[OMGGL98] OMG General Ledger revised submission: omg.org - finance/98-12-03 and finance/99-02-01

[LVM63] Ludwig Von Mises, Human Action: A Treatise on Economics, Regnery, 1963.

About the Authors

Jack Hassall and **John Eaton** are founders of UK based Stanford Software International and are the founding co-chairs of OMG's Financial Domain Task Force. As long time supporters of both the OMG and CORBA spanning several years, they also act as OMG's "Ambassadors at Large".

Chapter 8

COMPONENT-BASED ALGEBRAIC SPECIFICATION

behavioural specification for component-based software engineering

Shusaku Iida

Graduate School of Information Science
Japan Advanced Institute of Science and Technology
(Research Fellow of the Japan Society for the Promotion)
s_iida@jaist.ac.jp

Kokichi Futatsugi

Graduate School of Information Science
Japan Advanced Institute of Science and Technology
kokichi@jaist.ac.jp

Răzvan Diaconescu

Institute of Mathematics of the Romanian Academy
diacon@stoilow.imar.ro

Abstract   Component-based software development becomes an important technique to build reliable, huge and distributed systems. An important characteristic of components is that components are usually provided in binary code and users of components cannot debug them. So, components should be carefully implemented and the users need rigorous specifications of them. Specifications of components should provide information not only of their interface but also their behaviour with highly abstracted representation. In addition, a system specification (consists of several component specifications) should provide the architecture of the system (how the components are combined). In this article, we propose a formal method based on algebraic specification, which supports component composition. Our component composition technique can handle synchronization between components, so that it can be used to specify distributed systems. We use the algebraic specification language CafeOBJ which supports behavioural specification based on hidden algebra.

1.   INTRODUCTION

The rapid adoption of Internet/Intranet technologies has led to an explosive increase in demand for the construction of reliable distributed systems. To meet this important technical challenge, new technologies such as component-based software engineering, software architecture [SG96] and design patterns [GHJV95], attract many software researchers and engineers. Moreover, several standardization activities, such as OMG CORBA [OMG99], for defining uniform system interfaces between so-called distributed objects have been undertaken. These are considered to be the key technologies for developing reliable distributed systems in sufficiently short time.

If we have an adequate set of components and a good design pattern, a system development process may become easier and the quality of the product may be greatly improved. Component businesses seem to be starting up and many companies are offering their products (such as components based on ActiveX/DCOM [M99], JavaBeans [J99], etc). In the near future, a huge market of business components may appear on the Internet (or may be it is already appearing).

However, there remain some technical problems to be solved. How can we get an adequate set of components or how can we know the components we get are adequate for our systems? One answer from a social viewpoint is that we need human component brokers who gather information on components and advertise on the Internet [A98]. However, we still need a language to precisely express the characteristics of the components. Natural languages are of course insufficient because they may contain ambiguities.

We propose using a formal specification. The following properties are required or recommended for a formal specification:

- can specify the interface of components,
- can specify the behaviour of components,
- supports a precise semantics of composition, and
- be executable or have tools supporting testing and verification.

We use the algebraic specification language CafeOBJ, which meets all the above requirements. The semantics of composition in CafeOBJ has already been defined by our group [IMD 98, I99], and in this paper we are going to propose how it can be applied to component-based software development. We call our new specification style **component-based algebraic specification** (CBAS).

1.1   CAFEOBJ

CafeOBJ [DF98a, FN97, DFI99] is a multi-paradigm algebraic specification language which is a successor of OBJ [FGJM85, GWM 93]. CafeOBJ is based on the combination of several logics consisting of order sorted algebra [GM92], hidden algebra

[GM97] and rewriting logic [M92]. According to its semantics [DF98b, DF98a, D98], CafeOBJ can fit several specification (and programming) paradigms such as equational specification (and programming), rewriting logic specification (and programming), behavioural concurrent specification. The equational part is mostly inherited from OBJ3. In CafeOBJ, there are (at least) two sources of object-orientation given by rewriting logic and behavioural specification (hidden algebra). CafeOBJ does not make any specific choice on the kind of object-orientation since it regards the object-orientation as a derived feature [1] rather than a primary paradigm of the language. This gives the user the freedom to choose the most suitable form of object-orientation for their applications. In this paper we concentrate on the behavioural specification approach. CafeOBJ has a powerful module system: several kinds of module imports, parameterized modules, and for each module one can choose between loose and initial semantics (see next section for more details).

CafeOBJ is executable which means that it can be used for rapid prototyping and theorem proving. Its operational semantics is based on term rewriting, and the proof calculi are the equational and rewriting logic proof calculi. There is an interpreter (JAIST-SRA implementation) and two compilers (called **brute** and **TRAM** [OF97]) for CafeOBJ. All the specifications in this paper are executed by CafeOBJ version 1.4.2. Other information can be found at the CafeOBJ home page at http://caraway.jaist.ac.jp/cafeobj/ including the manual, the system and some basic documents. Basically, the system can be used freely (the details can be found in the above CafeOBJ home page).

2.   BEHAVIOURAL SPECIFICATION

In general, behavioural specifications abstract the internal structure of the systems and focus on their behaviour by using observations on the systems. In CafeOBJ, behavioural specifications are based on an extension of hidden algebra [GM97] called *coherent hidden algebra* [D98]. One of the advantages of behavioural specification is that we can abstractly specify systems and are able to focus on their important properties. Another good point is that the proofs can be greatly simplified. Behavioural specification can be used to specify encapsulated objects and components used in component-based software development.

The space of the states of an object (or a component) is distinguished from ordinary data and represented as a **hidden sort** ("sort" is the algebraic specification counterpart of "type" in programming languages) which should be regarded as a kind of black box in the sense that we can observe the state of an object by using some operations called **observations**. One of the advantages of hidden algebra compared with process algebra is that we can handle not only the behaviour of systems but also data structures by using ordinary sorts (we use a term **visible sorts** for ordinary sorts representing the sorts of data). The state of an object can be changed by **actions** and "constructed" by the so-called **hidden constructors**.

Let's consider the simple counter object with of integer numbers. This object has an action (add) which takes an integer value to count up (or count down if the value is negative). The data part of this behavioural specification is INT which is a system built-in module of integer numbers.

```
mod* COUNTER {
  protecting(INT)

  *[ Counter ]*

  op init : -> Counter                      -- initial state
  op add : Int Counter -> Counter {coherent} -- hidden constructor
  bop amount : Counter -> Int               -- observation

  var I : Int
  var C : Counter

  eq amount(init) = 0 .
  eq amount(add(I, C)) = I + amount(C) .
}
```

The name of this module (COUNTER) is specified after mod*. The keyword mod is the abbreviation of module and * means this module has loose denotation and if ! is specified instead then it means the module has initial denotation. In loose semantics, there are several models for the specification, for example, if we want specify monoids, what we want to specify is a theory of monoid not a specific monoid. In initial semantics, we consider only one model (which is the initial algebra) for the specification. In the above example, we use mod* so we consider several models for the COUNTER according to the possible data structures of the hidden sort Counter. Sorts are specified by using [ ] for visible sorts and *[ ]* for hidden sorts. The COUNTER imports the module INT which is a built-in integer number with protecting(INT). Operators are specified by using op for ordinary operations and bop for behavioural operations which are actions or observations. We can use ops or bops to specify several operations simultaneously. A behavioural operation has exactly one hidden sort and possibly several visible sorts in its arity (arity is a list of arguments) and if its sort is a hidden sort then it is called **action** and if its sort is a visible sort then it is called **observation**. In the above example, the only bop is the observation amount. The operator add is a hidden constructor and is specified with the operator attribute **coherent**, which means it preserves the behavioural equivalence defined by the observation amount. This constructor is **conservative** [D98], which means its coherence is a direct consequence of the rest of the specification. For the purpose of using this specification below in this paper, we may consider add as action rather than hidden constructor:

```
  bop add : Int Counter -> Counter      -- action .
```

Each sequence of actions determines an object state. Variables are specified by using var (vars for several variables). Equations are specified by using eq for ordinary equations and beq for behavioural equations (see Section 2.1). Conditional equations are specified by using ceq (bceq for behavioural conditional equations). Comments are given after the keyword --.

CafeOBJ is executable so we can test the specification by doing some reductions. We can observe the state of Counter with reduce command (red) by using the observation amount [2]:

```
COUNTER> red amount(add(4, add(6, init))) .
10 : NzNat
```

CafeOBJ methodologies introduce a graphical notation extending the classical ADJ diagram [G89] notation for data types to behavioural specification in which

G1. *Sorts are represented by ellipsoidal disks with visible (data) sorts represented in white and hidden (state) sorts represented in grey, and with subsort inclusion represented by disk inclusion, and*

G2. *Operations are represented by multi-source arrows with the monadic part from the hidden sort thickened in case of behavioural operations.*

The version of the counter specification with add as action can be therefore visualized as follows:

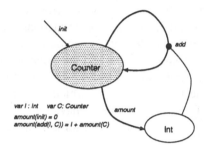

2.1   BEHAVIOURAL PROPERTIES

Behavioural specifications are always based on loose semantics because we consider several implementations (models) according to the structure of the hidden sorts. For example, we can think of the following two implementations of COUNTER:

- **history model** $\cdots$ the system records all the add action (by using models of lists, arrays or queues, etc), or
- **cell model** $\cdots$ holds just one integer number which is the result of the last addition.

Let's consider the following property in the above two implementations (where x, y : Int, c is a state of a counter):

$$\text{add}(x, \text{add}(y, c)) = \text{add}(y, \text{add}(x, c))$$

By using the ordinary equality (in CafeOBJ, this is denoted == and means that both sides of == are gets reduceded to the same term), this property holds in the cell model but not in the history model. However, we expect the system to behave as the above property, but in a *behavioural* rather than a strict sense. We call this kind of property **behavioural**, and the above one should be regarded as **behavioural equality** [3]. The semantic counterpart of behavioural equality is the behavioural equivalence relation on hidden sorts. Intuitive understanding of behavioural equivalence is that two states are behaviourally equivalent when they cannot be distinguished under all the specified observations after applying any sequence of actions. The **behavioural equivalence** denoted as $\sim$ is defined as follows [GM97]:

$$s \sim s' \text{ iff } c(s) = c(s') \text{ for all visible contexts } c$$

where s, s' are states of an object, a **context** is a term consisting of behavioural operations (i.e. actions and observations) that has only one hidden sorted variable with one occurrence, and a **visible context** is a context which has an observation as the outermost operation. The following are examples of visible contexts of COUNTER ([ ] represents the Counter-sorted variable and x, y : Int):

```
amount([ ])
amount(add(x, [ ])
amount(add(x, add(y, [ ])
```

In principle, the definition of behavioural equivalence may contain an number of infinite equations. Several proof methods are proposed such as: **coinduction** [GM97], **context induction** [H90], and **test set coinduction** [MF98]. Using these methods, we can obtain a simpler form of behavioural equivalence (which can be represented by finite CafeOBJ equations and can be used for reductions). CafeOBJ has a support mechanism for coinduction and under some conditions it automatically provides this simpler behavioural equivalence (in CafeOBJ this behavioural equivalence is represented by =*= and it means equality under all observations only). In the case of COUNTER this support mechanism succeeds (which is strongly related to the hidden constructor nature of add). So, we can prove behavioural properties as follows (open COUNTER opens the COUNTER module to add some temporary constants playing the role of variables):

```
COUNTER> open COUNTER
%COUNTER> ops x y :  → Int .
%COUNTER> op c :  → Counter .
%COUNTER> red add(x, add(y, c)) =*= add(y, add(x, c)) .
true : Bool
(0.000 sec for parse, 6 rewrites(0.010 sec), 58 matches)
%COUNTER> close
```

3.   COMPONENT-BASED ALGEBRAIC SPECIFICATION

In this section, we propose a new specification style – **component-based algebraic specification** (CBAS). Components can be specified by using hidden algebra as shown in the previous section. Now, we need a method to compose components for building a compound object. For such compositions, we use **projection operations** [IMD 98, I99]. A projection operation is a map from the state space of a compound object to the state space of its component. They are defined for each component of the compound object. Projection operations are specified as behavioural operations [4]. The precise mathematical definition [IMD 98, DF98a, I99] of projection operations (see Appendix) can be informally summarized as follows:

- all actions of the compound object are related via projection operations to actions in each of the components, and
- each observation of the compound object is related via the projection operations to an observation of some component.

In specifications, these conditions appear as strict equations about the projection operations.

The following UML figure shows the structure (i.e., **component composition**) of a system specified by CBAS.

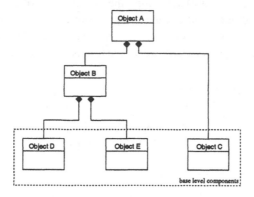

The compound object A represents the whole system. The components C, D, and E are called **base level components** which are the primitive components of this system. These base level components correspond to the specifications of components provided by component vendors. Therefore, the system designer can collect the components (like JavaBeans components) referring to the specifications of these base level components.

Projection operations correspond to the lines between the compound object and the components. Projection operations have the following crucial property [5] which means that we can reuse simple equational formulations of the behavioural equivalence of components for the behavioural equivalence of the compound object.

Theorem 1 *Given the states s and s' of a compound object then the behavioural equivalence $\sim$ of the compound object is defined as follows:*

$$s \sim s' \;\; iff \;\; \pi_n(s) \sim_n \pi_n(s') \;\; for \; all \; n \in Obj$$

where Obj is a set of the labels for the components (you can consider these labels as the names of the component modules), π_n is the projection operation corresponding to the component object n, and $\sim_n$ is the behavioural equivalence of the component n. □

Notice that this result holds both in the case of parallel composition and synchronized composition (see Section 3.2). Also, in the case of dynamic composition (see Section 3.1) which the set of components might change. In this case, *OBJ* is a possible infinite indexed set of all possible components and in the absence of the component n, $\sim_n$ $\pi_n(s) \sim_n \pi_n(s')$ is considered true.

3.1 UML AND CBAS

CBAS can be related to the class diagram of UML notation [S 97] as we already showed in the previous section. Each component can be represented as a class in UML where the hidden sort of the component relates to the name of the class, actions in CBAS correspond to methods in UML, and observations in CBAS correspond to methods for access the attributes in UML. Initial states in CBAS can be regarded as object constructors in UML. A projection operation can be represented as a composition in UML (line with filled diamond). If a composition is a one-to-many relation (we call this **dynamic composition**), then the initial states of components in CBAS should have an object identifier as their arity. For example, we can compose several Counter to build a dynamic system of Counters. In the following figure, we attach the name of the projection operation to the line between the compound object and the components.

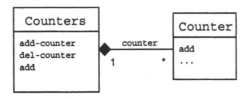

The object constructor (i.e., initial state) of Counter should be changed to:

```
op init : Id -> Counter
```

where Id is an appropriate data for the object identifier for Counter (such as integers, set of labels, etc) [6]. The projection operation for Counter is in fact a family of projection operations produced by the object identifier.

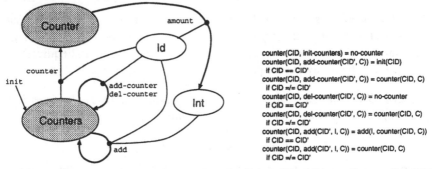

Aggregation (line with white diamond) and relation (line with no diamond) in UML can also be related to CBAS by using object identifiers [I99]. Notice that in dynamic compositions the set of components may be changed by add (add-counter) and delete (del-counter) actions at the level of the compound object.

3.2   SYNCHRONIZATION

Synchronization happens when:

1. the projected state of the compound object (via a projection operation) depends on the states of different (from the object corresponding to the projection operation) component (we call this **client-server computing**),
2. actions of the compound object change simultaneously the states of several components (we call this **multi-casting**).

As mentioned above, handling of synchronization amounts to conditional equations for the projection operations (see the Appendix for details).

3.3   EXAMPLE

Here, we consider a counter with a switch (COUNTER-WITH-SWITCH). By using the switch, we can specify which action should happen: add or subtract.
COUNTER-WITH-SWITCH has actions put to add or subtract the value to the counter, add and sub to operate the switch. If we push the sub button and put 5 then it means subtract 5 from the counter. Recall that the action add in COUNTER takes an integer value and we can subtract a value from counter by giving a negative number to it. So, COUNTER-WITH-SWITCH can be considered as a user friendly version of COUNTER. If we have a switch component, it is natural to think that we can build COUNTER-WITCH-SWITCH by composing the switch component and COUNTER. The following is the behavioural specification for a switch and COUNTER-WITH-SWITCH in UML.

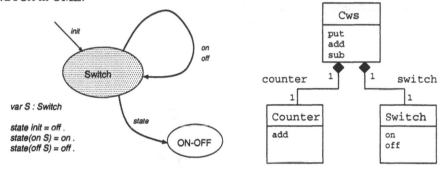

Note that there is a synchronization in the above specification such that the state changes (by add) of Counter depend on the state of Switch (client-server computing).

We can test this specification as follows:

```
COUNTER-WITH-SWITCH> red amount(put(5, add(put(3, sub(init))))) .
2 : NzNat
```

3.4   PROVING BEHAVIOURAL PROPERTIES OF COMPOUND OBJECT

We can automatically obtain the behavioural equivalence of COUNTER-WITH-SWITCH by using Theorem 1. The following CafeOBJ module defines it:

```
module CWS-PROOF {
   protecting(COUNTER-WITH-SWITCH)
   op _R_ : Cws Cws -> Bool          -- behavioural equivalence relation
   vars C1 C2 : Cws
   eq C1 R C2 =   switch(C1) =*= switch(C2) and
                  counter(C1) =*= counter(C2) .
}
```

Using this behavioural equivalence we can prove a behavioural property similar to the one in 2.1 (commutativity of add) also holds:

```
CWS-PROOF> open CWS-PROOF
%CWS-PROOF> op c :   → Cws .
%CWS-PROOF> ops n1 n2 :   → Nat .
%CWS-PROOF> red put(n2, sub(put(n1, add(c)))) R
```

```
sub(put(n1, add(put(n2, sub(c)))))  .
true : Bool
%CWS-PROOF> close
```

4.   CASE STUDIES

We have done several case studies using CBAS, for example ATM (Automated Teller Machine) and ODP Trading Function [IITO97].

4.1   ATM

An ATM system is a client-server system and contains several aspects of distributed systems like concurrency and synchronization.

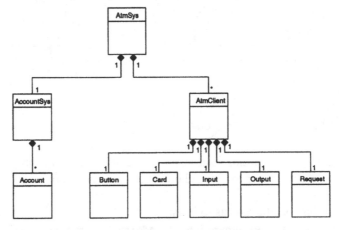

In the above ATM specification [IMD 98, DF98a, I99] there are six base level components but some of them are essentially the same and can be obtained by just renaming primitive components. We only need three primitive components to build the above specification. We proved a behavioural property that the withdrawal operations by different users can be done concurrently. This proof needs about 30,000 rewrites so it seems almost impossible to accomplish this proof by hand, but with the CafeOBJ compiler it takes only about 0.3 second (executed by PC with Pentium 233Mhz). The behavioural equivalence of all the components in the ATM system are provided automatically by CafeOBJ, so we can immediately obtain the behavioural equivalence the ATM systems by using **Theorem** 1. The rather complex case analysis for this proof is generated automatically as a big proof term by the CafeOBJ rewrite engine by metalevel encoding in CafeOBJ (for details see [DF98a, I99]). The ATM specification itself can be seen as a component of an ATM system, so it seems easy to specify a federation of banks connecting their ATM system to each other.

4.2   ODP TRADING FUNCTION

The ODP Trading Function provides a standard specification of trading systems over networks and it is now a DIS (Draft International Standard) [IITO97] drawn up by

ISO, ITU-T and ODP. The specification consists of three views which correspond to enterprise specifications (overview of ODP Trading Function, written in English), information specifications (types of information and the relationships between them, written in Z), and computational specifications (interfaces of a trader with its environment, written in ODP IDL). There are three main categories of players in the ODP Trading Function, trader, exporter, and importer. Exporters export the services to a trader and the trader advertises the services to networks. Importers pass a query to a trader to find out the services they need.

service interaction

Our case study of writing the ODP Trading Function in CBAS is an on going project [MIF99]. The goal of our project is to provide: (1) a pattern of ODP Trading Function in CBAS, and (2) a learning system based on CBAS.

Suppose we have a virtual shopping street on the Internet based on the ODP Trading Function and some company wants to add their shop to it. The shop should satisfy the specification of the exporter. How can we check it? We can check that the shop has the correct interfaces by using the computational specification. However, it is not easy to check or prove that the shop behaves correctly with respect to the specification of the exporter. This happens because any of the three viewpoints does not provide the information about how the exporter component should behave.

We defined the architecture of the trading system as follows and built a CBAS based on it (we omit the detailed structure of each component: trader, exporter and importer; they also consist of several components).

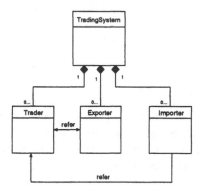

By using CBAS it is easy to focus on the exporter component specification and check the shop is satisfied with it by using refinement techniques. The designer does not have to consider the other parts of the specification. The exporter component in

CBAS consists of several components and the projection operations show how they are composed, so system designers can know the architecture of the exporter easily. The architecture information helps system designers/implementers to select an adequate set of components to build the system.

Understanding ODP Trading Function in detail is not so easy because [IITO97] has 84 pages with few figures. We think a learning system understanding the ODP Trading Function is therefore necessary. CBAS is an executable specification so it can be used as an underlying technique of the learning system. For example, we can prove that each service advertised in a trading system should have a unique identifier. System designers/implementers can obtain precise image of the ODP Trading Function from these kinds of proofs and testing. The learning system will be built on the CBAS technique and have hyper-links to other important information such as figures or examples.

5.   CONCLUSION AND FUTURE WORK

We present a new specification style called **component-based algebraic specification** (CBAS). By using CBAS, we can specify each component's interface and behaviour and compose them to build a specification of huge and complex systems. The key technology is the **projection operation** which allows the reuse not only of the specification code of the components but also the behavioural equivalence relation of the components (**Theorem 1**). This theorem and the coinduction support mechanism of CafeOBJ greatly helps the process of verification of a system.

Our work on CBAS is based on an extension of hidden algebra [GM97] which is presented in [DF98a, D98]. Earlier work on algebraic semantics for the object paradigm can be found in [GD94]. The technical basis of CBAS is in [IMD 98] which also presents how to prove the correctness of a composition, object inheritance, etc.

Finally, we would like to present our opinion regarding the question we posed in the introduction. If the component vendors provide behavioural specifications (based on CBAS) of their products and open up the specifications via the Internet, then system designers can down load the specifications and compose them to check whether they can be used for their system. Of course, they can test and verify each component specification and also can test and verify how they behave when they are composed. After checking the specification, system designers/implementers can purchase and use the binary components with confidence.

5.1   FUTURE WORKS

5.1.1   Using UML as an interface of CBAS.   We are planning to use UML as an user interface of CBAS. We discussed the relationship between CBAS and UML class diagram in **3.1**. We are now working for a precise semantics to UML by using projection operation and other capabilities of CafeOBJ. Especially, the relationship between the state chart diagrams of UML and CBAS represents and interesting future work. The learning system of ODP Trading Function will be built based on this research [MIF99].

5.1.2   Handling non-functional aspects of a system.   When building a complex system, difficulties are not only in functional aspects (such as the structure of a system) but also in the non-functional aspects such as performance of the system (response speed, required memory space, etc). Many formal methods try to provide a way to check or prove logical correctness of systems but few of them mention non-functional aspects. We are planning to supply a technique to check non-functional aspects in CBAS. The idea is to apply special observations to a base level object, which returns non-functional aspects. For example, we can consider the observation cost of Counter which returns the amount of calculation costs of the add operation. Base level components are usually small so the corresponding implementation of components is also small and it is not so difficult to measure its non-functional aspects. In a compound object, these (special) observations can be defined by using the projection operations and the (special) observations in the components, and they can be categorized by the types of synchronization between the components. We are now analyzing these types to formalize this technique.

5.1.3   Alternative methodologies.   Finally, another research direction would be to explore alternative object composition methodologies based on the behavioural specification paradigm and study the relationship between them. Each such methodology should be the basis for a corresponding CafeOBJ development tool.

Acknowledgments

We would like to thank Michihiro Matsumoto and Dorel Lucanu for close collaboration on many technical details. We are grateful to all members of the Language Design Laboratory to at JAIST for the stimulating research atmosphere. We thank Haim Kilov for proof reading an earlier version of this report, and the organizers of the Seventh OOPSLA Workshop on Behavioural Semantics of OO Business and System Specification for their great work.

Notes

1. See [GD94], [GM97], [DF98a] for further information.

2. COUNTER> is a CafeOBJ system prompt which means that the user is in the module COUNTER. The bold-face part is the string inputted by the user.

3. CafeOBJ admits another kind of behavioural properties, but we do not consider them here.

4. We are currently investigating methodology with projection operators as ordinary operations rather as behavioural operations.

5. You can find the proof property in Appendix.

6. The one-to-one case can be seen as a particular case of one-to-many case such that the data for the object identifier has only one element.

References

[A98]   AOYAMA, Mikio: New Age of Software Development: How Component-Based Software Engineering Changes the Way of Software Development? *In: ICSE'98 International Workshop on Component-Based Software En-*

gineering, 1998

[DF98a]   DIACONESCU, Răzvan ; FUTATSUGI, Kokichi: *AMAST series in Com-*
            puting. Bd. 6 : CafeOBJ Report: The Language, Proof Techniques, and
            Methodologies for Object-Oriented Algebraic Specification. World Sci-
            entific, 1998

[DF98b]   DIACONESCU, Răzvan ; FUTATSUGI, Kokichi: Logical Semantics for
            CafeOBJ. **In:** *ICSE'98 Workshop on Precise Semantics for Software*
            Modeling Techniques, 1998. – obsolete version in the technical report of
            Japan Advanced Institute of Science and Technology (IS-RR-96-0024S)

[DFI99]   DIACONESCU, Răzvan ; FUTATSUGI, Kokichi ; IIDA, Shusaku:
            Component-based Algebraic Specification and Verification in CafeOBJ.
            In: *Proc. of The World Congress on Formal Methods '99*, 1999. – to
            appear

[D98]   DIACONESCU, Răzvan: Behavioural Coherence in Object-Oriented Alge-
            braic Specification / Japan Advanced Institute of Science and Technology.
            1998 (IS-RR-98-0017F). – Forschungsbericht

[FGJM85]   FUTATSUGI, Kokichi ; GOGUEN, Joseph ; JOUANNAUD, Jean-Pierre ;
            MESEGUER, José: Principles of OBJ2. **In:** *Proceedings of the 12th ACM*
            Symposium on Principles of Programming Languages, ACM, 1985, S.
            52–66

[FN97]   FUTATSUGI, Kokichi ; NAKAGAWA, Ataru: An Overview of Cafe Speci-
            fication Environment — an algebraic approach for creating, verifying and
            maintaining formal specifications over the NET —. **In:** *First IEEE Inter-*
            national Conference on Formal Engineering Methods, IEEE, 1997

[GD94]   GOGUEN, Joseph ; DIACONESCU, Răzvan: Towards an algebraic seman-
            tics for the object paradigm. **In:** EHRIG, Harmut (Hrsg.) ; OREJAS, Fer-
            nando (Hrsg.): *Recent Trends in Data Type Specification* Bd. 785. Bd.
            785, Springer, 1994

[GHJV95]   GAMMA, Erich ; HELM, Richard ; JOHNSON, Ralph ; VLISSIDES,
            John: *Design Patterns: Elements of Reusable Object-Oriented Design*.
            Addison-Wesley, 1995

[GM92]   GOGUEN, Joseph ; MESEGUER, José: Order-sorted algebra I: Equational
            deduction for multiple inheritance, overloading, exceptions and partial op-
            erations. **In:** *Theoretical Computer Science* 105(2) (1992)

[GM97]   GOGUEN, Joseph ; MALCOLM, Grant: A hidden agenda / UCSD Techni-
            cal Report. 1997 (CS97-538). – Forschungsbericht

[G89]   GOGUEN, Joseph: Memories of ADJ. 36 (1989), S. 96–102. – Guest
            column in the 'Algebraic Specification Column'. Also in *Current Trends*
            in Theoretical Computer Science: Essays and Tutorials World Scientific,
            1993, pages 76-81

[GWM 93]   GOGUEN, Joseph ; WINKLER, Timothy ; MESEGURE, José ; FUTATSUGI,
            Kokichi ; JOUANNAUD, Jean-Pierre: Introducing OBJ / SRI International,
            Computer Science Laboratory. 1993. – Forschungsbericht

[H90]   HENNICKER, R.: Context Induction: a proof principle for behavioural abstractions. **In:** MIOLA, A. (Hrsg.): *Design and Implementation of Symbolic Computation Systems. International Symposium DISCO 1990.* Springer-Verlag, 1990 (LNCS 429)

[I99]   IIDA, Shusaku: An Algebraic Formal Method for Component based Software Developments. 1999. – PhD. thesis

[IITO97]   ISO ; ITU-T ; ODP: Information technology - Open Distributed Prosessing - Trading Function-Part1: Specification, Revised 2nd DIS text. 1997. – Draft ITU-T Rec. X950-1, ISO/IEC 13235-1(E)

[IMD 98]   IIDA, Shusaku ; MATSUMOTO, Michihiro ; DIACONESCU, Răzvan ; FUTATUGI, Kokichi ; LUCANU, Dorel: Concurrent Object Composition in CafeOBJ / Japan Advanced Institute of Science and Technology. 1998 (IS-RR-98-0009S). – Forschungsbericht

[J99]   JAVASOFT: JavaBeans   Documentation.   1999.   – http://www.javasoft.com/beans/docs/

[M92]   MESEGUER, José: Conditional Rewriting Logic as a Unified Model of Concurrency. **In:** *Theoretical Computer Science* 96 (1992), S. pp.73–155

[MF98]   MATSUMOTO, Michihiro ; FUTATSUGI, Kokichi: Test Set Coinduction - Toward Automated Verification of Behavioural Properties. **In:** *Proc. of Second Workshop on Rewriting Logic and its Applications*, Elsevier Science Publishers B.V., 1998

[M99]   MICROSOFT: COM   Home.   1999.   – http://www.microsoft.com/com/default.asp

[MIF99]   MATSUMIYA, Chiyo ; IIDA, Shusaku ; FUTATSUGI, Kokichi: A Component-based Algebraic Specification of ODP Trading Function and the Interactive Browsing Environment. 1999. – submitted for publication

[OF97]   OGATA, Kazuhiro ; FUTATSUGI, Kokichi: TRAM: An Abstract Machine for Order-Sorted Conditional Term Rewriting System. **In:** *Proc. of RTA-97*, 1997

[OMG99]   OMG: Object   Management   Group   Home   Page.   1999.   – http://www.omg.org/

[S 97]   SORTWARE, Rational [u. a.] : UML Notation Guide. September 1997. – version 1.1

[SG96]   SHAW, Mary ; GARLAN, David: *Software Architecture - Perspectives on an Emarging Dicipline -*. Prentice Hall, 1996

Appendix

Definitions and Proofs for Projections

In this Appendix we present the mathematical definitions for the projection operations and give the proof of Theorem 1. The reader of this Appendix is assumed to be familiar with the basic hidden algebra formalism underlying CafeOBJ (we recommend [DF98a, D98]).

Definition 1 *Given a compound object O (with signature $(V \cup H, \Sigma)$ for which V is a set of visible sorts and H is a set of hidden sorts), a set of the labels of its components Obj, and the components $\{O_n\}_{n \in Obj}$ of O (with signatures $(V_n \cup H_n, \Sigma_n)$), there exists a projection operation $\pi_n : h \to h_n$ (with $h \in H$ and $h_n \in H_n$) for each $n \in Obj$ such that :*

1. *for each observation o of O, there exists $n \in Obj$ and a data (possibly derived) operation $f : v_{n_1}...v_{n_i} \to v$ ($v_{n_i} \in V_n$ and $v \in V$ where i is a natural number), and for each n_k with $k \in \{1,...,i\}$ a visible O_{n_k}-context c_{n_k} (i.e., made only of operations of the signature of O_{n_k}) such that:*
   $o(X) = f((c_{n_1} \circ \pi_{n_1})(X),...,(c_{n_i} \circ \pi_{n_i})(X))$ *for all states X,*

2. *for each action a of O, and for each $n \in Obj$, there exists a sequence of actions a_n such that:*
   $\pi_n \circ a = a_n \circ \pi_n$, *and*

3. *for each constant const of O, and for each $n \in Obj$, there exists a constant $const_n$ such that:*
   $\pi_n(const) = const_n$
   (i.e., the initial state of a compound object should be is related to the initial state of each component.)

As mentioned above in this paper, in the case of synchronized compositions, the equations of the previous definition are conditional rather than unconditional. Their conditions are subject to the following:

Definition 2 *In the case of synchronized compositions, the conditions for the equations for the projections (as defined by the previous definition) should fulfill the following:*

- *each condition is a finite conjunction of equalities between terms of the form $c_n \circ \pi_n$ (where π_n is a projection operator and c_n is an O_n-context) and terms in the data signature, and*

- *disjunction of all the conditions corresponding to a given left hand side (of equations regarded as a rewrite rule) is true.*

We complete this Appendix with a concise proof of Theorem 1:

Proof 1 *The "only if" part of the theorem follows directly from the fact that projections are behavioural operations.*
For the 'if" part of the theorem, we consider two states s and s' of O such that for all components $n \in Obj$, $\pi_n(s) \sim_n \pi_n(s')$. We also consider a visible context c for the compound object O. We have to prove that $c(s) = c(s')$. We have two cases:

1. *$c = c_n \circ \pi_n \circ a$ for some $n \in Obj$, a sequence a of O-actions, and c_n is a visible O_n-context, and*

2. $c = o \circ a$ for some sequence a of O-actions and an O-observation o.

Let's concentrate first on case 1. If a is empty (i.e., empty sequence) then we can apply directly the hypothesis. Therefore we may assume a is a single "atomic" action (the other case can be proved by iterating the "atomic" case by usual induction).

Because of the first condition of the previous definition, all conditions cond of the equations having $\pi_n \circ a$ as the left hand side are equalities of terms which are either of the form $c_k \circ \pi_k$ (for some $k \in Obj$ and some visible O_k-context c_k) or terms in the signature of the data, we have $cond(s) = cond(s')$ for all these conditions. Therefore, by the second condition of the previous definition, we can pick the condition cond for which both $cond(s)$ and $cond(s')$ are true, and let $a_n \circ \pi_n$ be the right hand side of the corresponding equation. Then

$$c(s) = c(s') \quad \textit{iff} \quad c_n(\pi_n(a(s))) = c_n(\pi_n(a(s')))$$
$$\textit{iff} \quad c_n(a_n(\pi_n(s))) = c_n(a_n(\pi_n(s')))$$

which holds because $c_n \circ a_n$ is a visible O_n-context and $\pi_n(s) \sim_n \pi_n(s')$.

Finally, case 2 can be reduced to case 1 by a similar argument with the above.

About the authors

Shusaku Iida received his Ph.D. from Graduate School of Information Science, Japan Advanced Institute of Science and Technology (JAIST) in 1999. He is a Research Fellow of the Japan Society for the Promotion of Science. His research interests include formal methods, algebraic specification, and software engineering (especially object-oriented methodologies).

Kokichi Futatsugi is a Professor at the Graduate School of Information Science, Japan Advanced Institute of Science and Technology (JAIST). After getting his Dr.Eng. degree from Tohoku University, Sendai, Japan, he got a research position at ETL, MITI, Japanese Government in 1975. From 1984 to 1985, he worked at SRI International, California, as a visiting researcher. During his stay at SRI, he designed and implemented the OBJ2 language. In 1992 he was appointed Chief Senior Researcher of ETL. He got a full professorship at JAIST in 1993. His current research interests include algebraic formal methods and their application to software engineering, and language design as a foundation for system design.

Răzvan Diaconescu received his Ph.D. from the Faculty of Mathematical Sciences, University of Oxford in 1994 and is now Associate Professor at the Institute of Mathematics of the Romanian Academy. His main research results are in the areas of algebraic specification, software engineering, and applications of category theory and logic to computing. He received several prestigious international research awards, such as the J. William Fulbright Award and a US National Research Council Award. During the CafeOBJ project, he was working at Japan Advanced Institute of Science and Technology as designer of the CafeOBJ language.

Chapter 9

A META-MODEL SEMANTICS FOR STRUCTURAL CONSTRAINTS IN UML

Stuart Kent
University of Kent, UK
s.j.h.kent@ukc.ac.uk

Stephen Gaito
Nortel Networks, UK
stga@nortelnetworks.com

Niall Ross
Nortel Networks, UK
nfr@nortelnetworks.com

Abstract   The UML standard has adopted a meta-modelling approach to defining the abstract syntax of UML. A meta-modelling approach is taken essentially to aid the construction of automated tools, but the semantics is defined by statements in English. A meta-model that incorporates precise semantics would support the construction of tools that could perform semantically-oriented tasks, such as consistency checking. One approach to defining the formal semantics of a language is denotational: essentially elaborating (in mathematics) the value or instance denoted by an expression of the language in a particular context. However, instances must also be expressed in some language: in UML, instances of the static model are expressed using object diagrams. Thus a meta-model can be constructed which incorporates (a) the modelling language itself, (b) the modelling language of instances, and (c) the mapping of one into the other. The current UML meta-model provides some support for (a) and (b), but not (c). (c) is the part that carries the semantics. This paper presents one such meta-model, for a fragment of UML suitable for describing and constraining object structures. The fragment includes parts of class diagrams and invariants in the style of OCL. An indication is given as to how the approach could be extended to models characterising dynamic behaviour.

1. PRELIMINARIES

The team responsible for standardising the Unified Modelling Language (UML, [UML99]) has chosen a meta-modelling approach to make precise its abstract syntax. A meta-model for a language is a definition of that language written in terms of itself. There are good reasons for adopting a meta-modelling approach:

- UML has been designed in part to support OO software development. The UML meta-model provides a blueprint for the core of any CASE tool built using an OO programming language.
- If a tool can be built which generates code from UML, or, more specifically from a particular UML model, namely the meta-model, then the tool can be used to *bootstrap* itself, provided every time the meta-model is changed or extended the code generation is suitably updated.

     (We envisage the following scenario. The meta-model is extended in a predictable way, for example a new kind of model specific to a particular kind of domain, i.e. a framework, with restrictions on the nature and structure of classes it can contain. The Java code for the extension is generated largely automatically, perhaps with some manual fine-tuning. The .jar file produced is dropped into the appropriate directory, and immediately the tool gains a new menu item allowing you to create instances of the domain-specific framework.)

- If the meta-model is written in UML, there is a greater likelihood that those using the language will be able to grasp its subtleties more easily.

The UML meta-model itself has little or no semantic content, although it is accompanied by an English commentary that states informally the meanings of the various constructs. Whilst this may be adequate for a developer to use UML effectively (and many doubt even that), it is certainly not adequate if you wish to be sure that the language is unambiguous and well-formed, or if you wish to build automatic tools which are able to make use of semantic content. Tools we have in mind include, for example, a consistency checker that makes sure invariants defined on a model do not conflict, an instance generator which allows examples satisfying a model to be easily generated, etc.

In order to give a semantics to a modelling language (which may not be directly executable) there are, essentially, two approaches: an axiomatic approach, which states what sentences in the languages can be derived from other sentences; and a denotational approach, where expressions are mapped to the "instances" they denote. For example, a program may be thought of as denoting the set of execution traces that would be produced, if the program was executed from every conceivable starting state with every conceivable set of external stimuli during its execution. For a good starting point on the different approaches to semantics see [S86], pages 3-5.

In the context of UML, an axiomatic semantics would be a set of rules that would dictate, for example, which diagrams were derivable from other diagrams. A denotational approach would be realised by a) a definition of the form of an instance of every UML language element (e.g. the objects that could be denoted by a class, the links that could be denoted by associations, etc.), and b) a set of rules which determine which instances are and are not denoted by a particular language element.

This paper adopts a denotational, meta-modelling approach to the semantics of a part of the UML. There are three main steps to the approach:
- Define the meta-model for the language of models: classes, roles, models.
- Define the meta-model for the language of instances: objects, links, snapshots.
- Define the mapping (also within the meta-model) between these two languages.

The part of the UML considered here is a subset for describing object structure. For characterising *models*, it includes the essentials of class diagrams, and a significant fragment of the *object constraint language* (OCL, [WK98]), a precise language based on first-order predicate logic, used for expressing constraints on object structure which can not be expressed by class diagrams alone. For characterising *instances of models*, it includes the language of object diagrams.

The paper does not consider constructs for describing dynamic behaviour, such as sequence diagrams and state diagrams (though state diagrams without transitions are considered).

We have chosen to start with a clean slate, rather than the existing meta-model of UML. The reasons are twofold:
- To ensure that only concepts essential to the semantics are introduced, thereby avoiding unnecessary distractions. A future task will be to incorporate the ideas set out here into the UML standard with as little disruption as possible.
- Because the existing meta-model is silent about the OCL. A major component of the meta-model presented here is a representation of the concepts underpinning OCL.

Thus the meta-model developed here elaborates the conceptual core of UML/OCL and is not tied to any particular concrete syntax. For example, the meta-model for the OCL fragment supports the visual syntax for constraints first described in [KENT1997] and further developed in [KG98] and [GHK99].

Section 2 describes the meta-model for simple models, involving only classes, roles and inheritance, where an association is represented by 2 roles. Section 3 describes the meta-model for instances of models, which are essentially object diagrams. Section 4 makes the connection between models and their instances, focussing, for the time being, on just the roles and classes. This introduces the basic form of the semantic approach described here. Section 5 then mixes in the meta-model for invariants, providing, essentially, the abstract syntax for OCL. Section 6 proceeds to extend the connection between model and instance with rules that take account of invariants. Section 7 concludes with a discussion of how to extend this meta-modelling approach into other parts of UML: work is already underway on handling model extension, composition and refinement as introduced by e.g. [SW99]; and dynamic behaviour (state diagrams, sequence diagrams, pre/post conditions).

2. MODELS, CLASSES, STATES AND ROLES

Figure 1 is a UML class diagram defining a model to be a set of roles and classes. A role is one end of an association, and has a source and target class. A role has a name, and upper and lower bounds on its cardinality (the number of links that any object of the source class may have to objects of the target class). A role may have an inverse. If it has, then the role and its inverse constitute an association. Thus in our model, associations are mapped to two roles, where each is the inverse of the other.

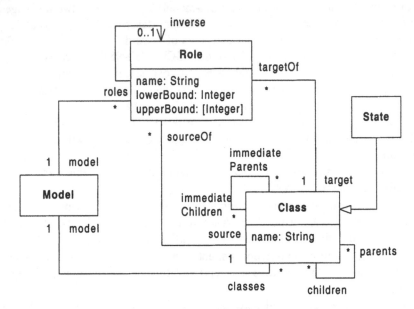

Figure 1. Models

It would be possible to introduce a class Association of objects constituted of two roles, each the inverse of the other, and have two kinds of role, one in association, and one without inverse. Roles are also restricted, here, to have a single source and target. Roles with multiple sources/targets represent relations between tuples – tuples of the sources are related to tuples of the targets, and could be used ot encode n-ary associations. However, the purpose of this paper is to show all the pieces of a denotational semantics embedded in a meta-model, focussing, in particular, on constraints expressed in OCL; roles with inverses are quite sufficient for this purpose. We envisage no fundamental difficulties in extending the semantics to n-ary associations; the constraints on the meta-model will just be a little more sophisticated.

Classes may have children and parents, where the parents of a class A are those classes from which A inherits. A simplified view of inheritance is taken in this paper, which admits multiple and single inheritance, but does not admit renaming of, or strengthening of cardinalities on, roles. (This can be handled, but requires a more sophisticated model of inheritance which there is not room to explore here.) Constraints on a class are carried down to children of that class.By the inverse nature of an association, if a class A is the parent of another class B, then A will have B as one of its children, and vice-versa. We distinguish the immediate children/parents of a class; the children/parents of a class are the immediate children/parents union their children/parents.

A state is a dynamic class: an object of a state may move into a different state, so it is not the case that an object created in a state (for a dynamic class) remains in that state (remains a member of that class) for its whole lifetime. The equation of state with dynamic class dates back to [S92], and is now embodied in the Catalysis method [SW99].

Roles and classes are here restricted to belong to a single model. This would not be the case in a meta-model that supported the notion of model extension, i.e. a model A being constructed by including everything in model B then adding some. However, the notion of model extension brings with it additional complications that there is not the space to consider in this paper.

As with the standard UML-meta model, we can make precise the well-formedness rules that apply to valid instances of the UML-meta model. That is, these rules further constrain the abstract syntax of UML to ensure that only valid expressions of the UML are permitted. The rules for this fragment of the meta-model are given below. They are written in OCL, the precise constraint language of UML.

```
context m:Model inv:
      the source and target classes of m's roles are classes in m
      m.classes->includesAll(m.roles.source
          ->union(m.roles.target))
context c:Class inv:
      the children/parents of c are the immediate children/parents union
      the children/parents of those
      c.children=c.immediateChildren
          ->union(c.immediateChildren.children)
      and c.parents=c.immediateParents
          ->union(c.immediateParents.parents)
context c:Class inv:
      the parents of c are in the same model as c
      c.parents.model=c.model
context c:Class inv:
      c is not a parent or child of itself
      not(c.parents->includes(c) or c.children->includes(c))
context r:Role inv:
      r.inverse->isEmpty or
      the inverse of the inverse of r is r
      (r.inverse.inverse=r and
      the inverse of r reverses the source and target of r
      r.inverse.source=r.target and r.inverse.target=r.source
      the inverse of r is in the same model as r
      and r.model=r.inverse.model)
```

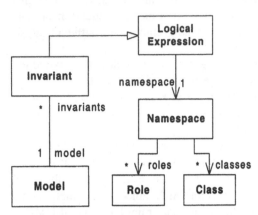

Figure 2 shows the relationships between models and invariants. An invariant is a logical expression, which always comes with its own namespace: the classes and roles referred to in the logical expression.

Figure 2. Invariants

A constraint is required to ensure that the language defined in the namespace of invariants of a model are provided by that model:

```
context m:Model inv:
    m.classes->includesAll(m.invariants.namespace.classes)
    and m.roles->includesAll(m.invariants.namespace.roles)
```

The full structure of logical expressions will be revealed in Section 5. However, there is already enough in this part of the meta-model to consider the semantics of a UML model.

3.   INSTANCES

The semantics of a UML model is given by constraining the relationship between a model and possible instances of that model. That is, constraining the relationship between expressions of the UML abstract syntax for models and expressions of the UML abstract syntax for instances. The latter requires a meta-model representing the abstract syntax of instances.

Figure 3 defines a *snapshot* (Catalysis parlance; represented in UML as an *object diagram*) to be a set of objects and a set of links. Snapshots, links and objects are instances of models, roles and classes, respectively. The UML standard meta-model does not make the connection between models and snapshots, but the symmetry between the two halves of the diagram is too hard to resist.

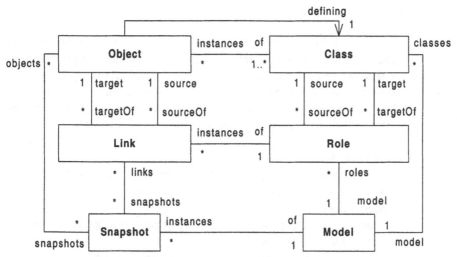

Figure 3. Objects, links, snapshots

A snapshot can only be an instance of a single model, because, here, models are self-contained and disjoint from other models (excepting the special case where a model is behaving as a namespace for an invariant). Snapshots could be instances of more than one model in a context where models could be extensions of other models, and thus have components in common.

On the other hand, objects are instances of one or more classes, hence they may be of one or more types. With no further constraints, it is possible for an object to change the classes of which it is an instance; thus this meta-model supports dynamic types. Indeed, as mentioned earlier, it is our view that states (as in state diagrams) are just dynamic classes.

There is one well-formedness rule for instances (i.e. the left-hand side of the diagram), which is given below:

```
context s:Snapshot inv:
     the source and target objects of s's links are objects in s
     s.objects->includesAll(s.links.source
          ->union(s.links.target))
     links between two objects are unique per role
     & s.links->forAll(l | s.links->select(l'|
     l'.source=l.source & l'.target=l.target & l'.of=l.of)=l)
```

Other invariants are required constraining the relationships between models and instances. These constitute the semantics and are the subject of the next section.

4. SEMANTICS: THE BASICS

Our semantics for UML focuses on the relationship between a model and its possible
instances. The constraints on this relationship are relatively simple, ignoring
invariants for the time being, but they do demonstrate the general principle.

Firstly, there are two constraints relating to objects and links, respectively. The
first shows how inheritance relationships can force an object to be of many classes.
The second ensures that a link connects objects of classes as dictated by its role.

context o:Object inv:
> the classes of o must be a single class and all the parents of that class
> ```
> o.of->exists(c | o.of=c->union(c.parents))
> ```

context l:Link inv:
> objects which are the source/target of links are of classes which are at the
> source/target of the corresponding roles
> ```
> (l.of.source)->intersection(l.source.of)->notEmpty
> and (l.of.target->intersection(l.target.of)->notEmpty
> ```

Secondly, there are four constraints which ensure that a snapshot is a valid snapshot
of the model it is claimed to be a snapshot of. Of these four constraints, the first and
second ensure that objects and links are associated with classes and roles known in
the model. The third constraint ensures that within the snapshot cardinality
constraints on roles are observed. The fourth that reverse links are in place for roles
with inverses.

context s:Snapshot inv:
> the model, that s is a snapshot of, includes all the classes that
> s.objects are instances of
> ```
> s.of.classes->includesAll(s.objects.of)
> ```

context s:Snapshot inv:
> the model. that s is a snapshot of, includes all the roles that
> s.links are instances of
> ```
> s.of.roles->includesAll(s.roles.of)
> ```

context s:Snapshot inv:
> the links of s respect cardinality constraints for their corresponding role
> ```
> s.links.of->forAll(r | let links_in_s be
>         r.instances->intersect(s.links) in
>             (r.upperBound->notEmpty implies
>                 links_in_s->size <= r.upperBound)
>             and links_in_s->size >= r.lowerBound)
> ```

context s:Snapshot inv:
> if a link is of a role with an inverse, then there is a corresponding reverse link
> ```
> s.links->forAll(l | l.of.role.inverse->notEmpty implies
>         s.links->select(l'| l'.source=l.target &
>         l'.target=l.source & l'.of=l.of.inverse)->size=1
> ```

5. INVARIANTS

This section provides the abstract syntax for a fragment of the OCL used to write invariants, many examples of which have appeared already as constraints on the meta-model. The OCL fragment under scrutiny includes navigation expressions, logical connectives and set comparisons, but does not include number denoting expressions, general quantification or filtered sets. These latter three concepts bring in other layers of complexity into the semantics, which there is not space to consider here.

Invariants are logical expressions, which appear in the context of models (see also *Figure 2*). This paper only considers invariants on a single class, as embodied in OCL. We realise that this can be too restrictive and that, often, model-wide invariants are required (indeed there is one such invariant in Section 6). It should not be difficult to extend our approach to cover this situation.

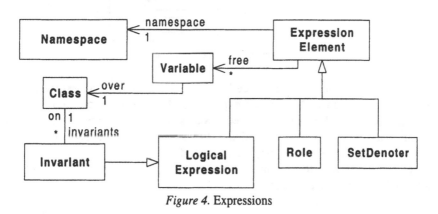

Figure 4. Expressions

An invariant has a single free variable which ranges over its class:

```
context i:Invariant inv:
    i.free.over=i.on and i.free->size=1
```

As will be shown in Section 6, this variable is universally quantified. Thus our treatment of this restricted form of invariant does show the way for a more general treatment of quantification.

Logical expressions are one kind of expression, the others being roles and set denoters. All expressions are associated with a namespace and one or more free variables (though sub-expressions of invariants considered here will have at most one free variable). The remainder of this section explores the different kinds of set denoter and logical expression.

5.1.   Logical connectives

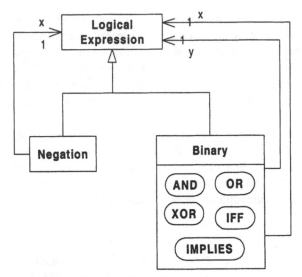

Figure 5. Logical connectives

The logical connectives are introduced via two kinds of logical expression (see *Figure 5*): a negation and a binary expression. The binary expression has state indicating the kind of connective used. (States are shown here using the state diagram shape – a box with rounded corners. They can be read as dynamic subclasses of the class in which tney are contained.)

There are constraints to propagate namespaces and free variables up through the structure of a complex expression.

```
context n:Negation inv:
    n.namespace=n.x.namespace & n.free=n.x.free

context b:Binary inv:
    b.namespace.classes=b.x.classes->union(b.y.classes)
    & b.namespace.roles=b.x.roles->union(b.y.roles)
    & b.free=b.x.free->union(b.y.free)
```

5.2. Set comparison

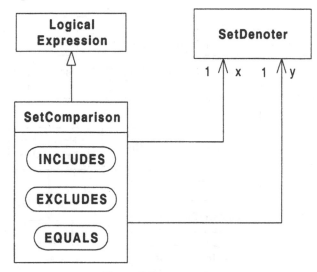

Figure 6. Set comparison

Logical expressions are also formed by comparing sets, here by containment, exclusion or equality. A set S excludes T if S has no elements in common with T; clearly if S excludes T, then T excludes S. A more usual term for *includes* is *contains*; a more usual term for excludes is *disjoint*. We have used includes and excludes as they are the terms used in OCL.

Namespaces and free variables are propagated in the same way as for binary logical expressions.

5.3.   Set denoters

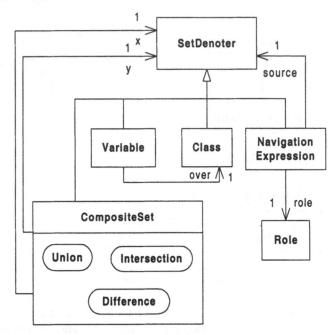

Figure 7. Set denoters

Finally, there are different kinds of set denoters, as indicated by *Figure 7.* Set denoters denote sets of objects. All are obvious except, perhaps, navigation expressions. In OCL, a navigation expression takes the concrete form `source.role`, where source denotes a set and role is a role. Of course source may itself be a navigation expression, allowing arbitrary length navigation expressions to be recursively defined.

Namespaces and free variables are propagated as follows:

```
context c:Class inv:
    c.namespace.classes=c & c.namespace.roles->isEmpty
    & c.free->isEmpty
```

```
context r:Role inv:
    r.namespace.roles=r & r.namespace.classes->isEmpty
    & r.free->isEmpty
```

Composite sets are treated like binary logical expressions. Finally:

```
context v:Variable inv:
    v.namespace.classes->isEmpty
    & v.namespace.roles->isEmpty
    & v.free=v
```

```
context ne:NavigationExpression inv:
    ne.namespace.roles=ne.source.namespace.roles->union(role)
    & ne.namespace.classes=ne.source.namespace.classes
    & ne.free=ne.source.free
```

6. SEMANTICS OF INVARIANTS

The semantics of invariants requires constraints that ensure that a snapshot of a model satisfies the invariants of the model, which in turn requires each invariant to hold for all objects in the snapshot of the class which the invariant is on. This requires the relationship between instances and models to be enriched. The two main problems when checking against an invariant are:

- To derive all the sets required by the invariant for the particular snapshot concerned, for example the sets represented by particular navigation expressions, classes etc.
- To work out a system for calculating the denotation of an expression for a particular substitution of the variable ranging over objects of the class the invariant is on.

These problems are solved in *Figure 8* by a qualified role from Expression to Denotation. Provide an expression with a snapshot and an object, and it will return the denotation of that expression in that snapshot for that object. Rules for each kind of expression determine the exact nature of the denotation returned.

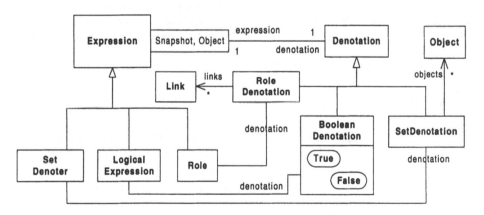

Figure 8. Denotations

With this in place, it is now possible to state the main constraint that ensures a snapshot satisfies the invariants of the model of which it is claimed to be an instance.

```
context s:Snapshot, o':Object inv:
    s.model.invariants->forAll(i |
    i.on.denotation(s,o').objects->forAll(o |
    i.denotation(s,o).oclIsInState(BooleanDenotation::True)))
```

(Strictly, OCL only allows an invariant to be applied to a single class. However, using quantifiers it is possible to write an invariant with variables that range over many classes. The syntax used here is far less cumbersome that the latter approach, and, we feel, fits naturally within OCL.)

That is, for every invariant of the model that s is an instance of, and every object o, which in s and of the class that the invariant is on, the denotation of the invariant in s for object o must be true. Note that o' is just a placeholder: when obtaining the denotation of a class in a snapshot, the object argument is ignored.

All that now remains is to give the rules stipulating the denotation returned for each kind of expression, for a particular snapshot and object. These rules work compositionally: they state how the denotation of a complex expression is built up from the denotation of its parts.

We consider each kind of expression in the same order as they were introduced in Section 5.

SECTION 5.1, LOGICAL CONNECTIVES, *FIGURE 5*

```
context b:Binary::AND, s:Snapshot, o:Object inv:
b.denotation(s,o).oclIsInState(BooleanDenotation::True) =
    b.x.denotation(s,o).oclIsInState(BooleanDenotation::True)
 &  b.y.denotation(s,o).oclIsInState(BooleanDenotation::True)
```

Similarly for OR, XOR, IFF, IMPLIES & NOT.

SECTION 5.2, SET COMPARISON, *FIGURE 6*

```
context sc:SetComparison::INCLUDES, s:Snapshot, o:Object inv:
    sc.denotation(s,o).oclIsInState(BooleanDenotation::True)=
        sc.x.denotation(s,o).objects
            ->includesAll(sc.y.denotation(s,o).objects)
```

Similarly for EXCLUDES and EQUALS.

SECTION 5.3, SET DENOTERS, *FIGURE 7*

```
context cs:CompositeSet::UNION, s:Snapshot, o:Object inv:
    cs.denotation(s,o).objects=
        cs.x.denotation(s,o).objects
            ->union(cs.y.denotation(s,o).objects)
```

Similarly for INTERSECTION and DIFFERENCE.

The denotation of a variable is the object passed to it as argument, as that object represents its substitution for this denotation:

```
context v:Variable, s:Snapshot, o:Object inv:
    v.denotation(s,o).objects=o
```

Although not very general (any variable will be substituted for the object that is passed as an argument), this approach is sufficient for generating the denotation of the restricted form of invariant considered here, which only has a single variable. A more general treatment of variables and quantification will be given in a future paper.

The denotation of a class in a snapshot is all the objects of that class in the snapshot:

```
context c:Class, s:Snapshot, o:Object inv:
    c.denotation(s,o).objects =
        s.objects->select(o'| o'.of->includes(c))
```

Similarly for roles.

Finally, the denotation of a navigation expression in a snapshot collects together the target objects of all the links of its role in the snapshot that are sourced on an object of the denotation of its source:

```
context ne:NavigationExpression, s:Snapshot, o:Object inv:
    ne.denotation(s,o).objects = ( ne.role.denotation.links
        ->select(1 | ne.source.denotation(s,o).objects
            ->includes(1.source)) ).target
```

7. FURTHER WORK

The meta-model for a significant part of the UML/OCL for models has been provided, and its semantics expressed within the meta-model by constraining the relationship to model-instances, also captured within the meta-model. Some shortcuts were taken, and some generalisations need to be made:

- Quantification in OCL has not been modelled, although the treatment of invariants should easily be extended to accomodate quantifiers.
- Set filtering (select & reject in OCL) should follow on from a treatment of quantifiers, as it, too, requires a general treatment of variables.
- Numerical expressions remain to be dealt with. This will require a tie up between pre-defined expressions (e.g. set size) and user-defined expressions, e.g. roles targeted on the class Number.
- A treatment has only be given for simple roles, i.e. ones with a single source and target. Qualified roles, as used, for example, in *Figure 8*, require roles with

multiple sources. Roles with multiple sources/targets, will be required to capture n-ary associations.

The above issues should provide a rich basis for producing a single static model. We have also been working on the meta-model (including semantics) for:

- Model extension, including class/role renaming, strengthening of role cardinalities and strengthening of invariants. A model extension mechanism would allow a model to be constructed from other models, which may include models representing patterns. This work may be viewed as a formalisation of the template mechanism described in Catalysis [SW99].

- Model refinement, focusing on the mapping of object structures at one level of abstraction to object structures at a more concrete level. This is in fact the most important aspect for us. We are interested in realising services (e.g. a guaranteed throughput) over concrete networks (e.g. IP networks). Formalisation of the modelling language and refinement and their semantics is essential to support the development of tools that will, for example, walk the refinement relationships to configure a network to support certain services.

It is also intended to extend the meta-model to incorporate *dynamic* modelling. This will require formalisation of operations (actions), state diagrams, sequence diagrams, and, of course, the corresponding instances of these constructs. We have a good idea how to handle some of this. Actions have arguments and pre/post conditions, for which the logical expression infrastructure already exists. States have already been introduced, as a kind of class, and transitions in state diagrams are effectively constraints on how an object configuration can change when certain actions are invoked with particular participants, that is a particular kind of post condition. Sequence diagrams impose constraints on how actions may be sequenced, and these constraints may depend on which objects participate in the actions. On the instance side, a notion of *trace* will be required, where a trace is a sequence of snapshots (in Catalysis [SW99], a *filmstrip*), with action instances between each pair. Traces must satisfy the constraints derived from the pre/post conditions, the sequence and state diagrams.

We have started work under the auspices of the pUML (precise UML) group (http://www.cs.york.ac.uk/puml) to incorporate many of the semantic ideas into the UML standard meta-model.

Finally, tools incorporating parts of the meta-model are being developed at Nortel to support network modelling and management of network services. We hope, and expect, that these tools will have a wider application in the general area of conceptual modelling and will serve to improve the lot of the practising modeller.

REFERENCES

[S92] D. D'Souza, Education and Training: Teacher! Teacher!, *Journal of Object-Oriented Programming*, vol. 5, pp. 12-17, 1992.

[SW99] D. D'Souza and A.C. Wills. *Objects, Components and Frameworks with UML: The Catalysis Approach*, Addison Wesley, 1999.

[GHK99] Y. Gil, J. Howse, and S. Kent, Formalizing Spider Diagrams, submitted for publication, 1999.

[K97] S. Kent. Constraint Diagrams: Visualising Invariants in Object Oriented Models. In: *Proceedings of OOPSLA97*, ACM Press, 1997.

[KG98] S. Kent and Y. Gil, Visualising Action Contracts in OO Modelling, *IEE Proceedings: Software*, vol. 145, 1998.

[S86] D.A. Schmidt, *Denotational Semantics: A Methodology for Language Development*, Allyn and Bacon, Massachusetts, 1986.

[UML99] UML task force. *UML 1.1. Specification*, Object Management Group, 1999.

[WK98] J. Warmer and A. Kleppe. *The Object Constraint Language: Precise Modeling with UML*, Addison-Wesley, 1998.

About the Authors

Stuart Kent is a Senior Lecturer in Computing at the University of Kent, UK. He researches, teaches and mentors in design/modelling notations and techniques. He has publihsed some 30 refereed papers and regularly presents at major international conferences. This work arose out of a collaboration with the co-authors whilst on a consultancy engagement at Nortel Networks.

Stephen Gaito is a senior software engineer working for Nortel Networks. He is currently researching designs for, and helping to build, a model repository capable of managing complex multi-layer multi-protocol telecomms networks and services. Stephen's previous work with Nortel Networks was on a KBS based configuration engine capable of configuring complex Nortel Networks PBXs given a set of customer requirements.

Niall Ross is a senior employee of Nortel Networks. He leads a team researching how to manage complex multi-layer multi-protocol telecomms networks and services. Niall's previous work includes leading edge research on object-oriented methods, type systems and databases, and on software metrics. His current development unites KBS and OO approaches.

Chapter 10

ON THE STRUCTURE OF CONVINCING SPECIFICATIONS

Haim Kilov   **Allan Ash**
Genesis Development Corporation[1]   *Software Arts, Inc.*
hkilov@gendev.com, haim_kilov@omg.org   *software_arts@compuserve.com*

Abstract   Recent popular management literature suggests that when you solve problems you ought to "think outside the box". You should not get too constrained by the (existing?) problem statement, but think about better ways of restructuring the problem so that it can be more effectively solved. In recent papers describing systems development based on rigorous business requirements, the authors have sketched a framework for realizing solutions which encourages such feedback from the solution to the problem set. This may be successfully applied to various, even seemingly quite different, businesses — including the business of creating an information management system.

In "thinking outside the box" we have, first and foremost, to establish a context for our thinking. In other words, we ought to describe the box since you do not even know whether you think outside something if that "something" was not described. *Describing the Box* is otherwise known as "Defining the Business Domain". *Thinking inside the box* means attempting to realize a solution for that domain. And *reshaping the box* means feeding back the insights gained from solving the problem to restate the problem so that it is more effectively understood and solved.

These same stages are used when we deal with specifications, or even code, at various levels of abstraction — business, system and technological. All these specifications ought to be convincing and elegant. Writers and readers need to be assured that the specifications describe whatever they are supposed to describe. Elegance ensures that they are written and read with pleasure. This paper will share our experience with you.

The physicians call a medicine which contains efficient ingredients in a small volume, and of a pleasant or tolerable taste, an elegant medicine.

1788 V. Knox Winter Even. I. vi. 67

1   AN INFORMATION MANAGEMENT PROJECT

When we want to build a house, we don't just hire a builder and say — "build a house". Even if everyone knows what a house is, and all houses are built from the same components, we need much more than that. Specifically, we need to know – and be able to express! – something that is true about all houses that would satisfy our needs, no matter what. We may be able to "hack a hut", but building anything more sophisticated requires a more formal approach[2].

An Information Management Project is a means by which an organization improves business operation efficiency or effectiveness through achieving specific business objectives. Usually, this results in a new computer system, since technology is a very powerful way to improve business processes to achieve efficiency and effectiveness. It should be noted, though, that even a "less-tech", "low-tech" or "no-tech" solution to a problem can be a cost-effective way to deliver these improvements.

A project is a *complex effort* with a specific set of objectives. For our purposes here[3], it is composed (see [KS96a]) of the processes of:

- Business Specification
- Business Design
- System Specification and
- System Implementation

These activities constitute an ordered composition. They are carried out, generally in order (from business specification to system implementation), to build the material – documents, systems and procedures – which are the objective of the project. Each activity builds its own material – a description of the system from its viewpoint – which then is "realized" or moved to a more concrete (more implementation-bound) viewpoint by the next activity, i.e., by the next component in this ordered composition. This means that we instantiate a Realization relationship which relates the "source" activity and the "target" activity which realizes it[4] (see below).

A target is not uniquely determined by its source. There may be more than one business design that will realize a given business specification, for example, although only the "best" one will be chosen to be realized by the next activity.

Note that an "ordered composition" relationship, a "realization" relationship, and other relationships are defined *precisely* and *explicitly*, by means of their invariants – stable properties of these relationships that do not change no matter what operations are applied to these relationships and their participants[5]. More details are provided in [ISO95a, ISO95b, KR94, K99] and elsewhere.

1.1   Business Specification

A Business Specification is composed of a business domain specification, that describes the "things" and relationships manipulated within the scope of the project, and a business operation specification, which describes the business operations applied to those things and relationships. The basics of the *business domain* provide a solid foundation for both currently existing and possibly invented business operations. This constitutes a reference relationship from the Business Domain Specification to the Business Operations Specification[6].

1.2   Business Design

A business design – showing "who does what when" – is a realization of its business specification. The business design sets out the (abstract) model of the business as clearly as possible. It should be noted that even though some operations and fragments of the business domain are realized by humans, these are still to be defined as part of the business design.

1.3   System Specification

The system specification is the result of the realization activity of translating those business things, relationships, and processes which the business design activity decided to realize in a computer-based information management system, into the systems things (sometimes known as "objects"), relationships and processes which will implement them. Similarly, a System Specification is composed of a System Domain Specification and a System Operations Specification, with a reference relationship between them.

1.4   System Implementation

This activity is concerned with realizing – producing – the computer programs and/or operating procedures necessary to accomplish the designs done during system specification.

2   THE REALIZATION RELATIONSHIP

The Realization Relationship is sketched in Figure 1, below. It is applicable to any kind of realization. Its purpose is to build a "target" which realizes (in an Information Management Project makes more "real") the source. It is the specification or building of a number of potential targets (variants), and then the selection of the "best".

On the one hand, some properties of the target are determined by properties of the source; and this is shown by the "refinement" reference relationship between the two. For example, perhaps the most important properties of business design are determined by the properties of its business specification. On the other hand, in some cases, changes to the source may be needed as a result of building the target. This is described as a "feedback" reference relationship. During business design, for example, a conscious decision may be made to solve a business problem somewhat different from the one described in the original business specification (for example, due to various constraints or opportunities resulting from the choice of a technological architecture). This change of the source, an activity that we can term "Reshaping the Box", must always be a deliberate and explicit engineering decision, deemed acceptable under prevailing circumstances.

Note that this change to the source may result in a change to *its* source, within their own instance of a realization relationship. This constitutes part of the feedback relationship at that previous stage of development. When realizing a System Specification by a System Implementation, for example, the feedback relationship might cause changes to the System Specification. This, in turn, may necessitate reconsidering the Business Design from which the original System Specification was realized. This would constitute the feedback relationship at that level of abstraction.

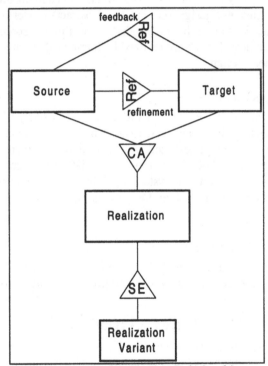

Figure 1. The Realization Relationship

In this figure, we show things as named boxes, and relationships as named triangles together with lines connecting them with their boxes. The kind of generic relationship is shown in the triangle — "Ref" (Reference), "CA" (Composition Assembly), and "SE" (Exhaustive Subtyping) — so that we can see the *abbreviated invariant* of the corresponding relationship in each triangle. The figure is short and understandable (and as you might have supposed, such figures exist also for the business specifications of an information management project, see below [KA98]).

We present here an example of a subset of a business domain for which this approach was used.

3   AN ACCOUNTING PROBLEM

3.1   Describing the Box (Defining the Business [Domain] Specification)

The Problem and Approach

The business problem to be solved was to provide moderately complex, globally uniform *accounting functionality* within a single organization, as part of a larger system development effort, intended to produce a deliverable which we will term the "System". A number of business practices were substantially changing as part of the introduction of the new system. In fact, the "System" was required to provide new and innovative facilities as a basis for accomplishing these functions.

The business analyst's problem was to describe both existing and novel business practices clearly enough to allow the subject matter experts (SMEs) to be convinced that it exactly represents both the current state of the business and their intent, and precisely enough to allow the design team to specify the implementation unambiguously. The latter was especially important for this project, since it was planned to enlist the aid of a development partner to help with implementation. Thus the business specification had to be not only precise and complete, but also understandable to everyone concerned (i.e., as concise as possible, and well-structured). In other words, abstraction[7] and precision are essential for success. In this manner, our specifications and our programs will be intellectually manageable, and we will be able to state, and justify, that our systems are what they are supposed to be.

For the purposes of this paper, the vast majority of the functionality of the "System" will not be described here. Our abstraction will deal with only the relevant pieces of the *accounting functionality* under consideration.

What is to be Included?

A business specification includes the fundamental properties of the business domain of interest – business "things", relationships among them, and operations applied to them. Things and relationships are described by means of invariants – predicates ("stable properties") that should be true all the time, independent of operations applied to these things. The very act of describing the business properties provided a good way to get rid of vagueness: to structure the analysts' (and SMEs') knowledge as well as providing a foundation from which to formulate questions. One of the SME's, noting the discipline which accrues to the process, "stopped to ask myself the invariant question in my own documents" [L97].

Operations (a.k.a. "business processes") are described by means of pre- and postconditions as well as triggering conditions. In other words, a business specification describes the "what" of the business, while the "how" of the business is described by a business design at which stage we have to decide "who does what when".

This approach is perfectly applicable to other specifications. For example, a system specification, in a similar way, describes system things (sometimes called "objects" of particular "classes") and relationships between them as well as operations (sometimes called "messages"). (The classical object-oriented approach to system specifications follows the approach presented in the Computational Viewpoint of RM-ODP [ISO95c].) Precise system specifications are accomplished by providing, for example, "class invariants" and pre- and postconditions for operations [M97, LBR99]. As another example, we have described the business of creating an information management system in a similar way, see the section "An Information Management Project", above, as well as [KA98].

Only some part of the business specifications may be realized by a computer-based system (and any potential realization is of no importance for a business specification) [KR94, KMS96, K99]. During business design it will be decided which parts of the business specification will be realized by humans, and which by a computer-based system. These parts have to smoothly interoperate, and specifically, it should be decided "who and when checks the invariants".

We did not use concepts like "collaborations", "messages", or even "objects" to formulate a business specification. These concepts may be used for certain system specifications (depending on the underlying technology and approach used); however, a business specification is technology-independent [KMS96, KS96, K99]. The usage of a message-oriented object paradigm in a business specification not only enforces premature decisions (like choosing the "owner" of an operation or of an invariant, or the way to use attributes, pointers, or association ends to realize relationships), but also makes the specification quite unnatural for a business expert leading to frustration or worse (in business, as noted by several experts, you don't send messages to your paycheck or your account). To avoid this — and to make our specifications convincing to the business users — we need to separate concerns, and in particular, the concerns of structuring a business specification from the concerns of structuring a system specification so as not to impose certain technology-centric ways of thinking. Specifically, we used the generalized object model [KR94], with collective state and behavior, in accordance with such international standards as RM-ODP [ISO95a] and GRM [ISO95b].

Goals of the Specification Task

The ultimate goal of the specification task is to create clear, precise, explicit, understandable business (functional) requirements, independent of the existing or planned system (so that, for example, new business processes will be specified independently of whether a human or a system will execute them; and so that this decision is not even made within the business specification process). In other words, the specification has to be *convincing* to its users — otherwise it will not be even read! A good specification ought to be a pleasure to read, in the same manner as a good program. These considerations about good (and otherwise) programs were presented and justified a relatively long time ago by E.W.Dijkstra [D63, D65]; the same is true for all kinds of specifications. Specifically, since any specification — from a business specification to a program — will be read much more often than written, substantial intellectual effort when writing a convincing specification is essential for success.

This set of business specifications provides the baseline for formulating the business design and, especially, the system specification, which is to happen later. Since the business domain specification defines those properties of the business fragment that remain stable (invariant) within the context of the business operations applied to the things and relationships of this domain, we will concentrate on these invariant properties. In order to discover and formulate them, we use business patterns — in particular, specifications of generic constructs, such as different kinds of *composition*, reusable for various application areas. These are our tools; and, as in programming, "the tool should be charming, it should be elegant, it should be worthy of our love. This is no joke, I am terribly serious about this. ... The greatest virtues a program can show: Elegance and Beauty." [D63]

Observe that there should be no restrictions of the constructs used to express a business specification as long as the constructs and their relationships are precisely defined. Specifically, since in business a thing may have several types (in the RM-ODP sense, i.e., predicates), may acquire and lose types, may be subtyped using different (mutually orthogonal) subtyping hierarchies, may be decomposed using different compositions, and so on, these mechanisms ought to be available to a business specifier even though some existing system technologies cannot directly support them.

By way of example, we present below a small fragment of our accounting business specification.

A Transaction

In the context of this accounting business (specification), a *transaction* is the complete information about a particular movement of cash. From the accounting viewpoint, a transaction consists of *basic components*, optional (Omnibus) accounts, optional fee components, and other components (see Figure 2, below). In order for a transaction to exist, at least its basic components have to exist.

Basic components of a transaction are composed (or more precisely constitute a Fixed Composition Assembly relationship) of: money, cash account, booking account (e.g., a client account, or a processing account), direction (from or to the firm), and value date. Each of these components has to exist in order for basic components to exist. Money, in turn, is a fixed composition of value and currency (not shown here).

It should be noted that Omnibus accounts are targeted to a future implementation phase, and are shown here only for completeness.

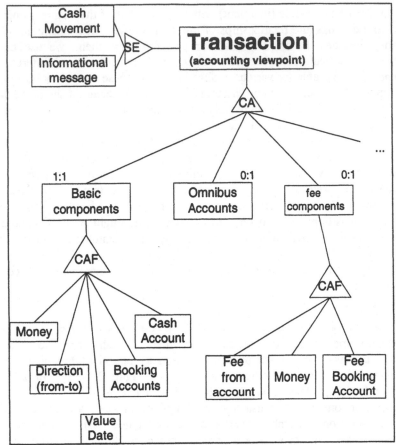

Figure 2 - A Transaction

We did not have to use any "5-day courses" to train customers and developers in specification constructs: they were introduced as and when needed. Thus, reading a specification was very easy: even if users did not want to use graphics, the corresponding English text (see above) was quite understandable.

Recording a transaction

A business transaction is a subtype of a transaction shown in Figure 2, above. In this context it is a money transfer. A system transaction is another subtype of a transaction and is the accounting representation of the different stages of a business transaction. It is composed of one or more *postable account pairs* (debits and credits) representing which of the accounts mentioned above need to be updated ("posted") with what money. Posting is accomplished with respect to a particular *account* – a component of the transaction from this viewpoint – and means determining and recording the account-related information (see Figure 2) about it. This information is then sent to an appropriate *ledger* (a component of the books of the firm) to be included there.

After the appropriate business decisions about a system transaction have been made, it needs to be recorded (posted) as a payment transaction in the appropriate ledgers. The effects of this transaction (those *components of a system transaction that are posted by the system*) on the appropriate *accounts* can be determined; and transformed into their ledger-specific representations – *transaction accounting entries* – which will be sent to the appropriate ledgers in the format and mode (batch or online) each ledger requires.

Figure 3 is a specification that includes a lot of the above and some additional business context information which we hope is in most cases self-explanatory. See also [KA97] for more details.

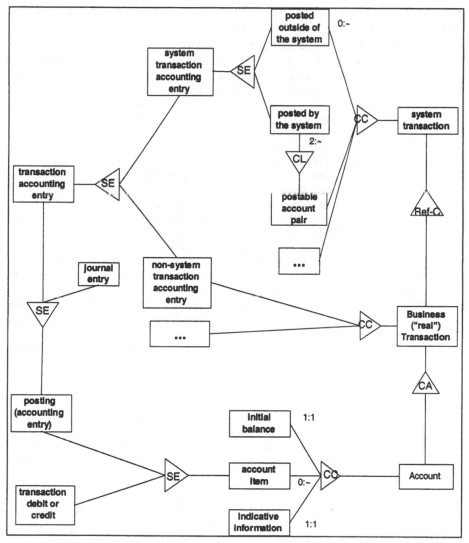

Figure 3. Account representations

Observe that substantial fragments of invariants for a business domain specification follow immediately from the instantiation of such generic business patterns as *subtyping exhaustive* (SE) or *composition-containment* (CC) (invariants for some generic relationships are shown in endnotes 5 and 6; see also [KR94, K99].) In addition, the specification of our business domain — as any other business domain — includes appropriate actual parameters for these generic patterns, such as actual properties that differentiate between subtypes of a particular supertype; or actual properties of the composite that are determined by properties of its components; etc.

Operations are defined by their pre- and postconditions which, in turn, refer to things and relationships of the business domain and satisfy the invariants of this domain. This is as it should be: RM-ODP states that dynamic schemas (that define operations) are subject to the constraints of the invariant schema.

Aside: on representation mechanisms

In our specifications we used two representation mechanisms: stylized English and graphics. Clearly, if a graphical representation is used then each element and relationship between elements ought to be precisely defined; and if English is used then this should be done with open eyes since natural language is prone to incompletenesses, ambiguities, etc. To quote E.W.Dijkstra [D72] about the English used for the Algol60 Report, "The report gloriously demonstrated the power of the formal method BNF... and the power of carefully phrased English, at least when used by someone as brilliant as Peter Naur. I think that it is fair to say that only very few documents as short as this have had an equally profound influence on the computing community." The international (ISO) standard — Reference Model for Open Distributed Processing (RM-ODP) — is even shorter, and seems also to have a very profound influence. We followed these approaches, in particular, when we used English to represent invariants and pre- and postconditions. When we say that a (business or system) specification includes the specification of invariants that describe things and relationships, and specification of operations in terms of pre- and postconditions, we have the very basic patterns — some may call them "templates" — in terms of which we say precisely what we want to say. Generic relationships like *composition* provide higher-level patterns encountered and used everywhere. In this manner, the specification in "English" becomes explicit, unambiguous, and convincing (like a legal contract which uses various legal patterns).

Using some "CASE tools" to represent specifications ought to be done with caution for the reasons eloquently noted by Dijkstra in his Turing Award Lecture in 1972 when he described PL/I — "a programming language for which the defining documentation is of a frightening size and complexity. Using PL/I must be like flying a plane with 7,000 buttons, switches, and handles to manipulate in the cockpit. I absolutely fail to see how we can keep our growing programs firmly within our intellectual grip when by its sheer baroqueness the programming language – our basic tool, mind you! – already escapes our intellectual control. And if I have to describe the influence PL/I can have on its users, the closest metaphor that comes to my mind is that of a drug."

3.2   Thinking inside the box (Defining the Business Design)

After specifying the business domain, various things, relationships and operations of that domain are grouped into subsystems which are realizable by humans or by information management systems. This is done during business design, when we consider one or more realization variants — different implementations of the same set of requirements (see also [KS96a]). The properties of the variant chosen are determined by the (business, system and technological) environment as well as by the strategy [KA98]. In the case of the domain described above, the small piece of the domain which transforms the representation of the entity described as the *system transaction accounting entry which is posted by the system* into *transaction accounting entries* was identified as a separate subsystem. The strategic reason for instantiating this piece as a subsystem was that this functionality bridges a physical gap in the domain between the [main] transaction processing part of the "System" and the external, already existing, Posting Ledger systems (PLS) (a fragment of the environment) which require various types of input representations, in various modes (batch or online), and via different platforms. Thus, explicit consideration of environments and strategy leads to making, justifying, and describing explicit choices. This corresponds very well to the enterprise viewpoint of RM-ODP [ISO95c] that describes the purpose, scope and policies of any system.

It should be noted that, in the case of more than one set of users, the economics of doing this transformation resulted in generating a realization variant using a manual link from system to system (i.e. rekeying information for a very small number of "large" transactions was cheaper than building an automated bridge to a ledger system which was planned to be replaced shortly). Considering a "low-tech" or "status quo" variant to realize all or part of a business requirement might result in a more cost effective solution overall.

In this simple case, business design consisted of determining the scope of the subsystem, i.e., the relevant things and relationships from the business specification and operations we were interested in, and making decisions about agents (human or computer-based systems) for implementing these operations.

In more general situations, business design may include a substantial amount of Business process reengineering (BPR) (a.k.a. business re-design) which involves not only rearrangement of existing actions, but also replacement of compositions of actions with other compositions of possibly different actions to achieve the same or a different objective. Some of these actions may be performed by humans, and some by computer-based systems. Thus, we think inside the existing box (of business domain), and by carefully and explicitly considering realization variants also think outside this box. As a result, the box may be somewhat or substantially changed.

3.3   Reshaping the box

The feedback from decisions made and specified during business design (and possibly during later project stages such as system specification) may and often will lead to changes in the business specification. This was mentioned in the description of the realization relationship (another business pattern) earlier.

In our case here, we had to include the existence and some relevant properties of the legacy general ledger subsystems as fragments of the business domain and operation specification (they were important and known to business people). We temporarily put these legacy fragments out of scope when we formulated our business specification since there were too many of them, and our goal was to understand and specify the business rather than the legacy systems that *happened to be* a part of the business. However, during business design it was understood that instead of including information about the properties of all these legacy systems, it was possible and desirable to abstract out ("supertype") a small number of the most important such properties, and thus drastically reduce possible clutter and "too much stuff" in the specification.

4   SPECIFYING A SOLUTION VARIANT (REALIZING THE BUSINESS DESIGN IN A SYSTEM SPECIFICATION)

We have now created a Business Design as part of moving the Information Management Project to a "more real" level of abstraction. As described in the section about an Information Management Project, above, and in more detail in [KA98], the next step in the *business of creating an information management system* is to realize the chosen fragment of the Business Design in a System Specification, with traceability from one to the other.

4.1   Thinking Inside the Box (Defining the System Specification)

By choosing a particular subsystem to be realized, we concentrate on a box which is a component (at a lower level of abstraction, in accordance with the definition of composition provided in RM-ODP) of our original box — the business domain specification.

Here again, in order to be able think inside this box at the next level (i.e., develop code), or think outside the box (i.e., decide what could be changed in the system specification), it is necessary to describe the box first. Let us, as usual, start with the purpose and scope of the box, in accordance with the enterprise viewpoint of RM-ODP.

As seen from the above choices made for this solution variant (The General Ledger Interface Module – GLIM subsystem), it has to transform collections of *system transaction accounting entries which are posted by the system* into corresponding collections of (Posting Ledger System [PLS]-specific) *transaction accounting entries*. Each input collection consists of several entries for any PLS. The input collections were realized as queues, and the output collections – in accordance with the requirements of the particular PLSs – are chosen to be realized as either files or PLS transactions. The input collections are created by the main transaction processing part of the "System" which realizes the bulk of the business specification described in [KA97] and which is not described here (see the subsection on the Problem and Approach, above).

Among some of the elements of the Business Design which were instantiated in the System Specification were the following:

- System Invariants

These are the properties which must be true across the entire system specification. Some examples from this specification are:

Invariant: The total value of debits for a PLS for any transaction equal the total value of credits for that PLS for that transaction.

<u>Invariant</u>: The total value of all PLS posting records representing a system transaction accounting entry equals the value of the system transaction accounting entry from which it was created.

- Queues

System Transaction Accounting entries are kept on separate queues which are segregated by Posting Ledger System (PLS).

- Interface Pipe

The Interface Pipe is the medium through which the main transaction processing part of the information management system and the GLIM will communicate

- Posting Records

A Posting Record (see Figure 4, below) is a transaction accounting entry which is sent to a Posting Ledger system to request a debit or a credit to an account.

- Operations

Operations were specified as usual by means of pre- and postconditions. Some examples of the more interesting ones are:

<u>Precondition (for creating a PLS posting record)</u>: There must exist a system transaction accounting entry in order to create a PLS posting record.

<u>Precondition (for creating a PLS posting record)</u>: There must exist a description of a PLS in order to create a PLS posting record.

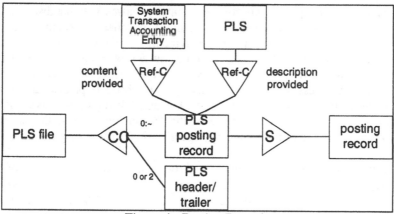

Figure 4 - Posting Records

4.2   Reshaping the box

This is the activity of feeding back insights gained during building the system specification to reshape the business design, which is the "box" at this point. Although, in this particular project, there was not sufficient feedback from the system specification process to affect business design, this feedback relationship should not be overlooked.

5   IMPLEMENTING A SOLUTION VARIANT (REALIZING THE SYSTEM DESIGN IN A SYSTEM IMPLEMENTATION)

Similarly to the preceding activity of realizing the system design variant, the realization relationship can now be instantiated with that system design as its source, and a System Implementation Variant as its target. Using the system design as the "box", we will do another round of thinking inside the box (writing code), as well as providing feedback to reshape the box (the design) to reflect better knowledge gained during the implementation process.

This piece of the "System" was realized very straightforwardly in C++, instantiating many of the "things" described by the system specification as the business classes of this implementation. We consider it prudent to explicitly check preconditions and postconditions. Even including code for that, the size of the code needed to implement the system specifications was manageable. The precise specifications provided by the system design phase contributed to simplifying the coding task, rather than, as might be anticipated at first glance, burdening the coding with artificial overhead.

6   REFINEMENTS; BRIDGING THE GAP

Because of the very nature of software code, a programmer who builds a system has to make precise and explicit decisions, and cannot get away with handwaving. If the business specification is too vague, or too complex, or relies on defaults, or is otherwise incomplete or inconsistent (i.e. not convincing) then bridging the gap between business needs and system "realities" becomes quite problematic: to build a bridge across a river, you have to be perfectly aware of *both* banks of the river. If, on the other hand, a business specification exists and is abstract, precise and explicit, bridging the gap becomes possible. The "business" bank of the river becomes known; and in order to become aware of the "technology" bank, the developers ought to become aware of the technology specifications. These may not be trivial to discover.

We use the same general concepts throughout lifecycle: the idea of using declarative specifications (invariants and pre- and postconditions) in "ordinary" programming goes back to Dijkstra and Hoare in the mid-1960's, and to Turing in 1949[8]. Similarly, the RM-ODP [ISO95a] uses the same basic constructs (like object, composition, type, subtype, invariant, refinement, contract, and so on) for all its viewpoints. This usage makes bridging the gap between a business specification and a system specification substantially easier: they are described in the same manner.

At least the following aspects of bridging the gap (refinement) deserve mention:
- Business specification things and relationships (described by invariants) are to be refined into collections of "data elements" and invariants (a business thing does not have to correspond to a system object, and neither does it have to correspond to a relational table). An implementation library can be used for this purpose. For example:
  - using attributes and their values – if appropriate – to implement subtyping

- • using primary and foreign keys and application-specific invariants for property determination to implement compositions
- pre- and postconditions for general relationship operations like "add a component" also are to be refined if these operations are to be implemented by the system
- It should be explicitly determined who (humans or computer-based systems) and when checks the business invariants (also, to a lesser extent, pre- and postconditions); and what to do if these invariants become violated
- some invariants may (but should not) be violated as a result of operations executed by humans
- Pre- and postconditions are to be explicitly refined from business to system specifications
- do not lose information (e.g., use an adequate CASE tool which provides for recording invariants, and pre- and postconditions)

The above aspects are determined by the technological architecture and the strategy chosen, as described in the section about an information management project.

7   RESULTS

7.1   Recommendations

Precision over Correctness. A precise specification should be provided to users even if it seems to be incorrect (or incomplete and has question marks in it); and the users can explicitly determine what is incorrect. If the specification is vague then no one can tell if it's wrong or even usable [G97].

Structure over Content. The same structure (e.g., generic relationships) can be reused for seemingly very different specifications — business and systems ones; or domain and operation ones. This approach leads to better understanding using deep and conceptually simple abstractions.

Explicitness. Even the things and relationships perceived as most obvious should be explicitly described at the earliest appropriate time, so that there is no doubt about their definition. This will avoid handwaving about them in the specifications, and will avoid leaving it to one of the programmers to invent a definition while in the process of coding them.

Context. Different business users work and think in different contexts with different ontologies. These contexts ought to be recognized and explicitly specified. A complete specification is composed of these context-dependent viewpoint specifications. This is not trivial since the components may be mutually inconsistent.

Clarity. In order to assure that everyone, including analysts and programmers, understands the specifications, a Business Domain Specification should be developed, which describes the user's business precisely and explicitly, and explains the business jargon in terms everyone can understand, reconciling the different ontologies, without losing the precision.

7.2   Observations on the Process

Tail Wagging the Dog. The existing systems should not determine the business (use a paper and pencil description of the business, like in [D01] for banking).

Asking Questions. It cannot be emphasized enough that the key to developing precise, clear, and understandable specifications is the continual questioning of all the audiences (specifiers, developers, SMEs, users, etc.) about their understanding of the emerging material. Does it say what you understand it to be? Are there any other things/relationships/properties that aren't written down? Does it ever happen any other way? How would you do it using only pencil and paper? These are among the leading questions that will help draw out the descriptions from the SMEs.

Abstraction. Abstraction — getting rid of "too much stuff" — is essential for human understanding and for providing specifications convincing to their readers.

Discovering Abstractions. This is clearly close to the need to articulate and may require non-trivial discovery (e.g., of supertypes and composites) within and sometimes outside of existing ontologies.

Ease of Change. Since changes are inevitable, they could as well be anticipated. A well-structured specification is conceptually simple and usually (serendipitously) leads to changes only in "contents" — parameters — leaving the structure unchanged.

Good Quality from the Beginning. High-quality specifications (abstract and precise, but not detailed) were provided from the beginning; and more details were added later based, in part, on user feedback.

What to do with Examples. Examples are important for illustrating the main ideas and concepts of the specification, perhaps in terms more familiar to some of the users; however, examples cannot and should not replace specifications since examples cannot and are not supposed to cover all possible situations.

What to do with Attributes. Such details often appear in various discussions about business specifications. Attributes, etc., do not belong to the frame of reference of business specifications, but should not be lost: they ought to be recorded explicitly for later use.

7.3   Conclusions

Project Management

- Reading is more important than writing: specifications were not trivial to write, but (perhaps therefore) much easier to read and understand
- Specifications should be clear and be able to describe both {business, system and technology} needs and possible {business, system and technology} changes
- Specification modules ought to be small
- Some (acceptable) learning period is needed; for specification reading it is mostly "learn as you go"
- Relatively quick results can be obtained in a short timeframe
- The goal is to be lucid and clear (à la RM-ODP)
- Examples should be used only to illustrate, but not to replace, specifications.

Technical

General

- Declarative specifications and rigor are possible not only for programs, but also for business specifications
- Abstraction and precision are essential throughout
- Separate business from system concerns
- Always search for business abstractions
- Postpone decisions as far as you possibly can
- Business patterns are everywhere — from basic (e.g., invariants) through generic (e.g., composition-assembly), business-generic (e.g., contracts) to more specific (e.g., General Ledger)
- No artificial restrictions should be imposed on a specifier by technology (e.g., use multiple subtyping when needed)
- Don't use exceptions - use (e.g.) subtyping for uniformity: what's exceptional for one person (viewpoint) is "normal" for another.

Specific

- Precision over correctness: precise but incorrect specifications can be understood and changed by their users; imprecise specifications are too vague and therefore useless. "Precise" is not the same as "detailed"
- Structure over content (values): the same structure (relationship "shapes") was successfully used in very different contexts
- RM-ODP and GRM were very useful both directly (as concept and pattern sources) and indirectly
- Use generalized object model for business specifications: messaging and "ownership" do not belong to the business frame of reference
- Components (not only things) are not isolated and neither are operations!
- Context should be considered and specified explicitly
- Articulation is needed not only for better understanding, but also for viewpoint integration (this includes recognition and handling of inconsistencies)
- Invariants first, operations later (operations "come and go", while invariants "stay the same").

Acknowledgements

This work was done for the Technology Strategy and Planning Department of Merrill Lynch & Co. as part of their efforts to improve the systems development process, and to provide an environment in which to realize it. The authors remain indebted to George Lieberman and Steven C. Wolfe for their interest in, and commitment of resources to the pursuit of these goals.

Thanks also to Maureen Linaugh-Nean for filling her role as SME with thoroughness, intelligence, and good humor.

Thanks to Ian Simmonds, for his always valuable observations and comments.

Endnotes

1 This work was done while the author was employed at Merrill Lynch & Co.

2 This comparison is due to Alan Kay's keynote at OOPSLA'97.

3 We are only concerned here with an Information Management Project. Other kinds of projects are not considered, and it is not known whether the same approach would be viable for them. At the very least, however, a precise and elegant specification of the business domain is needed for any project, not only an information management one (for example, RM-ODP is applicable to any "system", including a human one, and not necessarily to an IT system).

4 Fragments of this specification are a substantial incremental modification of the "satisfaction" business pattern [KS96]. Some ideas about composition (of source and target) have also been reused from [C97].

5 For example, the invariant of a composition states that a composite type corresponds to one or more component types, and a composite instance corresponds to zero or more instances of each component type. There exists at least one property of a composite instance determined by the properties of its component instances. There exists also at least one property of a composite instance independent of the properties of its component instances. The sets of application-specific types for the composite and its components should not be equal. Furthermore, the invariant of an ordered composition states, in addition to the invariant of a composition, that for a pair of component instances in a composition relationship instance, it is possible to define whether one is **before** the other ("for every pair" in the case of a total order, and "for some pairs" in the case of a partial order)..

6 The invariant for a reference relationship states that a maintained type corresponds to one reference type. The existence of a maintained instance implies the following: If a corresponding instance of the reference type exists, then the property values of the instance of the maintained type correspond (i.e., the result of an appropriate Boolean function with properties of the reference and maintained entities as parameters should be TRUE) to the property values of an appropriate version of the corresponding instance of the reference type.

7 "We all know that the only mental tool by means of which a very finite piece of reasoning can cover a myriad of cases is called "abstraction" .... In this connection it might be worthwhile to point out that the purpose of abstracting is not to be vague, but to create a new semantic level in which one can be absolutely precise. ... A byproduct of these investigations ... was the identification of a number of patterns of abstraction that play a vital role in the whole process of composing programs." [D72]

8 "How can one check a routine in the sense of making sure that it is right? In order that the man who checks may not have too difficult a task, the programmer should make a number of definite assertions which can be checked individually and from which the correctness of the whole programme easily follows." [T49]

References

[C97] B.Cohen. Set theory as a semantic framework for object-oriented modeling. In: *Proceedings of the ECOOP'97 Workshop on precise semantics of object-oriented modeling techniques* (Jyväskylä, Finland, 9-13 June 1997), ed. by H.Kilov, B.Rumpe, Munich University of Technology, TUM-I9725, pp. 61-68.

[D01] Charles F. Dunbar. *Chapters on the theory and history of banking.* (Second edition, enlarged and edited by O.M.W.Sprague). G.P.Putnams Sons, New York and London, 1901.

[D63] E W Dijkstra. Some meditations on advanced programming. *Proceedings of the IFIP Congress 1962*, North Holland, 1963, pp. 535-538.

[D65] E W Dijkstra. Programming considered as a human activity. *Proceedings of the IFIP Congress 1965*, Spartan Books, Macmillan and Co, 1965, pp. 213-217.

[D72] E.W.Dijkstra. The humble programmer. Communications of the ACM, Vol. 15, No. 10, 1972, pp. 859-866

[G97] Joseph Goguen. *Semiotic morphisms*. TR-CS97-553, University of California at San Diego, August 1997.

[ISO95a] ISO/IEC JTC1/SC21, Open Distributed Processing - Reference Model: Part 2: Foundations (IS 10746-2 / ITU-T Recommendation X.902, 1995).

[ISO95b] ISO/IEC JTC1/SC21, Information Technology. Open Systems Interconnection - Management Information Services - Structure of Management Information - Part 7: General Relationship Model, 1995. ISO/IEC 10165-7.2.

[ISO95c] ISO/IEC JTC1/SC21. Open Distributed Processing - Reference Model: Part 3: Architecture (ITU-T Recommendation X.903 | ISO/IEC 10746-3).

[KA97] H.Kilov, A.Ash. How to ask questions: Handling complexity in a business specification. In: *Proceedings of the OOPSLA'97 Workshop on object-oriented behavioral semantics* (Atlanta, October 6th, 1997), ed. by H.Kilov, B.Rumpe, I.Simmonds, Munich University of Technology, TUM-I9737, pp. 99-114.

[KA98] H.Kilov, A.Ash. An information management project: what to do when your business specification is ready. In: *Proceedings of the Second ECOOP Workshop on Precise Behavioral Semantics*, Brussels, July 24, 1998 (ed. by H.Kilov and B.Rumpe). Technical University of Munich, TUM-I9813, pp. 95-104.

[KMS96] H.Kilov, H.Mogill, I.Simmonds. Invariants in the trenches. In: *Object-oriented behavioral specifications* (Ed. by H.Kilov and W.Harvey), Kluwer Academic Publishers, 1996, pp. 77-100.

[KR94] Haim Kilov, James Ross. *Information Modeling: an Object-oriented Approach*. Prentice-Hall, Englewood Cliffs, NJ, 1994.

[KS96] Haim Kilov, Ian Simmonds. Business patterns: reusable abstract constructs for business specification. In: *Implementing Systems for Supporting Management Decisions: Concepts, methods and experiences*, Edited by Patrick Humphreys et al, Chapman and Hall, 1996, pp. 225-248.

[KS96a] H.Kilov, I.Simmonds. How to correctly refine business specifications, and know it. In: *Proceedings of the Fifth OOPSLA Workshop on specifications of behavioral semantics (Edited by H.Kilov and V.J.Harvey)*, San Jose, California, 6 October 1996, pp.57-69.

[K99] H.Kilov. *Business specifications: a key to successful software engineering*. Prentice-Hall, 1999.

[L97] Maureen Linaugh-Nean. *Private communication*. June 1997.

[LBR99] Gary T. Leavens, Albert L. Baker, and Clyde Ruby. JML: a Java Modeling Language. *Behavioral Specifications in Businesses and Systems*, Kluwer Academic Publishers, 1999 (ed. by H.Kilov, B.Rumpe, I.Simmonds).

[M97] B.Meyer. *Object-oriented software construction*. Second edition. Prentice-Hall, 1997.

[T49] A.M. Turing. Checking a Large Routine. *Report of a Conference on High Speed Automatic Calculating Machines*, University Mathematical Laboratory, Cambridge, England, June, 1949, pp. 67-69.

About the Authors

Haim Kilov's approach to information modeling has been widely used in industry, especially for business specifications. He described it in his books "Information Modeling" and "Business Specifications" and in many other publications. He has also edited books on behavioral semantics of business and systems, and has been co-chair, proceedings editor, speaker, tutorial presenter and program committee member for many international conferences. He is a subject area editor of *Computer Standards and Interfaces*. He has substantially contributed to several international standards on Open Distributed Processing (RM-ODP and GRM) and to the work of various OMG working groups and task forces.

Haim has over 30 years experience in various areas of information technology. His areas of expertise include business specifications, object-oriented information modeling, semantics (meaning) of specifications, formal specifications in distributed systems, international standards.

Allan Ash has been involved for the past 30 years in a wide range of systems development projects – as programmer, project manager and system architect – utilizing leading edge computer software and engineering techniques as they relate to business applications. Allan's experience includes several years with two major New York banks, followed by many assignments in systems projects ranging from programming message-switching systems to re-engineering an order-entry and billing process. He is co-author of a series of papers describing the practical application of Kilov's Information Modeling approach to building real systems.

Chapter 11

FORMALISING THE UML IN STRUCTURED TEMPORAL THEORIES

Kevin Lano
Dept. of Computing, Imperial College, UK
kcl@doc.ic.ac.uk

Juan Bicarregui
Dept. of Computing, Imperial College, UK
jcb1@doc.ic.ac.uk

Abstract   In this chapter we describe a possible semantics for a large part of the Unified Modelling Notation (UML), using structured theories in a simple temporal logic. This semantic representation is suitable for modular reasoning about UML models. We show how it can be used to clarify certain ambiguous cases of UML semantics, and how to justify enhancement or refinement transformations on UML models.

1. INTRODUCTION

The semantic model of UML used here is based on the set-theoretic Z-based model of Syntropy [CD94]. A mathematical semantic representation of UML models can be given in terms of *theories* in a suitable logic, as in the semantics presented for Syntropy in [BLM97] and VDM^{++} in [L98]. In order to reason about real-time specifications the more general version, Real-time Action Logic (RAL) [L98] will be used.

The semantics developed here should complement and be additional to the UML metamodel and OCL constraints on this defined in [R97].

A RAL theory has the form:

theory *Name*

types *local type symbols*

attributes *time-varying data, representing instance or class variables*

actions *actions which may affect the data, such as operations, statechart transitions and methods*

axioms *logical properties and constraints between the theory elements.*

Theories can be used to represent classes, instances, associations and general submodels of a UML model. These models are interpreted as *specifications*: they describe the features and properties which should be supported by any implementation that satisfies the model. In terms of the semantics, theory S satisfies theory T if there is an interpretation σ of the symbols of T into those of S under which every property of T holds:

$$S \vdash \sigma(\varphi)$$

for every theorem φ of T.

In addition to standard mathematical notation such as $\mathbb{F}$ for "set of finite sets of", etc, RAL theories can use the following notations:

1. For each classifier or state X there is an attribute $\overline{X} : \mathbb{F}(X)$ denoting the set of existing instances of X^1.

2. If α is an action symbol, and P a predicate, then $[\alpha]P$ is a predicate which means "every execution of α establishes P on termination", that is, P is a *postcondition* of α.

3. For every action α there are functions $\uparrow(\alpha, i)$, $\downarrow(\alpha, i)$, $\leftarrow(\alpha, i)$ and $\rightarrow(\alpha, i)$ of $i : \mathbb{N}_1$ which denote the activation, termination, request send and request arrival times, respectively, of the i-th invocation of α. These times are ordered as:

$$\leftarrow(\alpha, i) \leq \rightarrow(\alpha, i) \leq \uparrow(\alpha, i) \leq \downarrow(\alpha, i)$$

Also

$$i \leq j \Rightarrow \leftarrow(\alpha, i) \leq \leftarrow(\alpha, j)$$

Using these we can define concepts such as "every execution of α coincides with an execution of β" (α calls β):

$$\begin{aligned}
\alpha \supset \beta \equiv \\
\forall i : \mathbb{N}_1 \cdot \exists j : \mathbb{N}_1 \cdot \\
\uparrow(\alpha, i) = \uparrow(\beta, j) \wedge \downarrow(\alpha, i) = \downarrow(\beta, j)
\end{aligned}$$

We can also define the times that a given condition G becomes true or false for the i-th time: $\clubsuit(G := true, i)$ and $\clubsuit(G := false, i)$, for $i : \mathbb{N}_1$. Temporal operators $\diamond$ (sometime in the future), $\square$ (always in the future) and $\bigcirc$ (next) are also included.

Although for the sake of conciseness we will use Z-style notation for set comprehension, set unions, etc [S92], the OCL [R97] notation could be used instead. A systematic translation of OCL notation into Z is given in [LB98]. This produces Z predicates from OCL expressions.

Temporal logic makes representation and reasoning about dynamic models (state machines, interaction diagrams, etc) more concise than using a formalism such as pure Z. However it would be possible to work just in Z, by using sequences of states to represent the allowed behaviours of objects over time.

We focus on some areas where formalisation helps to clarify the meaning and consequences of certain UML constructs: aggregation, qualification, statecharts and collaboration diagrams.

2. OBJECT MODELS

A UML class C is represented as a theory of the form given in Figure 11.1. Each

---

theory Γ_C

types C

attributes
$\quad \overline{C} : \mathbb{F}(C)$
$\quad self : C \to C$
$\quad att_1 : C \to T_1$
$\quad \ldots$

actions
$\quad create_C(c : C) \quad \{\overline{C}\}$
$\quad kill_C(c : C) \quad \{\overline{C}\}$
$\quad op_1(c : C, x : X_1) : Y_1$
$\quad \ldots$

axioms

$$\forall c : C \cdot$$
$$self(c) = c \ \wedge$$
$$[create_C(c)](c \in \overline{C}) \ \wedge$$
$$[kill_C(c)](c \notin \overline{C})$$

Figure 11.1 Theory of Class C

---

instance attribute $att_i : T_i$ of C gains an additional parameter of type C in the class theory Γ_C and similarly for operations[2]. Class attributes and actions do not gain the additional C parameter as they are independent of any particular instance. We can denote $att(a)$ for attribute att of instance a by the standard OO notation $a.att$, and similarly denote actions $act(a, x)$ by $a!act(x)$.

Similarly each binary association lr can be interpreted in a theory which contains an attribute $\overline{lr}$ representing the current extent of the association (the set of pairs in it) and actions add_link and $delete\_link$ to add and remove pairs (links) from this set. Axioms define the cardinality of the association ends and other properties of the association. In particular, if ab is an association between classes A and B, then $\overline{ab} \subseteq \overline{A} \times \overline{B}$, so membership of $\overline{ab}$ implies existence for elements of a link.

More general n-ary associations can be transformed into n binary associations together with a new class and logical constraints [GR98].

Subclasses S of a class C may be static (ie, once an object is created as a member of S it remains in S for the rest of its life in C):

$$\forall a : C \cdot a \in \overline{S} \;\Rightarrow\; \Box(a \in \overline{C} \Rightarrow a \in \overline{S})$$

This axiom is omitted for states S in a statechart, or for dynamic subclasses. $\Box P$ means that P is true at the present time and always in the future.

2.1   AGGREGATION

There are two main forms of aggregation in UML: simple aggregation, represented by an open diamond at the 'whole' end of the aggregation between classes, and composition aggregation, represented by a filled diamond at the 'whole' end, or by physical containment of the part classes or model elements within the whole, as in Fusion [CABDGHJ94].

Simple aggregation is limited only by the constraint that there cannot be aggregation symbols at both ends of an association. It may also be reasonable to assume that a simple aggregation cannot be reflexive at the instance level:

$$\forall a : A \cdot \neg \left((a,a) \in \overline{r}\right)$$

where r is an aggregation from A to A.

In [R97] a semantics is suggested for composition aggregation, which we will formalise as follows, using ideas from [CD94]. If there is a composition aggregation ab from a whole class A to a part class B, then:

1. parts b cannot be deleted or removed from a whole object a, whilst a continues to exist:

$$(a,b) \in \overline{ab} \;\Rightarrow\; \Box(a \in \overline{A} \;\Rightarrow\; (a,b) \in \overline{ab})$$

2. parts b cannot be moved from one whole to another:

$$(a,b) \in \overline{ab} \;\wedge\; \Diamond((a',b) \in \overline{ab}) \;\Rightarrow\; a' = a$$

$\Diamond P$ means that P is true at the present time or at some time in the future.

Together, these properties mean that a whole may gain new parts but cannot lose or exchange existing parts.

Transitivity of composition.   Two composition aggregations can be put together to produce a third one (Figure 11.2) because

$$(a,c) \in \overline{ab};\ \overline{bc} \;\Rightarrow\; \exists b : B \cdot (a,b) \in \overline{ab} \wedge (b,c) \in \overline{bc}$$

$((1) \Rightarrow (2))$ and

$$\Diamond((a',c) \in \overline{ab};\ \overline{bc}) \;\Rightarrow\; \Diamond(\exists b' : B \cdot (a',b') \in \overline{ab} \wedge (b',c) \in \overline{bc})$$

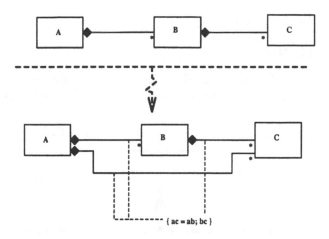

Figure 11.2   Transitivity of Composition Aggregations

$((3) \Rightarrow (4))$. But then $(1) \wedge (3)$ implies $(2) \wedge (4)$, so by 2 applied to b, c we have $b' = b$. Therefore, applying 2 to a, b we have $a' = a$ as required.

Also if $(a, c) \in \overline{ab}; \overline{bc}$ then $\exists b : \overline{B} \cdot (a, b) \in \overline{ab} \wedge (b, c) \in \overline{bc}$ and hence $\exists b : \overline{B} \cdot \Box(a \in \overline{A} \Rightarrow (a, b) \in \overline{ab}) \wedge \Box(b \in \overline{B} \Rightarrow (b, c) \in \overline{bc})$.   But then $\exists b : \overline{B} \cdot \Box(a \in \overline{A} \Rightarrow (a, b) \in \overline{ab} \wedge (b, c) \in \overline{bc})$ as required for 2.

An alternative interpretation of UML aggregation is described in [LE99] and a similar property derived for this semantics.

Moving Associations into Aggregates.   Another valid transformation on composition aggregations is to move an association between two part classes into the aggregation (Figure 11.3). This is a valid transformation because the new model has the extra

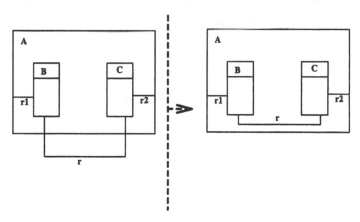

Figure 11.3   Moving Associations into Aggregates

axiom

$$\forall (b, c) \in \overline{r} \cdot \exists a : \overline{A} \cdot (a, b) \in \overline{r_1} \wedge (a, c) \in \overline{r_2}$$

In other words, r can only relate parts of the same aggregate.

2.2   QUALIFIERS

We could consider qualification as an abbreviation of a particular form of association class (Figure 11.4). That is, the qualification means that each $a : A$ has a number x of

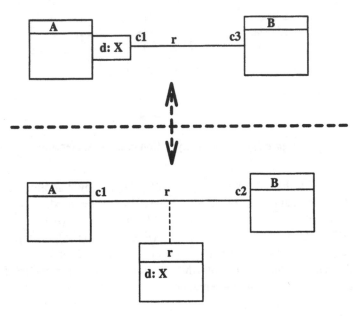

Figure 11.4   Qualification as Association Classes

$b : B$ elements associated with it, where $x \in c_2$:

$$\forall a : \overline{A} \cdot card(\{b : \overline{B} \mid (a,b) \in \overline{r}\}) \in c_2$$

and

$$\forall a : \overline{A}; \; x : X \cdot card(\{b : \overline{B} \mid (a,b) \in \overline{r} \land d(a,b) = x\}) \in c_3$$

so there is a function $f : \overline{A} \times X \to \mathbb{P}(\overline{B})$ where each $f(a, x)$ has cardinality in the set c_3.

   This equivalence means that a valid transformation is to introduce the qualification instead of the explicit association class – this is a useful transformation if c_3 is more restrictive (strictly smaller as a set) than c_2.

   The stronger interpretation suggested in [R97] would require the additional constraint

$$\forall b : \overline{B}; \; a_1, a_2 : \overline{A}; \; x_1, x_2 : X \cdot$$
$$d(a_1, b) = x_1 \land d(a_2, b) = x_2 \land (a_1, b) \in \overline{r} \land (a_2, b) \in \overline{r} \Rightarrow$$
$$a_1 = a_2 \land x_1 = x_2$$

in the association class version for the two models of Figure 11.4 to be equivalent. c_1 could then be taken as $0 .. 1$.

3. STATECHARTS

A statechart specification of the behaviour of instances of a class C can be formalised as an extension of the class theory of C, as follows.

1. Each state S is represented in the same manner as a subclass of C, and in general, nesting of state S_1 in state S_2 is expressed by axioms $S_1 \subseteq S_2$ and $\overline{S_1} \subseteq \overline{S_2}$ as for class generalisation.

2. Each transition in the statechart and each event for which the statechart defines a response yields a distinct action symbol. Each event e is the abstract generalisation of the actions $t_1, \ldots, t_n$ representing its transitions:

$$\forall a : C \cdot a!t_1 \supset a!e \land \ \ldots \ \land a!t_n \supset a!e$$

3. The axiom for the effect of a transition t from state S_1 to state S_2 with label

$$e(x)[G]/Post \frown Act$$

where G is the guard condition and $Post$ is some postcondition constraint on the resulting state, is

$$\forall a : C \cdot a.G \land a \in \overline{S_1} \ \Rightarrow \ [a!t(x)](a.Post \land a \in \overline{S_2})$$

4. The transition only occurs if the trigger event e occurs whilst the object is in the correct state:

$$\forall a : C \cdot a \in \overline{S_1} \land a.G \ \Rightarrow \ (a!e(x) \supset a!t(x))$$

We assume that distinct transitions from the same source state have non-overlapping guard conditions.

5. The generated asynchronous actions must occur at some future time (after t has occurred):

$$a!t(x) \ \Rightarrow \ \bigcirc \diamond (a!Act_1 \land \diamond(\ldots \diamond a!Act_m) \ldots)$$

where Act is a list $Act_1 \frown \ldots \frown Act_m$ of action invocations on objects associated to a.

Transitions γ with labels of the form $after(t)$ from source state S have an alternative axiom 4 defining their triggering, which asserts that they are triggered t time units after the most recent entry time $\clubsuit((a \in \overline{S}) := true, j)$ to state S [L97].

Likewise, automatic transitions α from a state S execute as soon as the activity of that state terminates.

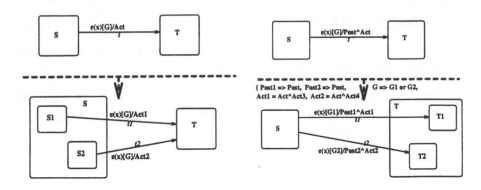

Figure 11.5   Source and Target Splitting of Transition

Source Splitting.   This transformation (Figure 11.5) can be justified in our semantics as follows.

The translation morphism σ from the old to the new model is:

$$\overline{S} \longmapsto \overline{S_1} \cup \overline{S_2}$$
$$t \longmapsto t_1 \sqcap t_2$$

$t \sqcap t'$ denotes the binary choice between two actions t and t'.

Axioms 1 of the new model are $\overline{S_1} \subseteq \overline{S}$ and $\overline{S_2} \subseteq \overline{S}$, which are additional to the existing axioms of the old model.

Axioms 2 of the new model are (for each object)

$$t_1 \supset e \,\wedge\, t_2 \supset e$$

Together these establish that $t_1 \sqcap t_2 \supset e$ as required.

Axioms 3 of the new model are

$$(\forall a : C \cdot a.G \wedge a \in \overline{S_1} \;\Rightarrow\; [a!t_1(x)](a.Post_1 \wedge a \in \overline{T})) \;\wedge$$
$$(\forall a : C \cdot a.G \wedge a \in \overline{S_2} \;\Rightarrow\; [a!t_2(x)](a.Post_2 \wedge a \in \overline{T}))$$

These imply the translation under σ of the axiom 3 of the old model because

$$a.G \wedge \sigma(a \in \overline{S}) \;\Rightarrow$$
$$a.G \wedge (a \in \overline{S_1} \vee a \in \overline{S_2}) \;\Rightarrow$$
$$[a!t_1(x)](a.Post_1 \wedge a \in \overline{T}) \;\vee\; [a!t_2(x)](a.Post_2 \wedge a \in \overline{T})$$

But by axiom 4 of the new model, $a!e(x) \supset a!t_1(x)$ in the first case where $a \in \overline{S_1}$, so, by the property $(\alpha \supset \beta) \Rightarrow ([\beta]P \Rightarrow [\alpha]P)$ of $\supset$ we have $[a!e(x)](a.Post_1 \wedge a \in \overline{T})$ in the first case (ie, if $a \in \overline{S_1}$).

But we already know that $t_1 \sqcap t_2 \supset e$, so $[a!(t_1 \sqcap t_2)(x)](a.Post_1 \wedge a \in \overline{T})$ in the first case, and hence, since $Post_1 \Rightarrow Post$, we have $[a!(t_1 \sqcap t_2)(x)](a.Post \wedge a \in \overline{T})$.

By similar reasoning the same holds in the second case. But this means the conclusion is exactly σ of the conclusion of axiom 3 of the original model for e, as required.

Axioms 4 in the new model are:

$$a \in \overline{S_1} \wedge a.G \Rightarrow (a!e(x) \supset a!t_1(x))$$
$$a \in \overline{S_2} \wedge a.G \Rightarrow (a!e(x) \supset a!t_2(x))$$

But because $t_1 \supset t_1 \sqcap t_2$ and $t_2 \supset t_1 \sqcap t_2$, this means that $a!e(x) \supset a!(t_1 \sqcap t_2)(x)$ in both cases, which establishes the translation of axiom 4 of the old model.

Target Splitting. Dual to source splitting, we can replace a single transition t from S to T by two or more transitions for the same event which go to distinct substates of T in particular cases, and may have additional postconditions and generations (left hand side of Figure 11.5).

The refinement mapping in this case is that $\overline{T}$ is interpreted by $\overline{T_1} \cup \overline{T_2}$, and t by $t_1 \sqcap t_2$.

As for source splitting, it is trivial that axioms 1 and 2 of the old model are validated by the new model. For axioms 3:

$$a.G \wedge a \in \overline{S} \Rightarrow$$
$$(a.G_1 \vee a.G_2) \wedge a \in \overline{S}$$

In the case that G_1 holds, we have:

$$[a!t_1(x)](a.Post_1 \wedge a \in \overline{T_1})$$

so by axioms 4 in the new model

$$[a!e(x)](a.Post_1 \wedge a \in \overline{T_1})$$

and by axioms 2 (that $t_1 \sqcap t_2 \supset e$), we therefore have

$$[a!(t_1 \sqcap t_2)(x)](a.Post \wedge a \in \overline{T})$$

as required, since $Post_1 \Rightarrow Post$.

But the same holds in the case that G_2 holds, so the axiom 3 for t is valid in the new model.

Axioms 4 in the new model are:

$$a \in \overline{S} \wedge a.G_1 \Rightarrow (a!e(x) \supset a!t_1(x))$$
$$a \in \overline{S} \wedge a.G_2 \Rightarrow (a!e(x) \supset a!t_2(x))$$

But $G \Rightarrow G_1 \vee G_2$, and $t_1 \supset t_1 \sqcap t_2$, etc, so the interpretation of axiom 4 of the old model is also valid here.

Similarly for axiom 5.

4. SEQUENCE DIAGRAMS

There is a mechanical translation of sequence diagrams into assertions on the sending times $\leftarrow(m, i)$ of the i-th instance of a message m, the arrival times $\rightarrow(m, i)$ of this message instance, and the initiation $\uparrow(m, i)$ and termination $\downarrow(m, i)$ times of this message instance.

For example, Figure 11.6 translates to the following assertions, where each message execution lifeline is interpreted by a particular message instance:

$$\forall i : \mathbb{N}_1 \cdot \exists j, k, l, l' : \mathbb{N}_1 \cdot$$
$$\rightarrow(Op, i) = \uparrow(create_{C1}(ob1), l)$$
$$\downarrow(create_{C1}(ob1), l) \leq \leftarrow(ob3!bar(x), j) = \rightarrow(ob3!bar(x), j)$$
$$\leq \leftarrow(ob4!do(w), k) = \rightarrow(ob4!do(w), k)$$
$$\downarrow(ob4!do(w), k) \leq \downarrow(ob3!bar(x), j)$$
$$\leq \downarrow(kill_{C1}(ob1), l') = \downarrow(Op, i)$$

These assertions can then be checked for consistency against detailed implementation level statecharts.

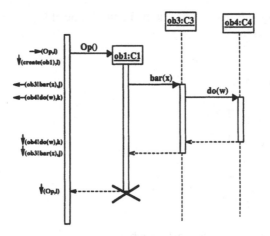

Figure 11.6   Example Sequence Diagram with Annotations

5.   COLLABORATION DIAGRAMS

The interaction elements of collaboration diagrams can also be interpreted as constraints on (generic) instances of objects and action invocations. Each message label in an interaction corresponds to a particular invocation instance of an action on an object. For example, a message $label_1 : m_1(x_1)$ sent to object obj_1 yields the association of $label_1$ to an invocation instance $(obj_1!m_1(x_1), i_1)$ for some $i_1 : \mathbb{N}_1$. The lexicographical ordering of labels determines the ordering of the executions of these invocation instances:

1. If $label_2 : m_2(x_2)$ sent to object obj_2 is an immediate successor of the $label_1$ message, ie: $label_1 = label.x[Name]$ for some integer x and optional string $[Name]$, and $label_2 = label.y[Name']$ where $y > x$, then the sending of $(obj_2!m_2(x_2), i_2)$ strictly succeeds that of $(obj_1!m_1(x_1), i_1)$:

$$\leftarrow(obj_1!m_1(x_1), i_1) < \leftarrow(obj_2!m_2(x_2), i_2)$$

If the first message send is synchronous, then the second send cannot occur until the first action instance has terminated:

$$\downarrow(obj_1!m_1(x_1), i_1) \leq \leftarrow(obj_2!m_2(x_2), i_2)$$

2. If the *label*$_1$ message is the immediate caller of a set of messages including *label*$_2$, ie, *label*$_2$ has the form *label*$_1$.*x*[*Name*] for integer *x* and optional string [*Name*], then if the *label*$_1$ message has procedural control flow (filled solid arrowhead), then the *label*$_2$ message must terminate before the *label*$_1$ message:

$$\uparrow(obj_1!m_1(x_1), i_1) \leq \leftarrow(obj_2!m_2(x_2), i_2) \land$$
$$\downarrow(obj_2!m_2(x_2), i_2) \leq \downarrow(obj_1!m_1(x_1), i_1)$$

However if the control flow of *label*$_1$ is asynchronous or flat (half stick or stick arrowheads), then the second constraint is replaced by:

$$\downarrow(obj_1!m_1(x_1), i_1) \leq \leftarrow(obj_2!m_2(x_2), i_2)$$

That is, the calling message terminates (at least from the viewpoint of the caller) before the subordinate messages are sent.

Synchronisation constraints place additional restrictions on the start time of messages. If we have a message *label*$_1$/*label* : $m(x)$ sent to *obj*, then this message cannot commence until the message labelled by *label*$_1$ has terminated:

$$\downarrow(obj_1!m_1(x_1), i_1) \leq \leftarrow(obj!m(x), i)$$

If we assume that the interaction diagram indicates the expected processing to be carried out for *every* invocation of a calling message (rather than just providing an *example* of what might happen), then for each calling message index i we can assert the existence of appropriate indices for the subordinate messages. In addition, for conditional messages, the condition must be true at the time the message is sent. For example, Figure 11.7 is formalised as:

$$\forall i : \mathbb{N}_1 \cdot \exists i_1 : \mathbb{N}_1 \cdot$$
$$(\uparrow(obj!m(x), i) \leq \leftarrow(obj_1!m_1(x), i_1) \land$$
$$(x > 0) \odot \leftarrow (obj_1!m_1(x), i_1) \land$$
$$\downarrow(obj_1!m_1(x), i_1) \leq \downarrow(obj!m(x), i)) \lor$$
$$(\uparrow(obj!m(x), i) \leq \leftarrow(obj_2!m_2(x), i_1) \land$$
$$(x \leq 0) \odot \leftarrow (obj_2!m_2(x), i_1) \land$$
$$\downarrow(obj_2!m_2(x), i_1) \leq \downarrow(obj!m(x), i))$$

$P \odot t$ denotes that P holds at time t. Time labels can be placed on message arrows as for sequence diagrams. The label A at the tail of a message arrow indicates the send time $A = \leftarrow(obj!m(x), i)$ of the corresponding message instance. The corresponding dashed label A' denotes the receive time of this message.

In the case that all message sends in an interaction are procedural, then in principle this semantic representation can be simplified by translating the interaction into an

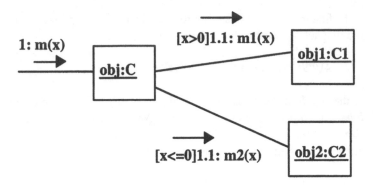

Figure 11.7   Example Conditional Interaction

abstract pseudocode using composite actions such as α; β (sequential composition), *if e then α else β* (conditionals), *for all* (unordered iteration), etc.

The semantics of sequence and interaction diagrams are defined in a similar way. Indeed there is considerable overlap in the expressiveness of these diagrams, suggesting that they may not be optimal choices for models of dynamic behaviour. A unified notation using timing annotations on interaction diagrams as proposed in [AW96] may be preferable in respect of eliminating redundancy.

6.   RELATIONSHIP WITH OTHER WORK

Representation of UML semantics in Z has been developed in [EFLR98]. This representation is a formalisation of the UML metamodel, whilst our approach shows how to associate theories to specific UML models. The set-theoretic models are similar: [EFLR98] represents each class by a set of instances, and each association by a set of links consisting of object tuples, as in this paper. Our notion of theory satisfaction agrees with the $\models$ relationship of [EFLR98]: if $\sigma : \Gamma \to \Gamma'$ is a theory interpretation then every model M of Γ' has a *reduct* $M' = M_\sigma$ of Γ with the interpretation $[\![\,\overline{C}\,]\!]_{M'}$ of the extension of classes C of Γ in M' being defined as $[\![\,\overline{\sigma(C)}\,]\!]_M$. But this means that $\Gamma' \models \Gamma$ in the terms of [EFLR98].

It is trivial to show that simple transformations such as adding a class or association *are* theory extensions in our formalism. Our approach has been chosen to simplify the task of proving transformations correct, but could be further formalised and generalised by using the Z semantics given in [EFLR98].

7.   CONCLUSIONS

We have proposed an axiomatic semantics of the UML notation, together with examples where this semantics helps to clarify issues of the meaning of UML constructs. Other areas which we have addressed elsewhere include dynamic classification (page 69 of [R97]), the meaning of interface specifications and the interpretation of OCL in conventional mathematical notation [LB98].

Notes

1. Alternative notation for $\overline{X}$ is $ext(X)$, the *extension* of X [WJS93].

2. The class theory can be generated from a theory of a typical C instance by means of an A-morphism [BLM97].

References

[AW96]   C Atkinson and M Weisskopf. An approach to process description using FUSION. In *Object-oriented Development at Work: The FUSION Method in the Real World*. Prentice Hall, 1996.

[BLM97]   J C Bicarregui, K C Lano, and T S E Maibaum. Objects, associations and subsystems: a hierarchical approach to encapsulation. In *ECOOP 97*, LNCS. Springer-Verlag, 1997.

[CABDGHJ94]   D Coleman, P Arnold, S Bodoff, C Dollin, H Gilchrist, F Hayes, and P Jeremaes. *Object-oriented Development: The FUSION Method*. Prentice Hall Object-oriented Series, 1994.

[CD94]   S Cook and J Daniels. *Designing Object Systems: Object-Oriented Modelling with Syntropy*. Prentice Hall, September 1994.

[R97]   Rational Software et al. UML documentation set version 1.1, http://www.rational.com/uml, 1997.

[EFLR98]   A Evans, R France, K Lano, and B Rumpe. The UML as a formal modelling notation, 1998.

[GR98]   M Gogolla and M Richters. Equivalence rules for UML class diagrams. In *UML 98*, 1998.

[L97]   K Lano. Transformations on syntropy and UML models, 1997. Technical Report, "Formal Underpinnings for Object Technology" project, Dept. of Computing, Imperial College.

[L98]   K Lano. Logical specification of reactive and real-time systems. *Journal of Logic and Computation*, 8(5):679–711, 1998.

[LB98]   K Lano and J Bicarregui. UML refinement and abstraction transformations. In *ROOM 2 Workshop*. Bradford University, 1998.

[LE99]   K Lano and A Evans. Verification of uml models, 1999. Technical Report, "Formal Underpinnings for Object Technology" project, Dept. of Computing, Imperial College.

[S92]   M Spivey. *The Z Notation: A Reference Manual*. Prentice Hall, 1992.

[WJS93]   R Wieringa, W de Jonge, and P Spruit. Roles and dynamic subclasses: A model logic approach. Technical report, IS-CORE report, Faculty of Mathematics and Computer Science, Vrije Universiteit, Amsterdam, 1993.

About the Authors

Kevin Lano. Dr Lano has carried out research and development using formal methods both in industry and academia. He is the author of "Formal Object-oriented

Development" (Springer, 1995) and "The B Language and Method" (Springer, 1996). His current research is on the integration of formal methods and safety analysis techniques, and on the formalisation of UML.

Juan Bicarregui. has a BSc and MSc in Mathematics from Imperial College and Queen Mary College, London and a PhD in Computer Science from the University of Manchester.

His research interests are in the technology transfer of formal software engineering techniques to industry through firstly, the application of formal techniques to practical software development with particular emphasis on the comparison and assessment of different approaches with a view to their effective integration; and secondly, the formalisation of techniques which are already established in industry.

These two strands of work are undertaken through positions as senior researcher at the Rutherford Appleton Laboratory and research fellow at Imperial College.

Chapter 12

JML:
A NOTATION FOR DETAILED DESIGN

Gary T. Leavens, Albert L. Baker, and Clyde Ruby

Department of Computer Science, Iowa State University
226 Atanasoff Hall, Ames, Iowa USA 50011-1040
leavens@cs.iastate.edu, baker@cs.iastate.edu, ruby@cs.iastate.edu

Abstract   JML is a behavioral interface specification language tailored to Java. It is designed to be written and read by working software engineers, and should require only modest mathematical training. It uses Eiffel-style syntax combined with model-based semantics, as in VDM and Larch. JML supports quantifiers, specification-only variables, and other enhancements that make it more expressive for specification than Eiffel and easier to use than VDM and Larch.

1.   BEHAVIORAL INTERFACE SPECIFICATION

JML [LBR99], which stands for "Java Modeling Language," is a behavioral interface specification language (BISL) [W87] designed to specify Java [AG98, GJS96] modules. Java *modules* are classes and interfaces.

A *behavioral interface specification* describes both the details of a module's interface with clients, and its behavior from the client's point of view. Such specifications are not good for the specification of whole programs, but are good for recording detailed design decisions or documentation of intended behavior, for a software module.

The goal of this chapter is to explain JML and the concepts behind its approach to specification. Since JML is used in detailed design of Java modules, we use the detailed design of an interface and class for priority queues as an example. The rest of this section explains interfaces and behavioral interface specification. In the next section we describe how to specify new types as conceptual models for detailed design. Following that we finish the example by giving the details of a class specification. We conclude after mentioning some other features of JML.

1.1   INTERFACES

A module's *interface* consists of its name, and the names and types of its fields and methods. Java interfaces declare such interface information, but class declarations

```
package edu.iastate.cs.jml.docs.kluwer;
public interface PriorityQueueUser {
 public /*@ pure: @*/ boolean contains(Object argID);
 public /*@ pure: @*/ Object next() throws PQException;
 public void remove(Object argID);
}
```

Figure 12.1 The JML specification of the Java interface named `PriorityQueueUser` (file `PriorityQueueUser.java-refined`).

do as well. As in the Larch family of BISLs [GHG⁺93, L98, W87, W90], interface information in JML is declared using the declaration syntax of the programming language to which the BISL is tailored; thus, JML uses Java declaration syntax.

An example is given in Figure 12.1. This example gives the information a Java program needs to use a `PriorityQueueUser` object, including the package to which it belongs, the accessibility of the methods (`public`), the names of the methods, the types of their arguments and results, and what exceptions they can throw.

Also included in Figure 12.1 are two annotations. These annotations are enclosed within annotation comments of the form `/*@ ... @*/`; one can also write annotation comments using the form `//@`, and such comments extend to the end of the corresponding line. Java ignores both kinds of annotation comments, but they are significant to JML. The annotations on the methods `next` and `contains` require both methods to be `pure`, meaning that they cannot have any externally-visible side effects.

1.2   BEHAVIORAL SPECIFICATION: A FIRST EXAMPLE

In JML, behavioral specification information is also given in the form of annotations. As in the Larch approach, such specifications are model-based. That is, they are stated in terms of a mathematical model [GHG⁺93, H72, W83, W87] of the states (or values) of objects. Unlike most Larch-style specification languages, however, in JML such models are described by declaring *model fields*, which are only used for purposes of specification. In JML, a declaration can include the modifier `model:`, which means that the declaration need not appear in a correct implementation; all non-model declarations must appear in a correct implementation.

As an example, we can specify a model for priority queues as in Figure 12.2. This specification is a refinement of the one given in Figure 12.1, which is why the `refine:` clause appears in the specification following the `package` declaration. The meaning of the `refine:` clause is that the given specification adds to the one in the file named, by imposing additional constraints on that specification. Such a refinement might be done, for example, when one is starting to make detailed design decisions or when starting to specify the behavior of existing software modules. In a refinement, existing specification information is inherited; that is, the method declarations in the interface `PriorityQueueUser` are inherited, and thus not repeated in Figure 12.2.

Following the `refine:` clause is a `model: import` declaration. This has the effect like a Java `import` declaration for JML, but the use of `model:` means that the

```
package edu.iastate.cs.jml.docs.kluwer;

//@ refine: "PriorityQueueUser.java-refined";
//@ model: import edu.iastate.cs.jml.models.*;

public interface PriorityQueueUser {

  //@ public model: JMLValueSet entries
  //@        initially entries != null && entries.isEmpty();

  //@ public invariant: entries != null
  //@     && \forall (JMLType e) [entries.has(e) ==>
  //@                             e instanceof QueueEntry];
  //@ public invariant:
  //@    \forall (QueueEntry e1) [
  //@       entries.has(e1) ==>
  //@         \forall (QueueEntry e2) [
  //@           entries.has(e2) && !(e1.equals(e2)) ==>
  //@             e2.iD != e1.iD
  //@             && e2.timeStamp != e1.timeStamp ] ];
}
```

Figure 12.2 A specification of a mathematical model for `PriorityQueueUser` (file `PriorityQueueUser-model.java-refined`).

import does not have to appear in an implementation, as it is only needed for specification purposes. The package being imported, `edu.iastate.cs.jml.models`, consists of several pure classes including sets, sequences, relations, maps, and so on, which are useful in behavioral specification. These fill the role of the built-in types used for specification in VDM and Z, or the traits used in Larch. Since they are pure (side-effect free) classes, they can be used in assertions without affecting the state of the computation, which allows assertions to have a well-defined mathematical meaning (unlike Eiffel's assertions). However, since they are Java classes, their methods are invoked using the usual Java syntax.

In Figure 12.2, we use the class `JMLValueSet` as the type of the model field `entries`. That is, for purposes of specification, we imagine that every object that implements the interface `PriorityQueueUser` has a public field `entries` of type `JMLValueSet`. This model field appears (to clients) to have started out initially as empty, as stated in the `initially` clause attached to its declaration [OSWZ94, M94].

The two `invariant:` clauses further describe the intended state of `entries`. The first states that it is not null, and that all of its elements have type `QueueEntry`. The `\forall` notation is an addition to the Java syntax for expressions; it gives universal quantification over the declared variables. The `==>` notation is another addition that means logical implication. The second invariant states that every such `QueueEntry` object has a unique `iD` and `timeStamp`.

In Figure 12.3 we make yet another refinement, to specify the behavior of the methods of `PriorityQueueUser`. This specification, because it refines the specification of Figure 12.2, inherits the model fields specified there, as well as the `initially` and `invariant`: clauses. (Inheritance of specifications is explained further below.)

The specification of `contains` shows the simplest form of a behavioral specification for a method: an interface followed by a single `normal_behavior`: clause. This specification says that the method returns true just when its argument is non-null and is the same as some object in the queue. The `normal_behavior`: clause in this specification consists of a single `ensures`: clause. This `ensures`: clause gives the method's total-correctness postcondition; that is, calls to `contains` must terminate (as opposed to looping forever or aborting) in a state that satisfies the postcondition. The use of `normal_behavior`: prohibits throwing exceptions as well. The meaning of `&&` and `==` are as in Java; that is, `&&` is short-circuit logical conjunction, and `e.iD == argID` means that `e.iD` and `argID` are the same object. The keyword `\result` denotes the return value of the method, which in this case is a boolean. The operator `<==>` means "if and only if"; it is equivalent to `==` for booleans, but has a lower precedence. The notation `\exists` is used for existential quantification.

The specification of the method `next` shows one way to specify methods with exceptions in JML. This uses a `normal_behavior`: clause for the case where no exceptions are thrown, and an `exceptional_behavior`: clause for when exceptions are thrown. The semantics is that a correct implementation must satisfy both of these behaviors [LB99, W94, W83]. In the specification of `next`, the `exceptional_behavior`: states that an instance of the `PQException` class (not shown here) must be thrown when `entries` is empty. The `requires`: clause gives a precondition for that case, and when it is true, the method must terminate (in this case by throwing an exception), as that case's postcondition must be satisfied.

The normal behavior of `next` must be obeyed when its precondition is true; that is, when `entries` is not empty. The normal behavior's postcondition says that `next` returns an object with the lowest timestamp in the highest priority level.

It would, of course, be possible to only specify the normal behavior for `next`. If this were done, then implementations could just assume the precondition of the normal behavior—that `entries` is not empty. That would be an appropriate design for clients that can be trusted, and might permit more efficient implementation. The given specification is appropriate for untrusted clients [M92a, M97].

The specification `remove` uses case analysis [LB99, W94, W83] in the specification of normal behavior. The two cases are separated by the keyword `also`:, and each must be obeyed when its precondition is true. The first case contains a `modifiable`: clause. This is a frame condition [BMR95]; it states that only the fields mentioned (and any on which they depend [L95b, L95a]) can have their values initialized or changed; no other fields or objects can be modified. Omitting the `modifiable`: clause means that no storage can be modified. Note that the precondition uses the method `contains`, which is permitted because it is pure.

The most interesting thing about the specification of `remove` is that it uses the JML reserved word `\old`. As in Eiffel, the meaning of `\old(E)` is as if E were evaluated in the pre-state and that value is used in place of `\old(E)` in the assertion.

```
package edu.iastate.cs.jml.docs.kluwer;
//@ refine: "PriorityQueueUser-model.java-refined";
//@ model: import edu.iastate.cs.jml.models.*;
public interface PriorityQueueUser {

  public /*@ pure: @*/ boolean contains(Object argID);
  //@ normal_behavior:
  //@    ensures: \result <==>
  //@             argID != null
  //@             && \exists (QueueEntry e) [
  //@                    entries.has(e) && e.iD == argID];

  public /*@ pure: @*/ Object next() throws PQException;
  //@ normal_behavior:
  //@    requires: !entries.isEmpty();
  //@    ensures:
  //@       \exists(QueueEntry r) [
  //@              entries.has(r) && \result == r.iD
  //@           && \forall (QueueEntry o) [
  //@               entries.has(o) && !(r.equals(o)) ==>
  //@                   r.priorityLevel >= o.priorityLevel
  //@                   && r.timeStamp < o.timeStamp ] ];
  //@ exceptional_behavior:
  //@    requires: entries.isEmpty();
  //@    ensures: \throws(PQException);

  public void remove(Object argID);
  //@ normal_behavior:
  //@    requires: argID != null && contains(argID);
  //@    modifiable: entries;
  //@    ensures: \exists (QueueEntry e) [
  //@             \old(entries.has(e)) && e.iD == argID
  //@             && entries.equals(\old(entries.remove(e)))]];
  //@ also:
  //@    requires: argID == null || !contains(argID);
  //@    ensures: \unmodified(entries);
}
```

Figure 12.3 A JML specification of the Java interface named PriorityQueueUser (file PriorityQueueUser.java).

While we have broken up the specification of PriorityQueueUser into three pieces, that was done partly to demonstrate refinement and partly so that each piece would fit on a page. In common use, this specification would be written in one file.

2.   SPECIFYING NEW PURE MODEL TYPES

JML comes with a suite of pure types, implemented as Java classes, that can be used as conceptual models in detailed design. As mentioned above, these are found in the package edu.iastate.cs.jml.models.

Users can also create their own pure types, by giving a class or interface the pure: modifier. Since these types are to be treated as purely immutable values in specifications, they must pass certain conservative checks that make sure there is no possibility of observable side-effects from using such objects.

Model classes should also be pure, since, in JML, the use of non-pure methods in an assertion is a type error. However, the modifiers model: and pure: are orthogonal, and thus one must list both of them when declaring a pure model class.

An example of a pure model class is the class QueueEntry, specified in Figure 12.4. Since it is a model class, it need not be implemented, but is used only for specification purposes. Since it is pure, none of its methods can permit side-effects. It is written in a .jml file, and that filename suffix tells JML that it consists solely of annotations; in effect, the entire file is ignored by Java but is significant to JML. The class QueueEntry has three public fields iD, priorityLevel, and timeStamp. The invariant clause states that the iD field cannot be null in a client-visible state.

The specification of the constructor follows the invariant. The constructor takes three arguments and initializes the fields from them. The precondition of this constructor states that it can only be called if the argID argument is not null; if this were not true, then the invariant would be violated.

The clone and equals methods in QueueEntry are related to the interface JMLType, which QueueEntry extends. In JML when a class implements an interface, it inherits the specifications of that interface. The interface JMLType specifies just these two methods. The specifications of these methods are thus inherited by QueueEntry, and thus the specifications given here add to the given specifications. The specification of the method clone in JMLType (quoted from [LBR99]) is as follows.

```
public /*@ pure: @*/ Object clone();
//@ normal_behavior:
//@    ensures: \result instanceof JMLType
//@            && ((JMLType)\result).equals(this);
```

This says clone cannot throw exceptions, and its result must be a JMLType object, with the same value as this. (In Java, this names the receiver of a method call).

Inheritance of method specifications means that an implementation of clone must satisfy both the inherited specification from JMLType and the given specification in QueueEntry. The meaning of the method inheritance in this example is shown in Figure 12.5 [DL96]. (The modifier pure: from the superclass can be added in here, although it is redundant for a method of a pure class.) Satisfying both of the cases is possible because QueueEntry is a subtype of JMLType, and because JML interprets the meaning of $E1$.equals($E2$) using the run-time class of $E1$.

The ensures: redundantly clause allows the specifier to state consequences of the specification that follow from its meaning [LB99, T94, T95]. In this case

```
package edu.iastate.cs.jml.docs.kluwer;
model: import edu.iastate.cs.jml.models.JMLType;

public pure: model: class QueueEntry implements JMLType {

  public Object iD;
  public int priorityLevel;
  public int timeStamp;

  public invariant: iD != null && timeStamp >= 0;

  public QueueEntry(Object argID, int argLevel,
                    int argTimeStamp);
    normal_behavior:
      requires: argID != null && timeStamp >= 0;
      modifiable: iD, priorityLevel, timeStamp;
      ensures: iD == argID && priorityLevel == argLevel
              && timeStamp == argTimeStamp;

  public Object clone();
    normal_behavior:
      ensures: \result instanceof QueueEntry;
      ensures: redundantly
              ((QueueEntry)\result).equals(this);

  public model: boolean equals(Object o);
    normal_behavior:
      requires: o instanceof QueueEntry;
      ensures: \result <==>
            ((QueueEntry)o).iD == iD
        && ((QueueEntry)o).priorityLevel == priorityLevel
        && ((QueueEntry)o).timeStamp == timeStamp;
    also:
      requires: !(o instanceof QueueEntry);
      ensures: \result == false;
}
```

Figure 12.4   A specification of the model class `QueueEntry` (file `QueueEntry.jml`).

the predicate given follows from the inherited specification and the one given. This example shows a good use of such redundancy: to highlight important inherited properties for the reader of the (original, unexpanded) specification.

Case analysis is used again in the specification of `QueueEntry`'s `equals` method. As before, the behavior must satisfy each case of the specification. That is, when the

```
public /*@ pure: @*/ Object clone();
  normal_behavior:
    ensures: \result instanceof JMLType
          && ((JMLType)result).equals(this);
  also:
    ensures: \result instanceof QueueEntry;
    ensures: redundantly
                ((QueueEntry)\result).equals(this);
```

Figure 12.5 An expanded form of QueueEntry.clone's specification, showing the effect of specification inheritance.

argument o is an instance of type QueueEntry, the first case's postcondition must be satisfied, otherwise the result must be false.

3.   CLASS SPECIFICATIONS

Figure 12.6 gives a specification of a class, PriorityQueue, that implements the interface PriorityQueueUser. Because this class implements an interface, it inherits specifications, and hence implementation obligations, from that interface. The specification given thus adds more obligations to those given in previous specifications.

The pure model method largestTimeStamp is specified purely to help make the statement of addEntry more comprehensible. Since it is a model method, it does not need to be implemented. Without this specification, one would need to use the quantifier found in the second case of largestTimeStamp within the specification of addEntry.

The interesting method in PriorityQueue is addEntry. One important issue is how the timestamps are handled; this is hopefully clarified by the use of largestTimeStamp() in the postcondition of the first specification case.

A more subtle issue concerns finiteness. Since the precondition of addEntry's first case does not limit the number of entries that can be added, the specification seems to imply that the implementation must provide a literally unbounded priority queue, which is surely impossible. We avoid this problem, by following Poetzsch-Heffter [PH97] in releasing implementations from their obligations to fulfill the postcondition when Java runs out of storage. That is, a method implementation correctly implements a specification case if, whenever it is called in a state that satisfies its precondition, either the method terminates in a state that satisfies its postcondition, having modified only the objects permitted by its modifiable clause, or Java signals an error, by throwing an exception that inherits from java.lang.Error.

4.   OTHER FEATURES OF JML

Following Leino [L95b, L95a], JML uses depends and represents clauses to relate model fields to the concrete fields of objects. For example, in Figure 12.7 the depends: clause says that the model field size may change its value when

```
package edu.iastate.cs.jml.docs.kluwer;
//@ model: import edu.iastate.cs.jml.models.*;

public class PriorityQueue implements PriorityQueueUser {
 public PriorityQueue();
 //@ normal_behavior:
 //@  modifiable: entries;
 //@  ensures: entries != null && entries.isEmpty();
 //@  ensures: redundantly
 //@            entries.equals(new JMLValueSet());

 //@ public pure: model: int largestTimeStamp();
 //@ normal_behavior:
 //@    requires: entries.isEmpty();
 //@    ensures: \result == 0;
 //@  also:
 //@    requires: !(entries.isEmpty());
 //@    ensures: \forall (QueueEntry e) [
 //@            entries.has(e) ==> \result >= e.timeStamp];

 public void addEntry(Object argID, int argPriorityLevel)
                   throws PQException;
 //@ normal_behavior:
 //@  requires: argID != null && !contains(argID);
 //@  modifiable: entries;
 //@  ensures: entries != null
 //@       && entries.equals(\old(entries.insert(
 //@            new QueueEntry(argID, argPriorityLevel,
 //@                           largestTimeStamp()+1))));
 //@ exceptional_behavior:
 //@  requires: argID == null || contains(argID);
 //@  ensures: \throws(PQException);

  public /*@ pure: @*/ boolean contains(Object argID);
  public /*@ pure: @*/ Object next() throws PQException;
  public void remove(Object argID);
}
```

Figure 12.6 A JML specification for the Java class PriorityQueue (found in the file
PriorityQueue.java-refined).

```
 depends: size -> theElems;
 represents: size -> size == theElems.length();
```

Figure 12.7 Example of JML's depends and represents clauses.

theElems changes. The represents: clause says how they are related, giving additional facts that can be used in reasoning about the specification. This serves the same purpose as an abstraction function in various proof methods for abstract data types (such as [H72]). The represents: clause above tells how to extract the value of size from the value of theElems.

JML also has history constraints [LW94]. A history constraint is used to say how values can change between earlier and later states, such as a method's pre-state and its post-state. This prohibits subtypes from making certain state changes, even if they implement more methods than are specified in a given class. For example, the following history constraint

```
constraint: MAX_SIZE == \old(MAX_SIZE);
```

says that the value of MAX_SIZE cannot change.

JML has the ability to specify what methods a method may call, using a callable: clause. This allows one to know which methods need to be looked at when overriding a method [KL92], and to apply the ideas of "reuse contracts" [SLMD96].

5.   RELATED WORK

Our general design strategy for making JML practical and effective has been to blend the Eiffel [M92a, M92b, M97] and Larch [GHG+93, L98, W87, W90] approaches to specification. From Eiffel we have used the idea that assertions are written using Java's expression syntax as much as possible, thereby avoiding large amounts of special-purpose logical notations. JML also adapts the \old notation from Eiffel, instead of the Larch style annotation of names with state functions. Currently JML does not come with tools to execute pre- and postconditions to help debug programs, as in Eiffel. This is planned, however, as future work for JML.

However, Eiffel specifications, as written by Meyer, are typically not as complete as model-based specifications written, for example, in Larch BISLs or VDM [J90]. For example, Meyer partially specifies a remove (i.e., pop) method for stacks as requiring that the stack not be empty, and ensuring that the stack value in the post-state has one fewer items than in the pre-state [M97, p. 339]. However, the only characterization of which item is removed is given informally as a comment. Nothing is said formally that ensures that the other elements of the stack are unchanged. To allow more complete specifications, we need ideas from model-based specification languages.

JML's semantic differences from Eiffel (and its cousins Sather and Sather-K) allow one to more easily write more complete specifications, following the ideas of model-based specification languages. The most important of these is JML's use of specification-only declarations. These model: declarations allow more abstract and exact specifications of behavior than is typically done in Eiffel. For example, because one has a model of the abstract values of stack objects, one can precisely state both which element is removed by pop and that the other elements on the stack are unchanged. The use of model fields in JML thus allows one to write specifications that are similar to the spirit of VDM or Larch BISLs.

A more minor difference from Eiffel is that in JML one can specify frame conditions, using the modifiable: clause. Our interpretation of the modifiable: clause is very strict, as even benevolent side effects are disallowed if the `modifiable:` clause is omitted [L95b, L95a].

Another difference from Eiffel is that we have extended the syntax of Java expressions with quantifiers and other constructs that are needed for logical expressiveness, but which are not always executable. Finally, we ban side-effects and other problematic features of code in assertions.

On the other hand, our experience with Larch/C++ [L96, L99] has taught us to adapt the model-based approach in two ways, with the aim of making it more practical and easy to learn. The first adaptation is again the use of specification-only model (or ghost) variables. An object will thus have (in general) several such *model fields*, which are used only for the purpose of describing, abstractly, the values of objects. This simplifies the use of JML, as compared with most Larch BISLs, since specifiers (and their readers) hardly ever need to know about algebraic style specification. It also makes designing a model for a Java class or interface similar, in some respects, to designing an implementation data structure in Java. We hope that this similarity will make the specification language easier to understand.

The second adaptation is hiding of the details of mathematical modeling behind a facade of Java classes. In the Larch approach to behavioral interface specification [W87], the mathematical notation used in assertions is presented directly to the specifier. This allows the same mathematical notation to be used in many different specification languages. However, it also means that the user of such a specification language has to learn a notation for assertions that is different than their programming language's notation for expressions. (A preliminary study by Finney [F96] indicates that a large number of special-purpose, graphic mathematical notations, such as those found in Z [H93, S92] may make such specifications hard to read, even for programmers trained in the notation.) In JML we use a compromise approach, hiding these details behind Java classes. These classes are pure, in the sense that they reflect the underlying mathematics, and hence do not use side-effects (at least not in any observable way). Besides insulating the user of JML from the details of the mathematical notation, this compromise approach also insulates the design of JML from the details of the mathematical logic used for JML's semantics and for theorem proving. We believe that the use of slightly extended Java notation for assertions is appropriate, given that JML is used in detailed design, and thus will mostly be read and written by persons familiar with Java.

6.   FUTURE WORK AND CONCLUSIONS

One area of future work for JML is concurrency. Our current plan is to use `when:` clauses that say when a method may proceed to execute, after it is called [L91, S95]. This permits the specification of when the caller is delayed to obtain a lock, for example. While syntax for this exists in the JML parser, our exploration of this topic is still in an early stage. We may also be able to expand history constraints to use temporal logic.

Another area for future work on JML is to synthesize the previous work of Wahls, Leavens and Baker on the use of constraint logic programming to directly execute a significant and practical subset of JML's assertions [WLB98]. This prior work supports the "construction" of post-state values to satisfy ensures clauses, including such clauses containing quantified assertions. Successful integration of these assertion execution techniques with JML would support automatic generation of Java class prototypes directly from their JML specifications.

In conclusion, JML combines the best features of Eiffel and the Larch approaches to specification. This combination, we believe, makes it more expressive than Eiffel, and more practical than Larch style BISLs as a tool for recording detailed designs.

More information about JML can be found on the web at the following URL.

```
http://www.cs.iastate.edu/~leavens/JML.html
```

Acknowledgements

Thanks to Rustan Leino and Peter Müller for many discussions about the semantics of such specifications and verification issues relating to Java. For comments on JML we thank Peter, Jianbing Chen, Anand Ganapathy, Sevtap Oltes, Gary Daugherty, Karl Hoech, Jim Potts, and Tammy Scherbring. Thanks to Anand Ganapathy for his work on the type checker used to check our specifications.

The work of Leavens and Ruby was supported in part by a grant from Rockwell International Corporation and by the US NSF under grant CCR-9503168. The work of Leavens, Baker, and Ruby is supported in part by the NSF grant CCR 9803843.

References

[AG98]   Arnold, K. and Gosling, J. *The Java Programming Language*. The Java Series. Addison-Wesley, Reading, MA, second edition, 1998.

[BMR95]   Borgida, A., Mylopoulos, J., and Reiter, R. On the frame problem in procedure specifications. *IEEE Transactions on Software Engineering*, 21(10):785–798, October 1995.

[DL96]   Dhara, K. K. and Leavens, G. T. Forcing behavioral subtyping through specification inheritance. In *Proceedings of the 18th International Conference on Software Engineering, Berlin, Germany*, pages 258–267. IEEE Computer Society Press, March 1996. A corrected version is Iowa State University, Dept. of Computer Science TR #95-20c.

[F96]   Finney, K. Mathematical notation in formal specification: Too difficult for the masses? *IEEE Transactions on Software Engineering*, 22(2):158–159, February 1996.

[GHG+93] Guttag, J. V., Horning, J. J., Garland, S., Jones, K., Modet, A., and Wing, J. *Larch: Languages and Tools for Formal Specification*. Springer-Verlag, New York, N.Y., 1993.

[GJS96]   Gosling, J., Joy, B., and Steele, G. *The Java Language Specification*. The Java Series. Addison-Wesley, Reading, MA, 1996.

[H72]   Hoare, C. A. R. Proof of correctness of data representations. *Acta Informatica*, 1(4):271–281, 1972.

[H93]   Hayes, I., editor. *Specification Case Studies*. International Series in Computer Science. Prentice-Hall, Inc., second edition, 1993.

[J90]   Jones, C. B. *Systematic Software Development Using VDM*. International Series in Computer Science. Prentice Hall, Englewood Cliffs, N.J., second edition, 1990.

[KL92]   Kiczales, G. and Lamping, J. Issues in the design and documentation of class libraries. *ACM SIGPLAN Notices*, 27(10):435–451, October 1992. *OOPSLA '92 Proceedings*, Andreas Paepcke (editor).

[L91]   Lerner, R. A. Specifying objects of concurrent systems. Ph.D. Thesis CMU-CS-91-131, School of Computer Science, Carnegie Mellon University, May 1991.

[L95a]   Leino, K. R. M. A myth in the modular specification of programs. Technical Report KRML 63, Digital Equipment Corporation, Systems Research Center, 130 Lytton Avenue Palo Alto, CA 94301, November 1995. Obtain from the author, at rustan@pa.dec.com.

[L95b]   Leino, K. R. M. *Toward Reliable Modular Programs*. PhD thesis, California Institute of Technology, 1995. Available as Technical Report Caltech-CS-TR-95-03.

[L96]   Leavens, G. T. An overview of Larch/C++: Behavioral specifications for C++ modules. In Kilov, H. and Harvey, W., editors, *Specification of Behavioral Semantics in Object-Oriented Information Modeling*, chapter 8, pages 121–142. Kluwer Academic Publishers, Boston, 1996. An extended version is TR #96-01d, Department of Computer Science, Iowa State University, Ames, Iowa, 50011.

[L98]   Leavens, G. T. Larch frequently asked questions. Version 1.89. Available in http://www.cs.iastate.edu/~leavens/larch-faq.html, January 1998.

[L99]   Leavens, G. T. Larch/C++ Reference Manual. Version 5.41. Available in ftp://ftp.cs.iastate.edu/pub/larchc++/lcpp.ps.gz or on the World Wide Web at the URL http://www.cs.iastate.edu/~leavens/larchc++.html, April 1999.

[LB99]   Leavens, G. T. and Baker, A. L. Enhancing the pre- and postcondition technique for more expressive specifications. Technical Report 97-19a, Iowa State University, Department of Computer Science, February 1999.

[LBR99]   Leavens, G. T., Baker, A. L., and Ruby, C. Preliminary design of JML: A behavioral interface specification language for Java. Technical Report 98-06e, Iowa State University, Department of Computer Science, June 1999.

[LH94]   Lano, K. and Haughton, H., editors. *Object-Oriented Specification Case Studies*. The Object-Oriented Series. Prentice Hall, New York, N.Y., 1994.

[LW94]   Liskov, B. and Wing, J. A behavioral notion of subtyping. *ACM Transactions on Programming Languages and Systems*, 16(6):1811–1841, November 1994.

[M92a]   Meyer, B. Applying "design by contract". *Computer*, 25(10):40–51, October 1992.

[M92b]   Meyer, B. *Eiffel: The Language*. Object-Oriented Series. Prentice Hall, New York, N.Y., 1992.

[M94]   Morgan, C. *Programming from Specifications: Second Edition*. Prentice Hall International, Hempstead, UK, 1994.

[M97]   Meyer, B. *Object-oriented Software Construction*. Prentice Hall, New York, N.Y., second edition, 1997.

[OSWZ94] Ogden, W. F., Sitaraman, M., Weide, B. W., and Zweben, S. H. Part I: The RESOLVE framework and discipline — a research synopsis. *ACM SIGSOFT Software Engineering Notes*, 19(4):23–28, Oct 1994.

[PH97]   Poetzsch-Heffter, A. Specification and verification of object-oriented programs. Habilitation thesis, Technical University of Munich, January 1997.

[S92]   Spivey, J. M. *The Z Notation: A Reference Manual*. International Series in Computer Science. Prentice-Hall, New York, N.Y., second edition, 1992.

[S95]   Sivaprasad, G. Larch/CORBA: Specifying the behavior of CORBA-IDL interfaces. Technical Report 95-27a, Department of Computer Science, Iowa State University, Ames, Iowa, 50011, December 1995.

[SLMD96] Steyaert, P., Lucas, C., Mens, K., and D'Hondt, T. Reuse contracts: Managing the evolution of reusable assets. In *OOPSLA '96 Conference on Object-Oriented Programming Systems, Languagges and Applications*, pages 268–285. ACM Press, October 1996. ACM SIGPLAN Notices, Volume 31, Number 10.

[T94]   Tan, Y. M. Interface language for supporting programming styles. *ACM SIGPLAN Notices*, 29(8):74–83, August 1994. Proceedings of the Workshop on Interface Definition Languages.

[T95]   Tan, Y. M. *Formal Specification Techniques for Engineering Modular C Programs*, volume 1 of *Kluwer International Series in Software Engineering*. Kluwer Academic Publishers, Boston, 1995.

[W83]   Wing, J. M. A two-tiered approach to specifying programs. Technical Report TR-299, Massachusetts Institute of Technology, Laboratory for Computer Science, 1983.

[W87]   Wing, J. M. Writing Larch interface language specifications. *ACM Transactions on Programming Languages and Systems*, 9(1):1–24, January 1987.

[W90]   Wing, J. M. A specifier's introduction to formal methods. *Computer*, 23(9):8–24, September 1990.

[W94]   Wills, A. Refinement in Fresco. In Lano and Houghton [LH94], chapter 9, pages 184–201.

[WLB98]   Wahls, T., Leavens, G. T., and Baker, A. L. Executing formal specifications with constraint programming. Technical Report 97-12a, Department of Computer Science, Iowa State University, 226 Atanasoff Hall, Ames, Iowa 50011, August 1998. Available by anonymous ftp from ftp.cs.iastate.edu or by e-mail from almanac@cs.iastate.edu.

About the Authors

The authors are all at the Department of Computer Science, Iowa State University, in Ames, Iowa, 50011-1040 USA.
Gary T. Leavens is an associate professor. He received a Ph.D. in Computer Science from MIT in 1989. His research focuses on formal methods in OO programming, and includes the theory of abstract data types, specification, verification, as well as topics in programming languages such as type theory and semantics. He has been involved in the design of the specification language Larch/Smalltalk, and is a principal designer of both Larch/C++ and JML. He is the author of the Larch FAQ.
Albert L. Baker is an associate professor. He received a Ph.D. in Computer Science from The Ohio State University in 1979. His research focuses on specification languages, software testing, prototyping from formal specifications and CASE tools. He has been involved in the design of the specification language SPECS/C++ and is a principal designer of JML.
Clyde Ruby is a Ph.D. student. He has more than 15 years experience as an analyst, designer, and implementer of software systems. His current research focuses on formal methods in object-oriented programming, specification, and verification. He is working with Leavens on Larch/C++ and JML.

Chapter 13

AGENTS:
BETWEEN ORDER AND CHAOS

James J. Odell
James Odell Associates
Ann Arbor, MI 48103 USA
jodell@compuserve.com
www.jamesodell.com

INTRODUCTION

Nature has moments both of order and chaos. Interestingly enough, those forms that are considered most fit actually reside someplace in between. This phenomenon applies to business and software agents, as well. This chapter discusses how agent systems can actually perform better on the edge of chaos.

FIRST, BASIC AGENT BEHAVIOR

One of the earliest form of agents is called a cellular automata (CA). The idea was originally conceived by the Polish mathematician Stanislaw Ulam in the early 1950s and further developed by John von Neumann and Arthur Brooks. Basically, a CA consists of a lattice of cells, or sites. Each cell has a state whose value is commonly expressed as 0 or 1, black or white, on or off, or a color selected from a set of colors. At discrete "ticks" of the CA clock, this value is updated according to a set of rules that specifies how the state of each cell is computed from its present value and the values of its neighbors.

The most familiar example is John Conway's game, Life. As described in the October 1970 issue of *Scientific American*, only a checkerboard and an ample supply of markers are needed. The rules of Life are simple:

- A dead cell (state 0), with exactly three of its eight immediate neighbors alive (state 1), is born. Under the right conditions, the cell comes alives.
- A living cell with two or three living neighbors remains alive, that is, the cell stays alive when nurtured by its neighbors to the right extent.
- All other cells die (or remain dead) due to overcrowding or loneliness.
- Each cell is updated once per time period.

The checkerboard rules represent the laws of physics (or life) and, while the cells themselves are not mobile, an amazing amount of behavior emerges.

Figure 1a depicts how a CA society can die out over three generations. Figure 1b, on the other hand, shows how a society can form a fixed configuration. Lastly, Fig. 1c illustrates how some patterns oscillate indefinitely.

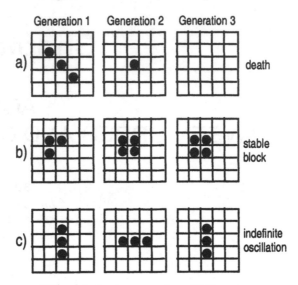

Figure 1 Some examples of Life patterns.

CLASSIFYING AGENT BEHAVIOR

Over the long run, CA societies have similar kinds of emergent behavior. The patterns of Fig. 2 illustrate the four classes of behavior identified by Stephen Wolfram in 1983 when he was at Princeton's Institute for Advanced Studies. Class I societies are those that exhibit a static, or *limit point*, behavior. Figures 1a and 1b are examples of this Class, because the lattice will not change after generation 3. Class II societies exhibit periodic, or *limit cycle*, behavior which is the indefinite oscillation depicted in Fig. 1c.

Class I and II can be considered one extreme of CA behavior because everything is predictable and orderly. Class III on the other hand is aperiodic, or *chaotic*, where chaos is the qualitative study of dynamical systems. Here, results can differ dramatically based on initial conditions, and its structures display no obvious order or uniformity. In between these extremes, is a mysterious and complex class of behavior: Class IV. Such automata exhibit considerable local organization, yet also have areas of irregular behavior. In other words, Class IV automata are some place in between the two extremes: they exhibit orderly behavior as well as some chaotic behavior. (Images are generated using the Discrete Dynamic Lab from http://www.santafe.edu/~wuensch/ddlab.html.)

ORDER VERSUS CHAOS

Cellular Automata offer a way to model natural and artificial processes, such as modeling crystallization, complex fluid flows, chemical reactions, and hardware architecture. Yet, CA involve an elementary form of agent. Imagine the kinds of systems that can be built with agents that are mobile and have sophisticated forms of communication and interaction. Such agent systems not only provide a richer way of modeling natural and artificial processes but provide a way of *implementing* such systems, as well.

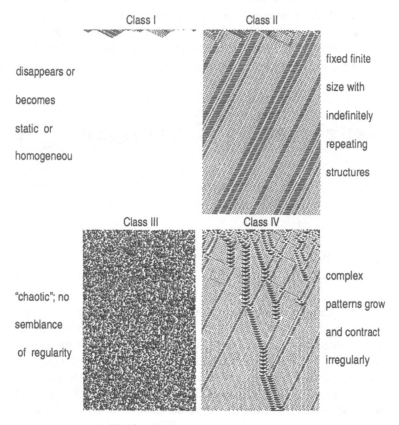

Figure 2 Wolfram's four classes of long-run behavior.

Such mature agents systems are still subject to the same Wolfram behavior. You can build agents systems that are orderly (Class I and II), and such orderly behavior is appropriate for some kinds of systems. However, when agents are expected to learn and change their behavior, an orderly system discourages change. In a business example, all the jobs in an organization would be subdivided so that employees have no latitude and only do the job for which they are hired. For an automated supply-chain system, the results would always be predictable. On the surface, such predictability would seem to be a good thing. However, when the business landscape changes (as it often does), the supply-chain operation would no longer suit the organization's needs. Instead, it would be predictably wrong. In both of these scenarios, everybody would benefit if the individual agents had the freedom to change. In short, orderly agent systems should become more fluid—and a bit closer to chaos.

Conversely, if agents are deep in a chaotic regime (Class III), they can never get the job done. For example, employees who do not know what they're supposed to do half the time end up working at cross purposes. A supply-chain system would not be able to deliver the right product, to the right person, at the right time. In both of these scenarios, if the individual agents could have tighter connections with fewer individuals, a greater degree of stability would be introduced. Chaotic agents, then, should become less fluid by adapting to what other agents are doing, resulting in aggregate behavior. This means pulling back from chaos.

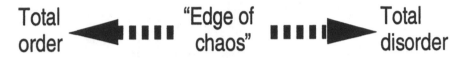

Figure 3   Systems poised between order and chaos are best able
to carry out ordered yet flexible behaviors.

THE EDGE OF CHAOS

Neither order nor chaos seems to be the best place for complex systems. Instead, such agent systems need to be someplace in between. With too much order, the system stagnates and dies in the face of new competition that needs to be only a little bit better. With too much chaos, the system will not survive because it can not make useful products. The edge of chaos is on average where fitness is best. Such systems can exploit what they have learned, as well as extend that learning through exploration. Complex systems are characterized by perpetual novelty. This approach can be scary: things can get out of control and errors will be made. Yet without this kind of approach, there will be no change—only status quo. To talk about complex adaptive systems being in equilibrium is meaningless because the system never gets there. It is always unfolding, always in transition. If a system ever reaches equilibrium, it is not just stable—it is dead.

Stability is probably something valued in accounting and payroll systems. However, the next generation business systems should be operating on the edge of chaos. Order entry, inventory control, and supply chain systems are particularly appropriate. These are systems whose agents are people, machines, and software. To work effectively, these agents must work together as a living system: requiring flux, change, and the forming and dissolving of patterns.

Complex systems theory points us away from isolated units and toward interactions between individuals and their environment. Strategy focuses on the management of volatility, not the achievement of specific goals. Growth comes from agent relationships and rules rather than through a significant increase in size. Opposing thoughts or points of view are held simultaneously. Mild instability is encouraged. Build something workable, rather than "optimal." Developing complex systems is not for the faint-hearted, which applies to both executives and IT system developers. We need to unleash our software and let it grow and learn like any living system. Only then can our systems mature beyond our limitations—and exceed our expectations.

> A greater kind of courage and a different psychology is now required—to be willing to let go and experience the creativity, innovation and disturbance which comes about when we risk the outer boundaries of trying to maintain a balance and the excitement of living, developing and coaching at the "edge of chaos." Learning will perhaps ultimately prove less valuable in the third millennium than the skill and attitudes of unlearning—in the same way that knowing what to do may become far less important than knowing what to do when you no longer know what to do. (Petruska Clarkson, psychologist, in UK)

REFERENCES

[COV95] Coveney, Peter, and Roger Highfield, *Frontiers of Complexity: The Search for Order in a Chaotic World*, Fawcett Columbine, New York, 1995.

[EPS96] Epstein, Joshua M., and Robert Axtell, *Growing Artificial Societies: Social Science from the Bottom Up*, MIT Press, Cambridge, MA, 1996.

ABOUT THE AUTHOR

James Odell is an IT consultant and practitioner specializing in the object-oriented and agent-based approaches. Throughout most of his 30 year career, he has been heavily involved in developing better methods to manage, understand, and express business system requirements. Now, he is one of the first practical implementers of object and agent modeling, and implementation--consulting to major companies worldwide. He is a very experienced and highly-regarded educator and speaker. James Odell is also the co-chair of OMG's Agent Work Group and Analysis and Design Task Force.

Chapter 14

UML, THE FUTURE STANDARD SOFTWARE ARCHITECTURE DESCRIPTION LANGUAGE?

Andy Schürr

Institute of Software Technology
University of the Federal Armed Forces, Munich
85577 Neubiberg, Germany
Andy.Schuerr@unibw-muenchen.de

Andreas J. Winter

Department of Computer Science III
Aachen University of Technology
52056 Aachen, Germany
winter@i3.informatik.rwth-aachen.de

Abstract   The object-oriented Unified Modeling Language (UML) which has become OMG standard offers a great variety of concepts for the definition of the structure and the expected behavior of a software system. It has the potential to replace many previously used software architecture description languages. This is especially true for the subset of so-called module interconnection languages. Compared with these languages UML has the main drawback that its module concept is continuously changing from version to version without reaching a well-defined stable state (until the current version 1.3). It is the purpose of this contribution to revisit the development of the UML module concept, to criticize its current form, and to present a compact and precise definition of its visibility rules. The integration of still missing concepts of component-based architecture description languages is out of the scope of this contribution. It is one of the main tasks of the OMG task force which is responsible for the development of a real-time modeling extension of UML.

1.   INTRODUCTION

The design of software system architectures is a discipline of rapidly growing importance. The software engineering community agrees on the fact that a software system's architecture plays a key role for planning its development process and for guaranteeing its quality concerning certain functional and nonfunctional requirements such as its "correctness", availability, performance, maintainability, portability, etc. [BCK98]. Many papers have been published in the last years about specific software architectures, design pattern languages, and architectural styles. Nevertheless, there is no common agreement on the definition of the term "software architecture". As a consequence, most books or papers about this topic start with just another definition of the term software architecture and introduce their own architecture description language. A rough classification of the literature shows that there are at least two main categories of these languages:

1. More recently published papers use the term *software architecture description language (ADL)* often as a synomym for component description languages; they favor the view that software architectures are "components + connectors + behavioral constraints" [GP95, SG96].

2. Elder papers usually adhere to the terminology of so-called *module interconnection languages (MIL)* [DK76], where a software architecture is a set of modules with different kinds of dependency relationships between them; the Ada-inspired hierarchical object-oriented design language HOOD is one famous example of this category [R92].

There is some hope that the invention of new ADLs and the associated discussion of "who's ADL is the best one and who's terminology is correct" may be terminated by using the *Unified Modeling Language UML* as a starting point for a standard software architecture description language [RJB99]. UML is the widely accepted OMG standard of an object-oriented modeling language. It is in our opinion the first OO modeling language which addresses all facets of a state-of-the-art module concept. Its modules, called packages, build shells around arbitrary types of diagrams. It overcomes thereby the serious scaling-up problems of previously used OO methods, when huge analysis or design documents had to be partitioned into manageable pieces with well-defined interfaces between them.

It is worth-while to notice that UML combines the standard elements of MILs with a rather broad spectrum of other sublanguages for modeling the logical behavior and the physical structure of a software system:

- Class diagrams and packages offer all important MIL concepts such as information hiding, import and generalization relationships, multiple interfaces for classes and packages, genericity, ...

- The object constraint language OCL allows for the definition of invariants as well as for pre- and postconditions and offers thereby the necessary means for "designing by contract".

- Various types of diagrams (state transition diagrams, collaboration diagrams etc.) may be used to model the dynamic behavior of networks of related objects.

- Finally, component and deployment diagrams may be used to define a mapping of logical software objects onto available hardware components.

Despite of its richness, UML has a number of drawbacks compared with component-based ADLs such as those presented in [SG96]. This is mainly due to the fact that UML's component diagrams are not intended to represent the *logical* decomposition of a software system into reusable and recombinable subsystems:

"a component is a physical unit of implementation"   ([RJB99], p. 93).

Furthermore, UML does not offer the concept of connectors as first-class objects, which would be a hybrid of an association (class) between some classifiers and an import dependency between a class and an interface of another class.

Fortunately, serious efforts are under way to incorporate a variant of ADL components and connectors into UML collaboration diagrams. These activities, discussed in [SR98], are out of the scope of this contribution. Here we will revisit the capabilities of UML as a "traditional" module interconnection language (MIL). We will see that UML offers all necessary elements of a MIL, but lacks a precise definition of their (static) semantics as well as an in-depth description of how certain combinations of the offered concepts shall be used in practice.

The following Section 2 starts with a short summary of the UML package concept. It shows why UML's package concept definition — as presented in the UML reference book [RJB99] and the accompanying standard document for UML version 1.3 [OMG99a] is neither consistent nor complete. Section 3 discusses the most questionable part of the UML module concept, the nesting of packages, in more detail. Section 4 explains afterwards why it is useful that package dependencies have their own visibility attributes. These visibility attributes are part of the UML meta model, but — as far as we can see — not mentioned in the UML reference book. Finally, Section 5 summarizes our discussion and presents a compact formal definition of the UML package visibility rules.

Please note that this paper is our third presentation of a consistent view of the UML module concept. Previously published papers presented formal definitions of UML visibiliby rules for version 1.0 in [SW97] and for version 1.1 in [SW98], respectively. In the mean time, the UML standard visibility rules have been changed radically, without solving the presented problems. Even worse, we have some doubts that the changes from UML version 1.1 to version 1.3 improved the UML package concept. It is, therefore, the main purpose of this paper to

- explain why we have some doubts that the visibility rules of version 1.3 are better than those of version 1.1,

- show how a precise, compact, and useful definition of UML's visibility rules might look like, and

- suggest how certain hidden features of the UML package concept might be used to express otherwise not directly available concepts.

2.   THE UML PACKAGE CONCEPT

The information hiding and modularization concept of UML packages was strongly influenced by the design of the OO programming languages C++ [ES94] and Java [AG96]. Furthermore, the design of Ada [C96] obviously influenced the development of the UML package concept, too. As a result, the package concept of UML has about the following properties:

- A package builds a shell around a group of closely related declarations; usually these declarations have the form of a diagram and define the data structures and/or the operations of a modeled software system.

- It is the single purpose of a package to regulate the *visibility* of its own declarations, i.e. to restrict the usage of the enclosed declarations to well-defined parts of a system model.

- As a conseqence, packages have *no run-time semantics* at all, i.e. the semantics of a system model is not changed if all its declarations are put into a single package.

- A *dependency* from a client package to a server package reveals some of the server's declarations (elements) while others remain hidden.

- Package elements as well as (nested) packages themselves either have *public* or *protected* or *private* visibility (denoted as +, #, and −).

- Packages may be *nested*, thereby granting a child (parent) package the access rights to all those elements, which are visible in its parent (child) package.

- *Import/access dependencies may be used to access public resources of a server package, whereas* generalizations relationships *(inheritance relationships) reveal the existence of protected resources, too.*

- Friend dependencies *between a client and a server package destroy the server package's visibility shell completely and allow the client package even to reference private declarations of the server package.*

For the discussion of all further details we have to clarify which version of the UML standard is used as a baseline. Consider for instance the history of the visibility rules associated with nesting of packages and the export of imported package elements in different UML versions:

1. In UML 1.1 [OMG99b] a parent package has an implicit import relationship to all its child packages. The implicit import relationship allows the parent package to reference all public elements of its child packages. Furthermore, these nested public elements as well as well as the explicitly imported (and referenced) elements from other packages with public visibility belong (probably) to the export of the regarded package.

2. The UML version described in the UML reference book [RJB99] reverses the visibility rules for nested packages. A child package sees all elements visible for its parent package, but not the other way round (as long as the parent package does not have an explicit import dependency to its child package). Furthermore, the reference book states on page 99 that

> "Elements with *private* visibility are visible only in the package containing them and any packages nested inside that package."

Finally, the reference book announces on page 120 that import relationships are not transitive. This means probably that public imported elements from other packages do no longer belong to the regarded package's export.

3. The UML draft version 1.3 (alpha R2) [OMG99a] finally agrees with the UML reference book concerning the treatment of nested packages. But it has a different opinion concerning transitive imports. It requires on page 2-170 that

> "A package with an import dependency to another package imports all the public contents of the namespace defined by the supplier package, including elements of packages imported by the imported package."

In the following we will use the UML draft version 1.3 as the reference point for our discussions. It contains the most precise specification of the UML visibility rules, although the critical parts of these visibility rules are not yet expressed in the form of object constraint language expressions (listed OCL expressions deal with renaming conflicts only and do not make any attempts to define the visibility of imported elements or the above mentioned transitive import relationships).

The UML draft version 1.3 distinguishes between two different kinds of permission dependencies. Normal *import dependencies* add all public elements of server packages (targets of import dependencies) to the name space of their client packages (sources of import dependencies). Client packages have the permission to introduce alias names for imported elements and to downgrade visibilities of imported elements. In this way a client package is able to resolve name conflicts between imported elements from different packages. Furthermore, it offers only those imported elements as part of its own export interface, which have an unchanged visibility. So-called *access dependencies* on the other hand do not change the namespace of a client package. They grant a client module merely the permission to reference an element e of a regarded server package S by using the *path expression* S : : e.

Figure 14.1 presents one example for a still rather trivial interaction of access and import dependencies with nesting of packages. We believe that the visibility rules of UML 1.3 have to be applied as follows:

- Package B sees the imported class identifiers a1, a2, and d as well as its own class identifier b, and its own package identifiers D and E, but not the class identifiers a3, a4, and e.

- Package D sees its own class identifier d as well as all class and package identifiers visible in its parent package (maybe except for the class identifier a1 with private visibility).

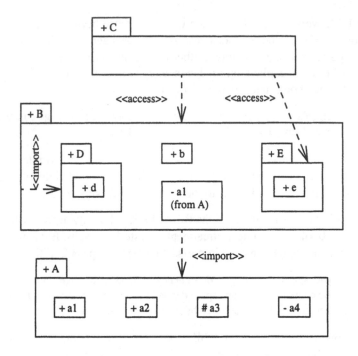

Figure 14.1   Interaction of package access, import, and nesting.

- Package E sees its own class identifier e as well as all class and package identifiers visible in its parent package (maybe except for a1).

- Package C sees the package identifiers B::D and B::E as well as the class identifiers B::a2, B::d, and B::b via its access dependency to B, it sees the class identifier E::e via its access dependency to E. It may not use the class identifiers B::a1, b, or B::D::d.

Please note that we have some doubts concerning the treatment of public identifiers of visible packages (such as B::D::d), the handling of access or import dependencies to nested packages (such as the access dependency from C to B::E), and the notation for imported elements with a changed visibility attribute value (such as a1 in B, whose visibility value has been changed from public to private). These doubts are mainly caused by the abstract example of Figure 13-6 on page 121 of the UML reference book, repeated in Figure 14.2 (except for some irrelevant classes). We cannot see any reasons why package X is allowed to access package V inside package Z without having an additional access or import dependency to package Z itself.

3.   VISIBILITIES OF NESTED PACKAGES

The previous section did already mention the differences between the visibility rules for nested packages in UML version 1.1 and version 1.3, respectively. Furthermore, it presented one example from the reference book with an access dependency between

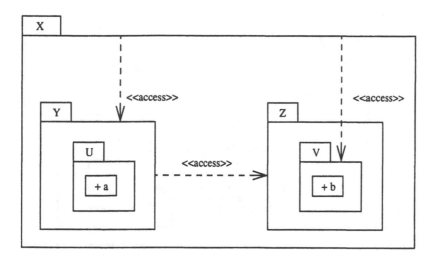

Figure 14.2   Interaction of package access, import, and nesting.

a package and a subpackage of one of its subpackages. As far as we can see such a dependency is forbidden in UML version 1.3, but permitted in version 1.1.

The following Figure 14.3 summarizes the main differences between the nesting (scoping) rules of UML version 1.1 and 1.3, respectively. In UML 1.1 a parent package sees all the public elements of its (public) child packages and exports them as if they were its own elements. This is the reason why the import dependency from X to Z is redundant in UML 1.1. Child packages, on the other hand, do not see any elements of their parent packages, which are not imported explicitly. As a consequence, the import dependency from package U to package Z is illegal as long as there is no import dependency from the parent package Y to package Z (which makes Z together with its contents visible in Y).

In UML 1.3 a child package sees all the (nonprivate) elements which are visible for its parent package. This is the reason why the import dependency from Y to X is redundant in UML 1.3. Parent packages, on the other hand, are not able to see inside child packages without first establishing an explicit import dependency. As a consequence, the import dependency from package Y to package V is illegal as long as there is no import dependency between the packages Y and Z (which makes the contents of Z visible for Y).

It is worth-while to notice that the visibility rules of UML 1.1 with the propagation of visible elements up the composition hierarchy are rather unusual. The new visiblity rules of UML 1.3 have the advantage that they are closely related to the visibility rules of Ada for packages and library units [C96] and to the scoping rules of any block-structured programming language. Nevertheless we believe that the new rules are rather dangerous from a software engineer's point of view due to the following reasons:

- Usually the realization (or model) of a software system depends on the realization (models) of its subsystems, but not the other way round. As a consequence the

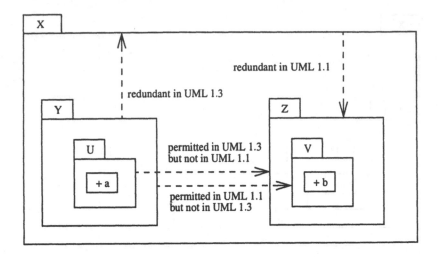

Figure 14.3   Interaction of package access, import, and nesting.

new propagation rules encourage the design of unwanted system/subsystem relationships.

- The dependencies of parent packages do no longer summarize the dependencies of their child packages if child packages are allowed to import packages not imported by their parent packages. A package is, therefore, no longer a proper abstraction of its subpackages.

- The propagation of visible elements from parent packages to child packages encourages the development of software architectures, where basic resources are not located in basic layers at the bottom of a software system, but in the topmost packages of the system model.

In Section 5 we will present a precise definition of UML visibility rules which is a kind of compromise between the nesting of rules of UML 1.1 and UML 1.3. These rules neither support the dangerous automatic propagation of element visiblities from parent to child packages, nor do they support the dangerous automatic extension of a parent package's namespace with the public elements of its child packages. They treat public elements of child packages as if they were made visible by access dependencies from parent to child packages. This has the following consequences for the scenario depicted in Figure 14.3:

- An access dependency from package X to package Z is redundant as it was the case in UML 1.1.

- An import dependency from X to Z is not redundant; it gives the clients of X the right to use the path expression X::e instead of X::Z::e.

- Neither an access nor an import dependency from Y to X is redundant if the new visibility rules are used (as it is the case in UML 1.3).

- The import or access dependency from package Y to package V is permitted due to the fact that the path name Z::V is visible and may be used inside X to reference the target package of the required dependency.

- The import or access dependency from package U to package Z is not permitted without the existence of an import or access dependency from Y to Z.

4.   VISIBILITIES OF PACKAGE DEPENDENCIES

The discussion of UML visibility rules in the preceeding sections ignored more or less the fact that import and access dependencies as well as generalization relationships are all subclasses of the meta class ModelElement of the UML meta model. They inherit from their common superclass the property to have one name and visibility attribute value in their owner package and a different alias name and visibility attribute value in any client package. In our opinion it makes no sense to provide these relationships with their own names and alias names.

The situation is a little bit different in the case of the inherited visibility attributes of import dependencies and generalization relationships. They could be used to distinguish between interface imports and implementation imports as well as between subtype inheritance and implementation inheritance in the usual sense. It is even probable that at least one author of the UML standard definition version 1.1 [OMG99b] had this possibility mind when (s)he wrote the sentence on page 142

"Private inheritance (generalization) ... hides the inherited features of a class (package) ...."

Nevertheless, the rest of UML 1.1 as well as all recently produced UML descriptions ignore the visibility attributes of dependency and generalization relationships. They rely exclusively on the existence of certain stereotypes for the distinction of different kinds of generalization relationships. Furthermore, they do not explain the interaction between the usage of these stereotypes (such as implementation and interface inheritance) and the visibility rules for generalization relationships.

It is the purpose of this section to explain how the visibility attributes of dependency and generalization relationships could be used in addition or instead of some of the previously mentioned relationship stereotypes. Furthermore, this section prepares the reader for the precise definition of the visibility rules of the following section, which take these visibility attributes into account. It explains the details of the following idea:

A protected or private import dependency or generalization relationship between two packages adds all public (protected) elements of the regarded server package with an appropriately reduced visibility to the client package's own namespace (optionally under a different alias name).

Please note that the discussion of reduced imported element visibilities is meaningless as long as these elements are not added to the namespace of the client package. As a consequence, access and friend dependencies between packages are out of the scope of this section.

Combining three different kinds of visibilities with two types of relationships results in six different kinds of relationships between packages:

1. *Public import:* a public import dependency adds the imported elements to its own export interface. This kind of transitive import dependency is for instance useful

if one package defines a set of operations which use elements from different packages as parameter types. Any client package, which imports (accesses) the exported set of operations automatically, imports automatically all needed parameter types, too.

2. *Protected import:* a protected import dependency adds all imported elements with protected visibility to the client package's namespace. It has to be used whenever certain implementation details based on imported resources have to be hidden from regular client packages, but must be revealed to all packages, which specialize (inherit from) the regarded package.

3. *Private import:* a private import dependency corresponds to the concept of implementation module imports in Modula-2 [WS84]. It allows to import all those resources, which are needed to construct the contents of the regarded package, without revealing (reexporting) these imports to its client packages.

4. *Public generalization:* a public generalization relationship between two packages defines a kind of subtype relationship between them. It is an assertion for all regular clients of these packages that the interface of the more specific package is an extension of the interface of the more general package.

5. *Protected generalization:* a protected generalization relationship between two packages defines an inheritance relationship, which is invisible for regular import/access dependency clients of these packages, but visible along further generalization relationships. The usefulness of this construct is still a matter of debate.

6. *Private generalization:* a private generalization relationship is closely related to the well-known concept of implementation inheritance. It allows us to construct a package based on the public as well as protected elements of another package without any restrictions concerning its exported set of elements.

5.   PRECISE DEFINITION OF THE PACKAGE CONCEPT

The informal discussion of UML's package concept could be continued by addressing new topics such as the characterization of pathological combinations of import dependencies and generalization relationships (cf. [SW98]) or a precise definition of the formal parameters of generic packages (package templates) and their permitted instantiations with actual parameters. Discussing these topics without having agreed on a solid definition of the basic package concept beforehand would be more or less fruitless. It is, therefore, the purpose of this section to finish our discussion with a precise definition of what we believe is a useful UML package concept. This definition reuses to a certain extent bits and pieces of a more complex and more formal definition presented in [SW98]. Here, we use natural language sentences only for this purpose.

We do hope that the following eight statements are comprehensible without any further explanations or the presentation of another set of examples. Please note that all statements rely on the fact that visibility attribute values are treated as an enumeration type with the following order of its elements:

private < protected < public.

Furthermore, they rely on the assumption that UML 1.3 no longer distinguishes between the fact that an element is imported and, therefore, visible inside another package, and the fact that this element is actually referenced (used) inside a client package (the UML 1.1 standard definition gave its readers the impression that only those imported elements are exported again which are actually referenced in the client package).

Based on these assumptions a precise definition of the UML visibility rules for package should have about the following form:

(1) *Packages add their own elements to their namespace containers:* package P owns element e with visibility v implies that P contains e with visibility v.

(2) *Packages see the elements of their own namespace container:* package P contains element e with visibility v implies that P sees e with visibility v.

(3) *Packages may not depend on or specialize invisible packages:* package P has an import or access dependency or a generalization relationship to package Q with visibility v requires that P sees Q with visibility greater equal v.

(4) *Packages add imported elements to their own namespaces:* package P has an import dependency to package Q with visibility v and Q contains a public element e implies that P contains e (under its old name or a new alias name) with a visibility less equal than v.

(5) *Packages see public elements of accessed or contained packages:* package P has an access dependency to package Q with visibility v or contains package Q with visibility v and Q contains a public element e implies that P sees e under the path name Q::e with visibility v.

(6) *Packages extend the namespace of specialized packages:* package P has a generalization relationship to package Q with visibility v and Q contains (sees) an element e with public or protected visibility v' implies that P contains (sees) e with the minimum of the visibilities v and v' as its own visibility.

(7) *Friends have access to all elements of server packages:* Package P has a friend dependency to package Q with visibility v and Q contains an element e with visibility v' implies that P sees e under the path name Q::e with the minimum of the visibilities v and v' as its own visibility.

6.   SUMMARY

The development of the UML package concept and its accompanying visibility rules seems to be a never-ending story. First versions of the package concept were mainly influenced by the design of the package concept of the programming language Java [AG96]. The fact that Java does not associate any visibility rules with the file-system-directory-like nesting of its packages had the consequence that UML got its own rules for propagating visible elements up the hierarchy of nested packages [OMG99b]. Later on the developers of UML decided that its package concept should be more similar to the well-defined package concept of the programming language Ada [C96]. As a consequence the direction for propagating visible elements was reversed in UML 1.3 [OMG99a] — in our opinion without taking all negative consequences of this decision for a system modeling and not a programming language into account.

This contribution explained why we believe that the UML package concept should be modified again. Furthermore, it showed how a precise definition of its visibility rules might look like. Please note that all rules presented in the previous section are probably valid for UML 1.3 (draft alpha R2), except for the treatment of nested packages in rule (5). Nevertheless, we have to admit (complain) that almost all presented rules are subject to further discussions. It is for instance a matter of debate

- whether generalization relationships preserve ownership of elements or whether the elements owned by the more general package are treated similar to imported elements in the more specific package and

- whether the generalization relationship propagates only the namespace of the more general package to the more specific package or whether it propagates visibility rights of access dependencies, too.

Finally, we have to emphasize that it is not always possible to evaluate the pros and cons of different solutions faithfully without conducting any real case studies. It would for instance be interesting to add different versions of visibility rules to UML case tools, and to check how often constructed models (the UML meta model itself would be an ideal candidate for this purpose) are in conflict with the implemented set of rules.

References

[AG96]   Ken Arnold and James Gosling. *The JAVA Programming Language*. The Java Series. Addison-Wesley, Reading, MA, 1996.

[BCK98]   L. Bass, P. Clements, and R. Kazman. *Software Architecture in Practice*. Addison Wesley, Reading, Mass., 1998.

[C96]   Norman Cohen. *Ada as a second language*. McGraw-Hill, New York, 1996.

[DK76]   F. DeRemer and H. Kron. Programming-in-the-large versus programming-in-the-small. *IEEE Transactions on Software Engineering*, 2(2):80–86, 1976.

[ES94]   Margaret Ellis and Bjarne Stroustrup. *The Annotated C++ Reference Manual*. Addison-Wesley, Reading, MA, 1994.

[GP95]   David Garlan and Dewayne E. Perry. Introduction to the special issue on software architecture. *IEEE Transactions on Software Engineering*, 21(4):269–274, 1995.

[OMG99a]   OMG. *Object Management Group (OMG) Unified Modeling Language Specification (draft), Version 1.3 alpha R2*, 1999. http://www.rational.com/uml/resources/documentation/index.jtmpl.

[OMG99b] OMG. *UML Semantics, Version 1.1*, 1999. http://www.rational.com/ uml/resources/documentation/semantics/index.jtmpl.

[RJB99] J. Rumbaugh, I. Jacobson, and G. Booch. *The Unified Modeling Language Reference Manual.* Addison Wesley, Reading, Mass., 1999.

[R92]   Peter J. Robinson. *Hierarchical Object-Oriented Design.* Prentice Hall, Englewood Cliffs, MA, 1992.

[SG96]   M. Shaw and D. Garlan. *Software Architecture - Perspectives on an Emerging Discipline.* Prentice Hall, Upper Saddle River, New Jersey, 1996.

[SR98]   B. Selic and J. Rumbaugh. *Using UML for Modeling Complex Real-Time Systems.* ObjecTime Limited, 340 March Rd., Kanata, Ontario, Canada, 1998. http://www.objectime.com/otl/technical/umlrt.html.

[SW97]   A. Schürr and A.J. Winter. Formal definition and refinement of uml's module/package concept. In J. Bosch and S. Mitchell, editors, *Object-Oriented Technology — ECOOP '97 Workshop Reader*, volume 1357 of *Lecture Notes in Computer Science*, pages 211–215, Berlin, 1997. Springer Verlag.

[SW98]   A. Schürr and A.J. Winter. Formal definition of uml's package concept. In M. Schader and A. Korthaus, editors, *The Unified Modeling Language — Technical Aspects and Applications*, pages 144–159. Physica-Verlag, Heidelberg, 1998.

[WS84]   Richard M. Wiener and Richard Sincovec. *Software Engineering with Modula-2 and Ada.* John Wiley, New York, 1984.

About the Authors

Andy Schürr is a full professor in the Institute for Software Technology at the University of the German Federal Armed Forces, Munich. He is the speaker of the GI (German Computer Science Society) working group GROOM on "foundations of object-oriented modeling". His research interests include visual languages in general as well as object-oriented development of embedded realtime systems.

Andreas J. Winter is researcher at the Aachen University of Technology. Among his interests is the formal definition of object-oriented and visual languages.

Chapter 15

USING INFORMATION MODELING TO DEFINE BUSINESS REQUIREMENTS

Mark A Shafer

United Services Automobile Association
Mark.Shafer@USAA.Com

Abstract   For the most part, developing business requirements is still treated as an art as opposed to a science. The concept of using the rigor and precision necessarily associated to code with the process of defining business requirements is not widely known or accepted. In a few instances at USAA, we have attempted to use our limited knowledge of Information Modeling to achieve that goal and make explicit all of the information necessary to develop systems that satisfy the business requirements. This document describes a small instance.

1.   OVERVIEW

My company, like many others out there, is looking for a definitive technique by which all business requirements can be developed, measured, and costed to move to a repeatable process. A large part of the problem is the lack of consensus about what a good business requirement is. Where I work, the majority of the time that requirements are addressed for software development, the term requirement is used interchangeably with the term 'business process' to describe the actual business processes being analyzed. This anomaly creates confusion about what is actually the requirement and what is actually the business process. Because requirements exist for all facets of an enterprise, it is very important to be able to separate the concept of the requirement from the associative facet it is describing. A requirement by definition is a need. A need cannot exist in isolation, but must be associated to the thing that is needed, or needing to be changed, based upon the objective (why). With software development the need is usually associated to new functionality (how) or changes to existing functionality. This functionality is realized via what we refer to as a business process or collection of business processes. The separation of the requirement (or need) from the business process is critical as the combination of the two inevitably contains implementation details (the requirement, or need, describes how the process needs to be accomplished). That is why the concept of a *business specification* [KR94, KS96] is invaluable for the separation of the information associated to the actual business process from the information about the requirement that describes the changes to the business process. By focusing analysis on the precision of the business specification and documenting the specification in such a way that it can be universally understood and agreed upon, a framework can be created that will be the basis for the implementation of a system that satisfies the business needs. The primary value of the business framework is the ability to continue to understand and change the business process(s) due to the common understanding of the core functionality and implications of changes to the underlying structure.

2.   BUSINESS SPECIFICATION PROCESS

For the most part, we have had the misfortune of learning through trial and error the process of developing business specifications and still have not perfected the practice. Haim Kilov and Allan Ash describe the process we tried to follow very eloquently in their paper 'How to ask questions: Handling complexity in a business specification' [KA97], so I won't walk through the approach, but instead concentrate on the actual experience. What's important to note is that even though rigorous and precise specifications are the ultimate deliverable, the initial stages are quite the opposite in regards to the Modeling that actually occurs. We began (and always begin) with a collection of business concepts and relationships. We don't worry about whether or not the concept is a physical "thing" or a state of a "thing" at this point in time, but instead start to form a collection of information about the business objective of the overall business process. Fowler and Scott refer to this as Domain Modeling [FS97], while Kilov and Ash refer to the information as *primitives*. Whatever you call it, it is invaluable for creating a medium of communication that the business subject matter experts and the business analysts can relate to. By focusing on the end result of the business processes via the business primitives, a very logical business process decomposition is arrived at naturally through information Modeling techniques, specifically the definition of pre-conditions and post-conditions. During this phase we are focusing on things, states of things, and relationships between things. The rules for aggregates will be derived at a later point in time, as this is one way we help hide some of the details. These current models therefore only contain relationships that represent elementary associations (with further definition to be added), static subtyping, and dynamic subtyping as defined by Kilov and Ross [KR94].

3.   PROJECT DESCRIPTION

We used (are using) information Modeling techniques to understand and document the business processes used for the project 'Originate Mortgages In House (IHOM)'. The project scope is fairly large as it entails developing the ability to Originating Mortgages internally as opposed to merely acting as a front end (or sales) of home mortgages as we do today. The scope embodies all of the business processes needed to Create a Home Loan Mortgage and have it ready to be sold to a 'Wholesale Purchaser'. The project had actually been under way for several months and had been focusing on the development of business requirements. The need to stop and add some structure to the effort was not well received initially by all of the business community as the feeling was that the information was very well understood and documented.

The results of the analysis effort to date had consisted of six very high level business processes, (Sales, Counseling, Fulfilment, Processing, Closing, and Post-Closing) and a myriad of low level steps that were described via the systems that were to be used to accomplish the individual steps. The business processes were largely based on organizational responsibilities as opposed to the activities actually performed. The majority of the effort had focused on how the system might work without much analysis of the actual business. There was a general level of agreement of what the overall scope of the project entailed and what was expected to be accomplished. But, the ability to do things differently (as stated in the project charter) was not easily understood due to the lack of definitiveness in the steps documented in the Originate Mortgage Process. Also the ability to develop a different organization in support was very difficult to analyze due to the organizational influence in the definition of the high-level business processes.

The first step in working with the SMEs was to create a common understanding of the result of the Originate Mortgage Process at an abstract level (post-condition). By gaining a general understanding of the kinds of things generated and used in mortgage origination, the team could focus on naming the business processes on the things that were generated by the processes, not on the organization performing the processes. The following diagram was generated and agreed upon as the main objective.

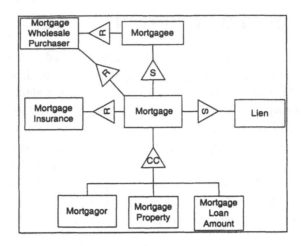

Figure 1. Originate Mortgages: Post-Condition

You can see that this is an extremely simple collection of business concepts, but the simplicity, and the importance of these particular concepts provide a very good foundation to base further analysis on. The next step was to work with the previously defined high-level business processes and gain an understanding of each of the post-conditions associated with those steps and map these to the concepts defined above. This exercise proved valuable for multiple reasons. The first thing it forced the team to do is to focus on the results of the individual processes, not the organization that performs it. Secondly it added clarity to the process by coming to some common agreement of the state of the business objects prior to continuation of the Originate Mortgage process. This helped clarify what changes to the business objects were performed during each phase of the process, and potential interfaces identified. Thirdly it helped identify gaps in the understanding of how the Originate Mortgage process would actually work. These breakpoints, based solely upon the business object development, helped us to look at changes to the business objects such as the Mortgage Customer, the Mortgage Property, the Mortgage Loan, and identify those primary business objects that undergo several state changes. The post-conditions included the states of the objects and were represented as dynamic subtypes. Two of the Post-Conditions are shown below as examples[1].

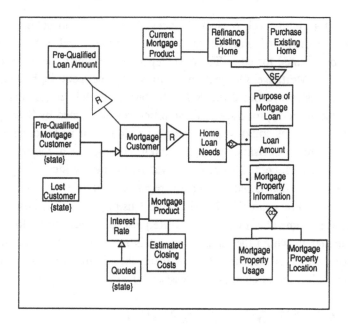

Figure 2. Mortgage Sales Post-Condition

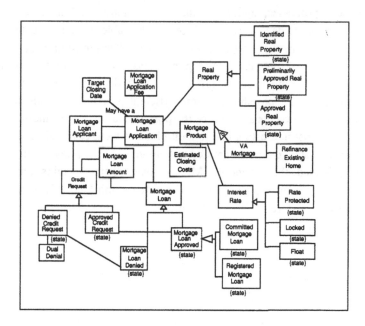

Figure 3. Mortgage Counseling Post-Condition

Each of the high-level business processes (Sales, Counseling, Fulfilment, Processing, Closing, and Post-Closing) were analyzed and the specific post-conditions documented for each. The next step was to identify the event or triggers that caused the Mortgage Origination to move to the next high-level business process. This was sometimes difficult for the business SME as (for example) they tended to think of Sales processes as those processes performed by Sales personnel. But the same processes could be performed by a Counselor under certain situations (difficulty of credit decision, property abnormalities) even though they were considered a Sales Process. This problem was overcome by identifying changes to the business model that acted as triggers regardless of who was performing the business process. For example, the Mortgage Customer leaves Sales and goes to Counseling at the time they make a formal Request for Credit for a Mortgage Loan. It doesn't matter to whom the Credit Request is made, or even which lower-level process from which it appears. The moment the Credit Request is made, the 'Counseling' collection of business processes is entered[2].

4.   BUSINESS SATISFACTION

By doing nothing more rigorous than defining explicitly the post conditions of each of the business processes, and removing the organizational influence from the business processes names, the project team was able to better categorize the information that had for the most part been a large collection of unmanageable data. This information was then used by the business SMEs to start to look at the opportunity of combining business processes that had previously been divided by organizational structure into shorter, more efficient processes. By focusing on the states of the business objects as a part of the post-condition, the business objects that proved to be the most interesting due to their changes were easily identified early on in the analysis and state diagrams created to help manage the points in time changes. This in turn helped the business SMEs manage their thoughts and verbalize information about the business objects as the process unfolded. The following state diagram shows the different views of a Mortgage Customer during the development of a Mortgage Loan.

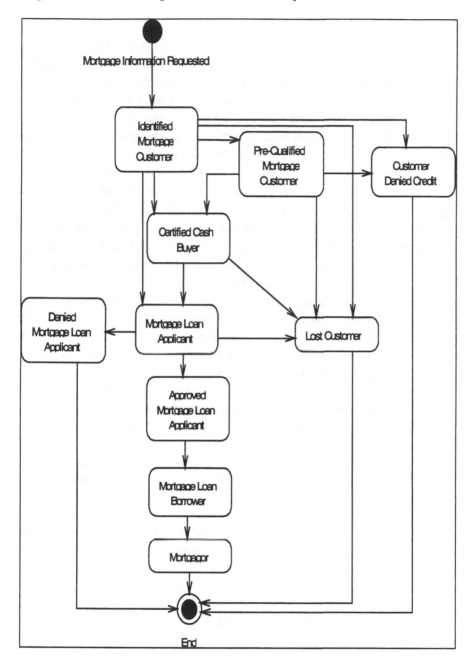

Figure 4. Mortgage Customer State Diagram

The quick realization of these states was made possible through the use of information Modeling. The business SME stated that subconsciously she understood that the she viewed the Mortgage Customer in each of these roles, but, had never had it explicitly defined for her. This helped the SME more easily define the processes that affected the business object at each of the specific points in time as opposed to treating the business object as a singular thing that did not change roles.

Another business SME was extremely happy with the ability to define 'when we're done' at each step along the way without having to complete the entire process. The creation of the post-conditions based upon changes only to the business model provided definitive start and stop points in the process that had previously been extremely fuzzy. This proved to be extremely valuable information when gathering tracking/monitoring requirements for the life of the mortgage. The gap analysis was also an extremely useful output to the business. The process helped crystallize those processes that are well understood and compartmentalized those areas that need better definition. The areas that lacked full understanding were documented as issues for future analysis. The ability to understand what specifically *isn't known* is almost as valuable as understanding what is known.

Pre-conditions were also created during the process. This information was used to define flow and dependencies between the business processes. This also served as a 'check' against the post-conditions from the original processes. As the post-conditions were defined, whether or not the business object had to exist, or be in a specific state prior to the next process initiating helped the business SMEs understand how the business processes overlap, execute simultaneously, or have start to finish relationships. These relationships were then used to create flowcharts. Much to my chagrin, the flowcharts have probably been perceived as the most valuable deliverable from the exercise, and are being used to distribute the information among the personnel who 'need to know'. I can take satisfaction in knowing that the flowcharts flow logically based upon the business model created during the first pass of analysis. Also, in only three weeks, the results of the exercise that had initially not been well received by the community is being used as the primary method of communication with external vendors and others. The output (which is still work in progress) is now being scheduled for session reviews and feedback with the Project Sponsor and become an integral part of the project plan. The business buy-in has been far greater than we had originally hoped for and is very encouraging for the project team as we progress in the development of the business requirements with the Information Modeling technique.

5.   REFERENCES

[FS97] M.Fowler, K.Scott. *UML Distilled, Applying the Standard Object Modeling Language.* Addison-Wesley,1997.

[KA97] H.Kilov, A.Ash. How to ask questions: Handling complexity in a business specification. In: *Proceedings of the OOPSLA '97 Workshop on object-oriented behavioral semantics* (Atlanta, October 6th, 1997), ed. by H.Kilov, B.Rumpe, I.Simmonds, Munich University of Technology, TUM-19737, pp.99-114.

[KR94] H.Kilov, J.Ross, *Information Modeling: an Object-oriented Approach.* Prentice-Hall, 1994.

[KS96] H.Kilov, I.Simmonds. How to correctly refine business specifications, and know it. In: *Proceedings of the Fifth Workshop on Specification of Behavioral Semantics (at OOPSLA '96),* ed. by H.Kilov and V.J. Harvey, Robert Morris College, 1996, pp. 57-69.

---

[1] We use additional documentation to support the association information due to our modeling tool. The simple associations are supported by rules stating dependencies, the cause of the association, etc.

[2] You may have noticed that even though I say we removed the organizational aspect from the business process decomposition, we retained the high level names that reflect the organization. This was an agreed upon compromise between the business community and the modellers. The 2nd level of decomposition on down reflects the results of the output.

About the Author

Mark Shafer is a Systems Architect at United Services Automobile Association (USAA) in San Antonio, TX. He has over 18 years experience in the development of information systems using multiple methodologies. He has been working with object-oriented development techniques for the last 6 years, and applying information modeling techniques for the last 3 years. He has written several white papers on requirements definition and business decomposition, helped developed the requirements definition process for the Software Engineering Process Group at USAA, and teaches a section on requirements modeling at USAA.

Chapter 16

A LAYERED CONTEXT PERSPECTIVE ON THE DESIGN OF ENTERPRISES AND INFORMATION SYSTEMS

Ian Simmonds

IBM TJ Watson Research Center
30 Saw Mill River Road
Hawthorne, NY 10532, USA
simmonds@us.ibm.com

David Ing

IBM Advanced Business Institute
Route 9W
Palisades, NY 10964-8001
daviding@ca.ibm.com

Abstract Most information systems requirements approaches mirror the techniques of business planning methods prevalent in the 1960s and 1970s. This was a period in which requirements, like plans, could be established in advance, and then implemented. Gradual changes in requirements could be analyzed and foreseen, and could result in slight modification requests.

Today, businesses operate in an increasingly complex, networked economy. They face changes that are discontinuous and increasingly less predictable. In contrast to the mechanistic, production-line view of work, enterprise processes are now considered as social activities founded in organizational knowledge. More and more business professionals perform information-intensive work within empowered work groups.

A new perspective is required. Firstly, enterprises which seek to be adaptive are finding their informational support systems to be mission-critical. The need for change in the enterprise outstrips the pace of change in existing information systems. Secondly, many traditional approaches to capturing requirements are inadequate. As the human-computer interaction and management information systems communities have long known, there are deep epistemological reasons why detailed system requirements cannot be simply captured into a static document prior to development.

We seek to develop practices, technologies and underlying theory that will ease change in information systems as enterprises adapt to changes in their environments. From Stewart Brand's study of built environments we borrow a model of change as layers that shear against each other at different rates. We follow the development of ideas by Christopher Alexander — best known in software circles for his 1970s work on patterns — towards a greater understanding of design and construction practice.

At the center of our approach are concepts of 'context,' 'context support,' 'context support machine' and 'mutual awareness.' We describe how these enable an enterprise to render its information technologies more adaptable.

1. INTRODUCTION

Many information system developers today still believe that an unambiguous, objective set of requirements for an information system can be obtained from pre-implementation analysis sessions with business professionals. They believe that these requirements, as objective specifications, should then be the absolute target towards which applications should be designed and constructed.

In his keynote speech at OOPSLA '96, Christopher Alexander criticized this perspective:

> Please forgive me. I'm going to be very directly blunt for a horrible second. But it could be viewed that the technical way in which you [software designers and theorists] look at programming at the moment is almost like 'guns for hire.' In other words, you are the technicians, you know how to make the programs work, 'tell us what to do Daddy, and we'll do it.'

Any analyst who has tried (and failed) to establish a durable set of requirements will concur. The quest for definitive experts — "Daddies" who will "tell us what to do" — is common. Since enterprises are social organizations, obtaining a uniform set of requirements in the reality of multiple reference sources is problematic. Requirements simply cannot be extracted from manuals and interviews to form a model on paper that can then be 'built' with no further involvement from potential users.

Overcoming this problem requires at least three changes to the knowledge and practices of information systems developers, including those of business analysts, architects, programmers and even users. Firstly, they must gain an appreciation of why requirements capture is problematic. We review this in Section 2. Secondly, they must develop a sense (a "warm and fuzzy feeling") that a better way may exist — an ideal towards which they can aspire. For this we reuse experiences with other forms of built structures, borrowing Stewart Brand's notion of shearing layers and Christopher Alexander's understanding of design and construction practices. We review these in Section 3. Thirdly, beyond a "warm and fuzzy feeling," they require a set of rigorous constructs that they can use for their own work in information systems development. Notions of 'context,' 'context support,' 'context support machine' and 'mutual awareness' are presented in Section 4.

These ideas provide a foundation for additional refinement. Section 5 hints at some of the difficult problems that remain to be resolved.

2. EVEN IF YOU COULD CAPTURE DETAILED REQUIREMENTS (WHICH YOU CAN'T), ENTERPRISE NEEDS CONSTANTLY CHANGE

Research in human-computer interaction, information systems and management theory demonstrates that it is naive to expect a business professional to be able to simply tell you what they want or need. The theory and practice of software requirements need to catch up with this realization.

2.1. A Model is a Very Poor Substitute for the Real Thing

The design of any complex thing is highly problematic. Designers usually rely upon models.[1] However, models inherently limit what can be learned about user needs. Alexander describes this phenomenon in building construction:

> Drawings serve as an important rough sketch of something that will be built, but must be executed with constant attention to room shape, light, wall and ceiling detail, openings — above all to the feelings which arise in each place, in the construction, as it is taking shape. These feelings are too complicated to predict, and *cannot* be predicted. When a building is built from plans that are conceived on the drawing board, and then simply built, the result is sterile at best — silly most of the time — and sometimes unthinkably bad. This is something familiar in virtually all large buildings that have been built since 1950. It is inevitable, given the process of construction used to build them. And it is inevitable that this process must lead to unsatisfactory results. [ABT95, p. 80, original emphasis]

The problem is one of epistemology and methodology. Epistemology is "the theory of knowledge, [especially] with regards to its methods and validation."[2] Just what does it take for someone to truly know something, about herself, about somebody else, or about anything in physical, virtual or social reality? In particular, what is the best way of finding it out, and how good an understanding should you expect to be able to develop? No wonder that "For most of the modern period of philosophy, from Descartes to the present, epistemology has been the central philosophical discipline" [G96, p.38].

The development of methods for determining the practical and theoretical knowledge of others is a particularly acute concern within sociological study [BW92]. The determination of the knowledge of other people, including their habits, language, dress, demeanor and all other aspects of their practices, relies on the knowledge of the researcher. In the process of studying people, the researcher must pay scrupulous attention to her use of her own knowledge. She needs to determine whether what she is studying is a phenomenon "out there" or something that her own expectations and prejudices are imposing upon the object of study.

Epistemology is of acute concern for all forms of design, since it implies — as Alexander pointed out above — that models are intrinsically inadequate. All forms of design are interventions into the practices of other people. Design not only requires scrupulous sociological attention to existing practices. It requires an understanding of what practices will be after they have been adapted to the use of the artifact being designed. Therefore, the best that a designer can do is to allow users to experience the designed thing as it is being conceived, prototyped and constructed.

2.2. The Human-Computer Interaction Community Approaches Design within the Usage Situation

These epistemological issues are not new to software. Since the mid-1980s, techniques such as user-centered design [ND86], prototyping, and participatory design [SN93] have emphasized the importance of involving users in system design. Kyng explains that more is needed [K95]:

> [System] designers may overlook crucial, obvious-after-the-fact issues due to lack of fit between their laboratory settings and the work situation of the users. A first important step toward bridging the gap is to get the users themselves into the design process; but it is not enough. As long as the users don't experience what it would be like to work with a system under development, their contributions will mainly be based on prejudice, that is, on prejudgment.

The ideal would seem to be to design human-computer interactions *in the situation in which the systems are used*, and as they are used.

Suchman has been highly influential in the community through the ideas presented in *Plans and Situated Actions* [S87]. People improvise with what they have "at hand" in the situation [WF87] rather than sticking to prescribed plans. Some get annoyed by highly procedural interfaces and those that limit their ability to improvise. Similar in spirit is Carroll's minimalist approach [C90] which can be extended from an application in user documentation to the design of information systems in general. By providing a flexible minimum set of tools that imposes no unnecessary constraints, each user is allowed to be creative as they use the software in different situations. She is able to take advantage of the unique human ability of sense making [W95].

Information systems development methodologies often fail to take heed of these lessons, even when they tackle complexity by means of abstraction, precision and rigor. This failure leads their disciples to inadvertent and inevitable errors [HKL95]. For example, Button and Harper describe a case of where methodology led to an "official story" of how work was done in a company which bore little or no relation to the way that work was actually performed [BH93]. As a result, the new information technologies were unusable. This case is by no means unique.

Suchman's thinking had a great influence on many other approaches within the human-computer interaction community, in addition to those listed above [DB98]. Reflection on the practice of information systems development has had notable effects on techniques such as prototyping and iterative development. The ideas place a focus on scenarios of use, although in techniques such as the capture of Use Cases the original spirit has not been fully preserved.

2.3. Management Theory Suggests that Adaptive Enterprises can Proactively Engage in Situated Learning and Change

The epistemological challenge of requirements specification is but one problem: with the rapid rate of change in the marketplace, business enterprises are being encouraged to adopt approaches to strategy that render a portfolio of information technologies obsolete ever more quickly.

Faced with an environment which is undergoing constant unpredictable and discontinuous change, the only feasible strategy for an enterprise is to design it to be adaptive. This is the premise of Steve Haeckel's Sense-and-Respond organization [H95, H99].

A Sense-and-Respond organization is conceived of and designed as a system[3] — an adaptive, purposeful, social system. General systems theory provides a range of useful foundations for understanding social systems, including an emphasis on *purposefulness* [AE72]. Purposefulness — both at the level of the system as a whole, and at the level of its component subsystems — distinguishes a social system from other kinds of system [AG96].[4] Governance of an enterprise requires the alignment of purposes in its parts (e.g., individual people and teams) with the purpose of the whole (i.e., function to its primary constituency). In the Sense-and-Respond organization, this alignment is achieved through "context-and-coordination," in which the leadership provides a context consisting of an enterprise "reason for being" and governing principles. Empowered employees coordinate their outcomes by making commitments consistent with the context in which the commitments are made [H95, H99].

The vector for adaptation is informed through continued inquiry into value to the primary constituency, and organizational purpose. To leverage the knowledge of multiple constituencies, a number of different methods of inquiry, and multiple perspectives are incorporated. Churchman describes a number of approaches in *The Design of Inquiring Systems* [C72], which have been extended to "unbounded systems thinking" by Mitroff and Linstone [ML93].[5] Since an enterprise is a purposeful system producing value for customers, it must focus inquiry on continually refining its understanding of what its customers consider to be of value, and the appropriateness of the declared purpose of the enterprise. The resulting 'tug of war' (or 'dialectic') between inquiries into customer value and organizational purpose allows the enterprise to determine in which direction it must adapt.

A strategy of adaptiveness embraces change through the expression of enterprise structure, both in terms of organizational capabilities and individual roles. This drives a need for adaptability in the information technologies supporting the enterprise.

3. CHANGE IS ACCOMMODATED THROUGH A LAYERED APPROACH TO DESIGN AND CONSTRUCTION

Our goal is to produce an information systems development approach that complements Haeckel's Sense-and-Respond design for an Adaptive Enterprise [H99].

The proposed approach shares theoretical foundations with the Sense-and-Respond organization: in management theory, sociology, learning organizations, epistemology and, above all, systems thinking. An understanding of the design of organizations, however, is not sufficiently prescriptive for the design of effective information systems.

These foundations must be augmented by an understanding of the adaptation of constructed things. Technology is not, in itself, adaptive. It is constructed and adapted by people. Stewart Brand offers a way of thinking about the adaptation of a building by the people occupying it. His work is complemented by a wide variety of practices for building design and construction developed by architect Christopher Alexander. These ideas can be carried over from the fields of built environments into the field of information systems development.

3.1. Change can be expressed as layers shearing against each other

In *How Buildings Learn* [B94], Brand sought to gain insight into organizational learning by studying buildings. "I wanted to see some physical trace of organizational learning (and failure to learn) in action. A study of buildings changing over time seemed like the right place to look" [B94a].

Brand's key finding was that buildings are subjected to several qualitatively different kinds and rates of change. He categorizes these kinds and rates of change in buildings as six *shearing layers*:[6]

> SITE — This is the geographical setting, the urban location, and the legally defined lot, whose boundaries outlast generations of ephemeral buildings. ...
> STRUCTURE — The foundation and load-bearing elements are perilous and expensive to change, so people don't. These *are* the building. Structural life ranges from 30 to 300 years ...
> SKIN — Exterior surfaces now change every 20 years or so, to keep up with fashion or technology, or for wholesale repair. ...
> SERVICES — These are the working guts of a building: communications wiring, electrical wiring, plumbing, sprinkler system, HVAC (heating, ventilation, and air conditioning), and moving parts like elevators and escalators. They wear out or obsolesce every 7 to 15 years. Many buildings are demolished early if their outdated systems are too deeply embedded to replace easily.
> SPACE PLAN — The interior layout, where walls, ceilings, floors, and doors go. Turbulent commercial space can change every 3 years; exceptionally quiet homes might wait 30 years.
> STUFF — Chairs, desks, phones, pictures; kitchen appliances, lamps, hair brushes; all the things that twitch around daily to monthly. Furniture is called *mobilia* in Italian for good reason. [B94, p. 13].

Much of Brand's book consists of illustrations of these kinds and rates of change occurring alongside each other.[7]

Brand observed that buildings considered as "livable" by their occupants are constructed to tolerate this variety of changes. They are constructed in appropriate shearing layers. Two buildings at MIT contrast successful and poor implementations of shearing layers. Building 20, which hosted the World War II team that developed radar for the United States and, later, the renowned Research Laboratory of Linguistics, "is a sprawling 250,000-square-foot three-story wood structure." "If you don't like a wall, just stick your elbow through it." "If you want to bore a hole in the floor to get a little extra vertical space, you do it. You don't ask." In stark contrast is the MIT Media Lab, designed by I.M. Pei in 1986: "Getting new cabling through the interior concrete walls — a necessity in such a building — requires bringing in jackhammers. You can't even move interior walls around, thanks to the overhead lights being at a Pei-signature 45-degree angle to everything else" (p. 53). In this case, the "structure" gets in the way of the "space plan." This forces the building occupants to adapt to the environment, rather than the environment being adaptable to their needs.

Brand's perspective on shearing layers within built structures provides a description of how 'good' design can be differentiated from 'bad' design, in terms of its robustness in the face of change.

3.2. Improving the Quality in Built Things Requires an Understanding of Design and Construction Practices

An understanding of shearing layers informs understanding as to why a built structure may or may not be adaptable. It is not a prescription for ensuring quality. It only provides guidelines for real world practice. In addition, the ability to adapt is just one measure of quality. More is required to suggest ways in which information systems development should change.

Christopher Alexander has devoted his career to reversing the cataclysmic decline in the aesthetic quality of the built world [G83]. His earliest work sought analytic approaches to the satisfaction of complex webs of requirements [A68]. Frustrated by this highly technical approach, he sought to return control of building to the building's users and purchasers by articulating the formerly tacit 'language' of what makes buildings satisfying [A79]. Having seen the limitations of the resulting pattern languages [AIS77] he then turned to a reexamination of the entire web of practices surrounding building construction. This included funding, organization, training institutions, materials, regulation, commissioning, and governing contracts, as well as construction itself [G83, ANAK87, ABT95, Ata].

The culmination of his work is a theory relating quality and aesthetics to the practices of design and construction. Most of his practices have been proven to be successful. Alexander's theory and practices complement Brand's intuitions on shearing layers. They recognize and unify phenomena that occur, change and are understood on qualitatively different scales and rates. They recognize that the achievement of quality in the built world requires a systemic engagement with that world.

3.3. Quality is Determined by the Relationships Between 'Centers'

According to Alexander, quality in any portion — large or small — of the built world is largely determined by the system of 'centers' that it embodies. Consequently, practices are founded upon a theory both of quality, and of the relationship between quality and practices in design and construction [A93,Ata].

A 'center' can be considered from at least three perspectives. In (1) a physical space, (2) a thing is constructed that results in (3) a site of possible social meanings. An example from Alexander's earlier work is a physical volume used by small groups of people (a physical space), called an alcove (a constructed thing), which provides an environment for semi-intimate, semi-private social interactions (social meaning).

The production of satisfying rooms, buildings, neighborhoods and cities is difficult, since *quality lies in the relationships between centers* rather than in the centers themselves. It is not any individual center which makes a building a success. It is the system of centers within the building which governs the way that social and psychological interactions will occur. For example, it determines the levels and gradients of intimacy throughout the building that determine where people are willing to behave or interact in certain ways, and how comfortable they will be in doing so in these physical surroundings.[8]

Any change or addition to a building disrupts its system of centers. The quality of the building as a whole is changed by the creation or destruction of centers, and the weakening or strengthening of relationships. An improvement in quality on any scale can only be achieved by considering each change as a part in a larger attempt to "heal" the whole — to reduce existing tensions within the system of centers, to make it richer or more satisfying [ANAK87]. This consideration must be at the foundation of all practices related to design and construction.

3.4. Appropriate Design is Revealed as the System of Centers is Understood

Since Alexander regards models as a poor substitute for the real thing, he creates full scale, *in situ* mockups rather than models [Ata]. The full nature of relationships between centers emerges only through the process of construction. Choices are framed by the unfolding situation. This requires that centers should be experienced in great detail, before the grand expense of construction commitments is incurred. His extensive use of cheap, throwaway materials such as sticks and corrugated cardboard makes *in situ* mockups of possible designs both practical and economically feasible.

In constructing a building, centers are layered as each new center is added to the set which has already been put into place. The first layer to be defined is obviously the site of the building as a whole [ANAK87, Ata]. The site, however, is not the first relevant center. The site is situated in the context of the existing neighbourhood.

People affected by centers at any level of scale are encouraged to participate in the design of those centers. For example, neighbors are invited to assist in the design of a building's boundaries. The use of physical mockups replaces the details of traditional "requirements" statements — of building specifications and blueprints — with a more tangible, *in situ*, representation of the proposed structure. There are two benefits of a more vivid representation of the building to those whose lives will be affected by the intervention: the emerging system of centers is reviewed at a time when changes are still feasible; and the role of the new building in helping to "heal" the whole — the neighborhood — can be experienced rather than just "imagined."

Each center completes and helps to define or create other centers, not only on its own scale, but also scales larger and smaller. From a merged process of design and construction, a building emerges as an "unfolding wholeness," even as it is occupied and used.

In situ mockups prior to and during construction are only one of the changes required to the practice of built environments. Alexander suggests changes in attitudes towards financing and contracting practices, as quality is a property which evolves over the entire duration of occupancy and cannot be foreseen before or as the first occupants move in [ABT95]. For example, a traditional approach to designing a family home would seek a list of requirements, such as the size of the family which the building would accommodate over the next decade. A layered approach to design allows design decisions to be made at a time when the family's situation is understood. What are the desired qualities of the home in which a young family will live for the next two years? Can the house accommodate one child (and then a second, or a third) without leaving rooms vacant today, or requiring major disruptions for renovation? Should bedrooms be constructed for easy access (e.g., for infants or disabled family members) or greater privacy (e.g., rebellious teenagers)?

In contrast to specifying the requirements of an "ultimate" family home prior to occupancy, design and construction can be viewed as *incremental and protracted activities* taking place over a twenty year horizon, or longer. Each requirement need not be specified until a time at which its attributes for choice can be properly understood. Not only does this approach better achieve the quality of a "livable environment" for both present and future occupants and neighbors; it can also change the economics of the industry. In contrast to an investment in a one-time megaproject, the sequential financing of increments may result in a lower overall cost. In effect, instead of contributing interest payments towards increasing the profitability of a bank, the homeowner's funds are directed specifically towards improving the quality of the building. The designer of the home should also take a stake in ensuring quality. The contract between the designer and homeowner can specify that some funds be held back, after each iteration or increment is completed, to permit the building to be experienced in reality. Based on these experiences, the homeowner and designer can engage in dialog about how these pre-committed funds should be applied, at that time, towards minor changes that are *known within the situation* to improve quality.

Alexander offers many other insights on the practice of building. Further insights into the relationship between quality and the practices of design and construction can only be appreciated by further study of his work. The interest in this chapter, however, is in applying the concepts that have been discussed towards the improvement of practices of building enterprise information systems.

4. THE CONTEXT PERSPECTIVE UNDERSCORES THE LAYERING IN INFORMATION SYSTEMS

The information systems which support an enterprise are produced in the contexts of (1) a business strategy expressed as organization structure, and (2) the practices of information systems development. We propose a *context perspective* appropriate to maintaining adaptability of information systems. This complements the Sense-and-Respond organization, which is a strategy for enterprise adaptiveness. The context perspective is derived as a refinement of Haeckel's notion of "context-and-coordination," and adapting Alexander's practices for design and construction.

4.1. An Enterprise and its Information Systems Form a System of Contexts

An enterprise is a complex system with human, social, and technological parts [H99]. It contains physical spaces, social spaces and virtual spaces, some of which are open to its environment (e.g., its customers). Individuals interact in physical spaces to produce tangible outcomes for the customers and constituencies of the enterprise. Hierarchies and networks (as formal and informal organizations) are social spaces which frame the relationships between people working in roles. In information intensive businesses, individuals increasingly communicate and exchange information with each other in virtual spaces — informational representations of business mediated through information and communication technologies.[9]

As the economy has moved from an industrial age to a postindustrial era, social spaces have become more important than physical spaces. "It's who you know that matters, rather than what you do." Simultaneously, physical spaces are gradually losing ground to virtual spaces. "I don't need to see her in person. I can just phone (or e-mail) her." Nevertheless, social spaces are embodied in, mediated by and partially determined by physical and virtual spaces. Trust is generated socially by face-to-face interaction, personal recommendation or other well-documented legitimation means. It is not uncommon (nor is it considered irrational) for individuals to feel more comfortable with people who dine in the same cafeteria[10] or who have jointly participated in electronic workgroups or long-distance dialogs. Working in social organizations requires that people seek common interests, meet, get to know each other, and then negotiate roles and relationships.

Context is an adaptable structure for the *formal* social spaces of the enterprise and their interconnections. At a top level, it is set by the leadership of the enterprise. At the same time, the spirit of 'coordination as self-organization amongst individuals' demonstrates the value of informal social spaces — including informal social networks — that emerge within the social system. Individuals are empowered to commit to outcomes on behalf of the enterprise as a whole, so long as the outcomes are consistent with the defined purpose and governing principles that are made unambiguous throughout the enterprise. Yet context is not solely generated hierarchially. Commitments are made by individuals who may play multiple roles. Commitments should be consistent not only across roles played by several people, but also for the many roles played by an individual. Each new commitment creates additional context not only for the parties who directly agree to the conditions of satisfaction, but also for others in the enterprise as a whole.

A context frames purposeful action towards the production of a specified outcome. Conditions of satisfaction unfold within this frame through conversation. Thus, 'context' is defined rather abstractly as a frame in which the conversations about purposeful action towards a particular outcome can unfold. The multiple contexts which situate commitments can be layered, and enable the spectrum from informal to formal social spaces. Accordingly, the layering of the information technologies which support purposeful action can be characterized in terms of the support they provide to particular contexts — that is, in terms of 'context support.'

4.2. Relationships Between Contexts may be Resultant or Emergent

Context-and-coordination is the governance model for a Sense-and-Respond organization. It supports scalable adaptiveness by emphazing the coupling of subordinate outcomes towards a primary outcome. This is in contrast to the "command-and-control" perspective, which couples subordinate activities towards a primary activity.

Context-and-coordination ensures enterprise adaptivity while maintaining enterprise coherence [H99]. Successive layers of context shear against each other, with each context subjected to the constraints of related contexts that may be more slowly or more rapidly changing [IS99]. The layer within the enterprise that should evolve most slowly is the purpose of the enterprise as a whole. The environment in which the enterprise is situated contains the even more slowly changing layers within society itself. These societal layers are called "culture."

Relationships between contexts are partially resultant and partially emergent. Some result from the commitments that lead to the creation of a context, corresponding to the chaining of outcomes towards a larger outcome. Others emerge within the activities of people as they work and coordinate to meet their commitments, constrained by higher levels of organizational or environmental context. For example, participants may discover that the outcomes of two or more contexts are either mutually supportive or in conflict. An example of mutually supportive outcomes in a consulting company is between a project to develop software for one customer and a higher-level organizational commitment that consulting become more asset-based. In this case, the company may decide that the project's outcome is of sufficiently broad application that it may become an asset. An example of conflicting outcomes is when the sale of either of two of a company's products can satisfy a single need for a customer. Here there is a danger that two product groups will fight for the customer's business, introducing risk into a more important and longer lasting context: the relationship between the company and its customer.

A key role for information technology is thus *mutual awareness*. Whether two context's outcomes are in conflict or mutually supportive, individual participants and the enterprise as a whole are usually better off if contexts and the people involved in them are mutually aware. Once contexts are mutually aware they are able to collaborate or compete. Information can be exchanged and coordination can occur.

While information technology can greatly simplify the establishment of mutual awareness between contexts, this must be done carefully. The flip side of easy mutual awareness is increased attention management. Much of the design of workflows — formal and informal — is highly pragmatic, with layers of formal social network introduced to free "in demand" people to focus their attention towards outcomes most in need of their expertise. Equally, mutual awareness between contexts should not imply mutual transparency. Once contexts become mutually aware they obtain information about each other through formal or situationally-improvised protocols that control information disclosure. The control of mutual visibility is an important phenomenon within organizations. Access to information can mean power or even abuse. If information technology does not grant users sufficient control over the disclosure of information then the users will simply not store that information in the technology. Information technology that is unable to disclose a person's information to others is in this sense more acceptable than that which is unable to withhold.

4.3. Adaptability of Information Technology requires a Strict Correspondence Between Units of Interaction and Technology

The context perspective is the recommendation that the emphasis of information systems development and resulting information technologies should be on contexts and coordination. Every interaction between individuals within an enterprise — whether or not it is towards the defining purpose of the enterprise as a whole — should be represented either as a commitment between roles, as a context, or both. The structure of commitment negotiation is informed by the procedures of contract law, such as offer, counter-offer and acceptance. The defining purpose and governing principles of the enterprise provide a top-level context, as do legal, moral and ethical standards in society at large.

Informational representations of commitments are common in business transactions. For example, an application form for a mortgage provides information gathered in a sales context for use in an underwriting context to determine whether a third, financing context should be established. And so on.

Structures of contexts should be recognized as foundational layers to be included in a business specification[11]. They are a natural basis for conceptual modeling [SI99]. Further, from a sociological perspective, each context comes with its own practices and terminology. The type of language used within the context can vary from highly stylized and technical "jargon" to "common usage" [S99b]. If the use of the stylized language is widespread, then it is more likely that many contexts are similar and will require a similar type of support. In such cases it is likely that investments in dedicated context support machines will be worthwhile. A portfolio including stable, context-specific context support machines (where language and practices are stylized), together with more general purpose, context-generic context support machines (where they are not) should provide a relatively stable foundational layer to support the enterprise as it adapts to its changing environment.

For information technologies to be truly adaptable, the shearing layers of social interaction, technological support and technological construction need to be transformed simultaneously. Information technology changes are too often expressed merely as a response to organizational changes. In reality, changes to information systems not only impact virtual spaces (as information technologies) but also social spaces (as the social interaction of individuals) and even physical spaces (for example, to colocate members of a new call center to foster informal social networks within the group). In the context perspective, the notions of "context," "context support" and "context support machine" are introduced to emphasize that units of social space (context), physical and virtual spaces (context support) and information and other technologies (context support machines) are three perspectives on the same thing.[12] We will discuss these three notions more fully in future publications.

4.4. The Layered Context Perspective Require Changes in Information System Development Practices

The Sense-and-Respond organization is presented as a transformation of the enterprise, rather than as a mere reformation [H99]. Similarly, the layered context perspective is seen as a discontinuous change in the practice of information systems development rather than as an incremental improvement.

Many — if not most — of Alexander's practices for the design of physical space can be carried over "as is" to the design of virtual space. They can, however, be enriched with lessons from human-computer interaction and Sense-and-Respond.

As we have seen, Alexander's insistence that each center be considered with respect to neighboring larger, smaller and peer centers translates naturally into Sense-and-Respond. Social relationships of commitment, mutual awareness and coordination between contexts replace aesthetic relationships between centers.

General Systems Theory suggests that information systems development, focusing on the design of virtual spaces, must be incorporated into the design of the adaptive enterprise as a whole. Whole businesses include physical, virtual and social spaces. The "perspective" in "context perspective" relates it as a perspective of Mitroff's unbounded systems thinking inquiry system [ML93].

The Sense-and-Respond organization's preoccupation with inquiry into purpose and value has a systemic impact on information systems development. For example, collection and consolidation of information about customers supports ongoing inquiries into what the customer considers to be of value.

Other practices corresponding to those mentioned in section 3.4 are the subject of current and future work.

5. CONCLUSIONS AND FUTURE DIRECTIONS

A Sense-and-Respond organization is a complex, purposeful, adaptive, social system. A basic premise for studying and intervening in social systems is that "social actions are irreducibly events-in-a-social-order and they cannot therefore be adequately identified independently of the social order in which they are embedded. Neither, on the other hand, can the social order in which the actions are sited be itself identified independently of the actions themselves" [SB91]. This leads us to a concern with epistemology, inquiry, situated design and a search for better practices.

As Shafer describes elsewhere in this book [S99], a focus on the outcomes of a context frees all participants in information systems development to be creative in the design of business processes. With explicit contexts we can reason about *why* in a way that procedural descriptions such as process and workflow diagrams simply do not allow. We see connections and transactions as what they are. Most importantly, we free people to act purposefully in the situations in which they find themselves rather than chaining them to rigid procedures. As Suchman observed [S87], only part of each situation is represented within the information technology. Only a purposeful actor has the awareness and ingenuity to improvise ways forward.

We have introduced a notion of "context" corresponding roughly to Alexander's "center."[13] This enables information systems developers to practice the design and construction of virtual space in much the same way as Alexander practices the design and construction of physical space. From the more limited perspectives of conceptual modeling and software implementation, the layered contexts perspective should enable a substantial separation of concerns at the level of the enterprise to be exploited at the level of information technology [SI99].

Much of our immediate work is focused on gaining experience with these ideas by applying and refining them in real business situations.

Like Alexander in his keynote speech at OOPSLA '96, we can envisage the merging of IT and architecture. This would lead to a unification of the design of the physical and virtual spaces that support the social spaces of a social system. The structure of physical space is a system of centers. That of virtual space is a system of contexts. In Brand's terms, information technologies are *precisely* (a subset of) the services shearing layers of the enterprise.

Future theoretical work involves an extension of the context model to Bourdieu's theory of practice (e.g., [BW92]) as well as other foundational assumptions from ethnomethodology (e.g., [B91], [DB98]), and the further integration of information systems development into the larger inquiries of the adaptive enterprise.

Acknowledgments

In developing the Sense-and-Respond organization, Steve Haeckel has produced a rich synthesis of a huge amount of useful material. This chapter is part of our ongoing effort to unravel and explore the consequences of both his synthesis and his sources.

Doug McDavid has forced us to dramatically improve our arguments by consistently insisting that metaphors for software and human organization borrowed from architecture are well known and worn out. With this chapter, we are a step closer to proving Doug wrong.

We wish to thank Haim Kilov for his constructive comments on this chapter, and our colleagues in the Sense-and-Respond and Enterprise Builder projects — Bard Bloom, Pat Brown, Steve Haeckel, Bob Kaiser, Marianne Kosits, Darrell Reimer and Mark Wegman — for many useful discussions on related topics. Ian also wishes to thank Gary Birch and Mark Skipper for a full day of discussions and sightseeing in San Francisco after we were thoroughly provoked by Christopher Alexander's speech at OOPSLA '96.

End Notes

1. A requirements specification — be it a business specification or a system specification — is both a model and a design, and therefore suffers from the same problems. However, the following argument is not intended as an excuse for not producing them.
2. Concise Oxford English Dictionary, 8th Edition, 1990.
3. In the remainder of this chapter we use the word "system" in the technical sense of general systems theory. Ackoff defines a system as: "a whole that contains two or more parts that satisfy the following five conditions. (1) The whole has one or more defining functions. ... (2) Each part in the set can affect the behavior or properties of the whole. ... (3) There is a subset of parts that is sufficient in one or more environments for carrying out the defining function of the whole; each of these parts is separately necessary but insufficient for carrying out this defining function. ... (4) The way that the behavior or properties of each part of a system affects its behavior or properties depends on the behavior or properties of at least one other part of the system. ... (5) The effect of a subset of parts on the system as a whole depends on the behavior of at least one other subset." [A94, pp.18-21]
4. A social system such as a business enterprise has a purpose (for example, "to manufacture information systems"). At the same time its parts — including individual people and teams or groups — act purposefully. This becomes a problem when the purpose of individuals (e.g., a desire to stick to a 9-to-5 work day) is out of line with that of the organization (e.g., a desire to offer 24-by-7 customer support). This is not a problem in a mechanistic system (which is not purposeful either in its whole or its parts), in an organismic system (which has purpose in its whole but not in its parts), nor in an ecological system (which is purposeful only in its parts) [AG96].
5. A structured approach to inquiry is described in the Dialog Decision Process [BKO95].
6. Brand's work is based upon earlier work on shearing layers by the architect Francis Duffy [D90, p.17]. Brand took "the liberty of expanding Duffy's 'four S's'— which are oriented toward interior work in commercial buildings — into a slightly revised, general-purpose 'six S's'" [B94].
7. One series of time lapse pictures in [B94], taken over a period of 6 years, shows changes to the stuff, space plan, services and even detailed structure of an old warehouse building. The startup company occupying it grows in size and complexity. Eventually the startup

moves out and is replaced with *several* other companies, each with radically different needs yet still able to fit into the same basic structure. The time lapse pictures allow you to see the shearing happening before your very eyes in a manner that goes unnoticed in daily life.

8. Our brief study of the pattern language that emerged in Alexander's 1970s work revealed that a large proportion of the patterns are about how physical space hosts and delineates transitory or more durable social relationships and interactions. This is particularly evident in patterns such as Intimacy Gradient and Alcove, but equally true for patterns including Subculture Boundary, Identifiable Neighborhood, Entrance Transition, Farmhouse Kitchen, Children's Realm and, perhaps, one hundred or more others [AIS77].

9. Like [CH98] and others, we use the terms *information system* and *information technology* precisely and to mean quite different things. An information system is typically a socio-technical system consisting of both people and technology, while information technology does not include people. The technological components of an information system are typically information technologies.

10. From this perspective, buildings can be seen as a form of groupware. In the same way that software supports the individual's or group's information-intensive practices, buildings and the built environment support many of their physical and social needs.

11. Kilov and Simmonds [KS96] introduced a notion of *business context* as a structuring device within larger *business specifications*. A business context is a composition of an information model and business obligations, and imposes constraints on the *business operations* that can be performed within the business context. This formulation recognizes that a business situation — as specified in the business specification — may deal with several distinct sub-situations, each of which has a distinct terminology and business rules.

12. A context may exist within the organization whether or not it is directly supported by information technology. Users may improvise, for example making do with e-mail, word processors and spreadsheets. When context support is provided it may be anywhere in a spectrum from dedicated support machines built at great expense for this kind of context, to the cheap application of readily available, generic context support machines.

13. Other inspirations for context are notions of 'habitus' and 'field.' Pierre Bourdieu uses these to explain the mutual dependence between the knowledge of an individual and the institutional knowledge that is shared and reproduced across a larger social grouping (see, for example [BW92]). Personal knowledge constitutes the 'habitus' of the individual. Slowly changing societal shared knowledge constitutes 'fields,' to which new individuals become accustomed through peripheral participation. Example fields include institutions such as the American justice system or the French education system [BW92]. The relationship between context, center, field and habitus will be the subject of a forthcoming publication.

References

[AE72] Russell L. Ackoff, Fred E. Emery. *On Purposeful Systems*. Intersystems Publications, 1972.

[A94] Russell L. Ackoff. *The Democratic Corporation: A Radical Prescription for Recreating Corporate America and Rediscovering Success*. Oxford University Press, 1994.

[AG96] Russell L. Ackoff, Jamshid Gharajedaghi. *Reflections on Systems and their Models*. Systems Research, Vol. 13, No. 1, pp. 13-23, 1996.

[A68] Christopher Alexander. *Notes On the Synthesis of Form*. Harvard University Press, 1968.

[AIS77] Christopher Alexander, Sara Ishikawa, Murray Silverstein with Max Jacobson, Ingrid Fiksdahl-King, Shlomo Angel. *A Pattern Language: Towns, Buildings, Construction.* Oxford University Press, 1977.

[A79] Christopher Alexander. *The Timeless Way of Building.* Oxford University Press, 1979.

[ANAK 87] Christopher Alexander with Hajo Neis, Artemis Anninou, Ingrid King. *A New Theory of Urban Design.* Oxford University Press, 1987.

[A93] Christopher Alexander. *A Foreshadowing of 21st Century Art: The Color and Geometry of Very Early Turkish Carpets.* Oxford University Press, 1993.

[ABT95] Christopher Alexander, Gary Black, Miyoko Tsutsui. *The Mary Rose Museum.* Oxford University Press, 1995.

[Ata] Christopher Alexander. *The Nature of Order.* Unpublished Manuscript. 3 volumes. Oxford University Press, to appear.

[BKO95] Vince Barabba, Michael Kusnic, Dan Owen. *Lead.* Chapter 7 of *Meeting of the Minds: Creating the Market-Based Enterprise.* Harvard Business School Press, 1995.

[BW92] Pierre Bourdieu, Loic Wacquant. *An Introduction to Reflexive Sociology.* Chicago University Press, 1992.

[B94] Stewart Brand. *How Buildings Learn: What happens after they're built.* Viking / Penguin, 1994.

[B94a] Stewart Brand. Review of [B94] for Global Business Network Book Club, May 1994. Available on-line at http://www.gbn.org/bookclub/Buildings.html

[B91] Graham Button editor. *Ethnomethodology and the Social Sciences.* Cambridge University Press, 1991.

[BH93] Graham Button, Richard Harper. *Taking the Organization into Account.* In Graham Button editor, *Technology in Working Order: Studies in Work, Interaction and Technology,* Routledge, 1993, pp. 98-107. Also Xerox UK Technical Report EPC-1992-103.

[C90] John M. Carroll. *The Nurnberg Funnel: Designing Minimalist Instruction for Practical Computer Skill.* MIT Press, 1990.

[CH98] Peter Checkland, Sue Holwell. *Information, Systems and Information Systems: Making Sense of the Field.* John Wiley and Sons, 1998.

[C72] C. West Churchman. *The Design of Inquiring Systems: Basic Concepts of Systems and Organization.* Basic Books, 1971.

[D90] Francis Duffy. *Measuring Building Performance.* In *Facilities,* May 1990.

[DB98] Paul Dourish, Graham Button. *On "Technomethodology": Foundational Relationships Between Ethnomethodology and System Design.* In *Human-Computer Interaction,* Vol 13. pp. 392-432, Lawrence Erlbaum Associates, 1998.

[G96] A. C. Grayling. *Epistemology.* Chapter 1 of *The Blackwell Companion to Philosophy,* Nicholas Bunnin and E. P. Tsui-James editors, Blackwell, 1996, pp. 38-63.

[G83] Stephen Grabow. *Christopher Alexander: The Search For A New Paradigm In Architecture.* Boston: Oriel Press, 1983.

[H95] Stephan H. Haeckel. *Adaptive Enterprise Design: The Sense-and-Respond Model.* Planning Review, May/June 1995, pp. 6-13.

[H99] Stephan H. Haeckel. *The Adaptive Enterprise: Creating and Leading Sense-and-Respond Organizations .* Harvard Business School Publishing, 1999.

[HKL95] Rudy Hirscheim, Heinz K. Klein, Kalle Lyytinen. *Information Systems Development and Data Modeling: Conceptual and Philosophical Foundations.* Cambridge University Press, 1995.

[IS99] David Ing, Ian Simmonds. *Designing Natural Tension into the Structure of Adaptive Enterprises — "Context and Coordination" in the Sense & Respond Organization.* Proceedings of the 1999 meeting of the International Society for the Systems Sciences, Asilomar '99, Asilomar, California, July 1999.

[K95] Morten Kyng. *Creating Contexts for Design*. Chapter 4 of John M. Carroll editor, *Scenario-Based Design: Envisioning Work and Technology in System Development*, John Wiley and Sons, New York, 1995, pp. 85-107.

[KS96] Haim Kilov, Ian Simmonds. *How to correctly refine business specifications, and know it*. In Haim Kilov, V. J. Harvey editors. Proceedings of the Fifth Workshop on Specification of Behavioral Semantics, pp. 57-69, 11th Annual Conference on Object-Oriented Programming Systems, Languages and Applications (OOPSLA '96), San Jose, California, 6 October 1996.

[ML93] Ian I. Mitroff, Harold A. Linstone. *The Unbounded Mind: Breaking the chains of traditional business thinking*. Oxford University Press, 1993.

[ND86] Donald A. Norman, Stephen W. Draper editors. *User Centered System Design: New Perspectives on Human-Computer Interaction*. Lawrence Erlbaum Associates, 1986.

[SN93] D. Schuler, A. Namioka editors. *Participatory Design: Principles and Practices*. Lawrence Erlbaum Associates, 1993.

[S99] Mark Shafer. *Using Information Modeling to Define Business Requirements: An Example of Business Modeling*. In Haim Kilov, Bernhard Rumpe, Ian Simmonds editors, *Behavioral Specifications of Businesses and Systems*, Kluwer Academic Publishers, 1999.

[SB91] Wes Sharrock, Graham Button. *The Social Actor: Social Action in Real Time*. Chapter 7 of [B91], pp. 137-175.

[SI99] Ian Simmonds, David Ing. *The Specification of Information Systems for the Adaptive Enterprise: Conceptual Modeling in the Context Approach*. Submitted for publication.

[S99b] Harold Solbrig. *The Integration of Terminology and Information Models – Progress from a Medical Informatics Perspective*. In Haim Kilov, Bernhard Rumpe, Ian Simmonds editors, *Behavioral Specifications of Businesses and Systems*, Kluwer Academic Publishers, 1999.

[S87] Lucy A. Suchman. *Plans and Situated Actions: The problem of human machine communication*. Cambridge University Press, 1987.

[W95] Karl E. Weick. *Sensemaking in Organizations*. Sage, 1995.

[WF87] Terry Winograd, C. Fernando Flores. *Understanding Computers and Cognition: A New Foundation for Design*. Addison-Wesley Longman, 1987.

About the authors

Ian Simmonds is a researcher at the IBM T.J. Watson Research Center. His research interests lie in all fields that may help improve the quality, and ease the development, of information systems. Currently this includes general systems theory, epistemology, human-computer interaction, social theory and design theory. He actively participates in research related to the IBM Advanced Business Institute's Sense-and-Respond design for an adaptive enterprise.

Ian has published many papers on information systems development, with a focus on software engineering environments and information modeling. He co-authored *Tool Integration: Environments and Frameworks* (Wiley, 1993). He co-organized three workshops (on behavioral semantics and subject-orientation) in ACM's OOPSLA conference series. He led a tutorial on *Business Specifications* at IFIP's Middleware '98 conference. His research work has involved consulting engagements on information technology, notably in the insurance industry. Before joining IBM he worked on ESPRIT and EUREKA projects related to the Portable Common Tool Environment (PCTE), was joint architect for the EAST software engineering environment, and participated in the standardization of PCTE for ECMA and ISO. He received a Bachelor of Arts degree in mathematics from the University of Cambridge.

David Ing is a marketing scientist with the IBM Advanced Business Institute. His principal focus is on the development of the Sense-and-Respond design for adaptive enterprises, and their supporting information systems. He is principal curriculum developer for ABI's course on the Sense-and-Respond organization. His research is focused on customer-orientation, organizational theory and information systems design, applying the rigor of general systems theory. Earlier, as a consultant with the IBM Consulting Group, he led an internal project into industry reference models and system envisioning technologies. As a consultant, he has played several roles in the planning and execution of consulting engagements, blending a knowledge of business processes, marketing science techniques and technology.

David is a co-author of *The Marketing Information Revolution* (Harvard Business School Press, 1995). He was a cofounder of, and continues as a technical advisor to, the Canadian Centre for Marketing Information Technologies. He is active at industry conferences including the Marketing Science Institute, and Direct Marketing Association. He has spoken at ten INFORMS Marketing Science Conferences.

David was a doctoral student in business strategy at the Faculty of Commerce at the University of British Columbia. He received a Master of Management degree from the Kellogg Graduate School of Management at Northwestern University, and a Bachelor of Commerce degree from the University of Toronto.

Chapter 17

30 THINGS THAT GO WRONG IN OBJECT MODELLING WITH UML 1.3

Anthony J H Simons

University of Sheffield, UK
a.simons@dcs.shef.ac.uk

Ian Graham

Ian Graham Associates, UK
grahami@compuserve.com

Abstract   The authors offer a catalogue of problems experienced by developers, using various object modelling techniques brought into prominence by the widespread adoption of UML standard notations. The catalogue is revised to reflect changes made between UML versions 1.1 and 1.3, in which a number of semantic inconsistencies in the notation were fixed. Notwithstanding this, developers still seem to create inordinate problems for themselves by pursuing unproductive development strategies that are apparently fostered by UML. This article shows how the biggest problem by far is *cognitive misdirection*, or the apparent ease with which the rush to build UML models may distract the developer from important perspectives on a system. This problem is more serious than the outstanding *inconsistencies* and *ambiguities* which still exist in UML 1.3. A number of *inadequacies* are also highlighted, where UML somehow still fails to express what we believe are important semantic issues. While UML itself is mostly neutral with respect to good or bad designs, the consequences of allowing UML to *drive* the development process include: inadequate object conceptualisation, poor control structures and poorly-coupled subsystems.

1. INTRODUCTION

The following catalogue of problems is a revision of an earlier survey of developer experiences using the OMG endorsed standard for object modelling, UML. In our original findings [SG98a,b] some 37 different difficulties associated with using UML 1.1 were reported. With the recent introduction of UML 1.3 [BRJ99] a number of semantic inconsistencies in the notation were fixed. However, a significant number of problems, both cognitive and semantic, still remain.

1.1   The context of this critique

The difficulties described below are drawn from the reports of developers managed by, or known to the authors, as they used UML on real projects, in academia and in industry. In analysing these experiences, the authors found that it was not just that UML contained semantic ambiguities and inconsistencies, but rather that the increased prominence given to particular modelling notations had in turn placed a premium on carrying out certain kinds of analysis and design activity. Analysts were enthusiastically adopting new approaches to conceptualising their system, eventually becoming trapped in unproductive arguments over the objects populating the system and the proper representation of the control structure of the system. Designers were then refusing to implement the models produced by the analysts, since it was often impossible to map from use case models and sequence diagrams onto anything that a conventional software engineer would recognise. We decided then that the problem of *cognitive misdirection* was at least as important an issue as *semantic inconsistency* or *ambiguity*.

The authors appreciate the benefits that a standard modelling notation such as UML is supposed to bring, by allowing developers to communicate in a common language. However, the UML standard *as currently defined* [BRJ99; R97] is open to some rather subtle differences in interpretation, leading to serious problems downstream, as we have discovered with our developers in practice.

1.2   The critical framework

The body of this article is an enumeration of the problems experienced by developers as they embraced the UML notations and engaged in what they considered to be the most appropriate sequence of activities for building UML models. Each problem is indexed, for ease of reference, and classified using a three-letter code, in the style: *(#2: MIS)*. The classification codes have the following interpretation:

- INC - inconsistency, meaning that parts of UML models are in contradiction with other parts, or with commonly accepted definitions of terms;
- AMB - ambiguity, meaning that some UML models are under-specified, allowing developers to interpret them in more than one way;
- ADQ - adequacy, meaning that some important analysis and design concepts could not be captured using UML notations;
- MIS - cognitive misdirection, meaning that the natural development path promoted by a desire to build UML models actually misleads the developer.

Each problem cited below was placed into one of these categories, representing the major perceived underlying cause of the fault. The categories are not intended to be mutually exclusive, nor necessarily exhaustive, but merely indicative.

In the following section, we discuss what we believe are some of the causes underlying the failures reported by developers in our survey. The subsequent sections form the body of our catalogue. In our conclusions, we discuss the significance of the numbers of problems in each category.

2. CRACKS IN THE HEART OF UML

UML is intended to be a general-purpose modelling notation, based on a few consistently applied principles. As a result of pressures brought to bear during standardisation, UML has accomodated heterogeneous elements from its precursor methods and notations. It is a difficult task to tread the tightrope between minimalism and expressiveness successfully; and UML does this moderately well by managing to apply the same conventions across a number of its models. However, these strengths of UML also eventually account for its weaknesses.

2.1 Universal notation has multiple interpretations

One of the claimed strengths of UML is that it is *universal*, that is, the same notation is used for analysis, design and documenting the implementation. This minimalism is typically cited as a benefit. However, the down-side is that one developer will interpret another developer's diagram under a different set of assumptions. What was intended as an analysis diagram in one context may be interpreted as a concrete design in another context. Our developers repeatedly ran into problems because they could not decide how concrete UML models were supposed to be. Should an association just represent a vague imagined connection in the problem domain, or should it mean a physical connection between classes in the solution domain? Diagrams representing one thing were often found to have been interpreted as the other. UML claims that its capacity to model both perspectives is an advantage; the fact that it offers no control over how diagrams are interpreted must then be considered a serious disadvantage.

2.2 Universal notation fosters naïve seamless development

Nowhere is this more obvious than when a class diagram, which is drawn as an initial analysis of relationships between concepts in the problem domain, is pressed into service as a concrete design. Associations are converted into pointers; many-to-many relationships are translated directly into set-valued attributes and strong, mutually-coupled *Observer* patterns appear in the design [GHJV95]. It would have been better if our developers had noticed that many-to-many relationships could be eliminated using *linker entities* (in Entity-Relationship Modelling) or *Mediator* patterns (in Responsibility-Driven Design) to reduce coupling between classes in the design [SSH98]. Yet, they repeatedly failed to perceive systems in terms of such co-ordinating structures (see also problem #28 below).

The practice of analysing the semantic relationships in the problem domain using classes and associations actively blinds developers to alternative practical structures. Gestalt theory predicts that the initial concepts formed during the perception of some phenomenon radically affect how subsequent constructs are formed. Following this, we have observed how early analysis modelling using classes tends to fix these concepts and suppress others. Development then becomes a steady elaboration of detail; the analysis classes and structures do not change, but merely add to their attributes and methods, in the style of some early naïve development methods [CY91a,b; WN95], which emphasised the *seamless transition* from analysis into design. This approach leads to systems which are overly coupled and exhibit poor modular structure [SSH98]. Well-structured systems typically do not exibit a 1:1 mapping from analysis to design objects.

2.3   Eclectic models fail to resolve competing design forces

Another of the claimed strengths of UML is that it is *eclectic*, that is, it keeps the best parts from a number of precursor methods and notations, in particular [B94; RBPEL91; JCJO92]. Eclecticism is regarded as a good thing, because this means that the notation contains something for everyone; no-one's point of view is left out. However, it is extremely difficult to ensure that all the parts work together all of the time. Like the old adage that a camel is an animal that was designed by committee, eclectic systems are often ugly because they borrow elements out of the original context in which they evolved. In UML, great care has been taken to ensure that the elements of the notation fit together, at least on the syntactic level.

However, if you examine the intent behind sets of model elements in a single UML diagram, you will often find that these are in conflict, because they were taken from contexts which originally supported mutually exclusive design approaches. For example, a class diagram blends associative relationships between data structures with client-server relationships equivalent to inter-module procedure calls. If one were to resolve the data model alone in terms of minimising data dependency, this would lead to one structure, equivalent to 3NF. If one were to resolve the client-server class coupling model (the sense in which RDD originally used the term *collaboration graph* [WWW90]) then this would lead to a completely different structure, minimising inter-module dependency [SSH98]. The down-side of an eclectic notation is that different design forces compete within a single UML model - rather than offering a single perspective, it offers multiple perspectives simultaneously. As a consequence, developers do not profit from the structure offered by either perspective; they are unable to proceed because the UML model fails to resolve the competing design forces.

This duality is not just a feature of the class diagram. The sequence diagram switches between a dataflow and a method invocation perspective. The state and activity diagrams switch between a finite state machine and a flowchart perspective. Models which were highly constrained in their original context lose their useful constraint when extra enhancements are added in UML: an example of this is the attaching of extra *guard conditions* to events on transitions in the state model, which undermines the purpose of the state machine perspective. The richness of UML is its own undoing, since it prevents its models from offering any clear perspective on the direction the design should take.

2.4   Universal definitions of notation elements transfer poorly

The elements of a universal notation must have an interpretation for analysis, design and implementation.   Developers often take the most concrete examples of notational elements in use (because this is what they can understand) and retrofit these interpretations higher up in the analysis process.   This impedes analysis, by imposing implementation concerns too early.   The problem is more subtle than simply asserting that UML definitions are too concrete;   it is rather that universalism fosters the transfer of elements and their definitions out of context.

Nowhere is this clearer than with the fundamental definitions of *association* and *dependency* in UML 1.3 [BRJ99].   An *association* is a concept from ERM that is used initially to represent some imagined relationship between entities.   It has no immediate concrete interpretation.   A *dependency* is likewise defined quite abstractly in UML as a directed relationship in which the behaviour of the source is functionally dependent on the behaviour of the target.   However, when proceeding to the design level, UML asserts quite categorically that associations represent structural relationships that would require pointers (or embedding) in the implementation, whereas dependencies correspond to non-structural relationships, such as when one class uses another as an argument in its method signatures.   This mutually exclusive definition is retrofitted on the analysis perspective and prevents *associations* from being seen as kinds of *dependency*;   instead, developers are encouraged to make early distinctions between associations and dependencies in analysis [BRJ99, p74], decisions which really concern the implementation structure of systems.   The notion of *dependency* is too important to be relegated to non-structural dependency only; several outstanding problems regarding the expressiveness of UML follow from this.

3. USE CASES AND USE CASE MODELS

Use cases were hailed in the field of object technology [JCJO92] as the first serious attempt to elicit requirements upstream of object modelling (though business tools such as *RequisitePro* may prove a better starting point).   In OBA [G90; RG92], *scenarios* were originally collected during interview as *instances* of user-interaction, each describing a single execution path, like a procedure invocation.   The view adopted by UML 1.1 [R97] gave a *use case* a *type*-level interpretation, rather like a procedure description.   UML 1.1 also established the «uses» and «extends» generalisation relationships between use cases as a kind of novel control structure in the analysis domain.   UML 1.3 now defines a *scenario* as an *instance* of a *use case* [BRJ99] and has replaced the «uses» and «extends» relationships with new «include» and «extend» dependency relationships.

3.1   Fixes made to use cases in UML 1.3

The UML 1.1 use case model was perhaps the most contentious and most widely misapplied part of UML.   Originally, the «uses» and «extends» relationships were defined as specialised subtypes of the inheritance relationship between use cases (*stereotypes of generalisation,* in the jargon [R97]), using the standard generalisation arrow. In our previous survey [SG98a,b], we reported how developers simply disbelieved the official UML 1.1 semantics, preferring to infer different meanings for «uses» and «extends», with a number of consequential problems in communication and model consistency. Nowhere was this more painfully evident than during the OOPSLA 1998 use cases panel, in which Jacobson and Cockburn gave conflicting definitions on the meaning of «uses» without realising it, and some 80% of those present indicated that they failed to understand the «uses» and «extends» relationships [FCJAG98].

Jacobson's «uses» relationship, adopted in UML 1.1, was analogous to subclassing, in which a concrete use case "inherited" elements of an abstract use case and inserted them into its own sequence. In contradiction of this definition, developers commonly imagined that «uses» had the semantics of a simple subroutine call, in which the using case invokes the used case as a whole; they thus ignored the *generalisation* arrow semantics and the interleaving of elements.

The «extends» relationship was inconsistently defined from the start. On the one hand, the extension case was modelled as "inheriting from" the base case, but simultaneously was regarded as "inserting behaviour into" the base case. Both views cannot be held consistently: the extension must either represent the extra behaviour (insertion semantics), or the combination of the base and extra behaviour (specialisation semantics). In practice, the former semantics were applied, in violation of the metamodel description. UML 1.3 addressed these problems by abandoning the old «uses» and «extends» relationships. Their replacements are known as «include» and «extend». The main change is that these are defined as *stereotypes of dependency* (kinds of functional dependency) [BRJ99]. The effect of this change has been to remove the earlier conflicts with the generalisation/ specialisation semantics.

A number of problems still remain. Although use cases are supposed to be independent of any formal design, such that they "cannot be forward or reverse engineered" [BRJ99, p239], the conceptual structures fostered by use cases mislead developers about design structures. Logical faults are introduced, which prevent the use case model from scaling up to large systems.

3.2   Inadequacies of the «include» and «extend» relationships

The semantics of «include» is under-specified (#1: AMB)

By abandoning the old view that «uses» specialises an abstract base case and interleaves procedural elements, it would appear that UML is bowing to popular pressure for a straightforward *compositional* semantics for «include», as recommended by OPEN [FHG97] and as practised already by [C97a,b] in disregard of the UML 1.1 semantics. All of the examples given in [BRJ99, p227, 230, 337] are *consistent* with subroutines, rather than interleaved routines, but the authors fail to make absolutely clear whether this semantics is intended, since at the same time the *included* case is called "an aggregation of responsibilities" (p227) that is determined by "factoring out" (p226) common behaviour, which is reminiscent of generalisation

[JCJO92, p170-173]. What we would like to see is a plain assertion that *included* cases are atomic subroutines that are executed as a whole.

The semantics of «extend» cannot handle exceptions (#2: ADQ)

By abandoning the inconsistent view that the old «extends» is both an insertion and a specialisation, this allows the new «extend» relationship to be considered purely as an insertion. The inserted optional behaviour is executed if a trigger condition is satisfied [BRJ99, p228]. This definition is equivalent to a guarded block, or a single-branch *if*-statement, in which control returns to the point of call afterwards.

As well as *optional* branches, developers commonly use «extend» to indicate *exceptions*; and this intention is also clear in [JCJO92, p165]. Unfortunately, the insertion semantics of «extend» does not support exceptions. When an exception is raised, control *never* returns to this point, but may return to the *end* of the failed transaction after the exception has been processed, or not at all.

The semantics of «extend» cannot handle alternative history (#3: ADQ)

Likewise, developers commonly use «extend» to indicate alternative history. Figure 1 overleaf shows a typical example (adapted from [C96]) in which *PayDirect* is intended as an alternative to *SignForOrder*; likewise *ReturnGoods* is intended as an alternative to *PayInvoice*. Under the insertion semantics of «extend», this diagram is nonsensical, because the base cases would still execute, once the inserted optional behaviour had terminated (see also problem #5 below).

Jacobson originally expected the «extend» relationship to be able to characterise insertions, exceptions and alternatives [JCJO92; p165]. It is clear from the published semantics of «extend» that it can only handle the first of these. Use case diagrams are therefore dangerously ambiguous; developers have to rely on intuitions about the labelling of the cases to establish the intended logic, in disregard of the official semantics. The «extend» relationship is not one, but several different relationships that have been conflated.

3.3 Misdirection fostered by use case development

Use case modelling misses long-range logical dependency (#4: MIS)

Use case modelling promotes a highly localised perspective which often obscures the true business logic of a system. As a result, developers fail to capture important long-range dependencies. In figure 1, the extension cases aim to capture local alternatives (problem #3 notwithstanding). However, UML does not capture explicitly the exclusive alternation of *PayDirect* with the more distant main cases *SendInvoice* and *PayInvoice*; likewise, the *PayDirect* and *ReturnGoods* extensions are secretly inter-dependent. A customer who paid direct should not only *not receive* an invoice, but must *obtain a refund* in addition to returning faulty goods. Even simple examples like this exhibit unpleasant mutual interactions between extensions and between these and other base cases. Most alarming is the fact that the redress for the cash-paying customer is not captured at all - this logical loophole is completely obscured in the use case model.

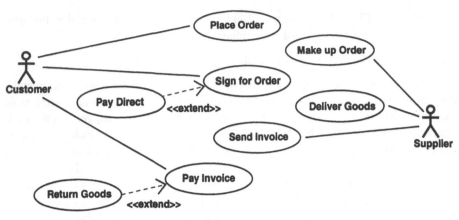

Figure 1: Pitfalls in a use case diagram

The granularity of use cases and logical task units are different (#5: ADQ)

Some of these problems could be fixed if UML admitted functional task units that were both larger and smaller than the nominal grain-size of use cases. A *use case* is defined as: "a sequence of transactions performed by a system, which yields an observable result of value for a particular actor" [JGJ97, p66]. The emphasis on *an observable result* is a deliberate constraint which seeks to ensure a minimum and maximum granularity: use cases may not be vacuous (they must deliver some useful result) and may not be multiple (they deliver a single result).

Unfortunately, to model alternative history requires *empty* base cases that may then be extended by each of the substantive alternatives. Unlike the doomed attempt to treat one alternative branch as the extension of the second branch (see problem #3), which fails under the semantics of insertions, both of the alternative branches could be legitimately modelled as insertions into some vacuous base case. Jacobson may even be accused of doing this [JCJO92; p164-165] where he considers *LogOn/LogOff* to be a base case into which the substantive alternative activities of a terminal session (such as *Compile, Mail* or *WordProcess*) are inserted. This base case is really of no observable benefit to the user!

Likewise, to model long-range logical dependency (see problem #4) requires *large scale* hierarchical units to co-ordinate the use cases that logically belong together. In figure 1, the true logical alternation is between the missing concepts *CreditPurchase* and *DirectPurchase*, not represented in UML, but which would appear as abstract intermediate nodes in a conventional structure chart. These are necessary to encode the long-range dependencies that exist between the use cases arranged under them. Neither of these would qualify a use case in UML 1.3, since they involve multiple transactions for many actors.

Use case dependency is non-logical and inconsistent (#6: INC)

The direction of dependency is misleading for «extend», flowing from the insertion to the base case that it modifies. This is an artefact of the order followed in the analysis procedure, rather than indicating any real logical dependency. Logically, it is the superordinate *selection* node, not represented in UML, but understood as the bundling of the base and all extension cases, which depends on all of its parts. The current UML 1.3 position is like saying that all branches of a multibranch-statement depend logically on one distinguished branch, clearly nonsense.

Whereas «include» can perhaps be construed as a genuine logical dependency, that of a *sequence* node on its subroutines, «extend» cannot; it merely records how the analysis paperwork was indexed. These are not stereotypes of the same dependency, they are two *completely different* kinds of relationship.

Use case modelling is unsound and must be deconstructed (#7: MIS)

This non-logical formulation of dependency also explains why «extend» cases break encapsulation, unfairly gaining access to the internal structure of the main cases they extend [G97]. In a logical formulation, all alternatives would be encapsulated inside the dispatching selection node. It also explains why «extend» seems to behave like a *come from* instruction, seizing control from the main flow.

While the UML authors may undermine attempts to impose logical consistency by asserting that use cases "cannot be forward or reverse engineered" [BRJ99, p239], the consequence of promoting non-logical relationships is that analysts will develop illogical use case models that have to be *completely deconstructed* later during design. Developers are misguided from the start.

4.   SEQUENCE AND COLLABORATION DIAGRAMS

Sequence diagrams and collaboration diagrams are two equivalent ways of illustrating object-to-object message interactions in UML [BRJ99]. A sequence diagram makes the time ordering of messages explicit, but hides the structural relationships between objects. A collaboration diagram displays the structural connections between objects and superimposes on this a sequence of messages. The sequence diagram may show the focus of control (stack frame invocation level), but is limited in the degree of branching it can accommodate; whereas the collaboration diagram may illustrate more sophisticated branching and iteration.

4.1   Fixes to sequence and collaboration diagrams in UML 1.3

A number of missing emphases have been added since UML 1.1, which address some of the criticisms raised in [SG98a,b]. A sequence diagram may be used to represent *either* a single execution of a single decision path, *or* a procedural view of the decision paths available for execution. In the former case, the sequence diagram models a *scenario*, whereas in the latter case, it models a *use case* (see 3 above). This still puts the onus on the developer to realise when the diagram is being used in either sense. The failure of sequence diagrams to handle all but the simplest kind of branching is acknowledged. The UML 1.1 policy of splitting and merging an object's timeline when it enters an alternative history seems to have been abandoned. Focus bars now have a clear stack-frame semantics and are correctly mandated for every *call-back* and every *self-delegation* [BRJ99, p247]. Unfortunately, the UML authors don't observe their own rule on p252, so we list focus bar interpretation as a continuing problem for developers.

Collaboration diagrams are largely unchanged. The interpretation of the complicated syntax for branching and iteration is explained briefly on p249, but the conventions for referring to iteration variables are not explained. An alarming new concept is the admission of *non-procedural message flow*. This serves to confuse further the object/messaging and dataflow/flowchart perspectives. In our previous critique [SG98a,b], we reported how UML had subverted the original meaning of the term *collaboration* from RDD [WWW90]. UML still lacks the concept of a *class-level* client-server functional dependency (see problem #29).

4.2   The method invocation and dataflow/workflow duality

Sequence diagrams developed from use cases produce dataflow (#8: MIS)

In a properly-constituted sequence diagram, the meaning of the arrow stimulus is a *message* sent to *activate a method* in the target object, the receiver. The arrow has the semantics of an invocation. Against this, we find time and again that developers do not have this perspective when drawing sequence diagrams. Instead, they tend to create *dataflow diagrams*, in which the meaning of the arrow is the transfer of information to destinations corresponding to imagined processes and datastores. This persistent failure to adopt a proper object-oriented mind-set is disturbing.

Eventually, we put this behaviour down to inadequate prior object modelling. If developers proceed directly to sequence diagrams from use cases, the kinds of object-concept available at this early stage relate almost exclusively to human actors and passive datastore concepts, such as letters, forms, price and stock records. There is a tendency to model the nouns in the description of the use-case literally in the sequence diagram. Sentences like: *the warehouse manager looks up the price and the stock-level* result in messages between the external *WarehouseManager* actor and object concepts representing a *PriceRecord* and a *StockLevelRecord*. Instead, price and stock-level should most likely be access methods of a *GoodsItem* object.

To counter this, developers must be prevented from drawing sequence diagrams as a primary model; instead, they should concentrate on eliciting responsible object abstractions [BC89, WW89, WWW90]. Sequence diagrams were deployed *much later* in OOSE to *confirm* that the object model covered the behaviour expected in use cases [JCJO92]; this has also been found useful in testing [M97].

Flat, or non-procedural message flow is workflow (#9: MIS)

In UML 1.3, the authors recognise both procedural and non-procedural message flow between objects in collaboration diagrams [BRJ99, p213]. The former is drawn with the filled arrowhead and has the semantics of method invocation, in which messages may nest. The latter is drawn with the stick arrowhead and has the flat semantics of "nonprocedural progression of control from step to step", in other words, the workflow in a flowchart. Workflow has no place in an object-messaging model and only serves to distract developers.

The return arrow is dataflow in an invocation model (#10: MIS)

UML 1.1 introduced the dotted-shaft return value arrow to distinguish the passing of return values from call-back invocations. A new problem is that this is now the only *dataflow* in an *invocation* model. It confuses developers about the intended meaning of arrows in sequence diagrams. If focus bars are used consistently (see problem #12), then return arrows are unnecessary - they should be dropped, except to express a request from a concurrent thread to resynchronise (a rendezvous).

Focus bars are misunderstood and used inconsistently (#11: INC)

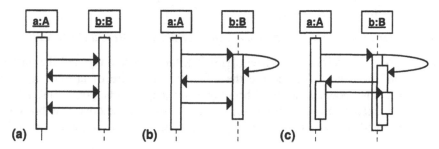

Figure 2: Thread, activation and stack-frame semantics of focus bars

Focus bars should have a *stack-frame* semantics, as shown in figure 2c. A nested focus bar must be shown for every *call-back* and *self-delegation* [BRJ99, p247]. It should be clear from the nesting and length of focus bars which messages are the master routines and which are the subroutines. In UML 1.1, a second *process thread* semantics was allowed [R97], shown in figure 2a. In this case, the length of the focus bar indicates the liveness of the thread. Most developers, including [BRJ99, p252] misuse focus bars in the style of figure 2b. The length of the bar conveys no useful logical information, corresponding only to the interval between when an object was first and last touched.

Absent, or misused focus bars promote dataflow over invocation (#12: MIS)

The style of figure 2b also visually promotes a conflicting *dataflow* semantics for the stimulus arrow, since it cannot now mean *invocation* (as no nested focus bar is raised). A similar visual conflict arises if no focus bars are displayed. The correct style of figure 2c promotes a proper *invocation* semantics. From this, it is always possible to determine when a subroutine terminates and to which caller the return value should pass. The value returned is implicit in the request, so need not be annotated, thus freeing the diagram from another dataflow (see problem #10).

4.3 Adequacy and expressiveness of interaction diagrams

The normal course plus extensions model is a fiction (#13: MIS)

Sequence diagrams are supposed to be drawn for each use case. A use case starts from the premise that you can construct a *normal course* of events and supplement this with various *extensions*. This works only for simple examples. In general, business logic is much more complicated, with multibranching decision paths. In a credit reinsurance system developed for BTR [HSR98], there were four ways a credit limit application could succeed and four ways in which it could fail.

The natural business logic is structured such that *early rejection* or *acceptance* cases are spun off the *continue to investigate* creditworthiness case, which in turn may lead to acceptance or rejection. It is impossible to decide which of these should be considered the *normal course*, since acceptance and rejection eventually occur with equal likelihood. The analysts were artificially constrained into accepting the *continue to investigate* case as the normal course, despite the fact that this is a fairly unlikely path through the system.

The granularity of use cases and logical sequence units is different (#14: ADQ)

In the same credit reinsurance system [HSR98], the designers rejected the analysis model from (problem #13), because the different cases were of unequal size and complexity. The modularisation of the system was judged to be poor. Instead, the designers wanted to truncate use-cases at points where conditions and branching were introduced, because of the weak support given to branching and iteration in sequence diagrams.

The designers represented in a single diagram the initial portion of the *continue to investigate* case up to the first *early rejection* point; then spun off a second sequence diagram to cover the continuation of the case up to the first *early acceptance* point; and so on. This was judged habitable, because each sequence diagram supported a single branch of the logic and was of a comparable modular size. However, the granularity principle for use cases was broken (see problem #5), since many cases were spun off which did not correspond to a single, complete interaction of a user with the system. Cases also acquired unlikely sounding names, such as: *Early Credit Limit Acceptance that was Previously Not Rejected Early*.

Decision logic in sequence and collaboration diagrams is limited (#15: ADQ)

In UML 1.3, a branching condition is indicated in [ ] brackets and placed as a guard on message stimuli. The guards for all branches at a fork must be mutually exclusive; only one branch is selected at one time. This allows client objects to dispatch requests to alternative servers, or to dispatch alternative requests to the same server, but cannot represent the client object entering a different timeline [SG98a,b].

UML 1.1 introduced the splitting of object timelines in sequence diagrams [R97], but this seems to have been dropped in UML 1.3 [BRJ99]. Instead, objects may occur multiple times in a collaboration diagram [BRJ99, p254] if they enter a substantively different state. In our earlier critique [SG98a,b] we noted how business logic tends to produce many overlapping and parallel timelines representing alternative ways of reaching the same outcomes, but which are contingent on having passed through different histories. To split and join multiple timelines is impossible in a single sequence diagram and clutters a collaboration diagram. The need to enter an alternative timeline forces the creation of another diagram (see problem #14) which also forces the premature truncation of use cases (see problems #5 and #14).

4.4   Conflicts between object messaging and decision logic

The sequence perspective generates incorrect control logic (#16: MIS)

Sequence diagrams are often used in ways that emphasize object interactions at the expense of proper decision logic. One of the models developed for the credit reinsurance system [HSR98] (see problems #13, #14) produced an example in which an *early rejection* point should logically have terminated the timeline; however, because of the CASE tool's inability to support branching and alternative timelines, the developer had continued using the same object timeline for the *continue to investigate* case, which was logically inconsistent.

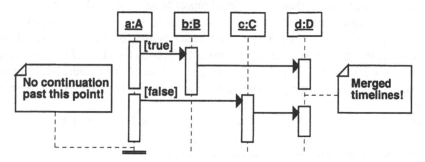

Figure 3: Pitfalls in a sequence diagram

This logic fault is equivalent to continuing past the termination point indicated in figure 3. Sequence diagrams are problematic where they suppress the developer's perceptions of proper decision logic. A timeline must either represent a single sequence of actions (with no branching), or a mutually exclusive set of guarded alternative histories, as in figure 3.

Alternative timelines are combined and misread (#17: MIS)

Sequence diagrams also merge object timelines which are logically distinct, especially when they are at several removes from the point of branching. These timelines are easily misread by designers and result in merged processing streams in the implementation. Figure 3 illustrates a case where the two alternative processing branches initiated by the object *a:A* are eventually merged as a single timeline in the object *d:D*. It is possible to view this as a single history for *d:D* when in fact this represents two alternative histories.

5.   STATE AND ACTIVITY DIAGRAMS

UML's *state diagram* derives from the *dynamic model* of OMT [RBPEL91] and ultimately from Harel's *statecharts*. It is a fusion of *Moore* and *Mealy* finite state machines in which computational activity may be attached to transitions (*Mealy*) and to states (*Moore*) [BRJ99, p336]. Each state at one level may be expanded to a substate machine, to model this computational activity. Arcs entering a superstate correspond to commencing the substate machine in its initial substate; arcs leaving the superstate boundary indicate exit transitions from *all* substates.

UML's *activity diagram* is a synthesis of a state machine, a flowchart and a Petri net. Described in state machine terms, the so-called *action* and *activity states* are really processing stages in a flowchart and the transitions represent program conditions rather than events. Diamond decision nodes indicate branching; and Petri-style synchronisation bars indicate concurrent fork and join points.

5.1   Status of state and activity diagrams in UML 1.3

Since UML 1.1, the scope of the state diagram has been widened to model whole system behaviour, rather than merely local object behaviour; and the importance of the activity diagram has been elevated, in line with our earlier recommendations [SG98a,b]. The activity diagram is much better suited to modelling real business processes than either of the interaction models (see problems #13-#17 above), since it models workflow, rather than object messaging. Alternate and parallel paths through the business logic may easily merge at points where the outcome is thereafter the same.

Nonetheless, we still find that developers make too little use of this model and proceed to interaction modelling at a far too early stage. Likewise, state models are under-used and we occasionally still see instances of the "use case too far" syndrome in which developers try to encode all the business logic in use cases [SG98a,b]. We have also identified a number of new inconsistencies since our last survey.

5.2   Interpretation problems with initial and final states

The initial state is both an indicator and a state (#18: AMB)

Developers do not know whether the *initial state* represents a true state, or merely points to the first substantive state. The Harel-semantics conflict with Mealy-semantics in which a free transition arrow proceeds to the first substantive state.

Harel-semantics encourages the view that the *initial state* is a real state, in which the system is dead, not yet switched on. However, when used to indicate the starting point of a substate machine, the *initial state* icon cannot represent a dead system state; it is used exactly like the Mealy initial free transition arrow. Similarly, since a majority of UML state diagrams place no event on the initial transition, the *initial state* may as well not be a state.

The final state is both an accept state and a halt state (#19: AMB)

Developers do not know whether the final state represents a true *accept state* in the system, or merely a *halt state* after the system has terminated and is deactivated. The Harel-semantics conflict with the Mealy-semantics in which the ringed state is an *accept state*, that is, the last substantive state in the machine.

The *accept state* view causes developers to place *final state* icons in substate machines [BRJ99, p303], to indicate that these eventually terminate. Under Harel-semantics, this indicates the premature halting of the whole system, rather than the successful completion of a substate machine. If the *final state* icon is reserved for a *halt state* (*after* the last substantive state), there is no way to indicate a true *accept state*. This mostly makes it harder to see where a substate machine terminates, without breaking the encapsulation of nested state machines (see problem #21).

5.3   Consistency problems when decomposing state machines

Transitions across a superstate boundary violate encapsulation (#20: ADQ)

The advantage of Harel statecharts is supposed to be that they allow the developer to view the control structure of a system at different levels of abstraction, hiding different amounts of detail inside substate machines. However, if major alterations to the state transition pattern are needed when a superstate is exposed as a substate machine, this negates the benefit of encapsulation and abstraction.

UML state diagrams routinely allow transitions to state boundaries at one level of description to be redrawn to connect with substates when these are exposed [BRJ99, p299, 301, 333, 437]. This breaks the encapsulation of state machines. The labelling of such transitions at the superstate and substate levels must often be different (see problem #21). Further problems of encapsulation are caused by admitting *shallow* and *deep history* connectors (see problem #24).

Boundary crossing makes a nested accept state redundant (#21: ADQ)

The most irritating example of boundary-crossing (see problem #20) is the practice of identifying an *accept state* in a substate machine (see problem #19) by a free transition, which exits this substate across the superstate boundary. This transition would have to be properly labelled with an *event* at the higher level (triggered by completion of the substate machine), thus illustrating the inconsistency of labelling at each level. Furthermore, a free transition exiting a nested *accept state* effectively makes this state redundant - it might as well not be there; instead, the penultimate states could exit directly when their events were triggered.

These points illustrate how boundary crossing breaks encapsulation by upsetting the state machine logic at both the higher and lower levels. Instead, substate machines should not connect directly across the superstate boundary. Reaching the *accept state* of a substate machine should be deemed equivalent to signalling a separate event at the higher level.

States with free exit transitions are not decomposable (#22: INC)

Sometimes, states representing processing stages, in the sense of a *Moore*-machine, have free exit transitions, meaning that the state may be quit automatically once its associated processing has terminated. However, if such a state is ever expanded, there is an immediate problem in interpreting the free exit transition consistently, since under Harel-semantics, a transition leaving the superstate boundary is equivalent to an exit transition from every substate. This would mean that every substate exits immediately! The substate machine cannot execute.

5.4   Misdirection in capturing the underlying control logic

Conditional guards conceal a duplication of control states (#23: MIS)

The admission of extra *conditional guards* on events in UML 1.3 undermines the purpose of the state machine formalism and conceals a duplication in control states. Figure 4a illustrates a simple heating system whose basic events are temperature triggers, which have been augmented by timing guards to introduce a delay in switching.

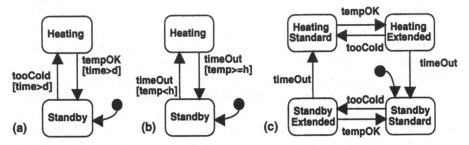

Figure 4: Pitfalls in state machine logic

This model is exactly equivalent to figure 4b, in which the basic events are timeouts, augmented by temperature threshold guards, illustrating how the augmented notation makes the choice of events essentially arbitrary! In figure 4c the guards are revealed for what they are: extra hidden control states.   Because conditional guards lead to self-deception about the real control structure of systems, we advise our developers to expand them away, so that they are at least aware of the real number of states and events in the system.

History connectors conceal a multiplication of state machines (#24: MIS)

UML 1.3 admits *shallow* and *deep history* connectors [BRJ99, p301]. Upon reentry to a superstate containing a *shallow history* connector, the substate machine resumes where it last left off, rather than starting in its initial state. This enrichment not only breaks encapsulation (problem #21), since it requires reasoning across state boundaries, but also corresponds to a *repeated duplication* of the *entire super state machine*, once for each alternative remembered substate! A *deep history* connector applies this expansion recursively, to all nested substate machines.

We appreciate that this approach is typically thought necessary to model interrupts and co-routines;   unfortunately it blinds most developers to the real complexity of what they have created. We discourage its routine use.

Entry/exit actions and internal transitions promote flowcharts (#25: MIS)

The simple logic of state machines is upset yet again by the concern to execute attached procedural elements in the correct order [BRJ99, 295-298]. For example, a distinction is drawn between standard *self-transitions*, which trigger entry/exit actions, and *internal transitions*, which do not. This imposes a procedural flowchart perspective, rather than an event-driven one, when designing state diagrams.

We think that a self-transition should always be equivalent to dwelling in a state, rather than exiting and re-entering. Self-transitions typically decompose into lower-level transitions in the substate machine. This leads us to conclude that there should only be *one* activity attached to a state, modelled by its substate machine.

6.   CLASS DIAGRAMS

Class diagrams are perhaps the most stable and widely used part of UML, since they translate in a straightforward way into program classes. Paradoxically, this can lead to developer overconfidence after the analysis stage and inadequate object modelling in the design stage. The strength, and also the weakness, of UML's class diagram is its ability to capture a wide variety of semantic relationships, which are *either* the anticipated, but as yet uninterpreted associations between entities in the analysis domain, cf. OMT [RBPEL91]; or the *actual* structural and functional connections between classes in the design domain, cf. *has* and *uses* in Booch '94 [B94].

Eventually, it is the richness of the representation which confuses developers. They are wrestling simultaneously with analysis and design perspectives, with data modelling and client-server functional dependency perspectives, all in the same diagram. A number of these problems were already described in section 2.

6.1   The premature curtailment of object modelling

Class diagrams tend to fix object abstractions too early (#26: MIS)

As we noted in sections 2.1 and 2.2, class diagrams drawn during the analysis phase exercise an undue influence on the eventual design. Initial class diagrams contain obvious domain concepts, related by uninterpreted associations. These are typically pressed into design in a naïve way. Developers do not reconsider the true nature of functional coupling between classes, so they simply add behaviour to the initial domain concepts, eventually overburdening them. They are hindered from thinking more imaginatively about classes as smaller, less concrete, agent or manager concepts exercising limited sets of responsibilities [WWW90].

Associations fix object connections and translate poorly into design (#27: MIS)

Again, in section 2.2 we noted how the recording of uninterpreted associations during analysis produces poorly-coupled designs, because these associations do not necessarily correspond to the optimal functional couplings in a design. As with the object abstractions, it is hard to undo initial perceptions. Associations are often pressed prematurely into physical class connections (viz. pointers). The universalism of UML fosters this (see 2.1).

We noted in [SG98a,b] how automatic translation schemes also resulted in overly-coupled designs, with set-valued attributes and *Observer*-style mutual connectivity between unimaginative domain classes (see also problem #26). In any case, the association perspective is not the correct one for optimal class coupling (see problems #29, #30).

Detailed analysis labelling impedes structural transformation (#28: MIS)

In [SG98a,b], we noted how developers worry inordinately over detailed labelling concerns, such as disjoint, versus overlapping, subclasses; or the difference between an association, a shared aggregation and a composite aggregation; or how far to go with adornments such as OCL constraints and stereotypes. While it is important to ensure that the semantic characterisation of the analysis domain is preserved in the design and implementation stages, many subtle annotations on analysis models are often irrelevant later in design, especially if model structure is transformed.

Consider the *Mediator* pattern [GHJV95], which can be applied systematically to reduce inter-object coupling [SSH98]. It matters little whether the *Mediator* itself is a true composition, a shared aggregation, or simply some kind of coordinating abstraction, so long as all cross-connections are removed between the mediated objects. Applying the *Mediator* pattern radically alters the structure of a system, deleting relationships and their adornments. This would seem to indicate that developers should be wary of investing too much effort in analysis labelling. Unfortunately, we find a reverse effect, which is that developers are motivated against applying radical structural transformations to the design, because of the earlier effort invested in labelling the structure of the analysis model.

6.2   The functional coupling and data dependency duality

The term collaboration *is misconstrued and the concept is missing (#29: ADQ)*

UML 1.3 still lacks an unequivocal concept for an abstract, class-level, client-server functional dependency. This is arguably the most important relationship in object-oriented modelling, the dual of an association in data modelling. In RDD, this concept is known as a *collaboration* [BC89; WW89; WWW90].

Unfortunately, the term *collaboration* has been subverted in UML to refer instead to a cluster of objects and their interactions; hence the use of *collaboration diagram* to refer to an object *interaction* diagram. This is an instance-level model, in which the arrows denote individual messages to objects. In RDD, a *collaboration* is an abstract, directed relationship between two classes, representing the functional dependency of one class on the other. This missing perspective is critical for the proper modular analysis and transformation of systems [SSH98, S98].

The available UML concepts do not cut the cloth in the same way: a *directed association* represents a concrete structural connection indicating navigability in one direction. A *dependency* indicates a non-structural dependency on method arguments (see 2.4). Both make premature assumptions about implementation and fail to capture the abstract notion of client-server dependency.

The class diagram mixes data and functional dependency (#30: MIS)

UML class diagrams freely mix *associations* with *dependencies*, thus confusing the *data modelling* and *functional dependency* perspectives. It is not clear whether *dependency* stretches to include *existence dependency* also (like the *derived* relationships in OMT [RBPEL91]). In section 2.3 we noted how such eclecticism leads to diagrams that offer no clear perspective on the direction in which a design should proceed. The class diagram fails to resolve the competing forces.

In its proper context, an *association* hails from data modelling (ERM) and is used to establish minimal coupling between data files. The RDD notion of a *collaboration* hails from responsibility analysis (CRC) and is used to establish minimal functional coupling between subsystem modules [BC89; WWW90; SSH98; S98]. Applying either technique will optimise a class diagram in a different way. UML class diagrams do not in any case offer an abstract *collaboration graph* [WWW90] perspective (see problem #29), which would allow subsystem optimisation to proceed from an analysis of inter-module functional dependency.

7.   CONCLUSIONS

Our survey has emphasised the way developers embrace and use UML 1.3. The cognitive issues surrounding the focus of developers' attention, how this is engaged and directed, are at least as important as the static issues of model semantics. By problem category, we identified the following counts (totalling 30):

INC	(inconsistency)	3 counts
AMB	(ambiguity)	3 counts
ADQ	(adequacy)	8 counts
MIS	(misdirection)	16 counts

The high level of misdirections (MIS) encountered in our survey is worrying. The ratio of MIS to the other three (INC, AMB, ADQ) has grown since our previous survey [SG98a,b], partly as a result of fixes made in UML 1.3 to inconsistencies and ambiguities in UML 1.1. However, the absolute increase in MIS scores (previously 12 out of 37) shows how developers are finding more ways to confuse themselves with UML. This is alarming, not just because it represents a waste of effort, but because it is not a problem which can be fixed simply by trying to clarify the semantics of UML as it stands; instead, large chunks of UML need to be reconstructed to take into account the ways in which developers' minds operate.

It is clear from Gestalt psychology how important initial conceptualisations are; and how much they influence subsequent concept formation. If the initial UML analysis view is of a pre-normalised data model, and if communications between entities are conceived initially as dataflow (or workflow), then substantial mental effort is required to undo these faulty perceptions. It involves going against the tide, fighting against the conceptual clutter in the minds of developers.

The INC and AMB scores reflect on problems with the *consistency* of UML, whereas the ADQ scores reflect on problems with the *completeness* of UML. These counts suggest that further revisions to UML are necessary. In particular, the authors identified problems with the control flow logic in use cases and sequence diagrams; and the absence of a proper model to illustrate client-server coupling for system design optimisation. The interested reader is referred to alternative treatments of these topics in the methods SOMA [G95], *Discovery* [S98] and OPEN [FHG97; HSY98]. Here, task analysis replaces use cases; and the relationship between tasks corresponds to clear sequence, selection and iteration compositions. Class diagrams correspond to proper client-server graphs, allowing the system design stage to proceed smoothly.

References

[BC89] K Beck and W Cunningham (1989), "A laboratory for teaching object-oriented thinking", *Proc. 4th ACM Conf. Object-Oriented Prog. Sys., Lang. and Appl.*, pub. *Sigplan Notices, 24(10)*, 1-6.

[BRJ99] G Booch, J Rumbaugh and I Jacobson (1999), The Unified Modeling Language User Guide, Addison Wesley Longman.

[B94] G Booch (1994), Object-Oriented Analysis and Design with Applications, 2nd edn., Benjamin-Cummings.

[CY91a] P Coad and E Yourdon (1991), *Object Oriented Analysis*, Yourdon Press.

[CY91b] P Coad and E Yourdon (1991), *Object Oriented Design*, Yourdon Press.

[C96] A Cockburn (1996), *Basic Use Case Template, TR.96.03a*, rev. 1998, Humans and Technology; also pub. *http://members.aol.com/acockburn/papers/uctempla.htm*

[C97a] A Cockburn (1997a), "Goals and use cases", *J. Obj.-Oriented Prog., 10 (5)*, 35-40.

[C97b] A Cockburn (1997b), "Using goal-based use cases", *J. Obj.-Oriented Prog., 10 (7)*, 56-62.

[FHG97] D Firesmith, B Henderson-Sellers and I Graham (1997), *OPEN Modelling Language (OML) Reference Manual*, March, SIGS Books.

[FCJAG98] M Fowler, A Cockburn, I Jacobson, B Anderson and I Graham (1998), "Question time! About use cases", *Proc. 13th ACM Conf. Obj.-Oriented Prog. Sys., Lang. and Appl.*, pub. *ACM Sigplan Notices, 33 (10)*, 226-229.

[GHJV95] E Gamma, R Helm, R Johnson and J Vlissides (1995), *Design Patterns: Elements of Reusable Object-Oriented Software*, Addison-Wesley.

[G90] E A Gibson (1990), "Objects born and bred", *BYTE magazine, 15(10)*, 255-264.

[G95] I Graham (1995), *Migrating to Object Technology*, Addison-Wesley.

[G97] I Graham (1997), "Some problems with use cases... and how to avoid them", *Proc. 3rd Int. Conf. Object-Oriented Info. Sys.*, eds D Patel, Y Sun and S Patel, (London: Springer Verlag), 18-27,

[HSY98] B Henderson-Sellers, A J H Simons and H Younessi (1998), *The OPEN Toolbox of Techniques*, Addison-Wesley.

[HSR98] K S Y Hung, A J H Simons and A Rose (1998), "Can you have it all? Managing the time and budget against quality issue in a dynamic business object architecture development", *Proc. 6th Conf. Software Quality Management* (Amsterdam: MEP), 21-34.

[JCJO92] I Jacobson, M Christerson, P Jonsson and G Övergaard (1992), *Object-Oriented Software Engineering: a Use-Case Driven Approach*, Addison-Wesley.

[JGJ97] I Jacobson, M Griss and P Jonsson (1997), *Software Reuse: Architecture, Process and Organisation for Business Success*, Addison-Wesley and ACM Press, Reading MA, USA, 497pp.

[M97] J D McGregor (1997), *Testing Object-Oriented Components, ECOOP '97 Tutorial 2* (Jyväskylä, AITO/ACM).

[R97] Rational Software (1997), *UML 1.1 Reference Manual*, September, *http://www.rational.com/uml/* .

[RG92] K Rubin and A Goldberg (1992), "Object-behaviour analysis", *Comm. ACM, 35(9)*.

[RBPEL91] J Rumbaugh, M Blaha, W Premerlani, F Eddy and W Lorensen (1991), *Object-Oriented Modeling and Design*, Prentice-Hall.

[S98] A J H Simons (1998), *Object Discovery - a Process for Developing Medium-Sized Applications, ECOOP '98 Tutorial 14*, (Brussels, AITO/ACM), 90pp.

[SG98a] A J H Simons and I Graham (1998), "37 things that don't work in object-oriented modelling with UML", *Proc. 2nd ECOOP Workshop on Precise Behavioural Semantics*, eds. H Kilov and B Rumpe, *Technical Report TUM-I9813* (TU Munich, Institut für Informatik), 209-232.

[SG98b] A J H Simons and I Graham (1998), "37 things that don't work in object-oriented modelling with UML", *British Computer Society Object-Oriented Programming Systems Newsletter*, *35*, eds. R Mitchell and S Kent (BCS: Autumn, 1998), *http://www.oopsnl.ukc.ac.uk/Issue35Autumn1998/contents.html.*

[SSH98] A J H Simons, M Snoeck and K S Y Hung (1998), "Design patterns as litmus paper to test the strength of object-oriented methods", *Proc. 5th. Int. Conf. Object-Oriented Info. Sys.*, eds. C Rolland and G Grosz (Paris: Springer Verlag), 129-147.

[WN95] K Waldén and J-M Nerson (1995), *Seamless Object-Oriented Architecture*, Prentice Hall.

[WW89] R Wirfs-Brock and L Wiener (1989), "Responsibility-driven design: a responsibility-driven approach", *Proc. 4th ACM Conf. Object-Oriented Prog. Sys., Lang. and Appl.*, pub. *Sigplan Notices, 24(10)*, 71-76.

[WWW90] R Wirfs-Brock, B Wilkerson and L Wiener (1990), *Designing Object-Oriented Software*, Prentice Hall.

About the Authors

Anthony Simons is a lecturer in Computer Science at the University of Sheffield, with 14 years experience using, researching and teaching object technology. He joined the department as a research assistant building speech recognisers; later he moved into mainstream software engineering. He has research interests in type theory, language design, analysis and design methods, and verification and testing. He is the author of over 50 research publications and the creator of the *Discovery Method* for developing object-oriented systems. He holds a PhD in object-oriented type theory and language design and a Masters degree in modern languages and linguistics.

Ian Graham is chairman of IGA Ltd, a consultancy specialising in advanced information technology and change management. Ian has over 20 years experience as a practitioner in IT. Previously, he was a VP at Chase Manhattan Bank and senior manager at the Swiss Bank Corporation (now Warburg Dillon Reed). Ian created the system development methods for both Chase and SBC. He is the author of 9 books and over 60 papers and the creator of the *SOMA* object-oriented development method. Ian is a Fellow of the British Computer Society, has a Masters degree in mathematics and holds an Industrial Chair in Requirements Engineering at De Montfort University.

Chapter 18

FORMALIZING ASSOCIATION SEMANTICS IN TERMINOLOGIES

Harold Solbrig
hrsolbrig@ibm.net

"Yet because there is no remedy, but that of necessity there must be some rules: therefore certain rules are here set forth, which, as they be few in number; so they be plain and easy to understand ... in such a language and order as is most easy and plain for the understanding, both of the readers and hearers. It is also more commodious, both for the shortness thereof, and for the plainness of the order, and for that the rules be few and easy."

Preface to the Episcopal Book of Common Prayer, 1549.

Abstract   The terminology of a scientific or technical community embodies an information structure that is meaningful to that community. The conceptual model underlying a terminology can serve as the basis for an information model, as well as providing a foundation upon which the external and internal information structures can be built. In order to be useful, however, the information content behind a terminology must be formalized - made precise and explicit. One of the roadblocks to this formalization process is the issue of association semantics. Different terminologies specify associations from different perspectives and at varying degrees of specificity. These associations need to be mapped into a common model that is useful to both the terminologist and the information modeler.

1. INTRODUCTION

The terminology of a scientific or technical community embodies an information structure that is meaningful to that community. The conceptual model underlying a terminology can serve as the basis for an information model, as well as providing a foundation upon which the external and internal information structures can be built. In order to be useful, however, the information content behind a terminology must be formalized - made precise and explicit. One possible means of accomplishing this task would be to specify a generalized conceptual model of terminology – a "terminology of terminologies." The conceptual model underlying a given terminology could then be mapped into this model, hopefully providing a precise, unambiguous and uniform external view. This approach was recently taken by the respondents to an RFP issued by the Object Management Group (OMG) Healthcare Domain Task Force (CORBAmed).[OMG97, OMG98]

The Healthcare DTF had requested an interface specification for read-only access to the content of various medical terminologies. As part of the response, the authors proposed an abstract model, the purpose of which was to define the useful characteristics and behavior of a terminology from the perspective of a computerized client. The respondents also proposed sets of uniform codes for designating such things as language, coding scheme name, syntactic type, etc. These codes were deemed necessary for a client to unambiguously communicate with a terminology service (e.g. give me the preferred *English* name for code *482.82* in the International Classification of Diseases coding scheme *ICD-9*).[1]

Among this set of codes were codes for naming associations. Associations play a central role in both the definition and retrieval of the concepts contained within a terminology. The usefulness of a formal definition, however, is heavily dependent upon the precision and clarity of the associations. Before the authors could propose a set of standard codes for associations, it was necessary to specify the *concepts behind the association codes*. To specify these concepts, it was fist necessary to determine which association characteristics were important – both from the context of the terminologist and that of the information modeler.

This has turned out to be a difficult problem. Many existing terminologies can be notoriously lax in their use of associations. Even where some degree of precision exists, terminologies have used different and potentially conflicting semantic formalisms.

2. TERMINOLOGY AND INFORMATION MODELING

"It must be left in each case to the specialist, who being familiar with the actual sign-situations involved can decide within his particular field of reference which symbols are true and which are not." [OR23]

The terminology of a scientific or technical community embodies an information structure that is meaningful to that community.

Semiotics, linguistics and terminology all deal with various aspects of signs and how they represent and communicate meaning. Terminology, in particular, focuses on how the conceptual space of a specialized area of knowledge is designated and partitioned. An excellent introduction to terminologies and their purpose can be found in the book, A Practical Course in Terminology Processing, by Juan Sager [S90]. In it he proposes the following definition:

"Terminology is concerned with the study and use of the systems of symbols and linguistic signs employed for human communication in specialised areas of knowledge and activities. It is primarily a linguistic discipline – linguistics being interpreted here in its widest possible sense – with emphasis on semantics (systems of meanings and concepts) and pragmatics. It is inter-disciplinary in the sense that it also borrows concepts and methods from semiotics, epistemology, classification, etc. It is closely linked to the subject fields whose lexica it describes and for which it seeks to provide assistance in the ordering and use of designations. Although terminology has been in the past mostly concerned with the lexical aspects of specialised languages, its scope extends to syntax and phonology. In its applied aspect terminology is related to lexicography and uses techniques of information science and technology."

Dr. Sager asserts that the "terms" and "terminology" of specialized areas of knowledge serve to distinguish and designate the concepts that are considered significant within the specific area, and contrasts these with the "words" and "vocabulary" used in everyday speech:

"The lexicon of a special subject language reflects the organizational characteristics of the discipline by tending to provide as many lexical units as there are concepts conventionally established in the subspace and by restricting the reference of each lexical unit to a well-defined region. ... The items which are characterised by special reference within a discipline are the 'terms' of that discipline, and collectively they form its 'terminology'; those which function in general reference over a wide variety of sublanguages are simply called 'words', and their totality the 'vocabulary'."

The language of everyday speech and writing is fraught with subtlety and nuance. It is the language of politics and poetry. It is a difficult, if not impossible task, to formalize the meaning and intention of everyday words and phrases. This task, however, is considerably easier when working with scientific and technical terminologies.

The conceptual model underlying a terminology can serve as the basis for an information model, as well as providing a foundation upon which the external and internal information structures can be built.

Terminologies develop in situations where conceptual space has been well defined. A terminology provides a link that enables practitioners in a given field to communicate in a precise and unambiguous way across the boundaries of space, time and function. Not unexpectedly, these turn out to be some of the same characteristics that are required to develop a rigorous information model for computerization.

The concepts defined within a terminology can serve to identify entities and entity instances within an information model. Definitions, synonyms, homonyms, etc. provide additional descriptive and identifying information. Taxonomies and other associative descriptions within a terminology can provide formal, computable definitions within an information model.

The terminology can also serve as a base for defining external information structures to represent the information model. A terminology can help to determine which entities in the information model will be represented as structures, what the various attributes of these structures will be, how the various structures are associated and which will be represented as constrained properties or domains.

It is not a difficult task to assign concise, unique identifiers to each concept within a terminology. Terminologies that have been used for data entry or other semi-automated data gathering purposes often already have an identifier scheme in place. Unique identifiers can be used as tags and codes for attribute values within the internal information model. If the contents of the terminology can be put into a machine-readable form ("IT enabled"), it then becomes possible to drive a significant portion of the input and output functions from the terminology itself.

For information acquisition, structural tags can serve to identify the names and possible values for required information. The compositional structure of a terminology allows lists of terms and/or synonyms to be displayed on input screens for selection. The words and phrases of the terms themselves allow selection of appropriate values by the entry of phrases and keywords.

An "IT enabled" terminology can also be used to format information displays and outputs in the form and language appropriate for the specific user in the specific setting. Terminologies can help with information retrieval and automated functions such as validation, workflow, diagnostics and alert generation.

Maintenance and revision of a terminology can be made considerably easier and robust has been computerized. With an "IT enabled" terminology it even becomes possible to generate and integrate new terms as the on the fly as the underlying information system is being used.

Not every business or enterprise has a well-developed terminologies. In situations where they do exist, however, they have the potential to provide both a precise behavioral specification and a readily available set of terms with which to communicate with the subject matter experts in the discipline.

In order to be useful, however, the information content of a terminology must be formalized - made precise and explicit.

Most of the terminologies in use today were developed well before the era of computerization. They were developed to aid in written and oral communication, and often exist in the form of dictionaries, textbooks, term lists, coding manuals, etc. The level of formalization can vary widely. Much of the background information and presumptions needed to use the terminology may be communicated via a secondary channel such as textbooks, college courses or simply by word of mouth. The process transforming the terms themselves into a digital form can be daunting.

It has been demonstrated, however, that the payoff for extracting and formalizing this information can be substantial. Not only does the analyst and information processing specialist benefit from a deeper understanding of the community that they are working with, but the community can benefit from the discovery of ambiguities and inconsistencies which may be uncovered within their own conceptual map.

One of the key elements in formalizing a terminology involves the explicit description of associations that exist between the different terms. Some of these associations may be stated implicitly by the organization of terms within hierarchical structures, while others may be named. It is not the norm, unfortunately, for the terminology of associations to be rigorously or precisely defined.

Terms such as *is-a* and *is-composed-of* are used with the presumption that the audience has a clear, *a-priori* understanding of their meaning. The intent of the author of an association is often anything but obvious. *Is-a* can be used in one situation to describe an exhaustive, mutually exclusive subtyping relationship and in a related situation to describe one that is overlapping, non-exhaustive. *Is-composed-of* can describe anything from the parts that make up a microscope to the compounds contained within a specific drug. The introduction of terms such as *has-laterality, has-member, has-etiology* only serve to further obfuscate the situation. For a terminology to be useful in the long term, the meaning *behind* the associations needs to be precisely and explicitly defined.

3. ISSUES WITH ASSOCIATION SEMANTICS

One of the major stumbling blocks to formalizing terminological content is the lack of a precise and well-agreed-upon set of association semantics.

The key to understanding the conceptual space that underlies a terminology is understanding the relationship of the terms to each other. There are at least three related issues that need to be resolved before any significant degree understanding can be reached:

- Terminologies come with widely varying degrees of precision in their association semantics
- Terminologies that do have a degree of precision in associations may still not be compatible with each other.
- Precision in the association semantics of terminologies opens up the possibility of doing direct, formal transformations between the characteristics of terminological associations and the behavior and characteristics required to specify and implement systems. These transformations, however, have yet to be understood and specified.

Issue 1: Terminologies come with widely varying degrees of precision in their association semantics.

This is especially true of terminologies that were developed before computerization. Juan Sager notes that, "While there is no doubt about the desirability of using conceptual relationships, there is no consensus about the importance of conceptual relationships in the clarification of the concept term relation."[S90] This is due in no small part to the fact that terminologies, until recently, existed for human-to-human communication and a degree of imprecision was tolerable. Dr. Sager also notes that, "It is widely accepted that they (relationships) are needed for determining conceptual fields, but it is not established how much useful information they provide. The fact, however, that we can now model relatively complex systems and their internal relationships on the computer has influenced theory to the extent that the number of relationships between concepts admitted as being useful for structuring conceptual fields has increased considerably."

We can take a couple of examples from the medical informatics field. Some of the terminologies within this field have little or no differentiation in their associations. Structures of the Medical Subject Headings (MeSH) [MESH87] organize concepts into hierarchical tree structures for the purpose of cross-referencing medical literature. In MeSH, the association between a parent and child node is often anything but obvious. A quick perusal of the structure will reveal examples of subtypes, dependency and composition, sometimes even combined underneath the same root! In addition, the same term sometimes appears in more than one sub-tree, with a different set of child terms for each appearance.

Other terminologies such as the International Classification of Diseases, ICD-9-CM [ICD97] and SNOMED [SMD97] have relied on an explicit hierarchy embedded within the codes for the concepts. While the association between two nodes is understood to be an "is-kind-of" relationship, further detail is lacking. This has resulted in several problems, not the least of which is the "NEC/NOS" issue.

The NEC/NOS problem arises because of the lack of precision in the specification of subtypes. Frequently hierarchical codes represent a taxonomy. It is presumed that the association between entities in the primary classification tree was *exhaustive* and *non-overlapping*. As many categories, however, are anything *but* exhaustive, nodes labeled "Not Elsewhere Classified (NEC)" or some similar wording began to appear. When a new node is added in the taxonomy, the *meaning* of the NEC term changes without the code changing. This results in a gradual drift in the meaning of previously recorded information.

One proposed solution to this problem is to change the definition of the association to *non-exhaustive* and *non-overlapping*. This way, the parent node can be used when none of the children apply, indicating simply that additional information was "Not Otherwise Specified (NOS)". While this solution addresses some of the problem space, it completely ignores subtypes that *are* exhaustive, or are overlapping.

It should be noted that SNOMED has recently released a new version, SNOMED-RT [SMD99], which separates the associations from the codes. SNOMED-RT goes a long ways towards clarifying the intent behind the associations, but is still lacking in the exact intent and meaning of a given association code.

There is not a tremendous amount that can be done right now with terminologies with imprecise or ambiguous associations. They exist and are used, so whatever the association model employed, it will need to be able to communicate the fact that information is lacking. In the long term, if we *can* develop a rigorous model of associations which will serve as a target for future terminology releases.

Issue 2: Terminologies which do have well-specified associations may still not be compatible.

Some terminologies do have a degree of precision in their association specifications. Unfortunately, however, terminological formalisms can come from a variety of different perspectives, including classical linguistics, conceptual analysis or, more recently, conceptual schemas and data modeling. While these approaches overlap, each of them stress different and possibly incompatible association characteristics. At the risk of painting with an overly broad brush, we attempt to characterize some of the general features of each approach in the next few paragraphs.

Classical linguistics is concerned with *lexical semantics* – the relationships among word and phrase "meanings." Classical linguistics defines several different types of "meaning", including referential meaning, social meaning and affective meaning. Referential meaning, "the person, object, abstract notion, state, or event to which a word or sentence makes reference."[F94] Social meaning "conveys information about the social nature of the language user or the context of utterance." Affective meaning conveys "what the language user feels about the content or the ongoing content."[F94] In a scientific discipline, the primary focus tends toward referential meaning.[2] The term *denotation* is frequently used when describing referential meaning while *connotation* is used when describing social and affective meaning.

Classic linguistics focus is on the relationships between words and phrases rather than on the relationships between the term referents. Among these basic relationships used to position the meaning of a word are *hyponymy* (a kind of), *synonymy* (similar meaning), *part/whole* (subdivision), *antonymy* (opposite meaning), *converseness* (reciprocal meaning), *polysemy* (many meanings), *homonymy* (same phonological shape), *metaphorical extension* (derived meaning) and *metonymy* (representative example).

The relationships in classic linguistics work reasonably well when it comes to creating an accurate image of the referents of a word or phrase in the mind of a human being. With the possible exception of hyponyms, however, these relationships are of limited value when attempting to create selection lists, make knowledge inferences or perform other computerized functions. Classic linguistic definitions also provide limited value when attempting to correctly categorize a new term.

Conceptual analysis focuses on entities, attributes and events. It is based on formal set theory, embodying the notion of *type*, a "function which maps concepts into a set." [S84] The *denotation* of a type is defined as the range of the type function

– a set of concepts. Entities, attributes and events are ordered in a network of *subtype* relationships defined over the denotations of the types.

The core of the conceptual analysis approach is founded on the classic Aristotelian notion of *genus* and *differentiae*. Information is organized into a lattice, with the topmost node denoting everything within the universe of discourse. Each subordinate node constrains the denotation of the superordinate node, with the terminus being the bottom-most node, which denotes the empty set.

With the exception of the subtyping association itself, associations occur within their own subtype lattice. These associations connect two or more types, with each type is associated with a specific role. Associations are described in terms of the "*maximal types* of concepts that may be linked to each arc of the relation." [S84]

Conceptual analysis is very strong in the area of classification of new terms and of determining the characteristics and attributes that an instance of a given type would be expected to possess. Its weakness, however, lies in the associations. Most systems based on conceptual analysis have only weak notions of dependency, part/whole, composition, etc. The "meaning" behind a given association – the characteristics and behavior that the association would exhibit – is left largely to the interpretation of the observer.

The conceptual schema approach is founded on the use of first or higher order predicate logic, in which a *term* is a linguistic object which refers to an "entity" and a *predicate* is a "verb, which says something about an entity or entities to which the term(s) in the sentence refer." [ISO87] A conceptual schema defines the permissible set of sentences that can be asserted (be "true") about a given universe of discourse. Subtyping associations are based on set membership. All other associations are represented as predicates over two or more entities.

The conceptual schema approach certainly has the potential to describe a wide variety of associations, and to do it precisely. As of yet, however, it doesn't seem to have arrived at the point of delivering association "patterns" – association names, attributes and behaviors that can be reused. This is a promising approach, however.

Issue 3: Precision in the association semantics of terminologies opens up the possibility of doing direct, formal transformations between the characteristics of terminological associations and the behavior and characteristics required to specify and implement systems. These transformations, however, have yet to be understood and specified.

An information model:
- Identifies the set of the possible entities within a system.
- Identifies the set of possible associations that may exist between the entities of the system.
- Defines which combinations of entities and associations are possible (valid) within the system.
- Defines the set of rules by which valid entity-association combination may be transformed.

To be useful, an information model must accurately abstract some "real-world" situation. The set of possible entities within the model must correspond to a set of mental images external to the system. The set of possible associations must correspond to a set of relationships that could exist between the images. The set of valid combinations in the model must correspond to a (subset) of the possible relationships that could exist between the external images, and the set of transformation rules must correspond to the set of ways that the mental images could be changed. In a nutshell, an information model must accurately represent some abstraction of the "real world", with the emphasis being on the word represent.

The purpose of a terminology is to provide mapping between a set of entity names and a system of external mental images. It does this by:

- Identifying a set of names.
- Providing a set of synonyms, homonyms, metaphors, etc. sufficient to allow a human being to fix each name with unique mental image within a given context.

To be useful, a terminology must provide sufficient precision such that any two people sharing pre-established experience and training would map the same name to mental images that are sufficiently similar that they could be considered to represent the same "concept" within a given context.

One of the key differences between a terminology and an information model is that an information model can be both descriptive and prescriptive. Invariants express the properties are consistently true within the system, while the behavioral portion of the specification states what the new state of a system will be given the current state and an external input. A terminology, on the other hand, is largely descriptive in nature. It provides a map of partition of an area of knowledge into a set distinct "concepts". It does not attempt to define how this system of concepts might change in response to external input. This difference turns out to have some profound ramifications when it comes to the semantics of associations.

As association semantics become more fully specified, it becomes important that the transformations between the terminological perspective and the information modeling perspective be formalized as well. As an example, take the notion of subtyping. From the information modeling perspective, subtyping involves the inheritance of structural and behavioral properties - "If an instance of a subtype belongs to its supertype, then the structural and behavioral properties of its subtype constitute a superset of the structural and behavioral properties of its supertype." [KR94]

The terminological perspective, however, tends to be more focused on the notion of inheritance of *meaning*. The statement, "a dog is a mammal" indicates that the set of mental images invoked by the term *dog* is a subset of the set of possible images that are invoked by the term *mammal*. It doesn't necessarily make any direct assertions about the structural or behavioral properties of either dogs or mammals – it is only an assertion about the set of mental images that each term refers to.

Another example would be the notion of *composition*. From an information modeling perspective, we are concerned whether the components of a composite can be ordered or not, whether the components can exist independently of the composite, whether a component may be associated with more than one composite, etc.[3][KR94]

From a terminological perspective, however, the concern is more with the various ways that a composite makes up a whole. A typical partitioning is described by Winston et al. [WCH87] and elaborated by James Odell [O94]. They utilize three characteristics:

- Configurable - whether or not the parts bear a particular functional or structural relationship to one another or to the object they constitute
- Homeomerous - whether or not the parts are the same kind of thing as the whole
- Invariance - whether or not the parts can be separated from the whole

to describe six different types of *meronomy* or composition:

	Configurational	Momoemeric	Invariant	Example
Component-integral object	yes	no	no	Wheels is part of a bicycle
Material-object	yes	no	yes	Steel made of iron
Portion-object	yes	yes	no	Sand pile part of a dune
Place-area	yes	yes	yes	Texas part of United States[4]
Member-bunch	no	no	no	Sand grain is part of a sand pile
Member-partnership	no	no	yes	husband is part of a marriage

Again, the focus is on the *meaning* of the association from an external or interface perspective rather than describing the behavior of the system.

CONCLUSION

The terminology of a scientific or technical community can provide a strong foundation for information models, external and internal schemas and the actual implementation of computerized systems. In order to be useful, however, the content of a terminology needs to be formalized – made precise and unambiguous. One of the keys to accomplishing this is arriving at a formal model of the contents of a terminology – a terminology of terminologies.

Significant progress is being made along this front, but one of the stumbling blocks is the semantics of associations. Further research is needed to determine:

- What characteristics and behaviors are needed to specify precise and useful association semantics from a terminological viewpoint?
- How should existing association semantics (or lack thereof) in current terminologies be mapped to these new semantics and behaviors?
- What is the correlation between the semantics and behaviors of associations from a terminological viewpoint and the semantics and behaviors of associations from an information-modeling viewpoint?

The answers to these questions should help to provide more exact, higher fidelity models of real-world businesses and problems.

Endnotes

[1] ESCHERICHIA COLI

[2] Many would argue that a scientific or technical discipline would want to minimize the impact of social and affective meaning in communication. Closer examination, however, often shows that all three forms still play a crucial role. The words and phrases used by a speaker serve to identify their particular field or specialty, allowing the listener to rate the message's validity and significance. Subtle queues are frequently included in communications, which serve to convey the speaker's certainty, sense of urgency, etc. Computerized communication can remove the social and affective content of a message, limiting its ultimate usefulness.

[3] Dr. Kilov notes that information modeling includes the "need to provide two kinds of composite's properties – those determined by properties of components and those independent of properties of components. Consideration of these properties is very important and may bring information modeling and classification closer than they might appear" [K99]

[4] Some might contest on the basis that Texas is not sufficiently similar to the rest of the United States to constitute a portion-object composition, and also that Texas could readily be removed without adversely effecting the rest of the country. This debate, however, is best left to more appropriate venues such as Friday night beer halls.

References

[F94] Edward Finegan, *Language - its structure and use*. Harcourt Brace, Fort Worth, TX. 1994 (Second Edition)

[ICD97] The International Classification of Diseases, 9th Revision, Clinical Modification (ICD-9-CM). US Department of Health and Human Services, Health Care Financing Administration, 1997.

[ISO87] ISO/TC 97, Information processing systems – Concepts and terminology for the conceptual schema and the information base. (ISO/TR 9007 : 1987 (E))

[KR94] Haim Kilov, James Ross, *Information Modeling: An Object-Oriented Approach*. Prentice-Hall, Englewood Cliffs, NJ, 1994.

[K99] Haim Kilov. Private correspondence with the author.

[L87] George Lakoff, *Women, Fire and Dangerous Things*. University of Chicago Press, Chicago, IL 1987.

[M97] Bertrand Meyer, *Object-Oriented Software Construction*. Second Edition. Prentice Hall, Upper Saddle River, NJ. 1997.

[MESH87] Medical Subject Headings – Tree Structures, 1988. National Library of Medicine, Bethesda, MD, 1987.

[OMG97] Object Management Group, CORBAmed Lexicon Query Services RFP. January 1997.

[OMG98] Object Management Group, Lexicon Query Services. April, 1998.

[O94] James J. Odell, "Six Different Kinds of Composition", Journal of Object-Oriented Programming, SIG Publications, Inc. New York, NY, Vol 5, No 8, January 1994.

[OR23] C.K. Ogden, I.A. Richards, *The Meaning of Meaning*. Harcourt, Brace & World, Inc, New York, NY, 1923. (reprint)

[S90] Juan C. Sager, *A Practical Course in Terminology Processing*. John Benjamins Publishing Company, Philadelphia, PA, 1990.

[S84] John F. Sowa, *Conceptual Structures – Information Processing in Mind and Machine*. Addison-Wesley, Reading, MA, 1984.

[SMD97] SNOMED – The Systemized Nomenclature of Medicine, College of American Pathologists, 1997.

[SMD98] SNOMED-RT – A Reference Terminology for Healthcare, College of American Pathologists, 1999.

[WCH87] Morton E. Winston, Roger Chaffin and Douglas Herrmann, "A Taxonomy of Part-Whole Relations," Cognitive Science, 11, 1987, pp. 417-444.

About the Author

Harold Solbrig is a computer systems architect and programmer. He has spent the majority of the last 24 years involved in medical computing, although he has had brief forays into operating systems, hardware design and television newsroom automation. His recent research has been focused on formalizing the relationship between terminologies and computerized data representation. He holds a BS in Mathematics, and has served on several standards committees involved medical and general information representation and transfer. He was employed by 3M Health Information Systems for the past ten years, but has recently accepted a position with the Mayo Clinic and is in the process of moving to the land of the truly cold.

Chapter 19

ON THE SPECIFICATION OF THE BUSINESS AND ECONOMIC FOUNDATIONS OF ELECTRONIC COMMERCE

Angelo E. Thalassinidis
EDS
thalassinidisa@acm.org

Ira Sack
Stevens Institute of Technology
Hoboken, NJ 07030
ira3@idt.net

Abstract: Using information modeling introduced in [KR94, K99], a specification framework and rationale of the business and economic foundations of E-Commerce is provided. A bifurcated approach to E-Commerce is undertaken. E-Commerce is partitioned into two subtypes: E-Macrocommerce (i.e., business-to-business electronic transactions) discussed in Part 1 and E-Microcommerce (i.e., business-to-consumer electronic transactions) discussed in Part 2. Our framework is founded on organizational theory, systems theory, classical economics, game theory, and business strategy. Further work is necessary in establishing the business and economic foundations of E-Commerce, but a core foundation employing business specifications, contracts, and game theory is established.

Keywords: E-Commerce, Information Modeling, Organizational Theory, Systems Theory, Classical Economics, Game Theory, Business Strategy, Business Contracts, Uniform Commercial Code, Prisoner's Dilemma, War of Attrition.

PART I: E-MACROCOMMERCE

Since the early 1960's, companies have been engaged in E-Macrocommerce–that is, business-to-business electronic transactions, such as electronic invoicing, electronic ordering, etc. These transactions are most effectively conducted among companies which have a strong and long-term business relationship. The relationship is necessitated by high switching costs that are incurred once an information system linking these companies has been established. With the advent of the Internet and especially the World Wide Web, organizations now have the opportunity to minimize entry/switching costs that enable the establishment of new trading partnerships.

In his groundbreaking book *Markets and Hierarchies* [W75], Williamson analyzes and compares markets and hierarchies. Expanding this work, in their seminal paper, *Electronic Markets and Electronic Hierarchies* [MYB87], Malone *et al.* examine how advances in information technology affect firm and market structure and discuss the impact of these changes on corporate strategies. Malone suggests the existence of two basic mechanisms for coordinating the flow of goods and services through adjacent steps in the business value chain[1]: *markets* and *hierarchies*. Whereas markets coordinate the flow of goods or services through supply and demand forces and facilitate external transactions between different individuals and firms, hierarchies coordinate the flow of goods or services by controlling and directing this flow at a higher hierarchical management level, i.e., suppliers are preselected by management.

Malone identifies the following determinants of coordination structure:

- *Asset Specificity*: An input used by a firm is highly asset specific if it cannot readily be used by other firms because of site specificity (e.g., natural resource available at a certain location and movable at great cost), physical asset specificity (e.g., a complex computer system designed for a single purpose), human asset specificity (e.g., highly specialized human skills), or time asset specificity (e.g., a perishable product that must arrive at its destination and be used within a short time after its production).

- *Complexity of Product Description*: This refers to the amount of information needed to specify the attributes of a product in enough detail to allow potential buyers to make a selection. Notice that the buyer selection involves both products of the same kind and products of different kinds that fulfil similar buyer's needs.

Malone argues that information technology has affected both of these determinants thus creating an overall shift from hierarchies to markets. The crux of his argument is that the widespread use of information technology is likely to decrease the "unit costs" of coordination. Such costs take into account gathering information (search cost), negotiating contracts, and protecting against the risks of "opportunistic" bargaining. Whereas high coordination cost promotes a hierarchy, low coordination cost promotes the creation of efficient competitive environments.

Consequently, when the coordination cost becomes smaller, companies will move to a more natural market structure.

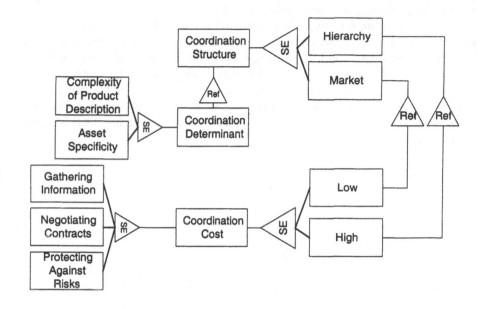

Figure 1. Market vs. Hierarchy

We should further explain the relationship between a market and a low coordination cost. When the coordination cost is low, a market is triggered. In the same way, when the coordination cost gets high, we have a shift to a hierarchy. The coordination cost is the determinant of the type of the coordination structure. (For a definition of the above and all other diagrams refer to Appendix A.)

Why Still Hierarchies?

Although information technology has made massive improvements since the publication of Malone's paper in 1987, a significant shift from hierarchies to markets has not been observed [SKP96, NB96]. Companies are using emerging technology–albeit they mostly implement industry standard systems (e.g., Web-EDI, VANs, etc.). Many analysts are wondering why the shift to markets has not occurred. We shall argue below that the failure of the shift to markets is due to an essential factor that Malone omitted in his analysis: the importance of long-term business relationships between companies.

Long-term relationships are defined and analyzed in still a broader context by John Kay [K95]. He emphasizes the essentiality of contracts among businesses. Kay identifies three types of business contracts: *Spot, Classical,* and *Relational.* Spot contracts are used in immediate bilateral exchanges such as the exchange of stocks in a stock market. Classical contracts are used for long-term exchanges whose terms are fully spelled out in legal relationships. An example of a classical contract is a standard mortgage agreement. Finally, relational contracts are used in exchange relationships that are not fully articulated such as a traditional marriage contract in the US. The rules of behavior are implicit, and the enforcement mechanism is the value of the continuing relationship between the parties.

Spot contracts are effective when individual selfish behavior works to the best joint interest of the contracting parties[2]. Unfortunately for spot contracts, much business is conducted using long-lived agreements. Although classical contracts can be used to establish a long-term relationship, they inhibit the free flow of information as such information might later be used against one of the parties. In a relational contract, however, information flows are most natural. Note that relational contracts are very difficult to make in a business environment in which business instability is customary[3].

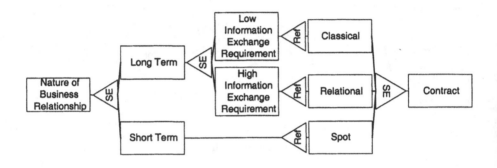

Figure 2. Contract Types and the Nature of Business Relationship

Having identified the significance of contract types to a business relationship, we now explain why a major shift from hierarchies to markets has not been observed. Long-term business requires a hierarchy, while short-term business dictates a market.

The reason for this can be seen by an examination of the well-known Prisoner's Dilemma of game theory [K95]:

> "Two prisoners are arrested and put in separate cells. The district attorney admits that he has no real evidence but presents the following alternatives: If one confesses, he will go free, and the other can expect a ten-year jail sentence. If both confess, each will be convicted, but they can expect a lighter sentence, seven years perhaps. If neither confesses, the likely outcome is a short one-year sentence for each one, based on a trumped-up charge."

The problem with this game is that both parties do better to confess (to look at the short-term profits), but the cost is seven-years (it costs much more to be in a market). The Prisoner's Dilemma may be resolved if the game is played repetitively (i.e., a long-term perspective is taken). A repeated game strategy establishes a *relationship* between the two players. It always pays to confess (look for short-term profits - market), but not doing so is to everyone's long-term benefit (look for long-term profits–hierarchy). Only the creation of a long-term relationship can achieve this outcome. An important feature of this solution is that both parties expect the venture to continue. If it is likely to end, each party will begin to see the benefits of holding something back–of behaving strategically rather than maximizing the joint gains from the revenue.

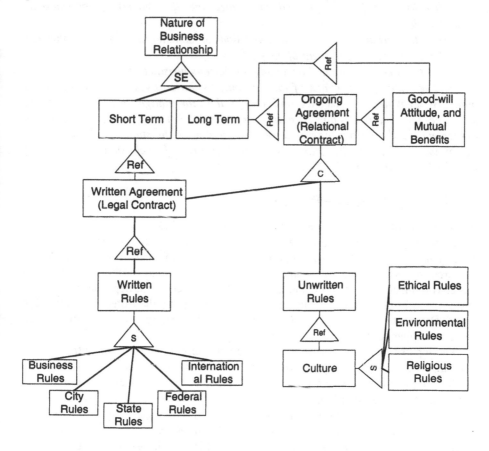

Figure 3. Nature of Business Relationship

A hierarchy is much more involved than the simple written contract that establishes it. The companies involved will be judged not only by a written contract, but also by unwritten rules which may well be of greater significance. Trust, cooperation, coordination, reputation: all these unwritten factors are key to establishing a long-term relationship–a company which breaks any of these factors will be punished by the loss of business. Unwritten rules are also essential to business law. For example, the Uniform Commercial Code (UCC) [CS90] examines not just the content of the contract but also the environment in which the contract was written; it also considers non-written contracts to be valid. Note also that UCC is explicitly applied within the context of the existing–written!–laws and regulations. There are a number of interesting questions, such as "What happens when these laws change?" and "Which has priority if they are inconsistent?" These questions do not have a clear answer. For this reason, mediation, bargaining, and negotiation are still invaluable instruments to dispute resolution.

" ...

(2) Underlying purposes and policies of this Act are

(a) to simplify, clarify and modernize the law governing commercial transactions;

(b) to permit the continued expansion of commercial practices through custom, usage and agreement of the parties;

(c) to make uniform the law among the various jurisdictions.

(3) The effect of provisions of this Act may be varied by agreement, except as otherwise provided in this Act and except that the obligations of good faith, diligence, reasonableness and care prescribed by this Act may not be disclaimed by agreement but the parties may by agreement determine the standards by which the performance of such obligations is to be measured if such standards are not manifestly unreasonable." [CS90]

The Need For Repetitive Business

But why is a company interested in a long-term relationship?

To better understand an organization, Churchman *et al.* suggest that it be viewed as a *system* [CAA57][D83]. An open system is a set of interacting elements that acquires inputs from the environment, transforms them, and discharges outputs to the environment. The need for inputs and outputs reflects interdependencies of the system with its environment. This approach is also used by the Reference Model for Open Distributed Processing (RM-ODP)–an ISO standard for open distributed systems (Appendix B).

The inputs that a company receives come from suppliers, while the outputs that a company produces go to buyers (who may be in the same company). Both the goods that a company uses and the goods that a company produces can be examined in terms of their *degree of uniqueness* (or asset specificity).[4] Porter explains why companies should try to produce unique value [P96]. He suggests that a competitive strategy is about being different: *"It means deliberately choosing a different set of activities to deliver a unique mix of value."* He adds that choosing a unique position is not enough to guarantee a sustainable advantage. A valuable position will attract imitation by competitors. As a solution he suggests that *"... a strategic position is not sustainable unless there are trade-offs with other positions. Trade-offs occur when activities are incompatible. ... Strategy is making trade-offs in competing. The essence of strategy is choosing what not to do. Without trade-offs, there would be no need for choice and thus no need for strategy. ..."*

In light of the above, we can now analyze the appropriateness of long-term and short-term commitments between companies. We first examine goods (both input and output) based on their *substitution cost* and *retooling cost*. Substitution cost is associated with a buyer substituting a particular good with another good from another or the same supplier. This includes the search cost defined by Malone and also any particular cost associated with modifying either the input or transformation process of the buyer. Certain goods, such as office supplies, are considered to be 'commodities'–they do not require any major investment in adjusting them to our needs. In contrast, there are goods that require major investment in order to fit a buyer's needs. For example, when a company moves into a new office, it incurs substantial fixed expenditures specific to that address: it must print stationary with this address, buy furniture that fit this office, install telephone and computer systems, and so on [K95].

Retooling cost is associated with a supplier changing his input process, and/or his transformation process, and/or his output process in order to manufacture another good for probably a different buyer. Certain goods require very little, if any, retooling for their production. For example, office supplies can generally be manufactured in a similar way, independent of the company that is going to use them. In contrast, there are goods that require a major retooling for their production. For example, an automobile part subcontractor will have to retool his plant, retrain employees, and more, in order to manufacture a part for a different car model.

The relationship between suppliers and buyers in both unique and not-so-unique cases of goods has been analyzed extensively by many economists, for example, see [K95]. Both the supplier and the buyer will prefer a long-term agreement in the case of high retooling cost and high substitution cost. In the case of low retooling cost and low substitution cost, both the supplier and the buyer will prefer a shorter term commitment.

The degree of uniqueness of a good is directly associated with the substitution and retooling costs associated with that good. If a good has either high substitution or retooling cost, then that good is considered to have a high degree of uniqueness. The degree of uniqueness of a good evolves according to a number of factors such as technology, the number of suppliers, the customizability of a good, and so on.

Contributions of E-Macrocommerce to the Evolution of Business

There are two opposing goals in today's business environment. The first goal is the creation of a market-like environment in which goods can be bought at close to cost. The limiting factor for the creation of this environment is related to the degree of uniqueness of goods. In goods with a high degree of uniqueness, a market-like environment is a virtual impossibility since there are not enough manufacturers who can produce the exact same product, whereas in goods with a low degree of uniqueness there are not many incentives for suppliers to participate.

The second goal is the creation of a repetitive business environment in which business relationships (trust, commitment, cooperation, etc.) are nourished. Similarly, the limiting factor for the creation of such an environment is related to degree of uniqueness. In goods with a high degree of uniqueness, there is a tremendous cost and risk for building such a relationship, whereas in goods with a low degree of uniqueness there are not enough incentives for such an investment[5].

The degree of uniqueness of a good has been the predominant reason why companies have not opened up their businesses to the extent forecasted by Malone. The limitation caused by the degree of uniqueness of a good is superseded by a business architecture known as a *network organization* in which a relatively small number of selected suppliers can participate efficiently in real time. In the network organization, companies can not only maintain long-term relationships, but they can also create a market-like environment among a few chosen parties. Network organizations stress the interdependence between organizational parties and thus pay considerable attention to the development and maintenance of (communicative) relationships. At the same time, the different organizational parties have their own particular interests, and can be allied to different network organizations. Thus, network organizational relationships can always be characterized by a tension between autonomy and interdependence, between team loyalty and individuality, and between competition and cooperation. Network organizations can be based either on horizontal, vertical, or symbiotic relationships. Within horizontal relationships, the organizations are one another's competitors. Organizations in vertical relationships follow each other in a (linear) value chain. The rationale behind symbiotic relationships is that the different organizations offer complementary services and products to the market[6]. Having only recently been examined in the business literature [BN96], symbiotic relationships are essential for Win-Win business scenarios as we will show in Part II of this paper.

The Internet and in particular the World Wide Web have provided the required infrastructure to effectuate a feasible network organizational architecture. Among the typical accomplishments of E-Macrocommerce are the following:

- Ease in implementing a network and its interfaces facilitated by industry standards such as SGML, XML, and EDI.

- Lack of a long-term commitment to the network infrastructure since parties can become participants in other network organizations with minor adjustments.

- Nonrestriction of a party from participating in other network organizations simultaneously. (Note that in this case, we have an example of a non-hierarchical composition.)

- Attraction of new members to the network organization since it is relatively inexpensive to participate.

- Customization of the network infrastructure to fit either a vertical or horizontal integration.

- Allowance of information richness through electronic links (i.e., extranets) with a company's suppliers, distributors, and partners. (Notice that a large quantity of information does not imply richness. Thus, the existence of electronic links is not the only determinant of information richness.)

In other words, business relationships now have the technological flexibility to be evaluated, created, or destroyed in real time with minimum effect on the performance of a corporation[7].

PART II: E-MICROCOMMERCE

Used to its fullest, E-Commerce creates a market-like environment especially in E-Microcommerce–that is, business-to-consumer electronic transactions. A consumer, with the assistance of intelligent agents, can evaluate numerous suppliers without being concerned about their specificity [HKLM95]. Notice that the usage of intelligent agent technology can be either implicit or explicit. An internet user can train an intelligent agent to perform comparative shopping or alternatively use existing specialized intelligent agents provided by third parties for this service. Third party intelligent agents may take the shape of web pages, such as eBay™. In [B96] Bakos states:

> "Efficiency and societal welfare are increased by reducing the cost of unproductive buyer searches and by enabling buyers to locate products better matching their needs. If the search cost is low enough, buyers look at all product offerings and purchase the one best serving their needs, resulting in a socially optimal allocation. Very high search cost, on the other hand, lead to efficiency losses and eventually cause the market to break down."

By using mobile intelligent agents, a consumer can locate and compare all suppliers (or a significant majority of them) simultaneously and negotiate for the lowest price without the necessity of being connected to the Web. Since the consumer will no longer have to leave his current location in order to search for suppliers and will only pay for the time logged on the Web, the "cutting a deal" cost is very close to zero. A spot market will eventually develop where suppliers are selected only on the basis of price. In theory, economic equilibrium will be reached where no suppliers can make a profit, i.e., goods will be sold at cost. This also may be true in the case of services which are standardized (outsourcing, financial advice, medical advice, etc.)

War of Attrition

But if this is the case, how can we explain the urgency by the suppliers to provide their goods to consumers using E-commerce?

Once again, the answer can be found by consulting game theory, this time specifically by examining the behavior of the players involved in a game commonly known as *War of Attrition* (or *Chicken*.) A typical version of Chicken involves two cars and two drivers. The rules are as follows:

> Two vehicles drive toward each other, waiting for one to swerve. The winner is the player who perseveres while the other swerves. If both swerve they are both considered to be "chicken." If neither does, they may not have an opportunity to play Chicken again.

Observe that in a War of Attrition game, matrix there is always a *symmetry* of the payoffs within the game matrix. Both players get almost identical payoffs if one player decides not to take an action but the other one does.[8]

Because of this symmetry, War of Attrition is a game with two pure strategy Nash equilibria[9]. Thus, in the Chicken game with two vehicles, in the first equilibria Player 1 swerves and Player 2 preserves, whereas in the second equilibria Player 2 swerves and Player 1 preserves. However, these solutions are not practical since it can not be known in advance who should swerve and who should preserve. (Thankfully, this acts as an incentive to drivers not to play Chicken in their everyday driving.)

We define this symmetry as *attrition equilibrium* since it is the essential component for a game to belong to the War of Attrition category.

Chicken may be played on a repeated basis. Examining a specific instance of the evolution of a War of Attrition may or may not enable us to identify the type of game that is being played. This is because during the game one of the players may accomplish an advantageous position against his opponents as a result of a strategic move. For example, in the traditional mode of business a supplier may achieve an advantage over his competitors after he announces a sale. During the period through which he enjoys the benefits of this move, the game does not share the typical 'look' of War of Attrition.

Examining numerical payoffs of a round of War of Attrition does not characterize the evolution of the game. To fully understand the forces that motivate the players of a War of Attrition game, we examine an associated category of "meta-level" games whose (parameterized) payoff pattern can be analyzed to reveal these forces [T98].

As a result of the above forces, in response to a move by a supplier, there always exists a countermove by the supplier's opponents that can at least level the game: A corresponding identical sale by an opponent is a countermove that will recreate the original structure of the game, whereas a corresponding larger amount sale by an opponent is a countermove that will tip the payoff towards him. Notice that a sale will not only hurt the profits of a supplier but will also create a *destructive momentum* in which any similar countermove will result in smaller and smaller profits for both players. In other words, the pie that the suppliers share becomes smaller and smaller and will eventually reach a size of zero [TS97]. This is a case of a limitation associated with any type of move (e.g., a sale) that brakes the attrition equilibrium. Every sequence of repeated moves of the same type will eventually reach a *saturation point* after which the usage of any similar type move will have no significant effects.

Every move that breaks the attrition equilibrium is temporary. This is attributable to the previous observation associated with the existence of a countermove by an opponent. Since a countermove always exists and since an opponent has incentives (originated from the forces underlying War of Attrition) for using it, it will be only a matter of time until the countermove is used and the original move gets neutralized.

With the advent of E-Microcommerce, suppliers are facing a similar dilemma as posed by a War of Attrition: if only a very limited number of suppliers engage in E-Microcommerce, they will be rewarded by gaining the business of a huge Web population. This brakes the attrition equilibrium giving them an advantage over their competitors. However, if many suppliers decide to enter E-Microcommerce, the attrition equilibrium will be restored and once again competition will become intense. As a result of the reduced search cost, E-Microcommerce may develop an economic equilibrium in which goods can be sold at close to zero profit.

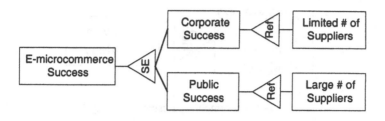

Figure 4. E-microcommerce Success Factors

This diagram characterizes the dilemma companies such as amazon.com™ are facing. As long as the number of competitors is relatively small, amazon.com™ is capable of reaping huge profit margins. But when the number of competitors increases, the consumer will enjoy the luxury of lower prices. This economic logic accounts for our choice of the non-overlapping subtyping of E-microcommerce success.

Contributions of E-Microcommerce to the Evolution of Business

As previously argued, suppliers can not expect to break the attrition equilibrium in other than a temporary way. The attrition equilibrium is the predominant force underlying every competitive environment. No single move can 'beat' an opponent. Instead, the name of the game is to 'wear down' your opponent. But even if you succeed in eliminating your opponent, another will rise to take his place. Is it then meaningless to compete? Of course not! The solution is to change the destructive momentum of competition into a constructive one. Instead of shrinking the pie, it can and should be enlarged. Contemporary business strategy has misleadingly adapted strategic foundations from the worlds of military and sports. But unlike war and sports, business is not solely about winning and losing. Nor is it just about how well you play the game [BN96]. Companies can succeed spectacularly without requiring others to fail. And they can fail miserably no matter how well they play if they make the mistake of playing the wrong game. Looking for win-win strategies instead of win-lose is increasingly seen as the invariant underlying contemporary business strategy[10].

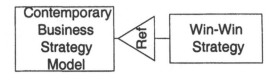

Figure 5. Contemporary Business Strategy[11]

In our opinion, the single largest contribution of E-Microcommerce to our business society is to provide the foundation for an essential shift in the economic evolution towards a cooperative mode of competing[12]. E-Microcommerce does not impart a solution to War of Attrition, but it definitely constitutes the environment for a more profitable way of playing this game.

The traditional way of competing has been based principally on price. E-Microcommerce suppliers have found a number of ways to both temporarily break the attrition equilibrium in a non-price based approach and also deal with the economic equilibrium in order to improve their profit margins. In contemporary business, for every move by a supplier that breaks the attrition equilibrium there exists a countermove by his opponents that reestablishes it. However, as a result of E-Microcommerce the resulting payoffs for all parties can be much larger at the end of each round than they were in the beginning of it.

Some characteristic moves of War of Attrition that enlarge the pie are as follows:

- *Information as part of the product:* Instead of supplying a traditional product by means of E-Commerce, many suppliers have 'enriched' their product or services with information. No longer is a consumer restricted to receiving selective facts about a product or service; they may also receive information about competitive products, about the usage of the product, training, customer support, and so on. Equivalently, the manufacturers can collect 'intelligence' information about the use of their product, the needs of their clients, the way their product is used, competitors' products, and so on. Suppliers have even saved money by adjusting their operational model to accommodate E-Commerce. For example, ORACLE was able to limit their technical support staff as a result of the creation of an ORACLE User Group.

- *Increased Specificity:* Other suppliers were able to increase the specificity (specialization) of their product in order to prevent customers from treating their product as a commodity. This also resulted in an improved customer satisfaction rate since the increased product selection allowed for a more suitable selection of goods based on their suitability to the customers' needs. The typical example is airplane tickets. Airlines have implemented extremely complicated and ever-changing fare structures, flight restrictions, and ticket availability—typically offering several hundred thousand possible fares at any one time.

- *New Products:* Other suppliers increased the differentiation of product offerings by offering additional new products, possibly using the technology to help differentiate what would normally be a commodity. Frequent flyer programs have been very successful in achieving this goal.

- *Marketspace*: Finally, other suppliers have changed the focus of their product. Instead of selling a specific product, they provide an environment (a marketspace) where similar goods from different suppliers can be exchanged. The typical examples of a marketspace are again from the airline industry. APOLLO (United), PARS (TWA), and SABRE (American) are just two examples of reservation systems which provide a central location for the purchasing of tickets. Increased competition, fueled by the deregulation of the airline industry and the computerized reservation systems, was adversely affecting the profitability of flight operations for the most airlines in the early 1980's. The airlines that pioneered reservation systems, however, were enjoying high profits from system-related revenues. In 1980-1982, American Airlines commanded a 40% gross margin on its SABRE revenues, while flight operation yielded as little as 5%. TWA made more money in the same period on PARS than from its airline.

- *Specification in real time of customized products*: E-Commerce catalyzes Advanced Manufacturing Technology (AMT). AMT allows for increased batch size and product variety at the same time.

As previously argued, there is no single type of move that can be effective forever. Every War of Attrition game with moves of the same type has a *saturation point*. Even contemporary E-Commerce has already been faced with a saturation point. The multitude of corporations that have entered E-Commerce has made it difficult for the buyers to locate appropriate suppliers [BRW97]. A partial response to this saturation point has been the development of E-Commerce databases that are accessed by (mobile) intelligent agents.

CONCLUSION

E-Commerce must be addressed in both of its aspects: E-Macrocommerce which is an enabler of flexible business-to-business relationships, and E-Microcommerce which is an enabler of Win-Win business-to-customer relationships. E-Commerce is a natural progression of our economic and business evolution. We emphasize that it is not the solution to the common cooperation and competition problems, but it constitutes a natural progression of the response to these problems. Moreover, as with any other system lifecycle, E-Commerce obeys the S-curve. It will eventually reach a saturation point, in which case we will have to invent and rationalize a new means of conducting business.

Our motivation for specifying the business and economic foundations of E-Commerce is to catalyze organizations to effectively exploit business opportunities in E-Commerce, to increase awareness of its advantages and limitations, and to understand the types of business adjustments required by this new electronic marketing environment. Once again, using the information modeling approach as formulated in [KR94, K99], the major components and their relationships of an evolving and complex business environment are clearly defined, thus giving the organizational decision-makers a common model for developing effective business strategies.

APPENDIX A — KEY TO DIAGRAMS

The diagrams show invariants in the form of 'entity' types and associations between them. Each association is an instance of a generic association invariant which is precisely specified (for reuse purposes) in [KR94][K99]. Therefore, each diagram has a precise and unambiguous meaning. There is insufficient space to repeat the full specification of each generic association invariant here.

In the diagrams, a triangle with a 'C' is a composition association. 'D' stands for a dependency. 'S' stands for (non-exhaustive non-overlapping) subtyping, while 'SE' stands for exhaustive (non-overlapping) subtyping, and 'S+' stands for overlapping (non-exhaustive). 'Ref' stands for reference. 'Ref-C' stands for reference-for-create and it is enforced only during the create operation.

APPENDIX B — RM-ODP

RM-ODP proceeds to define a system, actions, interactions, environment, behaviour, and so on as follows:

6.1 Entity: Any concrete or abstract thing of interest. While in general the word entity can be used to refer to anything, in the context of modelling it is reserved to refer to things in the universe of discourse being modelled.

6.2 Proposition: An observable fact or state of affairs involving one or more entities, of which it is possible to assert or deny that it holds for those entities.

6.3 Abstraction: The process of suppressing irrelevant detail to establish a simplified model, or the result of that process.

6.4 Atomicity: An entity is atomic at a given level of abstraction if it cannot be subdivided at that level of abstraction.

Fixing a given level of abstraction may involve identifying which elements are atomic.

6.5 System: Something of interest as a whole or as comprised of parts. Therefore a system may be referred to as an entity. A component of a system may itself be a system, in which case it may be called a subsystem.

NOTE - For modelling purposes, the concept of system is understood in its general, system-theoretic sense. The term "system" can refer to an information processing system but can also be applied more generally.

6.6 Architecture (of a system): A set of rules to define the structure of a system and the interrelationships between its parts.

REFERENCES

[A76] Aumann, R. "Agreeing to Disagree," *The Annals of Statistics*. 1976, Vol. 4, No. 6, pp. 1236-1239.

[B96] Bakos, J.Y. "Reducing Buyer Search Costs: Implications for Electronic Marketplaces," *Management Science*, Volume 43, Number 12, December 1997.

[BRW97] Barua, A., Ravindran, S., and Whinston, A. B. "Efficient Selection of Suppliers over the Internet," *Journal of Management Information Systems*, Spring 1997, vol. 13, No 4, pp. 117-137.

[BN96] Brandenburger A., Nalebuff, B. *Co-opetition*, Doubleday Dell Publishing Group Inc., 1996.

[CAA57] Churchhman, Ackoff, and Arnoff, *Introduction to Operations Research*, John Wiley & Sons Inc., New York 1957.

[CS90] Robert N. Corley, Peter J. Shedd. *Fundamentals of Business Law*. Fifth Edition. Prentice-Hall, 1990, pp. 893-979.

[D83] Daft, R. *Organization Theory and Design*, West, 1983.

[HKLM] Heilmann, K., Kihanya, D., Light, A., Musembwa, P. "Intelligent Agents: A Technology and Business Application Analysis", 1995, http://www.mines.u-nancy.fr/~gueniffe/CoursEMN/I31/heilmann/heilmann.html.

[K95] Kay, J. *Why Firms Succeed*, Oxford University Press, 1995.

[K99] Kilov, H. *Business Specifications: The Key to Successful Software Engineering*, Prentice Hall, Upper Saddle River, NJ, 1999.

[KR94] Kilov, H. and Ross, J. *Information Modeling: an Object-oriented Approach*, Prentice Hall, Englewood Cliffs, NJ, 1994.

[K90] Kreps, G.L. *Organizational Communication*, White Plains: Longman, 1990.

[MYB87] Malone, T. W., Yates, J., and Benjamin, R. I. "Electronic Markets and Electronic Hierarchies," *Communications of the ACM*, June 1987, Vol. 30, Num 6.

[M97] McKenna, R. *Real Time: Preparing for the Age of the Never Satisfied Customer*, Harvard Business School, 1997.

[NM96] Nouwens, J., and Bouwman, H. "Living Apart Together In Electronic Commerce: The Use Of Information And Communication Technology To Create Network Organizations," *Journal of Computer-Mediated Communication* Vol. 3, 1996 {http://usc.edu/dept/annenberg/vol1/issue3/nouwens.html}.

[P96] Porter, M. "What is Strategy?," *Harvard Business Review*, November-December, 1996.

[P90] Powell, Walter W. "Neither market nor hierarchy: Network forms of organization," *Research in Organizational Behavior*, 1990, vol. 12, pp. 295-336.

[SKP96] Steinfield, C., Kraut, R., and Plummer, A. "The Impact Of Interorganizational Networks On Buyer-Seller Relationships," *Journal of Computer-Mediated Communication* Vol. 3, 1996 {http://usc.edu/dept/annenberg/vol1/issue3/steinfld.html}.

[TS97] Thalassinidis, A.E., and Sack, I. "An Ontologic Foundation of Strategic Signals," OOPSLA 1997 *Workshop on Object-oriented Behavioral Semantics*, Atlanta, GA, USA.

[T98] Thalassinidis, A.E., "An Ontologic and Epistemic Meta-Game-Theoretic Approach to Attrition Signaling in a Globalized, Electronic Business Environment," Ph.D. Thesis, Stevens Institute of Technology, May 1998.

[W75] Williamson, O. E. *Markets and Hierarchies, Analysis and Antitrust Implications*, The Free Press, 1975.

ABOUT THE AUTHORS

Angelo E. Thalassinidis is a Senior Director at EDS. He has been a business consultant for over ten years, focusing in the alignment of organizational structures and information systems to business strategies. His research interests include business strategy, competitive intelligence, and negotiation theory.

Ira Sack is a Professor of information management at Stevens Institute of Technology. He has performed research in the areas of electronic commerce, information modeling, business strategy, and organizational architecture. He is a co-author of *Organization Modeling: Innovative Architectures for the 21st Century* to be published in June 1999 by Prentice Hall, Inc. Formerly, he was a Member of Technical Staff of Bell Laboratories and a consultant to NASA in the area of information management.

---

[1] We define the business value chain as the composition of the value-added activities of a business that translate resources into products and services.

[2] For a seminal paper on business behavior and knowledge, consult [A76].

[3] Also, relational contracts are characterized by *information richness* since their execution depends on human knowledge and judgement.

[4] With little change, our argument applies to services as well as goods.

[5] Investment, cost, and risk refer too the effects from associating the future of a company with the future of its partners, and any costs associated with building proprietary systems (information, distribution, payment, etc.).

[6] Details of network organizational architecture are addressed in [P90] and [K90].

[7] For a seminal work on the significance of real-time competition to corporations, refer to [M97].

[8] More generally, identical pattern descriptors of a Chicken game need not be numerically equivalent.

[9] Details of game theory, including equilibria, can be found in any standard game theory text.

[10] For an in-depth elaboration of win-win strategies, consult [BN96].

[11] Information modeling allows us to present complicated business concepts in a simple and understandable way. For example, the above *reference relationship* specifies contemporary business strategy in a minimal but sufficiently precise way.

[12] A major consequence of the usage of E-Commerce as a strategic tool is the reevaluation of tactical vs. strategic moves. Since the response time from an opponent to a move that breaks the attrition equilibrium can be more timely in E-Commerce, a long-term cooperative strategy is needed much more now than ever before.

Chapter 20

EMBEDDING OBJECT-ORIENTED DESIGN IN SYSTEM ENGINEERING

R.J. Wieringa

Department of Computer Science
University of Twente
roelw@cs.utwente.nl

Abstract   The Unified Modeling Language (UML) is a collection of techniques intended to document design decisions about software. This contrasts with systems engineering approaches such as for example Statemate and the Yourdon Systems Method (YSM), in which the design of an entire system consisting of software and hardware can be documented. The difference between the system- and the software level is reflected in differences between execution semantics as well as in methodology. In this paper, I show how the UML can be used as a system-level design technique. I give a conceptual framework for engineering design that accommodates the system- as well as the software level and show how techniques from the UML and YSM can be classified within this framework, and how this allows a coherent use of these techniques in a system engineering approach. These ideas are illustrated by a case study in which software for a compact dynamic bus station is designed. Finally, I discuss the consequences of this approach for a semantics of UML constructs that would be appropriate for system-level design.

1.   INTRODUCTION

It is an important principle of linguistics that the semantics of a notation cannot be separated from its intended use. This means that if you change the intended methodological use of a design notation, you have to change its semantics and vice versa. It also means that you cannot define a semantics for a notation without making assumptions about its methodological purpose, that should be made explicit. Object-oriented design techniques such as the Unified Modeling Language (UML) are intended to document design decisions about software. This intended methodological use of the UML corresponds to the intended semantics as sketched by the OMG [UML99]. This semantics stays close to the execution semantics of object-oriented programs.

If we want to use UML techniques at a higher level of abstraction, for example the level where we want to model the requirements of an entire system rather than the execution behavior of an object-oriented program, we have to define a different semantics. This higher abstraction level, which is called the essential modeling level, is more appropriate for system-level models, because at this level it has not yet been decided which part of the requirements will be implemented by software, which by hardware and which, perhaps, by people. In this paper I show how some of the UML techniques can be used at the essential model level, alongside with some of the techniques from the Yourdon Systems Method (YSM, [Y93]). The essential model level is the level at which we model purely system requirements and do not take implementation restrictions into account. To use an old phrase of McMenamin & Palmer [MP84], at the essential level, we assume perfect implementation technology.

Section 2. elaborates the relationship between meaning and use of a design notation. To show how UML techniques can be used at the essential modeling level, I give in section 3. an integrated framework for software and systems engineering in the next section. In section 4., I show how UML and YSM techniques fit into this framework and give an example of an essential-level specification where these techniques are used. The major conclusion is that techniques taken from YSM are suitable for the specification of external functionality and that techniques from the UML are suitable for modeling an essential-level system architecture. In section 5., I draw conclusions about desirable features of the semantics of UML techniques used as essential architecture modeling techniques in an integrated systems and software engineering process. The major conclusion of that section is that the UML semantics as currently proposed by the OMG is appropriate for the implementation level but not for the essential level.

2.   MEANING AND USE OF DESIGN NOTATIONS

When the central heating system of a house is designed, a subcontractor makes a drawing which represents the location of the central heater, the radiators, the pipes connecting the heater with the radiators, and other components that make up the central heating system. In the Netherlands, different symbols are used for radiators with one, two and three plates and for pipes through which warm or cold water flows. The symbols used in the diagram have a meaning that is directly related to their use: representing the topology of a central heating system. The diagram is used for communication among stakeholders, including installers, the house owner, electricians and other contractors, who can use it to plan their work, detect conflicts among their various views of the house, negotiate about the design, etc. For example, comparing the central heating view with the electrician's view, it may turn out that a radiator has been planned at a location where an electricity outlet is planned too.

Observe that to describe the meaning of a notation to designers is the same thing as to explain to them how to use it. Use a green fat line to represent a radiator; use a red line to represent a pipe that transports warm water and a blue line for a pipe that transports cold water; etc. A description of the meaning of a design notation is a description of the way how the notation is to be used.

The identification of meaning with use stems from the later Wittgenstein and is connected to the idea of language games [W71, paragraph 41]. It is opposed to the early

Wittgensteinian idea that meaning is a mapping from symbols to their denotation, that can be defined independently from any context of use. The identification of meaning with use of design notations does not entail that these notations have no denotational semantics. But it does entail that any such denotational semantics should be closely connected with methodological instructions about how to use the notation.

The identification of meaning with use does not go so far that, in the definition of the meaning of a design notation, we actually tell people how to design a system. The symbols in the design notation for central heating systems do not come with heuristics that tell the designer how to design a central heating system. They merely allow the designer to represent standard components that can be put together in various ways. However, they do help the designer of the central heating system to order his or her thoughts about the design and to communicate the design to others. And they do help the designer to some extent to make design decisions, for the notation says that a central heating systems consists of a central heater, pipes, and radiators, which have certain properties, such as the number of plates of a radiator. And the syntax of the notation disallows the representation of certain combinations of components that cannot work. Similarly, a UML model says that a software system consists of software objects that have certain properties, such as the messages they can exchange, and the syntax of the UML disallows certain combinations of objects that cannot work.

Two interesting aspects of the use of a design notation that should be defined for any practical design notation are the following:

- The intended practical context of use should be specified, including the purpose for which the notation is to be used, in this context. For example, the intended context of use of a design notation could be the design of a central heating system, and its purpose could be to describe the topology of a central heating system—as opposed to for example its energy efficiency or its esthetics.

- The permissible combinations of the symbols should be specified. For example, a line representing a pipe must must be connected to a symbol representing a radiator to a symbol representing another radiator and/or a central heater.

It is possible to identify structures in a context of use and study the properties of these structures mathematically, independently from the particular usage context. It is also possible to study symbol manipulations and the way they can be interpreted in mathematical structures, as is done in logic. Mathematics and logic tell us how certain notations can be used in contexts that exemplify certain abstractly defined structures. To actually use these notations in practice, these abstract structures have to be mapped to concrete usage contexts; and the abstract meanings must make sense with respect to the particular purpose for which the notation is used.

The definition of a practical design notation should therefore consist of a definition of its syntax and of its intended use, which includes at least a description of the intended context and purpose of use of the notation. In the UML, the intended context is software design, but even within this wide context, the purpose of the notations in this context is not fixed. For example, for every notation in the UML, Booch et al. [BRJ99] list many different possible uses. Since there is no single intended use of the UML notations, there is no single intended semantics of UML notations. Rather, there are many different possible semantics, that are useful for different purposes within the general context of software design.

In this paper, I investigate how design notations from the Unified Modeling Language [UML99] and the Yourdon Systems Method [Y93] can be used in a systems engineering context, that includes software engineering as a part. The answer that will emerge from our investigation is that we can use notations from YSM to represent system and software *requirements,* and notations from the UML to represent a software *architecture* at an essential level of abstraction. This differs from the way the UML is given a semantics in, for example, the Rhapsody Case tool [i-L99, HG97]. But this is just to say that these different semantics are useful for different software design purposes.

3.   SYSTEMS ENGINEERING

To define the usage context of the YSM and UML notation aimed at in this paper, we start from the traditional concept of a system as a set of interrelated components working together toward some common objective [BF90]. This very general definition applies to any kind of system, including software systems. It contains two elements.

- First, not any set of elements make up a system: They must work together in a coherent whole. In other words, they must fit together in an architecture.

- Second, the elements of the architecture must work together towards a common objective. In other words, the system architecture must match the system requirements.

Two concerns in any system engineering effort are therefore the design of the architecture of the system and the identification of the objectives to be served by the system. Hence, the two main dimensions of our framework are architecture and requirements. I discuss these in the next two subsections.

3.1   ARCHITECTURE

Systems can be decomposed into subsystems, which can be further decomposed, etc. This gives us a hierarchical architecture of systems. For software systems, this simple picture is incorrect because there are *two* different kinds of decomposition that are relevant, the conceptual and the physical decompositions. Software is a *state* of a physical system. We can decompose the physical system into subsystems, such as PC's and a connecting network, and partition these subsystems further in lower-level subsystems, such as printed circuit boards, plugs, wires, disks, screens, etc. But in a completely different decomposition hierarchy, we can decompose a software system into subsystems, such as a user interface subsystem and a database subsystem, but all the way down to the level of bits, these systems are conceptual. They are abstractions of states of hardware systems.

The conceptual (software) hierarchy and the physical system hierarchy are independent from each other. It is not the case that a component in one decomposition is a "part" of a component in the other decomposition. Rather, there is a many-many relationship between these two decompositions, in which a software component may be allocated to several physical components and a physical component may execute several software components.

This distinction is related to another, commonly recognized distinction in software engineering, namely that between essential architecture and implementation architdcture. An **essential architecture** is a decomposition defined solely in terms of the desired external functionality of the system. An **implementation architecture** is a decomposition motivated in terms of both external functionality and in terms of the underlying implementation platform. Both architectures are *software* decompositions and thus reside in the conceptual part of the system; they are decompositions of abstractions of hardware states. But where an essential architecture remains close to the concerns of the system user, an implementation architecture reflects the concerns of the engineer who must allocate the software to a network of physical resources.

There is nothing new in the concept of an essential architecture. It is called the logical architecture by some. It corresponds to the essential model of McMenamin & Palmer [MP84], to the specification model of Syntropy [CD94], and to the analysis model of Objectory [JCJO92] and the unified software development process [JBR99]. Typical techniques used to represent an essential architecture are the data flow diagram in structured analysis and the class diagram in object-oriented analysis. Since it does not take implementation limitations into account, it assumes perfect technology. This simplifies the design, improves our understanding of the requirements and facilitates the traceability from external requirements to lower-level implementation parts. The essential architecture should remain invariant under changes in implementation.

To clarify the distinction between the essential and implementation levels, it helps to give some decomposition guidelines for each of these two levels. Examples of essential architectural design guidelines are the following.

- *Functional decomposition.* Identify essential components that correspond to external functions. This is the major decomposition guideline in structured analysis and in systems engineering.

- *Event partitioning.* Identify essential components that correspond to events to which the system must respond. This is also one of the major guidelines in structured analysis [MP84].

- *Interface partitioning.* Identify components that correspond to entities at the interface of the system, such as for example devices with which the system must communicate, users of the system, other software with which the system must communicate, etc. This guideline is used in structured analysis [Y93, page 515] and in object-oriented analysis [JBR99, page 183].

- *Subject domain-oriented decomposition.* Identify components that correspond to subject domain entities, which are entities in the environment of the system referred to by messages that cross the system interface. (The concept of a subject domain is eleborated upon below.) This is the major guideline in object-oriented design.

Despite what some people may say, these criteria are very well compatible. For example, JSD uses subject domain-oriented decomposition to identify the stable part of a decomposition, and functional decomposition to identify functional components whose meaning is defined in terms of the subject domain-oriented part [J83]. Objectory [JCJO92] as well as the Unified Software Development Process [JBR99] identify entity objects, boundary objects and control objects, that can be found by subject domain-oriented decomposition, interface partitioning and functional decomposition, respectively.

At the essential level, no implementation errors occur, each component has unlimited processing power and memory space available, etc. At the implementation level, by contrast, software must be decomposed into parts that can be allocated to processor nodes in a network of physical resources. Each of these parts must be a sequential process and may be run in parallel to other sequential processes on the processor. They must deal with the finite capacity of the processor and with errors that may occur. Examples of guidelines for implementation architecture are the following.

- *Event-based.* Define one process for each event that must be responded to.

- *Actor-based.* Slightly less greedy in the number of processes that must be run in parallel on one processor is to define one process for each device that can generate events.

- *Time-based.* Still less greedy is to define one process for each group of devices that have similar temporal characteristics. For example if several input devices have to be polled within the same period, these can be dealt with by the same periodic process.

- *Geography-based.* Processes that must communicate with devices in a network must be allocated to a node close to those devices.

- *Purpose-based.* Tasks with a related purpose can be allocated to one process. For example, one process can deal with alarm-handling, another one with error-handling, etc.

More guidelines are given by Awad et al. [AKZ96], Cook & Daniels [CD94], Gomaa [G93] and Douglas [D98]. Some of these guidelines coincide with essential architectural design guidelines, others are different. This explains why the relationship between the essential and implementation architectures is many-many.

A final observation about architecture to make is that the parts into which a software system are decomposed are *processes* in structured analysis and *objects* in object-oriented analysis. Both are entities that have an interface and a behavior. But processes may be instantaneous data transformations, or control processes specified by a state machine, or reactive processes specified by an event list. Objects, by contrast, are uniformly modeled as state machines with local variables (called instance variables or attributes). An object may be specified by a trivial state transition diagram, with only one node. But even in this case, there are usually many different possible attribute values, and therefroe many different possible states. This difference in the kind of entities into which a software system is decomposed—processes or objects—is unrelated to the use of decomposition guidelines. All guidelines listed above, from functional decomposition to subject domain-oriented decomposition, can be used to yield architectures consisting of processes as well as to architectures consisting of objects.

3.2   REQUIREMENTS

The second main dimension of our framework is that of system requirements. I will not attempt a classification of kinds of system and software requirements; these may range from financial requirements to ergonomic requirements, performance requirements and functional requirements. However, one distinction is important to point out: the difference between business requirements and system requirements. The system under design is embedded in an environment, that I will call the *business environment* or simply the "business". This is the part of the world where the system must have its desired effects (called the problem domain by Jackson [J95]). It must be distinguished from the *implementation environment* of the system, which consists of the lower-level hardware and software components from which the system will be constructed or assembled.

Business requirements are desired properties of the business. They consist of the wishes and goals of people in the environment. They exist in the business and they are about the business, e.g. about a desired way of doing business or a desired way of behaving of people in the business. Business requirements are not about the system but about the business. Techniques to discover them include stakeholder analysis, business strategy analysis and task analysis.

System requirements are desired properties of the system under design. They are motivated by business requirements. They are derived from the business requirements by answering the following question: If these are the goals of the business, what can the system do to help people achieve these goals? An elevator system can help people to achieve the goal of easy transport across floors; an information system can help people to maintain organizational memory; a groupware system can help people to achieve asynchronous communication across time and space. This paper discusses system requirement specification techniques, not business requirement specification techniques.

An exhaustive survey of structured and object-oriented analysis methods [W98b] reveals that the system requirement specification techniques offered by these methods can be classified into three groups: techniques to specify the messages that pass the software boundary, techniques to specify behavioral properties of these messages and techniques to specify communication properties of these messages.

- *Messages.* Because software manipulates symbols, a software system communicates with its environment exclusively by exchanging symbols, or in other words messages, with its environment. I define the **subject domain** of a message as the part of the world referred to by the message, and the subject domain of a software system as the sum of the subject domains of all its messages. The subject domain is part of the business environment of the system. Techniques to specify messages that cross the software boundary include event–response lists (structured analysis), where each event and each response is a message, and use cases to specify message sequences that are of value to an external actor (UML).

- *Behavior* is the ordering of messages in time. Techniques offered for behavior specification include a large variety of state transition diagrams such as Moore (used by Shlaer & Mellor [SM92]), Mealy (used in YSM [Y93]), statecharts (used in Statemate [HP98] and the UML) and SDL state machines [BHS91] as well as a large variety of temporal and real-time logics.

- *Communication* is the ordering of messages over "space". Less metaphorically, it consists of the way in which the system is connected to actors in its environment and interacts with those actors. Techniques to specify communication include the context diagram and data flow diagram of structured analysis, the object communication model of Shlaer & Mellor [SM92], SDL block diagrams [BHS91] and various process algebras. The sequence and collaboration diagrams of the UML can be used to represent communication sequences, but I will argue below that, in the way they are currently defined, they are techniques for illustration rather than specification.

3.3   THE MAGIC SQUARE AND TRACEABILITY

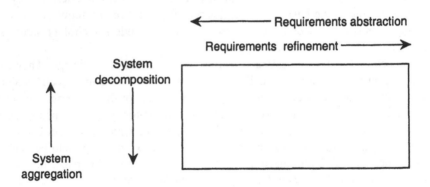

Figure 20.1   Harel & Pnueli's "magic square".

To sum up, our framework distinguishes two requirements and two architecture levels.

- **Business requirements** consist of desired properties of the business environment, such as a desired way of doing business, of working, of behaving, of playing.

- **System requirements** consist of desired properties of the system. We distinguish the desired *messages* between the system and its environment, its desired *behavior*, and its desired *communication* connections to its environment.

- The **essential architecture** is an implementation-independent architecture that realizes the system requirements.

- The **implementation architecture** is an architecture of implementation components, that maps the essential architecture to an implementation environment.

	Requirement 1	...	...	Requirement n
Component 1	X			X
...				
...	X			
Component m			X	

Figure 20.2 Traceability table.

The relationship between the system requirements and the different architecture levels can be represented by the rectangle shown in figure 20.1, called the "magic square" by Harel & Pnueli [HP85]. The upper left point in the square represents the system mission at the highest level of abstraction, and the upper right point represents the system requirements at the highest level of refinement. These include the messages that cross the system boundary and the behavioral and communication properties of these messages. In between these two extremes, we can find, for example, the required system functions and use cases. At the lower left point, we find the purpose of each low-level component of the system and at the lower right point, we find the detailed messages and protocols by which these components communicate with their environment. System engineering is a journey through this square that generally begins at the upper left point and ends at the lower right point. This journey may proceed in a top-down, bottom-up, inside-out or iterative manner. Discussion of engineering strategies is outside the scope of this paper.

Each point in the square identifies one level of aggregation and one level of requirements refinement. For each point, a **traceability table** such as outlined in figure 20.2 exists. This relates the requirements at one level of refinement to the parts of the system at one level of aggregation. For example, a traceability table can be used to show how external system functions are allocated to essential software objects. Each column would then show how a number of software objects collaborate to realize an external function.

Note that we can use traceability tables between any two different levels of abstraction: For example, to trace business requirements to system requirements, system requirements to essential architecture components, and essential architecture components to implementation components. Traceability tables are an important technique in systems engineering and they are a central technique in quality function deployment [L95]. For any non-trivial system, its traceability tables are too large to draw and we need software tools to store, manage and present this information. In section 5. I show how the UML techniques can be mapped to a traceability table that maps software requirements to software architecture.

Technique	Source	View	Abstraction level
Mission statement	YSM	External behavior	System requirements
Function refinement	IE		
Context/use case diagram	YSM / UML	External communication	
Event-response list	YSM	External messages	
Subject domain entity model	YSM	Subject domain decomposition	Subject domain architecture
Class diagram	UML	Essential decomposition	
Communication diagram	Shlaer-Mellor, SDL	Essential component communication	Essential architecture
Statecharts	UML	Essential component behavior	
Component diagram	UML	Implementation components (software)	Implementation architecture
Deployment diagram	UML	Implementation components (physical)	
Dictionary			

Table 20.1   Techniques in TRADE. YSM = Yourdon Systems Method [Y93], IE = Information Engineering [M89], UML = Unified Modeling Language [OMG97].

4.   A TOOLBOX FOR REQUIREMENTS AND DESIGN ENGINEERING (TRADE)

In this section I show how some techniques from YSM can be combined with some of the UML techniques in a coherent systems engineering approach. Table 20.1 lists the techniques to be used. I call this list a Toolbox for Requirements and Design Engineering, or TRADE for short. More information about the source of the techniques in TRADE is given by Wieringa [W98a]. In section 5., I discuss requirements on the precise syntax and semantics of the techniques listed in table 20.1. Here, I informally illustrate most of these techniques by means of a case study in which software for a compact dynamic bus station is specified. Due to space limitations, component and deployment diagrams are omitted. The list of specifications given below does not represent the temporal sequence in which these specifications have been produced. It should not even be taken to suggest that they have been produced in any sequence: They have, in fact, been produced in parallel.

A bus station consists of a number of platforms at which busses can park so that passengers can enter and leave busses. At any point in time, most platforms of a bus station are empty, which in densely populated areas is a waste of space. A *compact* dynamic bus station consists of a small number of platforms to which busses can be dynamically allocated so that, over time, the available space is used optimally. The software system to be designed is informed of the approach of all busses and has a database of preferred allocations of busses to platforms. It dynamically allocates an approaching bus to a platform that is expected to be available at the time the bus will enter the station, and informs the driver as well as waiting passengers about this allocation. The driver is then expected to drive to this platform and the passengers to walk to this platform to enter the bus. If there is unexpectedly no room at the platform for the bus, the bus will drive to a buffer area, from which it will drive to the platform as soon as there is room available. More requirements are given in the specification below. I will refer to the software system as the Bus Allocation System, or BAS for short. As part of a feasibility study in the application of formal description techniques, a specification of BAS was made in ASF/PSF, from which a prototype was generated [KVS96]. In order to make the structure of the ASF/PSF specification more explicit, we developed the model presented in this paper.

4.1   BUSINESS REQUIREMENTS

Even though table 20.1 does not contain techniques for the specification of business requirements, it is useful to illustrate what these requirements look like in this example. There are several stakeholders that play a role with respect to the system, including the bus drivers, the passengers, the bus company and the public in general, as represented by the municipality that maintains the roads. An analysis of their goals and needs would uncover such business requirements as the following:

- Passengers want to be informed in a timely manner about the approach of busses and the platform at which they can enter a bus.

- Drivers want to be informed in a timely manner about the platform they must drive to.

- The bus company wants efficient use of scarce platform space.

- The municipality wants to reduce the use of private cars and increase the use of public transport.

Requirements like these set the stage for design choices made in determining system requirements. The crucial step from business to system requirements is made by answering the following question: If this is what the business wants, then how can the system help the business achieve these goals? We now turn to the techniques in TRADE for specifying system requirements.

4.2   SYSTEM REQUIREMENTS

I simply work down the list of techniques shown in table 20.1. I should reiterate that this is *not* the sequence in which the specifications have been developed. They have been developed in parallel.

The mission of BAS is to dynamically allocate busses that approach a compact dynamic bus station to platforms. Its responsibilities are:

- To monitor the presence (arrival and departure) of busses at platforms;

- To respond to the approach of a bus by recomputing the optimal allocation of all busses to platforms;

- To announce the allocation to the driver in the approaching bus and to passengers waiting at platforms.

Figure 20.3 Mission statement for BAS.

Mission statement. A mission statement describes the required functionality of the system at the highest level of abstraction. It gives the reason for existence of the system, and links it to the business requirements. It summarizes the reason why some stakeholders in the business environment would pay money for acquiring the system. It consists of a one-sentence description of the functionality followed by a description of the main responsibilities of the system. Figure 20.3 gives a mission statement for BAS. Often, it is useful to additionally state a number of things that the system will *not* do. Although there are infinitely many things that the system will not do, the expectations of stakeholders may have to be managed by listing a few of those things explicitly.

Function refinement. A **system function** is a piece of external interaction of the system that is useful to some actor in the business environment of the system. Any execution of a function consists of a sequence of message exchanges with the business environment. In the UML, system functions are called **use cases.** Jacobson tries to distinguish use cases from functions by saying that functions are system interactions that might be good to have, whereas use cases are system interactions that are useful for particular classes of actors [JBR99, pages 5, 37]. This is a caricature of the definition of "function" in structured analysis, put up merely to maintain a fictional distinction between the use case approach and the functional approach to system requirements. Both structured analysis and object-oriented analysis start from desired system functions, both define them as external interactions useful for external actors, and both represent these actors in a diagram (the context and use case diagrams).

A function refinement tree is a hierarchic list of desired system functions, in which the system functions may be refined one or more times. The meaning of this refinement is that the functions $f_1, \ldots, f_n$ that refine a function f_0 jointly describe f_0 at a lower level of abstraction (a higher level of detail) and, conversely, that the desirability of f_0 explains the desirability of $f_1, \ldots, f_n$. Both levels of refinement refer to the same system at the same level of aggregation. In terms of Harel & Pnueli's "magic square", function refinement moves from left to right in the square but remains at one level of aggregation. Going to the more detailed level (to the right in the "magic square"), we

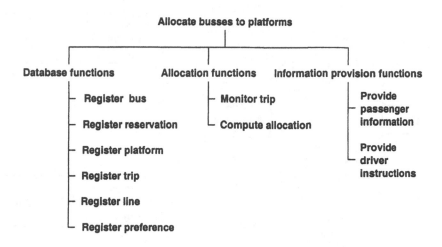

Figure 20.4 Function refinement tree.

answer the question *what* the system does. Going to the more abstract level (to the left in the "magic square"), we answer the question *why* the system does that.

A function refinement tree is a result of negotiation between the customer and the designer. There are many different ways to organize functions in a tree, that depend upon the perception of the functionality by the customer and the designer. What matters is that the function refinement tree bounds the discussion with the customer and acts as a means of communicating with the customer about desired functionality. The tree can be represented simply by an indented list of function names. If the tree is small, however, it may be represented by a tree diagram. Figure 20.4 shows a function refinement tree for BAS.

Context Model. A context model shows the way in which the system is embedded in its environment. The context diagram used in structured analysis shows the possible communications between the system and its external actors. The use case diagram of the UML does the same for use cases: For each use case (system function), it shows the external actors with which the system communicates when it is engaged in that use case. So the use case diagram is actually equivalent to a context diagram for a number of system functions. The UML provides several constructs that can be added to this basic picture, which I will not treat.

A non-trivial system may have dozens or even hundreds of use cases, too many to represent in one diagram. One can manage this complexity by maintaining a relationship with the function refinement tree. The root of the tree represents the system mission; this corresponds to the context diagram, which shows the external communications needed to realize this mission. The leaves of the tree represent elementary system functions, or elementary use cases in object-oriented parlance; a use case diagram provides a context diagram for all of these use cases. If there are too many elementary use cases to depict in one diagram, one can move up the tree until an

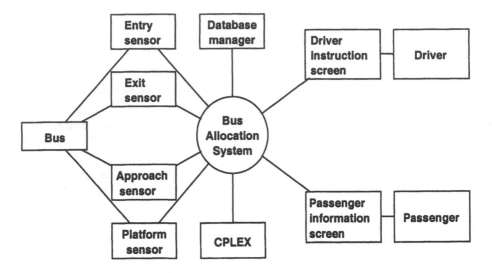

Figure 20.5   Context diagram of BAS.

abstraction level is reached with a manageable number of more abstract use cases, and draw a use case diagram at that level. Or one can just draw a context diagram for each use case separately without drawing a diagram that shows all of them.

Context diagrams and use case diagrams only show the actors with which the system communicates and omit the wider context of the system. As argued by Jackson [J95, page 35], it is actually very informative to include the wider context. The immediate context often consists of sensors and actuators, whereas the actors of interest, for whom the system performs a service, are one or two communication links removed from the system. Figure 20.5 gives a Yourdon-style context diagram for BAS, representing the system under design by a circle, external actors by rectangle and communication links by lines. CPLEX is a linear programming software library that performs the computations needed to optimize the bus allocation.

Event–response list.   Figure 20.6 lists the events to which the system must respond, the stimulus by which the system discovers that the event has occurred, the source of this stimulus, the desired response of the system, and the function to which this event–response pair contributes. The arrival of an event and the production of a response are input and output messages of the system, respectively. Other properties of event–response pairs that can be listed are the destination of the response message, performance requirements, safety properties, ergonomic requirements, etc. Cross–referencing the list to the function refinement tree acts as a coherence check: Each event–response pair should contribute to a system function, and each system function should be realized by one or more event–response pairs. The event list is also cross-referenced to the context model, because the sources of stimuli in the event list as well as the destination of the responses, must be actors in the context model that have direct communication links with the system.

Event	Stimulus	Source	Desired response	Function
Scheduled arrival 15 minutes from now		Time	Update trip status to Expected.	Monitor trip
Scheduled arrival time has arrived		Time	Trip status becomes delayed. Update passenger information board.	Monitor trip Provide passenger information
Bus approaches	approach	Approach sensor	Update passenger information board. Update trip status to Approaching.	Monitor trip Provide passenger information
Bus enters bus station	entry	Entry sensor	Update passenger information board. Instruct driver to drive to platform or buffer.	Monitor trip Provide passenger information Provide driver instructions
Bus arrives at platform	at platform	Platform sensor	Update trip status. Clear driver instructions.	Monitor trip Provide driver instructions
Bus departs from bus station	exit	Exit sensor	Clear passenger information board. Recompute position allocation.	Monitor trip Provide passenger information
Time to compute allocation (Every minute)		Time	Compute optimal allocation.	Compute allocation
Update database	update	Database manager	Update the database.	All database functions

Figure 20.6 Events to which the system must react, and their desired responses.

Subject domain. The messages received and sent by the system are messages about the subject domain. Figure 20.7 shows a simplified decomposition of the subject domain into entities and relationships. I use a subset of the UML class diagram syntax to represent entity-relationship diagrams. Boxes represent entity types and lines represent relationships, annotated with multiplicities. Attributes of entities can be listed in the entity type box.

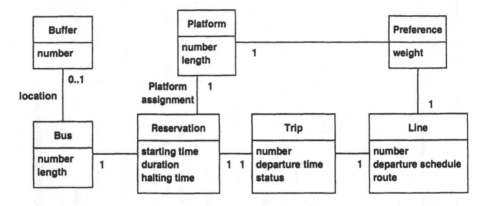

Figure 20.7 Class diagram of subject domain decomposition.

The figure shows that each trip belongs to one bus line and that a reservation relates a bus with a trip and a platform. Each line has a preference for a platform, which is indicated by a certain weight. Finally, a bus may (temporarily) be at the buffer.

Note that a subject domain model is not part of the system model. It is really part of the requirements dictionary, that documents the meaning of terms used in the requirements specification. The subject domain is the part of the business environment that is referred to by the messages that the system exchanges with its environment. A subject domain model represents a decomposition of this part of the business environment. The information about the subject domain represented by this model includes:

- Which classes of entities exist in the subject domain and

- what is the multiplicity of these classes and their relationships.

In addition, static and dynamic properties of the subject domain may be represented if this helps to understand the requirements of the system. The subject domain model must be cross–referenced to the event–response list, because the descriptions of the events and responses in that list can refer only to entities, relationships and attributes defined in the subject domain model.

4.3   ESSENTIAL ARCHITECTURE

Component classes. Figure 20.8 shows an essential decomposition of the system which shows the boundary between the software part of the system and the other parts. The software part duplicates the subject domain decomposition and adds software

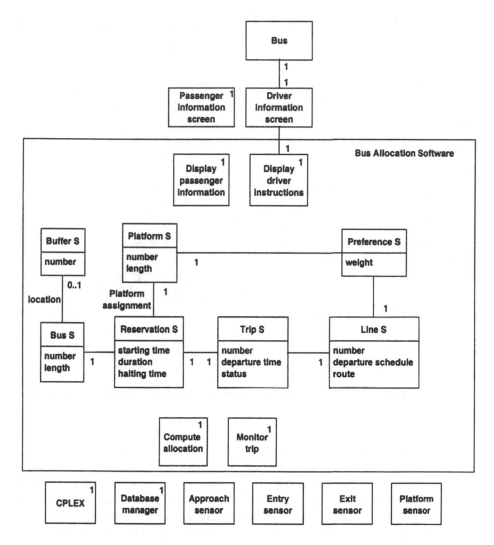

Figure 20.8 Class diagram of essential system decomposition.

objects that handle the desired system functions. The decomposition is represented by a UML class diagram. Two of the essential architectural software design guidelines mentioned in subsection 3.1 have been used: Identify software objects that represent subject domain entities and identify objects that perform required system functions. The class of a software object that represent a subject domain entity has been given the same name as the entity type, suffixed with an S.

The information provided by a class diagram the system architecture is the following:

- Which classes of objects make up the system, and

- what are the multiplicities of these classes and their relationships.

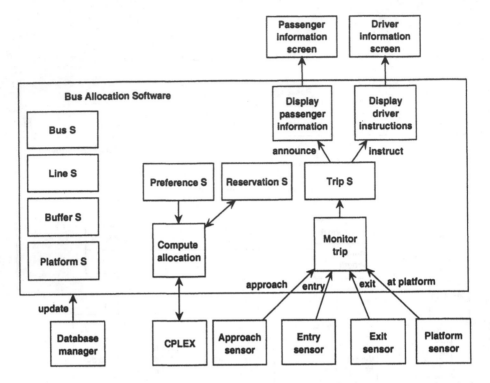

Figure 20.9 Essential communication diagram, showing the communications needed at the essential level.

Figure 20.8 shows that the function classes are singleton classes. The diagram also shows that there are many driver information screens (one per bus), but that there is one passenger information screen. Associations in the class model do not represent communication links but are used to represent multiplicity relationships. They are included only where they are needed to represent multiplicity information.

Depending upon the kind of subject domain and the desired system functionality, other information from the subject domain model can be used to design the software components, such as state invariants and behavioral properties of the software objects.

Component Communication.   It is useful to represent communication between essential components by a separate **communication diagram**, consisting of boxes and arrows. The boxes represent object classes just as in a class diagram, possibly including multiplicities, attributes and operations. In contrast to class diagrams, however, all lines in a communication diagram are arrows, and they represent communication links. Figure 20.9 shows the communication diagram for BAS.

Our communication diagram is similar to communication diagrams used by Shlaer & Mellor [SM92], to block diagrams in SDL and to architecture diagrams used in the literature on software architectures [SH96]. It must be cross-referenced to the class diagram, because there, all the boxes from the communication diagram must be declared as object classes. It must also be cross-referenced to the context diagram,

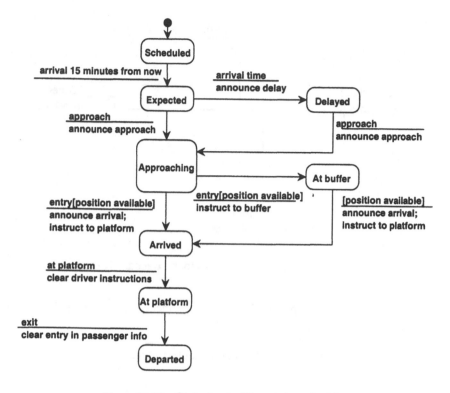

Figure 20.10   Statechart of the status of a trip.

because there, all the external communications of the communication diagram should appear.

Component behavior.   Figure 20.10 represents the desired behavior of a trip by a simple and informal statechart. In an executable model, the events, guards and actions of the statechart should be specified in some executable language.   The attribute status of a trip object represents the possible states in this diagram.   The statechart must be cross-referenced with the communication diagram, because it must describe the behavior of instances of a class in the communication diagram, and the events and actions in the statechart must appear as communications of that class in the communication diagram.

5.   USING UML TECHNIQUES IN SYSTEM ENGINEERING

The YSM function specification techniques in TRADE can be mapped in a simple way to Harel & Pnueli's "magic square":

- External system functionality at the highest level of abstraction (the upper left point in the "magic square") is represented by the *mission statement* and at the highest level of refinement (the upper right point of the "magic square") by the

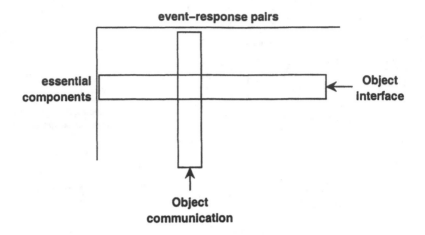

Figure 20.11   Mapping techniques to the traceability table.

event–response list. The two levels of refinement are related by the *function refinement list.*

The UML can be mapped to the traceability table format of figure 20.2; see also figure 20.11.

- The *class diagram* represents the classification and multiplicity of the components that appear in the leftmost column of the table.

- Each row of the table represents the interface of an object, that must be declared in the class diagram. The *statechart* of an object class constrains the behavior of this interface.

Each column of the table represents the operations of different objects that realize an event–response chain. The *communication diagram* shows the communication links needed for these collaborations. However, the communication diagram is not part of the UML. Instead, the UML defines two other kinds of diagrams to represent communication: sequence and collaboration diagrams. In their basic form, both diagrams can be used to represent a sequence of message exchanges between a finite (small) set of entities. These entities may be for example software objects, or processing resources in a network, or external actors exchanging messages with the system. Sequence and collaboration diagrams contain various constructs that allow one to specify control structures such as iteration, and to represent several independent processing sequences in different threads of control. In whatever form, these diagrams represent *possible* execution sequences in which a number of *individual* entities are involved. Their use as a specification technique is restricted to showing particular behaviors that the system must be able to perform. More properly, they can be used to document a particular implementation, for example, by illustrating a behavior pattern. For this reason, they are not included in table 20.1. Damm & Harel [DH99] have defined an extension to sequence diagrams in which one can express the requirement that all possible behaviors of a system must conform to the diagram.

The *component* and *deployment diagrams* from the UML, not treated in this paper, show the communications between implementation components and physical resources. These should be related to the essential level components by another kind of traceability table. Finally, UML *activity diagrams* can be used to represent a network of activities between which temporal dependencies exist. These seem more suitable to representing workflows in organizations, i.e. business requirements, rather than system requirements. However, the UML is a mulit-purpose notation and Booch et al. [BRJ99] also recommend using activity diagrams for documenting operations of software objects.

The use of UML techniques in TRADE has implications for the semantics of these techniques when they are used this way. Class diagrams and statecharts are used in TRADE to represent software architecture at the essential level, where we can assume perfect technology. This means, for example, that actions do not take time and that all objects perform their tasks in parallel. A first version of such an essential-level semantics is presented elsewhere [WB98, BW99]. This semantics differs from the OMG semantics [UML99], in which actions take time, there are several threads of control and one message queue per thread which can receive signals exchanged by objects. The OMG semantics is clearly intended for and appropiate to what I call the implementation architecture. This is called the design model in the Unified Software Development Process [JBR99]. The use of C++ as action language in the executable UML models of Rhapsody [i-L99] confirms this, as does the outline of the executable statechart semantics given by Harel & Gery [HG97]. As pointed out in section 2., I do not claim that one of these semantics is "better" than the other. Rather, I claim that they are good for different methodological purposes.

If we describe an intended semantics of a design notation without making its intended methodological purpose explicit, as is done in the OMG documentation, then we leave the user of the notation in the dark about the use of the constructs whose meaning has been defined. Conversely, if we omit a description of the semantics of a notation from a description of the method for which this semantics is intended, as Jacobson et al. [JBR99] do, then we leave the reader in the dark about the meaning of the constructs she uses. To repeat Wittgenstein once more, meaning is use.

As pointed out before, the UML user guide by Booch et al. [BRJ99] lists so many possible completely different uses for each of the UML diagrams, that there is no single semantics that corresponds to all of these uses. This places the UML semantics proposed by the OMG into perspective as one among a variety of possible semantics, suitable to different methodological purposes. The OMG semantics is suitable for documenting an object-oriented program by an executable model that closely reflects the implementation. The TRADE semantics is another possibly useful semantics, suitable for documenting the architecture and behavior of a system required at the essential level, independent from its implementation. This resembles very much the semantics of Statemate models [HP98].

6.   CONCLUSIONS AND FURTHER WORK

This paper gave a framework for system and software design that separates requirements from architecture, distinguishes business from system requirements, and essential from implementation architecture. System requirements are separated into required messages, required behavior and required communication. TRADE is a collection of techniques to specify system requirements and essential software architecture, that includes techniques from YSM for requirements specification and techniques from the UML for essential architecture specification. This entails an essential-level semantics for the used UML constructs, that differs from the intended OMG semantics. It was shown how this collection of techniques can be used in a systems engineering approach, that emphasizes the embedding of software in its system environment and of the system in its business environment and that explicitly maintains traceability between these different levels.

Our current work includes the elaboration of the formal semantics for a UML class and behavior diagrams that is appropriate for the essential modeling level, and application of the UML to a number of case studies to validate this semantics. After validation, the execution semantics will be implemented in TCM [DW96].

References

[AKZ96] M. Awad, J. Kuusela, and J. Ziegler. *Object-Oriented Technology for Real-Time Systems: A Practical Approach Using OMT and Fusion*. Prentice-Hall, 1996.

[BF90]   B. S. Blanchard and W. J. Fabrycky. *Systems Engineering and Analysis*. Prentice-Hall, 1990.

[BHS91] F. Belina, D. Hogrefe, and A. Sarma. *SDL with Applications from protocol Specification*. Prentice-Hall, 1991.

[BRJ99] G. Booch, J. Rumbaugh, and I. Jacobson. *The Unified Modeling Language User Guide*. Addison-Wesley, 1999.

[BW99]   J. Broersen and R.J. Wieringa. A logic for the specification of multi-object systems. In P. Ciancarini, A. Fantechi, and R. Gorrieri, editors, *Formal methods for Open Object-Based Distributed Systems*, pages 387–398. Kluwer, 1999.

[CD94]   S. Cook and J. Daniels. *Designing Object Systems: Object-Oriented Modelling with Syntropy*. Prentice-Hall, 1994.

[DH99]   W. Damm and D. Harel. LSC's: Breathing life into message sequence charts. In P. Ciancarini, A. Fantechi, and R. Gorrieri, editors, *Formal methods for Open Object-Based Distributed Systems*, pages 293–311. Kluwer, 1999.

[D98]   B.P. Douglas. *Real-Time UML: Developing Efficient Objects for Embedded Systems*. Addison-Wesley, 1998.

[DW96]   F. Dehne and R.J. Wieringa. Toolkit for Conceptual Modeling (TCM): User's Guide. Technical Report IR-401, Faculty of Mathematics and Computer Science, *Vrije Universiteit*, De Boelelaan 1081a, 1081 HV Amsterdam, 1996. http://www.cs.utwente.nl/~tcm.

[G93]   H. Gomaa. *Software Design Methods for Concurrent and Real-Time Systems*. Addison-Wesley, 1993.

[HG97]   D. Harel and E. Gery. Executable object modeling with statecharts. *Computer*, 30(7):31–42, July 1997.

[HP85]   D. Harel and A. Pnueli. On the development of reactive systems. In K. Apt, editor, *Logics and Models of Concurrent Systems*, pages 477–498. Springer, 1985. NATO ASI Series.

[HP98]   D. Harel and M. Politi. *Modeling Reactive Systems with Statecharts: The STATEMATE Approach*. McGraw-Hill, 1998.

[i-L99]   i-Logix. *Rhapsody Reference Guide, Version 2.1*. i-Logix Inc., 1999.

[J83]   M. Jackson. *System Development*. Prentice-Hall, 1983.

[J95]   M. Jackson. *Software Requirements and Specifications: A lexicon of practice, principles and prejudices*. Addison-Wesley, 1995.

[JBR99]   I. Jacobson, G. Booch, and J. Rumbaugh. *The Unified Software Development Process*. Addison-Wesley, 1999.

[JCJO92] I. Jacobson, M. Christerson, P. Johnsson, and G. Övergaard. *Object-Oriented Software Engineering: A Use Case Driven Approach*. Prentice-Hall, 1992.

[KVS96]   A.S. Klusener, S.F.M. van Vlijmen, and A. Schrijver. Compact dynamisch busstation. Technical Report CS-N9601, Centrum for Wiskunde en Informatica, May 1996.

[L95]   W.M. Lamia. Integrating QFD with object-oriented software design methodologies. In *The Seventh Symposium on Quality Function Deployment*, pages 417–433. QFD Institute, 1995. http://www.gfdi.org/.

[M89]   J. Martin. *Information Engineering*. Prentice-Hall, 1989. Three volumes.

[MP84]   S. M. McMenamin and J. F. Palmer. *Essential Systems Analysis*. Yourdon Press/Prentice Hall, 1984.

[OMG97]   OMG. *Unified Modeling Language: Notation Guide, Version 1.1*. Object Management Group, 1 September 1997. http://www.omg.com.

[SH96]   M. Shaw and D. Harlan. *Software Architecture*. Prentice-Hall, 1996.

[SM92]   S. Shlaer and S. J. Mellor. *Object Lifecycles: Modeling the World in States*. Prentice-Hall, 1992.

[UML99]   UML Revision Task Force. *OMG UML Specification*. Object Management Group, march 1999. http://uml.shl.com.

[WB98]   R.J. Wieringa and J. Broersen. A minimal transition system semantics for lightweight class– and behavior diagrams. In M. Broy, D. Coleman, T. Maibaum, and B. Rumpe, editors, *ICSE98 Workshop on Precise Semantics for Software Modeling techniques*, pages 129–151, 1998. Report TUM-I9803, Technische Universität München.

[W98a]   R.J. Wieringa. Postmodern software design with NYAM: Not yet another method. In M. Broy and B. Rumpe, editors, *Requirements Targeting Software and Systems Engineering*, pages 69–94. Springer, 1998. Lecture Notes in Computer Science 1526.

[W98b] R.J. Wieringa. A survey of structured and object-oriented software specification methods and techniques. *ACM Computing Surveys*, 30(4):459–527, December 1998.

[W71]   L. Wittgenstein. *Philosophische Untersuchungen*. Suhrkamp Verlag, 1971.

[Y93]   Yourdon Inc. *Yourdon^{TM} Systems Method: Model-Driven Systems Development*. Prentice-Hall, 1993.

7.   ABOUT THE AUTHOR

Roel Wieringa is professor of Information Systems at the University of Twente, the Netherlands. His research interests include design methods for software systems that integrate techniques for data-intensive and behavior-intensive systems, and the integration of formal description techniques with diagram-based techniques. In this context, he has studied the application of algebraic and logical techniques to information system specification. His current research interests are the application of temporal and real-time logics in information system specification. Together with J.-J. Ch. Meyer he edited a book on *Deontic Logic in Computer Science*. He wrote a book on *Requirements Engineering: Frameworks for Understanding* (Wiley, 1996), in which a number of classical software engineering methods are analyzed in a systems engineering framework.

INDEX

Printed in the United States
By Bookmasters